INTRODUCTION TO PRIVATE SECURITY

THEORY MEETS PRACTICE

Cliff Roberson

Kaplan University

Michael L. Birzer

Wichita State University

Prentice Hall
Upper Saddle River, New Jersey
Columbus, Ohio

Library of Congress Cataloging-in-Publication Data

Roberson, Cliff, 1937-
  Introduction to private security : theory meets practice / Cliff
Roberson, Michael L. Birzer.
      p. cm.
  Includes bibliographical references and index.
  ISBN-13: 978-0-205-59240-1
  ISBN-10:   0-205-59240-6
  1. Private security services—United States.   I. Birzer, Michael L.,
1960-   II. Title.
    HV8291.U6R63 2008
    363.28'90973—dc22

                                        2008043459

Vice President and Executive Publisher: Vernon Anthony
Senior Acquisitions Editor: Tim Peyton
Editorial Assistant: Alicia Kelly
Media Project Manager: Karen Bretz
Director of Marketing: David Gesell
Marketing Manager: Adam Kloza
Marketing Coordinator: Alicia Dysert
Production Manager: Wanda Rockwell
Creative Director: Jayne Conte
Cover Design: Bruce Kenselaar
Cover Illustration/Photo: Jupiter Images
Manager, Rights and Permissions: Zina Arabia
Manager, Visual Research: Beth Brenzel
Manager, Cover Visual Research & Permissions: Karen Sanatar
Image Permission Coordinator: Vickie Menanteaux
Full-Service Project Management/Composition: Anupam Mukherjee, Aptara®, Inc.
Printer/Binder: Hamilton Printing Co.

Credits: Pg 4, Steve Gorton © Dorling Kindersley; Pgs 6 and 8, Geoff Brightling © Dorling
Kindersley; Pg 30, Chen Chao © Dorling Kindersley; Pg 41, Max Alexander © Dorling
Kindersley; Pg 57 Michael Newman/PhotoEdit; Pg 61 AP Wide World Photos; Pg 66, Michael
Newman/PhotoEdit Inc; Pg 76, Corbis Bittmann; Pg 78, The Granger Collection; Pg 89, Andy
Crawford and Steve Gorton © Dorling Kindersley; Pg 110, Neil Lukas © Dorling Kindersley;
Pg 112, David Young-Wolff/Stone/Getty Images; Pgs 115, 147 © Dorling Kindersley, Pg 174,
Lucy Claxton © Dorling Kindersley; Pg 233, Kim Sayer © Dorling Kindersley, Pg 283, Spencer
Platt/Getty Images, Inc.-Getty News; Pg 286, © Dorling Kindersley; Pg 288, M. Kowal/Custom
Medical Stock Photo, Inc.; Pg 305, Jules Selmes and Debi Treloar © Dorling Kindersley; Pg 309,
Neil Fletcher and Matthew Ward © Dorling Kindersley; Pg 322, © Dorling Kindersley;
Cover, Colin Anderson/Jupiter Images/PictureArts Corporation/Brand X Pictures Royalty Free.

Pearson Education LTD.
Pearson Education Australia PTY, Limited
Pearson Education Singapore, Pte. Ltd
Pearson Education North Asia Ltd

Pearson Education, Canada, Ltd
Pearson Educación de Mexico, S.A. de C.V.
Pearson Education–Japan
Pearson Education Malaysia, Pte. Ltd

Prentice Hall
is an imprint of

www.pearsonhighered.com

10 9 8 7 6 5 4
ISBN-13: 978-0-205-59240-1
ISBN-10:   0-205-59240-6

CONTENTS

PREFACE

This book is designed as a comprehensive yet readable text on private security and security management. The material describes private security and security management concepts and is designed for a one-semester course in private security. Although the chapters are independent units, they also build on each other to provide a complete picture of private security.

Chapter 1 discusses the history of private security and how it relates to the present. Chapter 2 examines the relationships among security, crime, and the physical environment. In Chapter 3 the connection between private security and community policing is explored. Chapter 4 examines the management of private security. Retail and business security are examined in Chapter 5. Chapter 6 discusses the role of private security during terrorist acts and natural disasters. Chapter 7 looks at the investigation of crime, and Chapter 8 discusses computers and electronic information issues related to private security. Chapters 9 and 10 examine the criminal and civil court issues involved in private security, and Chapter 11 discusses testifying in court and report writing. In Chapter 12 the recruitment and training aspects of private security are examined. Chapter 13 looks at drug and alcohol issues, and the text concludes with Chapter 14, which discusses ethics.

Although we are listed as the authors, this text is actually the result of work by numerous people, including our former editor at Allyn & Bacon, David E. Repetto, and his associate, Jack Cashman, and especially our present editor at Pearson, Tim Peyton, and his associate, Alicia Kelly.

We are also grateful to our reviewers:
Joseph LeFevre
University of Wisconsin—Platteville
Platteville, WI 53818

Marie (Hansen) Hankinson
Husson College
Winterport, ME 04496

We have worked hard to provide readers and students with the whole picture, but any suggestions, errors, or omissions may be forwarded to the authors by email to croberson@kaplan.edu.

Dedications

To my sons Clif, Marshall, Kenneth, and Dwayne

—Cliff Roberson

To my wife Gwynne and my son Michael Jr.

—Michael L. Birzer

ABOUT THE AUTHORS

Cliff Roberson, LLM, Ph.D. Cliff is editor-in-chief of *Professional Issues in Criminal Justice.* His prior experience includes service as a Marine judge advocate; military judge; head, Military Law Branch, U.S. Marine Corps; director of programs, National College of District Attorneys; dean; associate vice president for academics, Arkansas Tech University; and director, Justice Center/professor of criminology, California State University, Fresno. Cliff is also professor emeritus of criminal justice, Washburn University, and a member of the Core Faculty, Graduate School of Criminal Justice, Kaplan University. Cliff has authored or co-authored over fifty texts and books. Cliff has an LLM from the National Law Center, George Washington University, in criminology, criminal law, and psychiatry. He also has a Ph.D. in human behavior and leadership.

Michael L. Birzer, Ed.D. Michael is an associate professor of criminal justice and director of the School of Community Affairs at Wichita State University. His research interests include ethnographic and phenomenological investigations of police behavior, criminal justice education and training, and applying multivariate analysis methods in studying criminal justice phenomenon. Michael's qualifications include both practitioner experience and academic experience. Prior to his entry into academia, he served with the Sedgwick County Sheriff's Department in Wichita, Kansas, retiring in 1999. His most recent book publication (with Cliff Roberson) is *Police Field Operations: Theory Meets Practice* (Boston: Allyn & Bacon, 2008).

CHAPTER 1

Introduction to Private Security

Private security plays the majority role in the United States in the protection of property, people, and assets. In both the private and public sectors, private security guards are relied on as the first line of defense against illegal, criminal, and terrorist activity.

(Ricci 2007)

CHAPTER OUTLINE

OBJECTIVES

After completing this chapter, you will be able to:

- Describe the magnitude of the private security industry.
- Explain the history of private security.
- Discuss how private security and the police interact.
- Explain how states regulate private security.
- List the types of private security.

Explain the current status of private security regulation.

> *Police are not experts when it comes to site security. Partnerships between the police and private security are necessary to assist in these types of homeland security efforts.*

—*Post-9/11 Policing Roundtable participant*

Private security:
The wide range of activities
used by nongovernment
organizations and persons to
protect themselves from
criminal endeavors.

C urrent estimates of public-sector policing strength by the U.S. Bureau of Justice Statistics indicate that in 2005 there were 16,661 state, local, and county law enforcement agencies in the United States, and they employed a total of 677,933 sworn officers. Studies on private security staffing indicate that there may be as many as 10,000 private security agencies employing slightly less than 2 million private security officers in the United States. Clearly, if these numbers are accurate, then private security officers are a vast potential resource that can assist law enforcement agencies in fulfilling their mission (Morabito and Greenberg 2005).

According to Morabito and Greenberg (2005, p. 5), "Private policing is considered as a big part of the response to today's increased security concerns, as citizens realize that security is much more than the presence of guards and the perception of safety." The Stockholm International Peace Research Institute is a worldwide private security company whose revenues exceed $100 billion. The institute, which studies issues involving worldwide security, estimates that private security industry income will double by 2010 (Wagner 2006).

Corporate security:
Security departments in
businesses or corporations.

Private security services fall into two categories: (1) proprietary or corporate security and (2) contract or private security firms. Corporate security generally refers to the security departments that exist within businesses or corporations. Contract security firms, by contrast, sell their services to the public, including businesses, homeowners, and banks. Private security is not a monolithic entity. Just as there are differences between state and local law enforcement functions, private security functions can differ considerably. A security practitioner might be an experienced director of security at a major multinational corporation, a manager of contract security officers at a client site, a skilled computer crime investigator, an armed protector at a nuclear power plant, or an entry-level officer at a retail store (Morabito and Greenberg 2005).

This chapter examines and discusses the concept of private security . For purposes of this text, the term *private security* refers to the wide range of activities used by nongovernment organizations and persons to protect themselves from criminal endeavors. Since at least the beginning of recorded history, people have used private security measures to protect themselves. The measures include possession of personal weapons, building barriers around the home, forming citizen groups for protection, installing home burglar alarms that are monitored by private companies, and hiring body officers, among others.

When we think of private security, we tend to think of night watchmen. Private security, however, is far broader in scope. For example, both authors of this text have contracts with private alarm monitoring companies under which the authors pay a monthly fee and the private company monitors security devices that have been installed in their homes. Recently, a major bank notified all their customers who use their online banking servies of the installation of a new protection system designed to help secure the customers' data and prevent unauthorized disclosure of their private information. Such activities, along with many others designed to protect individuals and their property, are also within the concept of private security.

Private security evolved from a natural desire on the part of individuals to provide protection for people and their property. By additional protection, we mean protection beyond that offered by the state or national government.

A BRIEF HISTORY OF PRIVATE SECURITY

People were taking steps to protect themselves long before the advent of government-controlled policing. The Bible reports the use of a guard or watchman in Psalm 127. In ancient times, individuals relied mostly on physical security devices such as weapons, lakes, cliff dwellings, walls, and gates. The Great Wall of China, which extends for thousands of miles, was a government-built wall designed to protect the Chinese people. Individuals built similar security devices on a much smaller scale around their homes and their villages.

In medieval England, brush and other possible ambush covers were removed from the sides of the well-traveled roads. The Anglo-Saxons brought with them to England a strong affinity for feudal contracts whereby an overlord would guarantee the safety of persons and property under his control. Healy (1983) stated that in Switzerland, alone, over 300 lake-dwelling sites were used in ancient times to protect individuals. Most of these dwellings had protected access, restricted by bridges and moats. Healy noted that on Lake Geneva, one dwelling provided living space for over 1200 people.

Development of Private Security in England

A study of the development of private security in England is also a study of the development of English policing. It was not until the nineteenth century that a clear separation between private security and the police occurred.

The Statute of Westminster was issued by King Edward I in 1285. This statute placed a duty on the English people to drop all work when the "hue and cry" was raised and to join immediately in pursuit of anyone in the process of committing a crime. The "hue and cry," which had been used by the Saxons to dealg with persons who resisted the watchman's arrest, was revised by the statute. The statute established the assize of arms, which required all free males between the ages of 15 and 60 to keep a weapon in their home as a "harness to keep peace." England was divided into districts, and every district was responsible for crimes committed within its boundaries. Towns built gates and were required to close the gates at night. All strangers were required to give an account for themselves to the magistrates.

Hue and cry:
A call to citizens to assist in an emergency situation.

During that period, the English middle class rebelled against compulsory night watch service and hired individuals to take their place. In addition, the English merchants were unhappy with the hue and cry system under the Statute of Westminster and began to hire their own security. Many of the merchants hired private police to guard their wares, to investigate thefts, and to recover stolen property. These attempts to control crime at the local level were not very successful, but organized agencies for the enforcement of the laws were almost nonexistent. For the most part, the only protection that the English people had was privately established night watches and patrols (Critchley 1978).

During the eighteenth century, private citizens carried arms for protection and bonded together to hire special police to protect themselves. In 1748, Henry Fielding, considered by many the father of the English novel (he was the author of *Tom Jones*), proposed a permanent, professional, adequately paid security force. He established the "Bow Street Amateur Volunteer Force" (Reynolds 1998).

As noted in the following advertisement; Henry Fielding was trying to establish a new tradition in law and order by having citizens make reports when they were the victims of crime, a practice that is routine today. Prior to that time, the attention of the

British Want Ad of the 1750s

All persons who shall for the future suffer by robbers, burglars, etc., are desired immediately to bring or send the best description they can of such robberies, etc., with the time and place, and circumstances of the fact to Henry Fielding, Esq. at his house in Bow Street.

people was directed primarily toward apprehending the thieves rather than tracing and recovering the property. Victims of property crime were left to rely on their own ingenuity to secure the return of their property. It was not until 1691 that the act of receiving stolen property was considered a crime. Fielding was later followed by his brother John Fielding, who was blind. It was said that the "blind beak," as John Fielding was known, could smell a thief.

One of the most influential predecessors to the Fieldings was Patrick Colquhoun (1745–1820). His *Treatise on the Commerce and Police of the River Thames* (Colquhoun, 1796) was considered one of the leading publications on crime and led to the creation of the Thames River Police. The Thames River Police became the first regular professional police force in London, but it began as a private security force. It was created in June 1798 by the West India Trading Company to curb the thefts that plagued the world's largest port. Officers in the Company were impressed by Colquhoun's treatise on how the thefts of merchandise should be treated, and they appointed Colquhoun as director of a permanent staff of eight men and an on-call staff of 1120. Two features of the force were unique. First, patrols were preventive; officers patrolled visibly to prevent thefts. Second, officers were not stipendiary police; they were salaried and were prohibited from taking fees. The West India Trading Company estimated that the force saved the company about 66,000 English pounds in its first

Thames River Police:
The first regular police force in London. It began as a private police force for Thames River merchants.

The Thames River Docks remains an important part of the London even today. This is a picture of how the docks looked in 2006.

First Order of the Metropolitan Police

It should be understood, at the outset, that the principal objective to be attained is the prevention of crime.

To this great end every effort of the police is to be directed. The security of person and property, the preservation of public tranquility, and all other objects of a Police Establishment, will thus be better affected, than by the detection and punishment of the offender, after he was succeeded in committing the crime. (Lipson 1975, 120).

eight months of operation (Reith 1975). In July 1890 the House of Commons passed a bill making the marine security force a publicly financed organization (Critchley, 1978). Colquhoun contended that nine-tenths of the property thefts committed along the Thames River docks were committed by persons whose presence in the area was essential or justified, and he listed them as "watchmen, sailors, revenue officers, and so forth." He noted that stolen goods were being transported in the same barges that did the regular loading and unloading of ships (Lipson 1975, 18–19).

When Sir Robert Peel became home secretary in 1822, he envisioned a strong, unified, professional police force. He also attempted to decentralize police forces and develop community responsibilities. Between 1825 and 1830 he effected the fundamental consolidation and reform of English criminal law, covering three-quarters of all criminal offenses. Rising crime statistics convinced him that legal reform should be accompanied by improved methods of crime prevention. In 1829, Peel was successful in getting the Metropolitan Police Act, which set up the first disciplined police force for the Greater London area, passed by Parliament. As a result of Peel's efforts, the London police force became known as "Bobby's boys" and later simply as "Bobbies." Neither the Police Act that established city and borough police forces nor the County Act that created county police resulted in adequate citizen security. English citizens, therefore, continued their use of private security for protection and to recover stolen property (Pringle 1979).

The First Order of the Metropolitan Police is considered the first document in which there was a distinct separation between "police" and "private security." Prior to the order, private security focused on protecting people and property from crime, and the police focused on catching criminals.

Lipson (1975) noted that by 1830 in England, and within a decade or so thereafter in the United States, the beginnings of a separation of the security function into two spheres of responsibility had started. Public police departments, with their sworn duties, were charged with maintaining law and order. The burden of security for private property and personal safety therefore had to be redefined. The establishment of public police departments, however, did not—as many people contended automatically—lead to a disbanding of private security (pp. 20–22).

Development of Private Security in the United States

Since the American Revolution, private security firms have played an integral role in the successful development and defense of the nation. The role of the private security firm has not changed that much over time. Providing specialized capabilities and search capacity to the U.S. government in flexible, cost-effective packages, and building capacity for friendly foreign governments, continue to be core competencies of the industry (Taylor 2006).

When the American colonies were founded, the watch system was imported from England. Outside of the night watch patrols, no formal security agencies existed in United States cities until New York established the first policing organization in 1783. New York was quickly followed by the cities of Detroit, Cincinnati, and Chicago. The early police departments were rudimentary, and they tended to be inefficient and corrupt. Note: It was not until 1844 that New York established the first public police force.

In the late eighteenth century, several moral societies existed, including the American Purity Alliance. These societies were interested in enforcing moral standards in the colonies. Also, in the nineteenth century a number of societies were formed as "evangelical police," whose functions were to act as a watchdog over the lower class and to enforce Puritan propriety.

Evangelical Police:
A private police force in the Colonies whose function was to act as a watchdog over the lower class and to enforce Puritan propriety.

Because of the slow development of public police agencies and the steady escalation of crime as the United States became more urban and industrialized; a need developed for private security agencies. This need was quickly filled in the 1850s with the establishment of private security and detective agencies.

Allan Pinkerton (1819–1884)

Allan Pinkerton, who formed Chicago's first private detective agency in 1850, also founded the North West Police Agency in 1857,which provided security for the growing railroad industry. In 1859 he founded the Pinkerton Protection Patrol, which provided guard services for industrial companies. For approximately fifty years, Pinkerton was the only vendor to provide interstate security services. Today, Pinkerton's Inc. remains one of the largest agencies providing security services in the United States.

Allan Pinkerton is considered by many to be the father of the private security industry in the United States. He was born in Glasgow, Scotland. His father, a police sergeant, died when Allan was a child, leaving the family in poverty. In Scotland, Pinkerton became involved in Chartism, a political and social reform movement. Because of his activities on behalf of the movement, an arrest warrant was issued for him in 1841. Pinkerton fled to the United States and planned to immigrate to Canada, but changed his mind en route and settled in Chicago. While working as a barrel maker, he discovered

A carefully preserved Pinkerton badge from 1860 identifies the wearer as an agent from New York.

and later helped capture a gang of counterfeiters. He was then appointed a deputy sheriff of Cook County, with his office located in Chicago. In 1850, Pinkerton resigned from the sheriff's department and organized his own private detective agency, which specialized in railway theft cases. By 1853 he had a staff of five full-time detectives, including one women detective, in addition to a secretary and several clerks. His 1855 contract with the Illinois Central Railroad for protection included a then unheard-of retainer of $10,000 a year. He also received a lot of publicity when his agency was hired to solve the theft of a package containing $40,000 in currency from Adams Express Company. The Pinkerton Agency established that the package was stolen by a local office manager of Adams Express Company.

In 1866 the Pinkerton Agency captured the offenders involved in a $700,000 Adams Express Company theft, and in 1861 the agency thwarted an assassination plot against President-elect Abraham Lincoln in Baltimore. Pinkerton's agents guarded the President-elect during his trip to Baltimore. According to Pinkerton, the popular rumor that Lincoln entered Baltimore dressed as a women was false. (At the time, proslavery feelings were very high in Baltimore, and the citizens were upset by Lincoln's antislavery feelings.)

The Pinkerton Agency is credited with chasing Butch Cassidy and the Wild Bunch across the West and into South America. Many photographs of the various members of the Wild Bunch were discovered years later in a photographer's office in Fort Worth, Texas, by a Pinkerton agent. Apparently, the gang members had posed for the photos while hiding out in the area (Lipson 1975, 33).

The Pinkerton Agency's harsh treatment of labor union members and strikers during the coal miners' labor strikes in 1877 resulted in considerable criticism in labor circles. Pinkerton was labeled an enemy of labor. Pinkerton himself, however, asserted that he was helping workers by opposing labor unions (Levine 1963; Lipson 1975).

An infamous incident in the history of private security involving the Pinkerton Agency was the "Battle of Homestead" in 1892. The Homestead mill was part of the Carnegie Steel works and was located in Munhall, Pennsylvania, along the bank of the Monongahela River. The Homestead steelworkers had been locked out of the mill. On July 6, 1892, the strikers and community supporters broke into the closed mill. At that time, 300 Pinkerton agents armed with repeating rifles attempted to land at the pump house on mill property. By the time order was restored, seven strikers and three detectives had been killed. Afterwards, the agents were humiliated in a gauntlet organized by women and children of the strikers.

Battle of Homestead:
An infamous incident between mill laborers and Pinkerton security officers.

The battle was the culmination of failed contract bargaining between the Amalgamated Association of Iron and Steel Workers and Carnegie Steel. One report noted that while this battle occurred, the owner of Carnegie Steel, Andrew Carnegie, vacationed at his castle in Scotland. The Battle of Homestead is considered one of the most famous events in U.S. labor history and one of its most significant (Battle of Homestead Foundation nd).

During the 1880s, no central agency maintained records on known criminals. Pinkerton established the practice in his agency of maintaining criminal records on all known criminals. For many years, he maintained the only general file of known criminals. The files contained detailed descriptions of the individuals, any known associates, their *modus operandi,* and descriptions of scars and tattoos. Many of the pictures used on wanted posters were obtained by police departments from the Pinkerton Agency (Lipson 1975, 76).

The Pinkerton Agency remained a privately owned company controlled by Pinkerton's descendants until it went public in 1967. The agency had been a proprietorship until 1925, when it was incorporated for the first time. In 1965 the agency's name was changed to Pinkerton's Inc. (Lipson 1975, 35).

Other Notable Private Security Agencies

In the 1850s, Henry Wells and William Fargo were partners in the American Express Company. Their company had a charter to operate an express freight service. As they expanded their services beyond the Mississippi River, they operated as the Wells Fargo Company. Wells Fargo used its own employees as security officers and as "shotgun riders." Wells Fargo gained a reputation as the carrier of trusted valuables. It was, however, robbed at least twenty-eight times in the State of California during the period from 1875 to 1883.

An infamous outlaw, Black Bart, was captured by J. B. Hume, an employee of Wells Fargo. Hume used Chinese laundry marks to locate Black Bart. Bart's real name was C. E. Bolton, and he committed each robbery while wearing a flour sack to mask his face. As Bolton robbed each stagecoach, he would leave a few lines of poetry with the stage driver. His most famous one reads:

> I've labored long and hard for bread
>
> For Honor and for riches,
>
> But on my corns too long you've tread
>
> You fine-haired sons of ——

It was signed "Black Bart, the PO8" (Lipson 1975, 33)

Washington Perry Brink started Brinks, Inc., also in Chicago, in 1859. Brinks was at first only a package delivery service. Brinks made its first payroll delivery in 1891, and has since become the largest armored car and courier service in the United

An early Wells Fargo Badge.

States. By 1900, Brinks and Wells Fargo were the major firms offering security for the transportation of valuables and securities (Kakalik and Wildhorn 1971).

Edwin Holmes established the first burglar alarm service in the United States in 1858. He had purchased the rights to an alarm system that had been designed by Augustus Pope. The American District Telegraph Company, better known as ADT, was established in 1909. Both companies installed home alarm systems, monitored and maintained them, and responded to alarm situations, usually for a monthly fee. ADT still follows this practice today. In 1909, Baker Industries started a similar service for businesses, and ADT expanded to business organizations. In a 2007 advertisement, ADT stated that it presently protects over 5 million homes and 2 million businesses worldwide.

In 1954, George R. Wackenhut left the FBI to start Special Agent Investigators, a private security company, with three of his former FBI colleagues. By 1955 his partners had left the business, and soon after, Wackenhut formed The Wackenhut Corporation. The company went public in 1967, trading first on the American Stock Exchange and later on the New York Stock Exchange. During Wackenhut's stewardship, the organization grew to become one of the largest security solutions companies in the contract security industry. During the mid-1960s, Wackenhut recognized the need to provide specialized services for sensitive U.S. government installations and formed Wackenhut Services, Inc., which is now the largest contract security provider to the federal government.

The Wackenhut Corporation eventually offered physical security services, which became the company's primary revenue source. In the mid-1980s, Wackenhut saw the need to integrate physical security personnel with electronic security equipment to improve security measures and drive efficiencies in service delivery. This was the forerunner to what is today commonly referred to as *integrated security solutions,* which Wackenhut offers today. In 1984, The Wackenhut Corporation began its nuclear division—Wackenhut Nuclear Services—which is designed to provide quality security services for the nation's nuclear energy plants. This division now protects more than half of the United States' commercial nuclear power-generating plants.

Development of Professional Associations

In 1955, the American Society for Industrial Security (ASIS) was founded as the first professional organization for security personnel. The ASIS is presently an international organization and is the largest organization for security professionals, with more than 35,000 members worldwide. The stated mission of the ASIS is increase the effectiveness and productivity of security professionals by developing educational programs and materials that address broad security interests, such as the ASIS Annual Seminar and Exhibits, as well as specific security topics. ASIS also advocates the role and value of the security management profession to business, the media, governmental entities, and the public.

ASIS administers three certification programs. The Certified Protection Professional designation indicates board certification in security management and is generally considered the highest certification that can be accorded a security practitioner. The other two certifications are technical certifications: Physical Security Professional (PSP) and Professional Certified Investigator (PCI). In 1996, the ASIS created a foundation,

Blackwater Security Services

Blackwater Worldwide is one of the world's largest security firms. The firm provides private security to U.S. government officials in many foreign countries. In 2007 there were some issues about how their professionals were accomplishing their missions in Iraq. Blackwater's website advertises that the firm:

Efficiently and effectively integrates a wide range of resources and core competencies to provide unique and

timely solutions that exceed our customers' stated needs and expectations. Blackwater is guided by integrity, innovation, and a desire for a safer world. Blackwater Worldwide professionals leverage state-of-the-art training facilities, professional program management teams, and innovative manufacturing and production capabilities to deliver world-class, customer-driven solutions.

which presently funds and manages endowments for a wide range of academic, strategic, and professional development activities, and which sponsors security industry reports and research.

The National Association of Security Companies (NASCO) is the nation's largest contract security trade association, representing private security companies that employ more than 400,000 of the nation's most highly trained security officers servicing every business sector. NASCO has worked to set meaningful standards for the private security industry and security officers by monitoring state and federal legislation and regulations affecting the quality and effectiveness of private security services. The NASCO is also working toward implementing legislation in several states, including Mississippi, Alabama, and Colorado, which do not currently regulate private security, to set standards for security officer licensing (Ricci 2007).

The National Council of Investigation and Security Services, Inc. (NCISS), is a cooperative effort of companies and associations responsible for providing private security and investigation services to the legal profession, business community, government, and the public. The NCISS states that the issues it is involved in include: overly restrictive legislation regarding training and standards, proliferation of legislation requiring local licensing, public misunderstanding and misinformation on the role and contribution of private investigators and security services, and an uninformed media. The stated role of the NCISS is to meet and solve these issues while seeking to uncover and recommend action on any hidden potential problems that may affect the private security profession.

PRESENT-DAY ROLE OF PRIVATE SECURITY

Today, private security firms perform a number of roles, from executive protection and static security to training partner nations, to providing both ground and aviation logistics support, all in dangerous environments. In the future, private security firms will likely be called on to support stability operations and peacekeeping efforts (Taylor 2006).

Private security agencies have moved beyond simply protecting private property. They are actively engaged in maintaining order, investigating crimes, and making arrests in public spaces. They are involved in activities that were once performed exclusively by public police forces. The line between what is public and private property—and who is responsible for policing public and private space—is becoming blurred.

There has been an increase in property that is now considered mass private property. *Mass private property* refers to large tracts of public-access, privately owned space that have traditionally fallen outside the domain of public police—for example, shopping malls, commercial centers, and gated communities. In policing mass private property and in other situations as well, public police and private security agencies often develop cooperative relationships with one another. This cooperation frequently causes a blurring of the relationship between the public and private sectors. The movement of retiring police officers to the private security sector often facilitates cooperation. Many executives who lead private security companies, forensic accounting teams, or security consulting firms were formerly public police officers (Rigakos 2002).

Although the private policing industry and public policing forces share a common goal of protecting the public, these two industries have rarely cooperated (Minnaar 2005, 1).

On May 1, 2007, Joseph Ricci, executive director of NASCO, testified before the U.S. House of Representatives Committee on House Homeland Security. At the hearing, he discussed the present-day state of private security. The following facts were taken from his testimony.

Nearly 2 million people are employed in private security domestically, compared to less than 700,000 law enforcement personnel. Private security officers are guarding federal facilities, critical infrastructure, businesses, and public areas; working with the armed forces in Iraq and at Department of Defense installations; supporting the operations of the Customs and Border Patrol; and providing screening at airports for the Transportation Security Administration (TSA). Private security officers are often the "first responders" at the scene of any security- or terrorism-related incident, and private security protects 85 percent of the nation's critical infrastructure. Nearly 75 percent of private security officers work for contract security companies, with the balance serving as proprietary or in-house security. The vast majority of contract security firms employ many former law enforcement personnel in senior management.

Contract security officers are trained to support law enforcement. The legal authority invested in a security officer varies by jurisdiction. Security officers may have other authorities or may face further limitations to their police power according to state licensing or other regulation, where it exists. Protecting people and property from accidents and crime, controlling access, observing and reporting are generally principal roles of security officers. They may enforce laws on their employer's grounds, conduct incident interviews, prepare incident reports, and provide legal testimony. They may be armed, as required by specific duty assignments, consistent with state and federal laws governing private ownership and use of firearms.

Private security companies and their officers are working to support and complement law enforcement and other first responders. There are thousands of examples of law enforcement and contract security personnel working together to solve crimes and improve security measures, making our country safer and more secure.

Tens of thousands of contract security officers are currently (as of 2007) protecting U.S. government facilities around the world. The training and qualification standards for contract security officers are subject to regulations of the state where the facility is located, but more so, by the regulations and requirements of the federal agency with which they are contracting. Contract security officers are qualified and able to perform the security functions required of them by federal agencies such as

Federal Protective Services (FPS). One large federal customer for contract security is the Department of Defense. In 2003, as a result of increases in security requirements after 9/11 and the number of active-duty and reserve personnel being sent overseas, it was necessary that contract security officers fulfill security roles previously performed by military employees. Congress passed legislation lifting a restriction against the use of contract security officers at U.S. military installations, and in 2007 there were 130 Department of Defense installations using contract security officers.

In 2007 there were 15,000 contract security officers working at facilities under the jurisdiction of Federal Protective Services. Training standards for contract security officers fulfilling FPS contracts are higher than any state requirements. FPS requires that all security officers complete eighty hours of preassignment training on access and traffic control, security and fire systems, reports and response, as well as eight-plus hours of onsite and annual in-service training. All contract security officers must pass an extensive background check, and must pass an exam prior to employment and additional background checks every two years, as well as complete annual refresher training, cardiopulmonary resuscitation (CPR) and domestic violence certification, annual weapons requalification, and medical and first-aid certification.

REGULATION OF PRIVATE SECURITY

A 2003 *USA Today* story characterized private security as "homeland defense's weak link." The article stated that although a few states had introduced or raised hiring or training standards, most states still do not impose minimum training standards or even require background checks. Moreover, according to the article, even in states that did require training programs, there was little effort to monitor the content or quality of the programs (Hall 2003, A1.). Many security experts contend that the story does not correctly describe the current situation in the regulation of private security.

Federal Regulation

Except for private security persons employed by the federal government or by the District of Columbia, the majority of individuals performing private security duties are regulated by the states. Individuals employed by or contracted to federal agencies are for the most part regulated by the federal agency involved.

The federal government also assists the states in their regulation of private security. One key assistance area was implemented by the U.S. Private Security Officer Employment Authorization Act of 2004. The Act as implemented by the U.S. Code of Federal Regulations (28 CFR 105.21) requires the U.S. Attorney General to "publish regulations to provide for the security, confidentiality, accuracy, use, submission, dissemination, destruction of information and audits, and record keeping" of the exchange of criminal history record information, as defined in 28 CFR 20.3(d), and related information. The attorney general is also required to develop standards for qualifying an authorized employer, and the imposition of fees. The purpose of this federal program is to provide a convenient procedure so that employers can obtain criminal histories from different states for individuals who are applying for private security certification. (Under our federalist system of government, one state may not just demand that another state provide such information.)

Under the provisions of the program, when a valid request for criminal history on an applicant is received by a state, the State shall notify an authorized employer as to the fact of whether the person has been convicted of a felony, an offense involving dishonesty or a false statement if the conviction occurred during the previous 10 years, or an offense involving the use or attempted use of physical force against the person of another if the conviction occurred during the previous 10 years; or charged with a criminal felony for which there has been no resolution during the preceding 365 days.

In addition, upon receipt of a request for a criminal history record information search from an authorized employer, submitted through the State identification bureau of a participating State, the U.S. Attorney General shall: Search the appropriate records of the Criminal Justice Information Services Division of the Federal Bureau of Investigation; and promptly provide any resulting identification and criminal history record information to the submitting State identification bureau requesting the information.

The Act also provides for criminal penalties when information obtained pursuant to the Act is used for any purpose other than determining the suitability of an individual for employment as a private security officer. The state submitting the record of criminal history may require that a reasonable fee be paid before forwarding the criminal history of an applicant.

State Regulation

In 2008, forty-three states licensed and regulated private security companies and security officers. Regulation at the state level varies greatly with regard to screening and training. Training requirements range from a minimum of four hours or less of preassignment and no in-service training to forty-plus hours of training combining preassignment, onsite, and in-service training. Background screening requirements range from local criminal checks to national checks. There are additional requirements for armed as opposed to unarmed officers, and they too vary by state. There is a trend toward increased regulation at the state levels, with leading states such as New York and California recently raising training standards and hours and including proprietary or in-house security officers in registration regulations. Training standards have also recently been raised in New Jersey, and there is pending legislation in the District of Columbia.

As a general rule, the states are getting more careful about who can work in private security and when. For example, in 2004, by Senate Bill 1241, California lawmakers amended the state's Private Security Services Act, which provides for licensing and regulation of private security officers.

Previously, the Act let a new employee begin working before receiving a registration card and before a background check was completed. Now, employees cannot begin work until they have hard-copy proof that both tasks have been done. California law also has changed regarding off-duty police officers who work security. Before, the law exempted police from having to provide a fingerprint for background checks on the security work; that exemption is now gone. However, unlike a private security officer, the off-duty police officer can start security work before completion of the background check.

To be licensed as a private security officer, individuals must usually be at least eighteen years old, pass a background check, and complete some classroom training in such subjects as property rights, emergency procedures, and detention of suspected criminals. Drug testing often is required and may be random and ongoing.

Commonwealth of Virginia

Statute on Private Security Services

§9.1-139. a. No person shall engage in the private security services business or solicit private security business in the Commonwealth without having obtained a license from the Department. No person shall be issued a private security services business license until a compliance agent is designated in writing on forms provided by the Department. The compliance agent shall ensure the compliance of the private security services business with this article and shall meet the qualifications and perform the duties required by the regulations adopted by the Board. A compliance agent shall have either a minimum of (i) three years of managerial or supervisory experience in a private security services business; with a federal, state or local law-enforcement agency; or in a related field or (ii) five years of experience in a private security services business; with a federal, state or local law-enforcement agency; or in a related field.

Q: What are considered to be Private Security Services in the Commonwealth of Virginia?

The providing of services conducted by armored car personnel, security officers, personal protection specialists, private investigators, couriers, security canine handlers, security canine teams, alarm respondents, central station dispatchers, electronic security employees, electronic security sales representatives or electronic security technicians and their assistants to another person under contract, express or implied.

(*Source:* Virginia Department of Criminal Justice Services, www. dcjs.virginia.gov/pss/aboutUs/faqs.cfm, accessed May 7, 2007.)

In most states, the state must license security officers before they may carry weapon. Many states provide for further certification as special police officers, allowing those officers to make limited types of arrests while on duty. Armed positions generally have more stringent background checks and entry requirements than those of unarmed officers because of greater insurance liability risks.

A typical state statute on private security regulation is the Commonwealth of Virginia's statute.

City Codes

Many cities and counties have codes that also regulate private security and supplement the state statutes. A typical city code is that of Seattle, Washington.

THE TRANSFORMATION OF POLICING

In 1993 in the small town of Sussex, New Jersey, after the entire four-officer police force was dismissed because of a drug scandal, the community contracted for police services with a private company, Executive Security & Investigations Services, Inc. (Hall 2003).

Seattle, Washington City Code, Chapter 5

5.20.020 Regulation of private security companies, private security guards and armed private security guards.

No person shall operate a private security company within the City, or perform functions and duties as a private security guard and armed private security guard within the City, without first applying for and obtaining a business license and paying the fee therefor, as prescribed in this title, and, in addition, without being licensed pursuant to State law. (Ord. 92-1036 §2: Ord. 91-1057 §6)

According to Bayley and Shearing (2001), policing is being transformed and restructured. The major transformation is that policing, meaning the activity of making societies safe, is no longer carried out exclusively by governments. Bayley and Shearing even question whether governments are the primary providers. According to those authors, gradually and almost imperceptibly, policing has been "multilateralized" in that a host of nongovernmental groups have assumed responsibility for their own protection, and a host of nongovernmental agencies have undertaken to provide security services. The two researchers consider that policing has entered a new era, an era characterized by a transformation in the governance of security.

Bayley and Shearing noted that a number of studies have attempted to document in particular countries the rise of what is loosely referred to as "private security," but the extent of the transformation of policing has yet to be determined. They believe, however, that the following statements about the current restructuring are true and amply justify their efforts to understand what is happening:

- In most countries, especially in the democratic world, private security officers outnumber public police.
- In these same countries, people spend more time in their daily lives in places where visible crime prevention and control are provided by nongovernmental groups rather than by governmental police agencies.
- The reconstruction of policing is occurring worldwide despite differences in wealth and economic systems.

Bayley and Shearing note that, viewed historically, what is happening to policing is not unprecedented, and it can be argued that the monopolization of policing by government is an aberration. That is, only in the last 100 to 200 years has policing been effectively monopolized by government, and even that was not uniform across countries. In Europe, for example, France led the way in the systematic nationalization of policing in the seventeenth century. Nationalization followed throughout the rest of continental Europe, concentrated largely in towns and often deferring to the private authority of the land-owning aristocracy. Prussia permitted the land-owning Junker aristocracy to police their large estates up until the unification of Germany in 1871. Russia, too, allowed policing to be shared between government and the landed gentry until the early twentieth century.

In England, policing remained largely in private hands until well into the nineteenth century. In the United States, where policing was gradually governmentalized by cities in the middle of the nineteenth century, private policing never really died. Most states did not begin to develop organized police forces until the early twentieth century, and the national government did not do so until a decade or so later.

Bayley and Shearing ask whether the current restructuring of policing is simply a return to the past, another cycle in the historical ebb and flow of policing power between governmental and nongovernmental agencies. They note that governments have shared, even conceded, the power of policing to nongovernmental groups before. Sometimes security has been so precarious that government could scarcely be said to exist at all in many parts of the world. However, the researchers concluded that at the same time, the restructuring that is taking place today is taking a different form than in the past, because contemporary societies are organized differently than previous ones. Indeed, the concepts and terminology inherited from the past are inadequate for understanding what is happening today. According to Bayley and Shearing, for policymakers to comprehend, and possibly deal effectively with, the current transformation in policing, it will be necessary to examine contemporary developments with a fresh intellectual eye.

Bayley and Shearing noted that their knowledge of what is occurring is based largely on studies from democratic countries. These, after all, are where information about policing can be most freely obtained. The character of government, then, affects what is known about policing and, as we shall discuss, probably the extent of restructuring as well. Although they believe the restructuring is worldwide, it remains for new research to document its extent across the globe. They contend that the change in policing is occurring across the divide of economic development, with developing democracies participating along with developed ones.

Bayley and Shearing point out that when they use the term "policing" it does not refer to all the means by which human beings provide safety for themselves—policing is not synonymous with social control. Societies create order, and hopefully thereby safety, through processes of socialization and informal discipline. Everyone plays a role in these processes—parents, siblings, peers, friends, acquaintances, colleagues, and a host of authority figures. Their research focused on intentional attempts to regulate the distribution of physical security produced by actual or potential use of force.

The shift from government to private policing includes the following types of activities:

- In gated communities, policing involves primarily regulating access, surveillance, and patrolling. Gated communities are especially popular in the United States, where they have been the fastest-growing segment of the housing market. Bayley and Shearing noted that creating gates for communities does not happen exclusively under private auspices. When the public police barricade streets to create cul-de-sacs that impede drive-by criminal activity, as in Houston and Los Angeles in the 1980s, they are creating gated communities, and often for the poor.
- Residents of ungated neighborhoods may agree to pay a small per-capita fee to support private security services. This has happened in parts of Glasgow, London, and Melbourne. Such a practice demonstrates again the problem with describing security services as being either public or private. The financial levies agreed to could be regarded as a form of local government or as nongovernmental self-help. In cases like these, cooperative activity looks very much like self-government.
- Residential neighborhoods may form ad-hoc advisory councils to mobilize in-kind community resources that address security needs. Residents undertake to watch one anothers' houses, alert police to suspicious strangers, patrol the streets at certain times of the day, improve dangerous physical conditions, mediate neighborhood disputes, and organize restorative justice conferences. In the United States, the federal government has given some communities grants to support the security plans they have developed. Similar initiatives have been undertaken in South Africa and Ireland. (Bayley and Shearing 2001, 122–3)

Bayley and Shearing conclude that policing today is not just being "privatized." It is being restructured though the development of new groups as both instigators and providers of policing. The public and the private are being combined in new ways, ways that sometimes make it difficult to separate public from private. Multilateralization, although an awkward term, is a more accurate way of describing what is happening to policing in the late twentieth century than privatization.

Summary

- The number of individuals employed in private security far exceeds the number of police officers in the United States. Private security officers constitute a potential resource to assist law enforcement agencies in fulfilling their mission.
- The private security profession has changed greatly from the 1970s.
- There are two categories of private security services: proprietary or corporate security, and contract or private security firms.
- The earliest recorded history indicates that private security measures existed long before the advent of government-controlled policing.
- An early English method of private security included the "hue and cry," whereby citizens were required to help defend neighbors who needed assistance.
- The first organized efforts to prevent crime in England relied heavily on private citizens.
- Colquhoun organized the Thames River Police in 1798. The police were financed by private companies until 1890.
- The American colonies imported the watch system from England. No formal security agencies existed until the 1780s.
- The first public police force was established in New York City in 1844.
- Allan Pinkerton founded Chicago's first private detective agency in 1850. He is considered by many to be the father of the private security industry.

- Other notable private security agencies formed in the 1800s in the United States included Wells Fargo, Brinks, and Wackenhut.
- Edwin Holmes established the first home burglar alarm service in the United States. The American Society for Industrial Security (ASIS), founded in 1955, was the first professional organization for security personnel.
- The National Association of Security Companies (NASCO) is the nation's largest contract security trade association, representing private security companies that employ more than 400,000 of the nation's most highly trained security officers servicing every business sector.
- The National Council of Investigation and Security Services, Inc. (NCISS), is a cooperative effort of companies and associations responsible for providing private security and investigation services to the legal profession, business community, government, and the public.
- Private security agencies no longer just protect private property. They are actively engaged in maintaining order, investigating crimes, and making arrests in public spaces. They are involved in activities that were once performed exclusively by public police forces. The line between what is public and private property and who is responsible for policing public and private space has blurred.
- Private security is regulated mostly by individual states, thus the regulations vary. As a general rule, most states require certification before an individual may work as a private security officer.

Review Questions

1. Why has public policing not replaced private security?
2. What is the role of the private security industry in today's world?
3. How did Colquhoun influence the evolution of today's private security agencies?
4. Explain the patterns of state and local regulation in the private security industry.
5. What are the two categories of private security services? How do they differ?
6. What is the future of private security?

Class Exercises

1. Discuss in class how private security has changed since the 1970s.
2. Individual members of the class may conduct interviews of a local security manager for his or her opinion as to the future of private security.

3. Discuss in class the present-day role of private security.

References

Battle of Homestead Foundation—Pennsylvania Labor History Society. nd. "http://www.home.earthlink.net/~homestead1892/boh/1892history.html" (accessed May 8, 2007).

Bayley, David H., and Clifford D. Shearing. 2001. *The new structure of policing: Description, conceptualization, and research agenda.* NCJ 187083. Washington, DC: U.S. Department of Justice.

Colquhoun, Patrick. 1796, 1969. *Treatise on the commerce and police of the River Thames.* London: H. Fry. Reprinted London: Patterson Smith reprint series in criminology, law enforcement, and social problems, Publication no. 41, 1969.

Critchley, T. A. 1978. *A history of police in England and Wales.* Monclair, NJ: Patterson.

Healy, Richard J. 1983. *Design for security,* 2nd ed. New York: John Wiley & Sons.

Kakalik, James, and Sorrell Wildhorn. 1971. Private police in the United States: Findings and recommendations. RAND report R-869-DO. Santa Monica, CA: Rand Corporation.

Levine, S. A. 1963. *Allan Pinkerton: American's first private eye.* New York: Dodd, Mead.

Lipson, Milton. 1975. *On guard: The business of private security.* New York: Quadrangle Books.

Minnaar, A. 2005. Private–public partnerships: Private security, crime prevention and policing in South Africa. *ACTA Criminologica* 18(1): 85–114. www.ncjrs.gov/App/

Publications/abstract.aspx?ID=209702 (accessed on May 6, 2007).

Morabito, Andrew, and Sheldon Greenberg. 2005. *Engaging the private sector to promote homeland security: Law enforcement–private security partnerships.* NCJ 210678. Washington, DC: Bureau of Justice Assistance.

Pringle, Patrick. 1979. *Hue and CRY.* New York: William Morrow.

Reith, C. 1975. *Blind eye of history.* Montclair, NJ: Patterson, Smith.

Reynolds, Elaine. 1998. *Before the Bobbies.* Stanford, CA: Stanford University Press.

Ricci, Joseph. 2007. Executive director National Association of Security Companies (NASCO) testimony before the U.S. House of Representatives Committee on House Homeland Security, 1 May.

Rigakos, George. 2002. *The new parapolice: Risk markets and co-modified social control.* Toronto: University of Toronto Press.

Taylor, Chris. 2006. Testimony of Chris Taylor, vice president, Blackwater USA, at a hearing of the National Security, Emerging Threats and International Relations Subcommittee of the House Government Reform Committee, Subject: Private security firms: Standards, cooperation and coordination. Washington, DC: Federal News Service, June 13

Wagner, Dennis. 2006. Private security guards play key roles post-9/11. *The Arizona Republic,* January 22, A1.

CHAPTER 2

Security, Crime, and the Physical Environment

CHAPTER OUTLINE

OBJECTIVES

After completing this chapter, you will be able to:

- Discuss the complexity of crime.
- Describe the Uniform Crime Report.
- Describe the National Crime Victimization Survey.
- Explain the similarities and differences between the Uniform Crime Report and the National Crime Victimization Survey.
- Discuss deterrence theory.
- Explain the difference between general deterrence and specific deterrence.
- Describe the significance of the "opportunity" component in the crime equation.
- Discuss the importance of crime opportunity reduction.
- Describe the objective of situational crime prevention.

- Describe crime prevention through environmental design.
- Identify and discuss target hardening techniques.
- Identify and discuss a few special security concerns.

Crime and the fear of crime have permeated the fabric of American life.

—*Warren E. Burger, Chief Justice, U.S. Supreme Court*

An important mandate of the private security industry is to prevent and deter crime. The actual amount of crime prevented by the private security industry is not known, but it is believed to be astronomical. Think about this for a moment. If society did not have the services of private security, the police would quickly become overwhelmed with many tasks that are routinely performed by the private security sector. For example, private security officers patrol property to protect against fire, theft, vandalism, terrorism, and other illegal activity. Many construction contractors hire private security officers to patrol construction sites to prevent lumber and equipment thefts. Supermarkets and commercial shopping malls hire private security officers to prevent and detect shoplifting and other crimes. Private security firms routinely conduct security risk assessments for business and industry. Major manufacturers employ security departments that protect their investment, enforce laws on the property, and deter criminal activity and other problems. Hospitals and medical facilities maintain security departments that ensure the safety of medical staff and other hospital employees, and patients. The private security industry in the United States plays an invaluable role in the prevention and detection of crime.

Crime prevention:
Any action taken to reduce crime risks and build individual and community safety.

This chapter examines what private security officers should know about crime prevention and deterrence, as well as providing an overview of the two major crime reporting systems used in the United States. The chapter also introduces the concept of environmental crime prevention theory. Environmental crime prevention theory is presented in a manner that shows how theory can affect fundamental security practice. In other words, the reader is not inundated with a theoretical discussion that has little use for the security practitioner in the field. The chapter concludes with an overview of target hardening techniques and examples of a few special security concerns.

CRIME REPORTING AND CRIME

The ability of the public police and private security authorities to prevent and detect crime has improved steadily. Advances in technology and sophisticated security systems greatly assist security organizations in carrying out their mission. Like the public police, private security authorities work to prevent both crimes against property and crimes against persons. The advances in crime prevention and detection are grounds for optimism in many respects; however, criminals still manage to manipulate even the most innovative technology and security measures to carry out their crimes.

Crime occurs every day and in every location, yet we cannot predict with any certainty how many crimes will occur this year or in the future. We simply do not have a measurement that captures all the crime that is committed in the United States. In fact, it would be virtually impossible to do so, because not every crime that is committed is reported to the authorities. Authorities are able to glean some estimate of the extent of crime based on two major data sources: the Uniform Crime Report (UCR) and the National Crime Victimization Survey (NCVS).

Uniform Crime Report

At some time you may have heard on a news report or read in your local newspaper an account that goes something like this: "The FBI reports that violent crime is down 6 percent," or "Murder is up 2 percent." Where do the media get these numbers? They are probably reporting information from the Uniform Crime Report.

The UCR was conceived in 1929 by the International Association of Chiefs of Police to meet a need for reliable, uniform crime statistics for the nation. In 1930 the FBI was tasked with collecting, publishing, and archiving these statistics. Several annual statistical reports, such as *Comprehensive Crime in the United States,* are produced from data provided by nearly 17,000 law enforcement agencies across the United States. The UCR is an annual report that includes the number of crimes reported by citizens to local police departments and the number of arrests made by law enforcement agencies in a given year.

The UCR prepares an annual crime index that separates crimes into two categories, Part I and Part II crimes. Part I offenses, also referred to as *index crimes,* are serious crimes by nature and/or volume. Part I offenses include crimes such as murder and non-negligent manslaughter, forcible rape, robbery, aggravated assault, burglary, larceny-theft, motor vehicle theft, and arson. Not all crimes are readily brought to the attention of the police.

Index crimes:
The eight major crimes included in Part I of the FBI's Uniform Crime Report: criminal homicide, forcible rape, robbery, aggravated assault, burglary, larceny theft, motor vehicle theft, and arson.

Arson was not originally part of the crime reporting process; it became the eighth Part I crime as the result of a limited congressional mandate in 1978. With the passage of the Anti-Arson Act of 1982, Congress permanently designated arson as a reportable offense. The UCR also collects arrest data on the Part I offenses and twenty-one other Part II offenses.

Can you think of any limitations to the UCR? One such limitation is that the UCR includes only reported crimes, that is, crimes that are reported to law enforcement authorities. Thus the UCR does not depict the actual amount of crime that has occurred in the United States.

A number of factors influence the reporting or nonreporting of crimes to authorities. Violent crimes are most likely to be reported to the police, and household crimes are the next highest reported types of crime (Roberson and Wallace 1998). The most common reason given for not reporting a violent crime is that the crime was considered by the victim to be a private or personal matter. In some cases, household crimes are not reported to authorities because stolen are subsequently recovered or because the crime was committed by someone known to the victim. The most common reasons for reporting household crimes were tax and insurance concerns. That is, a burglary is reported to authorities because the victim's insurance company requires a police report before it will compensate the victim for the loss.

Roberson and Wallace (1998) report that victims do not always report crimes even when the offender is not known to the victim. For example, victims of crimes committed by strangers gave the following reasons for not reporting the offense:

- The offender was unsuccessful.
- The victim considered the police inefficient.

The Uniform Crime Report: Part I and Part II Offenses

Part I Offenses

1. Criminal homicide
2. Forcible rape
3. Robbery
4. Aggravated assault
5. Burglary
6. Larceny-theft (except motor vehicle theft)
7. Motor vehicle theft
8. Arson

Part II Offenses

9. Other assaults
10. Forgery and counterfeiting
11. Fraud
12. Embezzlement
13. Stolen property: buying, receiving, processing

14. Vandalism
15. Weapons: carrying, possessing, etc.
16. Prostitution and commercialized vice
17. Sex offenses
18. Drug abuse violations
19. Gambling
20. Offenses against family and children
21. Driving under the influence
22. Liquor laws
23. Drunkenness
24. Disorderly conduct
25. Vagrancy
26. All other offenses
27. Suspicion
28. Curfew and loitering laws (persons under age 18)
29. Runaways (persons under age 18)

- The victim felt the police did not want to be bothered.
- It was not important enough to the victim to report the crime.

The National Crime Victimization Survey

The National Crime Victimization Survey has been reporting data on personal and household victimization since 1973. The NCVS attempts to correct the problems of nonreporting that are inherent in the UCR by contacting a nationwide sample of citizens and interviewing them about their victimizations.

Uniform Crime Report (UCR):
Official data on crime that are reported to law enforcement agencies across the United States, which then provide the data to the FBI. The UCR is a summary-based reporting system, with data aggregated to the city, county, state, and other geographic levels.

An ongoing survey of a nationally representative sample of residential addresses, the NCVS is the primary source of information on the characteristics of criminal victimization and on the numbers and types of crimes that are not reported to law enforcement authorities. It provides the largest national forum for victims to describe the effects of crime and the characteristics of violent offenders. Twice each year, data are obtained from a nationally representative sample of roughly 42,000 households comprising about 75,000 persons on the frequency, characteristics, and consequences of criminal victimization in the United States.

The NCVS collects information on crimes suffered by individuals and households, whether or not those crimes were reported to law enforcement. It estimates

Uniform Crime Report

The FBI's Uniform Crime Report compiles data from monthly law enforcement reports or individual crime incident records transmitted directly to the FBI or to centralized state agencies that then report to the FBI. Each report submitted for the UCR is examined thoroughly for reasonableness, accuracy, and deviations that may indicate errors.

the proportion of each crime type reported to law enforcement, and it summarizes the reasons that victims give for reporting or not reporting the crime. The survey provides information about victims (age, sex, race, ethnicity, marital status, income, and educational level), offenders (sex, race, approximate age, and victim–offender relationship), and the crimes (time and place of occurrence, use of weapons, nature of injury, and economic consequences). Questions also cover the experiences of victims with the criminal justice system, self-protective measures used by victims, and possible substance abuse by offenders. The survey is administered by the U.S. Census Bureau on behalf of the Bureau of Justice Statistics.

The NCVS was designed with four primary objectives: (1) to develop detailed information about the victims and consequences of crime; (2) to estimate the numbers and types of crimes that are not reported to police; (3) to provide uniform measures of selected types of crimes; and (4) to permit comparisons over time and types of areas. The survey categorizes crimes as personal or property crimes. Personal crimes include rape and sexual attack, robbery, aggravated and simple assault, and purse-snatching/pocket-picking; property crimes include burglary, theft, motor vehicle theft, and vandalism. The data from the NCVS are particularly useful for calculating crime rates, both aggregated and disaggregated, and for determining changes in crime rates from year to year.

Comparing the UCR and NCVS

Both the UCR and the NCVS provide invaluable information about crime and victimization. Because the NCVS was designed to complement the UCR, the two programs share many similarities. Both programs cover rape, robbery, aggravated assault, burglary, theft, and motor vehicle theft. Rape, robbery, theft, and motor vehicle theft are defined virtually identically by both the UCR and NCVS. Although males as well as females can be victims of rape, the UCR Crime Index reports the crime against women only, whereas the NCVS reports it for both sexes.

Although there are some similarities between the UCR and the NCVS, there are also significant differences between the two programs. The two programs were created to serve different purposes. The UCR's primary objective is to provide a reliable set of criminal justice statistics for law enforcement administration, operation, and management. The NCVS was established to provide previously unavailable information about crime, including crime not reported to police, and about both victims and offenders.

National Crime Victimization Survey (NCVS):
Conducted by the Bureau of Justice Statistics and the U.S. Census Bureau. The survey consists of questions asked of a carefully selected sample of victims regarding their experiences with criminal activity.

Property crime:
A category of crime that includes burglary, larceny, theft, auto theft, arson, shoplifting, and vandalism. Property crime involves only the taking of money or property and does not involve force or threat of force against a victim.

Crimes against persons:
A category of crimes that includes robbery, simple assault, aggravated assault, sexual assault, and murder.

National Crime Victimization Survey

The National Crime Victimization (NCVS) is the primary source of information in the United States on criminal victimization. The NCVS reports the likelihood of victimization by rape, sexual assault, robbery, assault, theft, household burglary, and motor vehicle theft for the population as a whole as well as for segments of the population such as women, the elderly, members of various racial groups, city dwellers, or other groups. The NCVS provides the largest national forum for victims to describe the effects of crime and characteristics of violent offenders.

Measuring Crime

You may have heard the expression, "The burglary rate is 740." What does this mean? Basically, this statement can be interpreted as meaning that there are 740 burglaries for every 100,000 persons in the population under consideration. Crime rates are computed according to the equation:

$$\text{Crime rate} = (\text{number of reported crimes})/(\text{total population}) \times 100{,}000$$

Prevalence of Crime

The FBI recently reported a slight increase in the number of violent crimes. Recall that the violent crime category includes murder, forcible rape, robbery, and aggravated assault. Also remember, when you read that the FBI reports that a specific crime has increased or decreased, the reference is to crime data measured as part of the Uniform Crime Report.

According to the Bureau of Justice Statistics (2007), the location of about a quarter of incidents of violent crime was at or near the victim's home. The most common locations for violent crimes were on streets other than those near the victim's home and accounted for about 19 percent. Of violent crimes, about half occurred within a mile from the victim's home, and 76 percent within five miles. Twenty-two percent of violent crime victims were involved in some form of leisure activity away from home at the time of their victimization, 22 percent said they were at home, and another 20 percent mentioned that they were at work or traveling to or from work when the crime occurred.

Over the past few years, property crimes have continued to decrease. Property crimes include burglary, larceny-theft, and motor vehicle theft. Arson is also a property crime, but data for arson are not included in property crime totals. Property crime makes up slightly more than three-quarters of all crime in the United States. Overall, in about 84 percent of all burglaries, the offender gained entry into the victim's residence or other building on the property. In about 79 percent of all motor vehicle thefts, the vehicle was stolen, not just taken for a joyride.

Property crime, regardless of the type, occurred more often to those living in rented property. Households in rented property typically experience more property crime, whereas people who own their homes usually experience less victimization. The Bureau of Justice Statistics reports that persons who rented their property had more than twice the rate of motor vehicle theft as persons living in owned property.

DETERRENCE THEORY

Deterrence:
A theory of justice whereby the aim of punishment is to prevent or deter persons from engaging in future criminal behavior because of the consequences associated with their being detected.

Deterrence theory proposes that the aim of punishment is to prevent or deter future criminal activity. *Deterrence* is the idea is that people will refrain from engaging in criminal activity because of the consequences associated with detection (Adler, Mueller, and Laufer 2006). Some proponents of deterrence argue that deterrence will prevent offenders from reoffending, whereas some contend that the labeling and stigma placed on the offender will result in more criminality. Thus, there is substantial debate on the validity of deterrence (Roberson and Wallace 1998). Deterrence is often contrasted with *retribution,* the idea that punishment is a necessary consequence of a crime and should be calculated based on the gravity of the wrong done.

Consider the following case. A Federal District Court recently sentenced Lewis ("Scooter") Libby, former chief of staff for Vice President Dick Cheney, to two-and-a-half years in prison and fined him $250,000 based on a jury's verdict that found Libby's guilty on four criminal counts, including obstruction of justice, perjury, and giving false statements. Mr. Libby was convicted for lying about his role in revealing the identity of Valerie Plame, a CIA officer, as part of a campaign to discredit her husband. The jail term was at the low end of what the prosecutor had recommended but much harsher than the probation sought by Libby's attorneys. When the judge handed down Libby's sentence, he was using deterrence. Can you identify the deterrence used in Libby's case? If you identified the deterrence as the prison sentence and the fine, you are correct. It should be noted that President George W. Bush subsequently pardoned Libby of the prison time, meaning that he will not have to serve two-and-a-half years in prison.

Deterrence has several objectives, one of which is to deter people from engaging in criminal conduct, which is referred to as *general deterrence. Special deterrence* focuses on the individual offender by punishing him or her. *Incapacitation,* which is considered to be a component of special deterrence, focuses on the imprisonment of the offender.

General Deterrence

Imagine walking into your favorite clothing store one afternoon. A large sign hanging near the entrance reads: "SHOPLIFTERS WILL BE PROSECUTED TO THE FULLEST EXTENT OF THE LAW." Do signs like this really deter shoplifting? The answer is yes, according to the general deterrence theory. General deterrence proposes that persons will engage in criminal activity if they do not fear apprehension and punishment. General deterrence uses punishment to deter others from following the example of the offender, for fear of the same punishment that has been inflicted on the offender. General deterrence theory assumes that most crimes are rational and that potential offenders will calculate the risk of being caught, prosecuted, and sentenced. As used in the criminal justice literature, *general deterrence* refers to crime prevention achieved by instilling fear in the general population through the punishment of offenders. General deterrence uses such controls as criminal statutes and laws, criminal sentencing, aggressive enforcement operations, and crime prevention literature and signs to induce the public to refrain from criminal conduct. Can you describe the role of the private security industry in general deterrence?

General deterrence:
A punishment with the objective of deterring other persons from following the example of the offender, for fear of the same consequences that have been inflicted on the offender. The theory of general deterrence is not concerned with the future behavior of the offender but rather with deterring others from committing criminal offences.

Special Deterrence

Special deterrence, sometimes referred to as *specific deterrence,* focuses on the individual offender. The aim of special deterrence is to discourage the offender from future criminal acts by instilling an understanding of the consequences (Lab 2007). Special deterrence as used in the criminal justice literature refers to crime prevention

Special deterrence:
Focuses on the individual
offender. The aim of
punishment is to discourage
the offener from performing
future criminal acts by
instilling an understanding of
the consequences.

that is achieved by instilling fear in the specific individual such that the person will refrain from violating the law in the future. According to this viewpoint, the fear of future suffering motivates individuals to avoid involvement in criminal activity. Returning to the Scooter Libby case presented a little earlier, the prison sentence and fine imposed by the judge was intended to deter Libby from making the same mistake in the future.

Incapacitation

Incapacitation:
A component of deterrence
proposing that if the offender
is locked up in jail or prison,
he or she cannot commit
crimes.

Incapacitation is sometimes considered a subset of special deterrence. Incapacitation aims to prevent future crimes by taking away the criminal's ability to commit such acts. Under this theory, criminals are put in jail or prison not so that they will learn the consequence of their actions but rather so that they will be unable to engage in criminal activity. Incapacitation deterrence holds that while a prisoner is in confinement, he or she is unlikely to commit crimes on persons outside of prison.

THE CRIME EQUATION

Some crime prevention experts suggest that for a crime to occur, three elements have to be present: The offender has to have the ability, the motivation, and the opportunity to carry out the crime. Private security professionals, in order to be informed and reflective practitioners, should have a working knowledge of the crime equation.

Ability

The ability component of the crime equation centers on whether the perpetrator has the ability to carry out the crime. In other words, does the burglar have the skills and tools necessary to successfully break into the residence or business? Or does the offender have the requisite skills and tools to break into a safe, or commit an auto theft? Strategies that can be used to reduce the "ability" include increasing the amount of effort that the potential offender has to use to commit the crime. For example, installing deadbolts on doors and windows will make it harder for an offender to break into a residence or a business. These techniques are referred to as target hardening and will be discussed in greater detail later in the chapter.

Motivation

Criminal motivation is sometimes used synonymously with criminal desire. What motivates a person to commit crime is a complex question. It may be difficult for security professionals to eliminate the motivation of a potential offender. How can you eliminate the motivation of a potential offender? Some argue that if the opportunity for criminal behavior is reduced, so too is the motivation. Others argue that even if the opportunity is reduced, it does little to take away the offender's motivation. For example, factors that motivate a person to steal a vehicle may include temporary joyriding, to get from one location to another, for systematic financial gain, for resale or breaking into parts—or perhaps the owner commits vehicle fraud by reporting a vehicle stolen when it hasn't been, in order to get money from an insurance company.

The most effective way security professionals can minimize the motivation of the criminal is by reducing the reward available to the offender. For example, training business owners to keep only small amounts of money in the cash register, and instructing employees to count cash out of site of the public, are techniques that will reduce the reward of a thief.

Opportunity

The opportunity component is a simple concept that can be summed up with one question. Does the offender have the opportunity to commit the crime? Criminal opportunity may be the most important component in terms of private security industry working to reduce or eliminate crime. Offenders must encounter opportunities that allow criminal inclinations to be given expression (Sacco and Kennedy 1996).

Imagine shopping one summer afternoon at your favorite mall. After making several purchases, you begin to drive home when suddenly you realize that you forgot to buy a birthday gift for a favorite relative. It's too late to turn around; you are in heavy traffic. As chance would have it, a small strip mall is located conveniently a few blocks away, and you decide to stop and pick up a birthday gift. After finding a place to park, you run into a department store without remembering to lock your car. Furthermore, the packages from the previous mall excursion sit in plain view on the back seat in your car. After about thirty minutes you return to your car to find the packages gone. A thief opened the unlocked car door, grabbed the packages, and carried them off. In this fictional account, the opportunity for the crime was created by leaving packages in plain view in an unlocked car. If the packages had been placed in the trunk, where they would be out of view, the opportunity for the crime would have been reduced.

Recent criminal opportunity theories have emphasized principles that are close to the real world and ready to put into practice (Felson and Clark 1998). Opportunity is a root cause of crime, and opportunity reduction should be a primary focus of crime prevention. Ten principles of crime opportunity are

1. *Opportunities play a role in causing all crime, not just common property crime.* For example, studies of bars and clubs show how their design and management play an important role in generating violence or preventing it.
2. *Crime opportunities are highly specific.* For example, the theft of cars for joyriding has a different pattern of opportunity than theft for car parts. Crime opportunity theory helps sort out these differences so responses can be tailored appropriately.
3. *Crime opportunities are concentrated in time and space.* Dramatic differences are found from one address to another, even in a high-crime area. Crime shifts greatly by the hour and day of the week, reflecting the opportunities to carry it out.
4. *Crime opportunities depend on everyday movements of activity.* Offenders and targets shift according to their routine activities (e.g., work, school, leisure). For example, burglars visit houses in the day, when the occupants are out at work or school.

5. *One crime produces the opportunities for another.* For example, a successful break-in may encourage the offender to return in the future; or a youth who has his bike stolen may feel justified in taking someone else's as a replacement.

6. *Some products offer more tempting crime opportunities.* For example, easily accessible electrical items such as DVD players and mobile phones are attractive to burglars and robbers.

7. *Social and technological changes produce new crime opportunities.* Products are most vulnerable in their "growth" and "mass marketing" stages, as demand for them is at its highest. Most products will reach a "saturation" stage, when most people have them and they are unlikely to be stolen.

8. *Crime can be prevented by reducing opportunities.* The opportunity-reducing methods of situational crime prevention cut across everyday life, though they can be tailored to specific situations. Crime prevention is firmly grounded in opportunity theory.

9. *Reducing opportunities does not usually displace crime.* Wholesale displacement is very rare, and many studies have found little or no crime displacement, that is, crime that has been displaced or moved to another geographic area.

10. *Focused opportunity reduction can produce broader declines in crime.* Prevention measures in one area can lead to a reduction in another nearby, a diffusion of benefits. This is because offenders may overestimate the reach of those measures (Felson and Clark 1998).

CRIME PREVENTION

An Ounce of Prevention Is Worth a Pound of Cure

According to the National Crime Prevention Institute, crime prevention is the anticipation, recognition, and appraisal of a crime risk and the initiation of some action to reduce it. The National Crime Prevention Institute (now named the Institute for Community Security and Public Safety) proposed ten operating assumptions for crime prevention. These ten assumptions are important to the private security professional:

1. Potential crime victims or those responsible for them must be helped to take actions that reduce their vulnerability to crimes and that reduce their likelihood of injury or loss, should a crime occur.

2. At the same time, it must be recognized that potential victims (and those responsible for them) are limited in the actions they can take by the limits of their social control over their environment.

3. The environment to be controlled is that of the potential victim, not of the potential criminal.

4. Direct control over the victim's environment can nevertheless affect criminal motivation in that reduced criminal opportunity means less temptation to commit criminal offenses and learn criminal behavior and, consequently, fewer offenders. In this sense, crime prevention is a practical rather than a moralistic approach to reducing criminal motivation. The intent is to discourage the offender.

5. The traditional approaches used by the criminal justice system (such as punishment and rehabilitation by courts and prisons and the investigative and apprehension functions of police) can increase the risk perceived by the criminal and thus have a significant (but secondary) role in criminal opportunity reduction.

6. Law enforcement agencies have a primary role in crime prevention to the extent that they are effective in providing opportunity-reduction education, information, and guidance to the public and to various organizations, institutions, and agencies in the community.

7. Many skill and interest groups need to operate in an active and coordinated fashion if crime prevention is to be effective in a community-wide sense.

8. Crime prevention can be both a cause and an effect of efforts to revitalize urban and rural communities.

9. The knowledge of crime prevention is interdisciplinary and is in a continual process of discovery, as well as discarding misinformation. There must be a continual sifting and integration of discoveries as well as constant sharing of new knowledge among practitioners.

10. Crime prevention strategies and techniques must remain flexible and specific. What will work for one crime in one place may not work for the same crime in another place. Crime prevention is a "thinking person's practice," and countermeasures must be taken after a thorough analysis of the problem, not before (National Crime Prevention Institute 1978).

Primary Crime Prevention

Imagine for a moment that you visit your physician for a physical examination that is way overdue. Suppose that after a few minutes of talking with your physician, he decides that you should receive an influenza vaccination to minimize your risk of getting the flu during the upcoming flu season. Furthermore, your physician draws a blood sample from you in order to test your cholesterol levels. In this fictional example, your physician is engaged in primary health prevention. In the medical community, primary prevention measures are those provided to individuals with the objective of preventing the onset of a targeted condition. Primary prevention measures include activities that help avoid a given health care problem.

In crime prevention, *primary prevention* addresses the conditions in the natural environment that may lead to the development of crime. Neighborhood disorder such as broken windows, abandoned buildings, lack of street maintenance, and broken-down cars are precursors that could lead to social disorganization and crime. Primary crime prevention seeks to alleviate these factors directly. In other words, primary crime prevention measures suggest that if these precursors or risk factors for crime are eliminated, then the chances of criminal activity occurring are greatly reduced. A few techniques that may be used in primary prevention initiatives include neighborhood watches, environmental design, neighborhood initiatives, property identification programs (marking items with the owner's initials, for example, for later identification if necessary), neighborhood clean-ups, security risk inspections, and crime prevention education initiatives. Primary care prevention is directed at modification of potential crime conditions that exist in the physical and social environment at large (Gray 1982).

Secondary Crime Prevention

In medicine, secondary prevention measures identify and treat asymptomatic patients (patients who are not exhibiting symptoms) who have risk factors or preclinical disease even though the condition is not yet clinically apparent. These activities are focused on early finding of asymptomatic disease that occurs commonly and has significant risk for a negative outcome without treatment. Screening tests are examples of secondary prevention activities, as these are done on those without clinical presentation of disease that has a significant latency period, such as hypertension, or breast and prostate cancer. With early case finding, the natural history of the disease, or how the course of an illness unfolds over time without treatment, can often be altered to maximize the patient's well-being and minimize suffering.

Secondary prevention measures used in crime prevention are similar to those used in medicine. *Secondary crime prevention* is intended to prevent crime by focusing on potential offenders or potential opportunities that nurture criminal activity. The objective of secondary crime prevention is to identify high-crime areas that have the potential to result in criminal behavior. Once these high-crime areas are identified, the criminogenic factors can be treated (Lab 2007).

Secondary prevention is also directed at early identification and intervention in the lives of individuals or groups in criminal circumstances. There are many secondary crime prevention programs. Secondary crime prevention techniques include the use of public police and private security patrols to keep the peace, diversion programs, educational intervention programs, predelinquent screening, employee screening, crime location analysis, and neighborhood watch groups. Once potential

Substandard lock which creates criminal opportunity.

places, people, and situations that are at risk for criminal activity are identified, it may be possible to predict and prevent future criminal occurrences. By reducing criminal opportunity, increasing the risk(s) of the crime, and minimizing the potential gain of the criminal act, it is more likely that the criminal will not engage in such behavior.

Tertiary Crime Prevention

In medicine, tertiary prevention generally consists of the prevention of disease progression and patient suffering after the disease becomes clinically obvious and a diagnosis is made. This activity also includes rehabilitation of disabling conditions. *Tertiary crime prevention* deals with the actual offenders and involves intervention techniques. Tertiary prevention is directed at the prevention of recidivism though post-adjudication diversion, reform, rehabilitation, incapacitation, job opportunities for ex-offenders, aftercare services, and other techniques (Gray 1982). Incapacitation (jail or prison) is a common type of tertiary prevention used in the United States. Although it does not prevent criminals from committing crimes once they leave prison, it does protect the larger population from victimization while the offender is incarcerated.

SITUATIONAL CRIME PREVENTION

Situational crime prevention is a primary prevention measure that focuses on opportunity reduction. It is directed at stopping crime problems before they occur. Like other primary crime prevention measures, situational prevention tends to focus on reducing crime opportunities rather than on the characteristics of criminals or potential criminals. Situational prevention seeks to reduce opportunities for specific categories of crime by increasing the associated risks and reducing the rewards (Clarke 1997). For example, neighborhood watch programs, alarm systems, "light the night" programs, video surveillance, and a uniformed private security or police presence are all aimed at increasing the associated risks and reducing the crime opportunities.

> ***Situational crime prevention:*** *Seeks to reduce opportunities for specific categories of crime by increasing the associated risks and difficulties and reducing the rewards. Situational prevention focuses on reducing opportunities to commit crimes rather than on the characteristics of offenders or potential offenders.*

Research on crime patterns has shown that crime events are not simply a function of where criminals live but also reflect the concentration of opportunities for crime. Crime is much more likely to occur in certain places or "hot spots," theft is highly concentrated on particular hot products, and some repeat victims are more likely to experience crime than other people. The Center for Problem Oriented Policing, which maintains a comprehensive website (www.popcenter.org) proposes that assessing opportunities that specific situations offer for crime can go a long way in prevention efforts. The Center for Problem Oriented Policing suggests the following:

1. Increasing the effort the offender must make to carry out the crime
2. Increasing the risks the offender must face in completing the crime
3. Reducing the rewards or benefits the offender expects to obtain from the crime
4. Removing excuses that offenders may use to "rationalize" or justify their actions
5. Reducing or avoiding provocations that may tempt or incite offenders into criminal acts

Twenty-Five Tips for Situational Crime Prevention

Increase the Effort	Increase the Risks	Reduce the Rewards	Reduce Provocations	Remove the Excuses
1. Harden targets Immobilizers in cars Antirobbery screens	6. Extend guardianship Cocooning Neighborhood watch	11. Conceal targets Gender-neutral phone directories Off-street parking	16. Reduce frustration and stress Efficient queuing Soothing lighting	21. Set rules Rental agreements Hotel registration
2. Control access to facilities Alley gating Entry phones	7. Assist natural surveillance Improved street lighting Neighborhood watch hotlines	12. Remove targets Removable car radios Prepaid public phone cards	17. Avoid disputes Fixed cab fares Reduce crowding in pubs	22. Post instructions "No parking" "Private property"
3. Screen exits Tickets needed Electronic tags for libraries	8. Reduce anonymity Taxi driver IDs "How's my driving?" signs	13. Identify property Property marking Vehicle licensing	18. Reduce emotional arousal Controls on violent porn Prohibit pedophiles from working with children	23. Alert conscience Roadside speed display signs "Shoplifting is stealing"
4. Deflect offenders Street closures in red light district Separate toilets for women	9. Utilize place managers Train employees to prevent crime Support whistle blowers	14. Disrupt markets Checks on pawn brokers License street vendors	19. Neutralize peer pressure "Idiots drink and drive" "It's ok to say no"	24. Assist compliance Litter bins Public lavatories
5. Control tools/weapons Toughened beer glasses Photos on credit cards	10. Strengthen formal surveillance Speed cameras CCTV in town centers	15. Deny benefits Ink merchandise tags Graffiti cleaning	20. Discourage imitation Rapid vandalism repair V-chips in TVs	25. Control drugs/alcohol Breathalyzers in pubs Alcohol-free events

Source: D. B. Cornish and R. V. Clarke, Opportunities, precipitators, and criminal decisions: A reply to Wortley's critique of situational crime prevention, *Crime Prevention Studies 16* (2003): 41–96.

Opportunity-Reducing Measures

Phone Crime Problem	Situational Prevention Method
Phone booth vandalism	Improved design and sighting
Cash theft from public phones	Phone cards, stronger coin boxes
Theft of cellular phones	Phone programmed for one user
Massive phone fraud, NY bus terminal	Phones bar international calls
Jail brawls over phone use	Phones ration each inmate's time
Public phones for drug sales	Removing phones, limiting incoming calls
Obscene and threatening calls	Caller ID devices
Fear of calling the police	Free private phones provided for some

Source: M. Felson and R. V. Clarke, *Opportunity makes the thief: Practical theory for crime prevention,* Police research series paper 98, Policing and Reducing Crime Unit, Research, Development and Statistics Directorate (London: Home Office, 1998).

Routine Activities Theory

1. Motivated offender:
    - Tempted
    - Provoked
    - Idle
    - Bored
2. Suitable target:
    - Ease of access
    - Some reward

- Ease of escape
- Portability
- Ease of disbursement
3. Absence of capable guardians:
    - Parents
    - Neighbors
    - Authorities
    - Friends

ROUTINE ACTIVITIES THEORY

In 1979, criminologists Lawrence Cohen and Marcus Felson published an article theorizing that offenders evaluate a potential target before committing their crimes. They coined the term "routine activities" to describe their theory. *Routine activities theory* focuses on the characteristics of the crime rather than the characteristics of the offender. The theory contends that criminal offenses are related to the nature of everyday patterns of social interaction.

Routine activities theory proposes that for crimes to occur, there must be a convergence in time and space of three minimal elements: (1) a suitable target, (2) the absence of a capable guardian against crime, and (3) a likely offender. A suitable target can be a person, object, or place. Guardians may include security officers, police officers, neighborhood watch groups, neighborhood associations, video surveillance cameras, and the like. Only when all three factors are present do the chances of criminal activity increase substantially. Thus, the rate in which crime rises is equal to the number of suitable targets and the absence of individuals to protect those targets.

CRIME PREVENTION THROUGH ENVIRONMENTAL DESIGN

According to criminologist C. Ray Jeffery (1971), direct controls of crime are those that reduce the environmental opportunities for crime, and indirect controls include all others such as police enforcement, imprisonment, court action, probation, and parole. Crime prevention through environmental design (CPTED) proposes that the physical environment can play a role in determining the opportunities for crime in two ways, directly and indirectly. Directly, it can reduce access to property and can remove criminal opportunities through target hardening. Indirectly, the physical environment can reduce crime, fear, and related problems by influencing the social behavior and social perceptions of residents and/or potential offenders (Rosenbaum, Hernandez, and Daughtry 1991).

The National Crime Prevention Institute describes CPTED as the proper design and effective use of the built environment that may lead to a reduction in the fear and incidence of crime and an improvement of the quality of life. Environmental security measures involve the proper design and effective use of the built environment in a manner that can lead to a reduction in the fear and incident of crime, and an improvement in the quality of life (Crowe 2000). Environmental crime prevention provides a physical structure in which individuals have the opportunity, encouragement, and means to extend their use and sphere of responsibility for their neighborhood (Gardiner 1982).

Crime prevention through environmental design (CPTED):
A multidisciplinary approach to deterring criminal behavior. CPTED strategies rely on the ability to influence offender decisions that precede criminal acts. Most implementations of CPTED occur solely within the built environment.

CPTED strategies rely on the ability to influence offender decisions that precede criminal acts. Research into criminal behavior shows that the decision to offend, or not to offend, is influenced more by cues to the perceived risk of being caught than by cues to reward or ease of entry. Consistent with this research, CPTED strategies emphasize enhancing the perceived risk of detection and apprehension by addressing natural surveillance, natural access control, territorial reinforcement, and continued maintenance. CEPTD differs from other crime prevention or security measures in that CPTED focuses specifically on aspects of design, whereas other measures tend to be directed at target hardening, such as denying access to a target by using locks and bars, or using sensors and cameras to detect and identify an offender (Crowe and Zahm 1994).

Generally, there are three important components to CPTED strategies: natural surveillance, natural access control, and territorial reinforcement.

Natural Surveillance

Natural surveillance entails the placement of physical features, activities, and people in a way that maximizes visibility and is directed toward keeping intruders easily observable and therefore less likely to commit criminal acts. Oscar Newman (1972), an architect and city planner, proposed the theory of *defensible space,* which proposes that natural surveillance is a key component of preventing crime. According to Newman, physical space should be designed so that legitimate users can monitor and maximize visibility of the activities that occur in that area. The features that maximize visibility may include unobstructed doors and windows, pedestrian-friendly sidewalks and streets, front porches, and appropriate nighttime lighting. Natural surveillance relies on the assumption that criminals want to limit the possibility of being seen before, during, or after committing an illegal act. Providing parking areas in business environments as well as driveways in residential communities that are easily visible by other people, and making sure that all areas are visible from the street or from inside the building, reduces the opportunities for criminal activity. Another aspect of natural surveillance is providing good lighting during nighttime hours. Natural surveillance is the ability to intercept those who do not belong.

Natural Access Control

Natural Access Control is another design concept that is directed primarily at decreasing crime opportunities by denying access to crime targets and creating a perception of risk for offenders. People are physically guided through a space by the strategic design of streets, sidewalks, building entrances, landscaping, and neighborhood gateways. Design elements are very useful tools to clearly indicate public routes and discourage access to private areas.

Territorial Reinforcement

Physical design can also create or extend a sphere of influence. Residents or legitimate users of an area are encouraged to develop a sense of territorial control, while potential offenders, perceiving this control, are discouraged. This concept includes features that define property lines and distinguish between private and public spaces using landscape plantings, pavement designs, gateway treatments, appropriate signage, and open fences.

Crime Prevention Through Environmental Design

- *Territoriality:* Using architectural or other features to show the boundary between public and private space
- *Access control:* Signage, gates, doors, or more subtle visual effects limit access to private spaces
- *Natural surveillance:* Allowing visual observation of indoor and outdoor spaces—such as windows into a basement computer lab, glass-enclosed stairwells, preventing landscaping from creating secluded spaces
- *Image/maintenance:* Asserting responsibility and ownership—fixing broken windows, cleaning up derelict properties
- *Environment:* How the people who circulate or live around the site affect it

Professor Diane L. Zahm of Virginia Tech University developed a comprehensive outline for conducting a CPTED evaluation at a building or facility. Professor's Zahm's outline is presented as a guide to assist private security officials when evaluating environmental security in buildings or facilities.

Crime Prevention Through Environmental Design

Before the Site Visit
Request and review information:

- Administrative organization (to identify appropriate contacts)
- Relevant statutes, ordinances, codes, policies and procedures
- Site and facility background (maps, plans, manuals, design/development review and approval processes, maintenance procedures, etc.)
- Police/security, central fire services (CFS), and crime data

Develop an evaluation strategy and schedule appointments

During the Site Visit
Owner/manager orientation to CPTED and the evaluation process
Evaluator orientation:

- Overview of the organization
- "Tabletop" review of location, site, and facility (assignment of spaces, activities and schedules, etc.), noting problem areas

Constituent/stakeholder meetings and facility tours
Independent facility examination (without stakeholders):

- Morning, afternoon, evening, and night
- Multiple weekdays, and weekend visits

[Break—to organize materials, analyze data, identify information needs, document the process, and reflect on observations, if needed]

[Return visit—to fill gaps in data and information, to reconsider the findings from an earlier visit, to evaluate the facility during an alternate schedule, etc., if needed]

Client debrief

Following the Site Visit
Review data and other materials (photographs, floor plans, notes)
Develop recommendations:

- Changes to physical design and layout
- Modifications to laws, rules, regulations, policies, procedures
- Target hardening/security enhancements
- Community and social programs and activities
- Crime prevention education and awareness

Draft the report:

- Introduction to the problem and report overview
- Description of methods (data collection and analysis, survey and interview protocols, site and facility evaluation activities, dates and times)
- Discussion of issues and findings
- Recommendations for future action (including additional or follow-up evaluation)
- Supporting documentation in appendixes
- Disclaimer*

Submit draft report for review and comment (specifically, for factual accuracy)

(continued)

Crime Prevention Through Environmental Design (*continued*)

Redraft, re-review, and rewrite
Present and deliver final report

*Example disclaimer: "The recommendations outlined in this report are based on research and experience that suggest certain design and policy approaches can be adopted to reduce *opportunities for crime*. It is not pos-

sible to guarantee that *actual crime* will be reduced or eliminated if these recommendations are implemented."

Source: D. Zahm, *Using crime prevention through environmental design in problem solving*, Problem oriented guides for police problem solving tools series no. 8 (Washington, DC: U.S. Department of Justice, 2007, 46–7).

TARGET HARDENING

Target hardening:
A crime prevention technique that involves strengthening the security of a residence, business, or other structure with a view toward reducing or minimizing the risk of attack.

Target hardening is a technique that makes it physically more difficult for a potential offender to carry out a crime. Installing deadbolt locks on doors, using steering wheel locks on cars, and putting iron bars on windows are a few examples of target hardening.

In order to keep a residence or business from being targeted for criminal activities, it is important to make it more difficult for an offender to carry out the crime. The private security officer can have a significant impact on target hardening. Private security authorities should work with their customer base to harden the target. Target hardening focuses on the idea that criminals often seek an easy target to prey on. If a location is a hard target, the criminal will most likely move to a more vulnerable location to commit a crime. Criminals typically select easy targets that minimize the likelihood of being detected. The more of an obstacle is presented, the more likely a potential offender will be discouraged.

Research has shown that target hardening is an effective prevention tool. Professors Paul Cromwell and James Olson (2006) found that on-site practices such as target hardening and increasing visibility and surveillance from the street and from neighbors' homes do have a deterrent effect.

Although it would be virtually impossible to provide an exhaustive list of target hardening techniques, in the following pages we provide a few examples.

Doors and Locks

One of the most basic target hardening techniques for residences and businesses is to install durable locks on doors. Of course, ensuring that the doors themselves are

---

Techniques That Focus on Opportunity-Reducing "Target Hardening"

- Alarms (silent or audible)
- Burglar proofing—installing additional and more effective locks
- Bars on windows
- Steering column locks and ignition interlocks on automobiles
- Vandalism proofing—toughened glass, tamper-proof seals
- Access control—locked gates, fenced yards
- Entry phones at building entrances
- Enhanced lighting
- PINs (personal identification numbers)
- Deflecting offenders—bus stop placement, bar locations, street closures, graffiti boards
- Controlling facilitators—spray can sales, gun control, photos on credit cards

closed and locked is a first step. A significant number of home burglaries occur because a door was left unlocked. Burglars use unlocked rear doors, open bathroom windows, and unsecured garage service doors to enter target residences and businesses. Keeping doors and windows locked will dramatically reduce the likelihood of becoming a victim. Private security officers should insist to their clients that doors be locked even if the clients are leaving the house for only a moment. A brief trip can give a skilled burglar enough time to make his way through your house.

For optimal protection, exterior doors should be fiberglass, solid wood, solid wood core (a layer of veneer over solid wood), or metal. Hollow doors are merely sheets of veneer over a cardboard core and can be broken with ease. Metal doors should be reinforced inside and have a lock block. Otherwise, they can be bent out of the frame using a car jack.

Deadbolt locks should be installed on all external doors. A deadbolt lock is a type of door lock in which the bolt, which is square in cross section, is operated by the door key or a turnpiece. A deadbolt lock adds enough strength to the door to keep the door from being kicked in by most attackers. Most important, however, it keeps a potential burglar from "jimmying" a spring-latch locking mechanism. A deadbolt should at least be 1 inch in size, and 3 inches is optimal.

There are essentially three types of deadbolt locks. The single-cylinder deadbolt lock opens and locks with a key from outside the house and a knob or lever from inside. The single-cylinder deadbolt is commonly used in residences. In order to unlock a single-cylinder deadbolt, a person has to use a key to release the lock from outside, although a person inside can turn a door knob to secure or release the lock.

A double-cylinder deadbolt lock requires a key to open or lock the door from either side. These locks are ideal if the lock can be made accessible by breaking out an adjacent side light. Private security officers should caution homeowners, however, that if the double-cylinder lock is locked on the inside, it may prevent someone from exiting in a hurry in the event of a fire or some other emergency.

The third type of deadbolt is the keyless deadbolt lock. The keyless deadbolt lock allows a person to open or lock the door without using a key. Authorized users can activate a remote control, or in the case of a touchpad lockset, push a few buttons to enable entry. Other keyless entry or electronic locks are evolving for use in a large number of residential or nonresidential structures. One example is a fingerprint-sensitive electronic lock. The user of the lock simply swipes his or her finger to engage the locking device.

For maximum security, the bolt mechanism should extend a minimum of 1 inch and be made of case-hardened steel or contain a hardened insert. It is also recommended that the cylinder guard be tapered, round, and free-spinning, to make it difficult to grip with pliers or a wrench. It should be solid metal—not hollow casting or stamped metal. A heavy-duty strike plate installed in place of a regular strike plate will help strengthen the door frame. The heavy-duty plate uses four to six 3-inch wood screws, not the two ¾-inch screws used in regular plates. These longer screws go through the frame into the jamb, making it harder for someone to split the frame by kicking the door.

In cases where entry doors have decorative glass panels, double-cylinder locks are recommended because they require that a key be used from the inside in order to open the door. The double-cylinder lock may prevent someone from being able to break the near-by glass and then manipulate the interior lock.

Doors and their hardware need maintenance occasionally. Poorly maintained doors make it that much easier for an offender to enter your house. It is especially important to make sure that the tracks of sliding doors are in good repair and that the door stays in the track.

Sliding Doors

Sliding doors present special security challenges. Many offenders get into residences through a sliding door by lifting the sliding door out of its track from the outside. One way to prevent this from happening is to secure two metal screws through the track above the sliding part of the door. The screw should be adjusted to allow the door to operate correctly. Another effective way to secure sliding doors is to install keyed locks at the top and bottom. For optimal protection, a Charlie bar should be installed. A Charlie bar is a metal bar that is mounted between the end of the sliding door and the frame. A Charlie bar can be installed so that it swings down from the door frame to the middle of the door to prevent the door from sliding. If a Charlie bar is not installed, at the very least, place a rod (a thick wooden dowel, for example) in the bottom track of the door to keep it from being opened.

Windows

Poorly secured windows present golden opportunities for offenders. The same information that applies to securing doors also applies to windows. When addressing the security of windows, a secure frame and quality construction materials are important. Laminated glass is best. Have you ever witnessed a car window being broken? If you have, you probably observed that after the window was struck with an object, the glass seemed to stick together. This is because vehicle manufacturers use laminated glass. Laminated glass made up of several glass sheets and interlayers can provide protection in medium- to high-security applications. Laminated glass has a significant amount of rigidity and tear resistance. If an offender attempts to break laminated glass, the glass will not break into a million pieces and fall to the ground like some ordinary glass. Laminated glass will remain firmly bounded to the interlayer even if it is broken. This makes it more difficult for the offender to gain entry. Laminated glass is also manufactured to withstand bullets and bomb blasts by using multiple layers.

Window grills that can be installed over windows to provide increased security. Although window grills add security to a structure, they can also create a hazard in the event that a fast exit is required in a fire or other emergency situation. Some window grills are manufactured with quick-release levers for exit during an emergency.

For increased security, window pins are recommended. Window pins can be installed relatively easily and at minimal expense. To install window pins, drill about a 3/16-inch hole on a slight downward slant through the inside window frame and halfway into the outside frame, then place a nail in the hole to secure the window.

Windows located at ground level present an additional security risk. An offender can break the glass to obtain entry into the structure. Keeping windows clear of sight obstructions such as shrubbery and bushes may reduce the risk. On the other hand, a thorny shrub or bush might deter an offender from trying to crawl through.

Reinforcing windows with good locking devices should also be considered. Private security officers should recommend to property owners to consider replacing the standard glazed window with a high-security glass window.

Alarm Systems

With advances in technology, security alarm systems have made quantum leaps and have evolved into sophisticated crime detection and prevention tools. Security alarm systems greatly decrease the chances of burglaries and other criminal activity. Simply put, alarms systems prevent crime. Research has shown that criminals tend to avoid businesses and residences that have a security system (Wright and Decker 1994). Most systems rely on a combination of contacts and motion sensors placed at doors and windows. For the most effective security, all exterior points of entry should have contacts that sense when they are open. Glass break sensors are also recommended. Motion sensors should not be used as the primary means of detection, because they do not detect someone until he or she is already in the house.

Security systems may be either silent or audible. Silent alarms are just that— silent. When intruders enter a building, they have no way of knowing that they have tripped an alarm. The silent alarm sends a signal to the security company, which in turn notifies police and field security officers.

Auditable alarms emit a loud siren or other audible signal when a building or structure has been entered. The mere volume of the audible alarm will usually scare off the perpetrator. An audible alarm system that has been tripped can usually be heard for several blocks.

There are many alarm systems available, and the selection of a system can be a perplexing task. Private security officers should become knowledgeable about the types of alarm systems available, and be prepared to inform citizens which one would

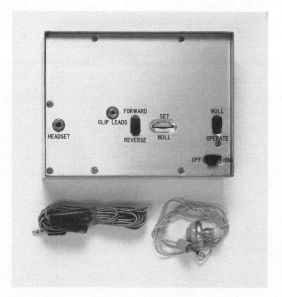

Burglar alarm evasion kit.
Source: © Dorling Kindersley, Courtesy of the H. Keith Melton Collection

best serve their security needs. Rolf (1982) presented several questions that should be answered when determining the requirements of an individual alarm system:

- The threat or risk—what is the system to protect against?
- The type of sensor needed—what will be protected?
- What methods are available to provide the level of protection needed?
- The method of alarm signal transmission—how is the signal to be sent, and who will respond?

The basic elements of a home security system include:

- *Control panel.* This is where the system wiring terminates, where the backup battery is located, and where it is connected to the phone lines if it is a monitored system.
- *Keypad.* This is where the system is armed and disarmed.
- *Siren.* Emits a loud, piercing signal when triggered by the alarm system control panel.
- *Motion detectors.* Detect movement within a preset range of a given environment. Motion detectors are among the most important and widely used security alarm sensors. They can be installed in many locations within the structure, including at corners, on walls, and on ceilings. Many motion detectors now can be set not to detect pets.
- *Infrared motion detectors.* Infrared or passive infrared sensors alert the alarm system to certain changes in the levels of heat and/or movement in a particular room or space.
- *Outdoor motion detectors.* Detect when a person or vehicle is within a certain range of the motion detector and alerts the alarm system to turn on lights.
- *Door and window contacts.* Trigger the alarm when the door or window is opened (and the system is on).
- *Glass break detectors.* Detect the breaking of windows or glass doors by listening for the specific sound frequency of breaking glass. A glass break detector will alert the alarm system if glass is broken within approximately 35 feet of the detector.

Burglary Deterrence Tips

- Make sure your street lights are in good working order.
- Make your home look occupied.
- Lock all outside doors and windows before you leave the house or go to bed. Even if you will be leaving for only a short time, lock your doors.
- Stop delivery of newspapers and mail when you are going to be away for an extended period.
- Install lights in your driveway and at your property boundaries. Make sure you have spotlights and motion-sensitive lights on or near your house.
- Trim back all shrubs and bushes. Keep your windows clear of trees and shrubbery. Keep your grass cut, and display a defined boundary between you and your neighbor's property line. If you are going to be gone for an extended period of time, arrange to have the lawn mowed.
- Keep your yard and property in good condition. Keep the lawn mowed. Pick up trash cans and other litter as soon as possible. Don't leave children's toys, ladders, or tools lying around.
- Make sure your house number is clearly visible.
- Keep the garage door closed. Leave a radio on when you are away from your residence. If a burglar knocks on your front door to see if anyone is home, he or she will hear the radio.

Lighting

Perhaps you have heard the old adage popularized by McGruff, the crime dog: "Light the night and take a bite out of crime." Research generally supports this seemingly simple advice (Painter 1994). Good lighting is the single most cost-effective deterrent to crime (Girard 1982). Interior lighting is great to show signs of life and activity inside a residence at night. A home that is dark night after night sends the message to offenders that the residents are away.

Light timers are inexpensive and strongly recommended. Light timers should be used on a daily basis, not just when occupants are away. In this way, a routine is established that neighbors become familiar with. They in turn can observe and become suspicious when your normally lighted home becomes dark. Typically, light timers should be used near the front and back windows with the curtains closed. The pattern of lights turning on and off should simulate actual occupancy.

Perhaps from time to time you have returned home late at night and entered into a dark residence. If you have done this, and most of us have, sometimes we may have a sense of insecurity about entering a totally dark house. Light timers are ideal in that they provide the security and comfort of not having to enter a dark residence upon returning home. The same light timers can be used to turn on radios or television sets to further enhance the illusion of occupancy.

Exterior lighting is also important. It becomes critical if you park in a parking lot or underground garage and need to walk a distance to your front door. The primary purpose of good lighting is to allow a person to see a potential threat or suspicious person. If a potential threat can be seen in advance, then you have a chance to avoid it. Exterior lighting should be bright enough to see at least 100 feet and bright enough to be able to distinguish colors.

Well lit exterior of building.

SPECIAL SECURITY CONCERNS

Automated Teller Machines

Automated teller machines (ATMs) have eliminated the inconvenience to having to rush to the bank before five o'clock in order to make a deposit or withdraw cash. Unfortunately, ATM machines have also made it convenient for robber to stake out the ATM and then rob patrons of the ATM when they pull up to withdraw money.

According to the Center for Problem Oriented Policing, robbery of patrons at ATMs is only one of several related problems that authorities must address. Other problems include:

- Robbery of couriers who fill ATMs with cash
- Theft of PINs (including theft by "shoulder surfing)"
- Theft by electronic data interception
- Theft by fraudulent electronic transactions
- Theft of money from ATMs by bank or ATM service employees
- Burglary of ATMs (including theft of entire ATMs)
- Homeless people sleeping in ATM vestibules
- Vandalism of ATMs
- Fraudulent use of ATM cards obtained from customers through dummy ATMs that keep their cards

Security professionals can play a pivotal role in the prevention of ATM-related crimes by offering some basic prevention advice to persons who use ATMs and to businesses that house ATMs on their premises. When choosing an ATM, especially after dark, chose one that is in a well-lighted area. Regardless of whether it is day or night, patrons should look over the area before approaching an ATM. Don't initiate a transaction if there is anyone around that you find suspicious. Put away cash, cards, and receipt before leaving the ATM machine.

A number of factors should be taken into consideration by businesses and banking facilities that have ATMs on their premise. It is important to ensure that the view of the ATM is not obstructed. An offender is less likely to commit a robbery if there is a chance that he or she will be seen and subsequently identified and arrested. Shrubbery and other vegetation growing in proximity of the ATM should be removed or pruned on a regular basis. Landscaping that prohibits public view of the ATM should also be removed or altered. The ATM should be well lighted. Businesses and banks should not place ATMs in areas that have a high incidence of crime. Likewise, in areas where ATMs are located, crime rates should be analyzed periodically.

Auto Theft

Each year in the United States, well over 1 million auto thefts are reported to law enforcement authorities. The FBI reports that there is an auto theft every twenty-six seconds in the United States. Although it is true that the FBI reports that auto thefts have decreased slightly in recent years, auto theft remains a significant but in many respects preventable problem.

In some auto theft cases the victim affords the offender with the opportunity to carry out the crime. Perhaps you have been guilty of this. How many times have you started your car in the winter to warm it up and then returned inside your residence or

Auto Theft Prevention Tips

- Lock your car doors and close your windows.
- If applicable, park in the garage and lock it.
- Always park in a well-lighted area.
- Leave only the ignition key with the parking attendant in a commercial parking lot.
- Car keys left at home (or at work) should always be hidden. This will prevent the theft of your vehicle if you are burglarized.
- Install a locking gas tank cap to help prevent gasoline theft and limit an offender's driving range to one tankful.

- Park the front wheel turned sharply to the right or left, making it difficult for the professional thief to tow your car away backwards.
- If you have a front-wheel-drive car, when you park, pull on the emergency brake and place your vehicle in park. If you have a manual (standard) transmission, pull on the emergency brake and shift into forward or reverse gear. All four wheels will be locked, making it difficult for an offender to tow your car.

office for a few moments? How many times have you ran into the convenience store or gas station and left your car running? How many times have you left the keys in your car? In these examples the opportunity for a motivated offender to steal your vehicle is ever present. Security professionals have the opportunity to play a prevention role by educating the citizenry about auto theft, as well as their own alertness while performing security duties.

Anti–auto theft techniques are usually presented in four layers. Common sense techniques such as door locks and ignition keys are considered the first layer of antitheft devices. Second-layer antitheft devices offer the best deterrence, and security professionals should be fully aware of these. Secondary-layer prevention techniques include:

- Steering wheel locks—metal bars designed to prevent the steering wheel from turning. These offer an excellent visual deterrent.
- Armor column collars—steel collars that wraps around the steering wheel and prevent a thief from cracking open the ignition. They offer the same benefits as steering wheel locks.
- Audible alarms—triggered by motion or impact sensors.
- Antitheft stickers
- Brake locks

Third-layer antitheft devices are basically vehicle immobilizers. These include "kill switches" that prevent the flow of electricity to the engine unless a special hidden switch is activated, ignition-system disablers, and "smart keys," which are computer-coded keys that must be inserted before the vehicle will start.

Fourth-layer antitheft devices are electronic transmitters that allow the police to track a vehicle after it is stolen. Although they are not very effective in preventing the original theft, these devices increase the chance of recovery. By the time the car is recovered, of course, it may be stripped or burned.

Carjacking

Carjacking is stealing a car by threat or use of force. For example, the victim is sitting at an intersection waiting for the traffic light to turn green when suddenly a carjacker rips the driver's door open and pulls the victim out of the car. The carjacker subsequently jumps into the car and drives off. Carjacking has become a serious problem in recent years. Motivated carjackers are looking for the easiest opportunity and the most vulnerable victim in order to carry out their crimes. The objective of the private security industry is to reduce the opportunity for carjacking by educating citizens as to how they can become less vulnerable.

Driving with the windows closed and the doors locked are good habits. Avoid unfamiliar shortcuts. When approaching an intersection, leave enough room to be able to pull out and get away from the car in front of you. If you are actually confronted by a carjacker, don't resist. Get out of the car promptly and walk or run in the opposite direction. Always check your surroundings before getting in or out of the car. Check inside and under the car before getting in. Keep plenty of gas in the tank, and try to avoid using self-service gas stations after dark. If you are bumped from behind and you feel suspicious, don't get out of the car; this is a ploy used by carjackers.

Another common ploy of carjackers is to try to get potential victims to stop by tricking them into believing that they have a flat tire or other mechanical problem. Private security officers should inform citizens that if they do not feel safe, they should drive carefully to a gas station or other high-traffic area. The recommended action is to motion the other driver to follow you and then go to the nearest well-lit public place. Of course, if the carjacker has a weapon, don't resist. No car is worth risking your life for.

Carjacking Prevention Tips

- As you approach your vehicle, pay attention to your surroundings. If you see suspicious persons or vehicles, do not go to your vehicle. Instead, walk to a safe place and call the police. Don't confront suspicious persons or vehicles.
- Always have your keys or remote ready to unlock your vehicle. Don't spend time fumbling for your keys. The more time you take, the greater is your risk of being carjacked. When shopping for a car alarm or remote unlocking system, consider a system that unlocks the driver's door only on the first button push, and the rest of the doors on the second push.
- Always drive with your doors locked and window up.
- Keep your vehicle well maintained and full of gas. Not only will this minimize break downs, the car will probably perform better during an emergency.
- Plan your trip ahead of time, so you know which route to take, and avoid high-crime areas.
- If you have a cellular (mobile) phone, make sure the batteries are charged and take the phone with you.
- Pay attention to other vehicles that are following you. If you think you are being followed, drive into and out of high-traffic parking lots (shopping centers and shopping malls), drive to a police station, or use your cellular phone to ask for help.
- Avoid driving in the far right lane. This lane is most vulnerable to carjackings.
- Always leave room between your car and the car in front of you. Not only can you see more, you will also have room to drive away in an emergency.
- If you are approached by a stranger, drive away. Sound your horn to draw attention or help.
- Do not stop for hitchhikers or prostitutes. Carjackers could be hiding nearby.
- Carjackers may try to get you to stop by tricking you into believing you have a flat tire or other mechanical problem. If you do not feel safe, then drive carefully to a gas station or other high-traffic area.
- When selling a vehicle, obtain the potential buyer's name and driver's license number before offering a test drive, and do not go on a test drive alone with a potential buyer.
- If you are carjacked, do not resist. Immediately abandon your vehicle, run, and call 9-1-1

Source: Sonoma County District Attorney's Office, www. sonoma-county.org/Da/auto_theft_taskforce4.htm.

Summary

- The private security industry plays a major role in crime prevention efforts. Much of this role involves eliminating criminal opportunities.
- Crime is measured by two sources, the Uniform Crime Report and the National Victimization Survey. The Uniform Crime Report consists of crime indexes, published annually by the FBI, which summarize the incidence and rate of reported crimes within the United States. The National Crime Victimization Survey is a national survey conducted by the Bureau of Justice Statistics for the purposes of building a crime index. The survey consists of questions regarding the respondents' experiences with criminal activity.
- Deterrence is a theory of justice whereby the aim of punishment is to prevent or deter future criminal activity. General deterrence is a philosophy that contends that punishing an individual offender deters others from offending. Special deterrence referrs to crime prevention techniques that are achieved through instilling fear in the specific individual being punished, such that the person refrains from future violation of the law. Incapacitation is considered by some to be a subset of specific deterrence. Incapacitation aims to prevent future crimes not by rehabilitating the individual but rather by taking away the person's ability to commit such acts.
- In order for a crime to be committed, three elements have to be present: ability, desire on the part of the offender, and opportunity for the offender to carry out the crime.
- Crime prevention is usually described by a three-pronged approach. Primary, secondary, and tertiary crime prevention all involve some level of community involvement with private security efforts.
- Situational prevention seeks to reduce opportunities for specific categories of crime by increasing the associated risks and difficulties and reducing the rewards. Situational crime prevention proceeds from an analysis of the circumstances that give rise to specific kinds of crime.
- The routine activities theory proposes that for a crime to occur, there must be a convergence in time and space of three elements: (1) a suitable target, (2) absence of a capable guardian against crime, and (3) a likely offender. Routine activities theory hypothesizes that criminal offenses are related to the nature of everyday patterns of social interaction.
- Crime prevention through environmental design is a unique approach to preventing crime that focuses on the physical environment. The CPTED model assumes that offenders are rational and look for unguarded targets in the selection of a crime site. According to CPTED theory, police and private security authorities, architects, city planners, landscape designers, and resident volunteers working coactively can create a climate of safety in a community.
- Target hardening is the concept of reducing the opportunity for an offender to carry out a crime. Opportunity reduction is a technique whereby persons seek to deter criminal activity by making it difficult for an offender to carry out a crime.
- The basis of target hardening is to strengthen the defenses of a site to deter an attack and/or to delay the success of an attack. Examples of target hardening include secure doors, locks, windows, alarm systems, and adequate lighting.

Review Questions

1. Define and discuss criminal prevention strategies.
2. Explain the differences between the UCR and the NCVS.
3. Identify and describe an index crime from the Uniform Crime Report.
4. Describe how general deterrence is different from special deterrence, giving examples of each.

5. Identify and describe situational crime prevention.
6. Describe the process of target hardening.
7. Describe crime prevention thorough environmental design.
8. Identify and discuss carjacking prevention tips.
9. What should you look for when choosing an ATM machine?

10. Identify ways in which an ATM machine can be altered and target hardened to protect it from potential criminal activities.
11. Identify auto theft tips or ways you can prevent a car from being stolen.

Class Exercises

1. Discuss the two major crime reporting techniques, the uniform crime report and the national crime victimization survey. Discuss similarities and differences in these two reporting techniques. Can these data assist private security? If so, how?
2. Review crime stories in the local and national newspapers and discuss in class examples of general and specific deterrence.

3. Visit a convenience store in your community and look for opportunities that may exist for criminal opportunity. Discuss in class ways that you could reduce the opportunity.

References

Adler, F., G. Mueller, and W. S. Laufer. 2006. *Criminal justice: An introduction.* Boston: McGraw-Hill.

Bureau of Justice Statics. 2007. *Crime characteristics: Summary findings.* www.ojp.usdoj.gov/bjs/cvict_c.htm#vtrends.

Clarke, R. V. 1997. Introduction. In *Situational crime prevention: Successful case studies,* ed. R. V. Clark. Guilderland, NY: Harrow and Heston.

Cromwell, P., and J. N. Olson. 2006. The reasoning burglar: Motives and decision making strategies. In *In their own words: Criminals on crime,* ed. P. Cromwell, 42–56. Los Angeles: Roxbury.

Crowe, T. 2000. *Crime Prevention Through Environmental Design,* 2nd ed. Boston: Butterworth-Heinemann.

Crowe, T., and D. Zahm. 1994. Crime Prevention Through Environmental Design. *Land Development,* Fall, 22–7.

Felson, M., and R. V. Clarke. 1998. *Opportunity makes the thief: Practical theory for crime prevention.* Police Research Series Paper 98, Policing and Reducing Crime Unit, Research, Development and Statistics Directorate. London: Home Office.

Gardiner, R. A. 1982. Designs for safe neighborhoods. In *Handbook on loss prevention and crime prevention,* ed. L. J. Fennelly, 43–57. Boston: Butterworths.

Girard, C. M. 1982. Security lighting. In *Handbook on loss prevention and crime prevention,* ed. L. J. Fennelly, 95–109. Boston: Butterworths.

Gray, B. M. 1982. History and principles of crime prevention. In *Handbook on loss prevention and crime prevention,* ed. L. J. Fennelly, 1–20. Boston: Butterworths.

Jeffery, C. R. 1971. *Crime prevention through environmental design.* Beverly Hills, CA: Sage.

Lab, S. P. 2007. *Crime prevention: Approaches, practices, and evaluations,* 6th ed. Nantucket, MA: Lexis Nexis.

National Crime Prevention Institute. 1978. *Understanding crime prevention.* Louisville, KY: Crime Prevention Library.

Newman, O. 1972. *Defensible space.* New York: Macmillan.

Painter, K. 1994. The impact of street lighting on crime, fear, and pedestrian street use. *Security Journal* 5(3): 116–24.

Roberson, C., and H. Wallace. 1998. *Introduction to criminology.* Incline Village, NV: Copper House Publishing.

Rosenbaum, D. P., E. Hernandez, and S. Daughtry. 1991. Crime prevention, fear reduction, and the community. In *local government police management,* 3rd ed., ed. W. A. Geller, 96–125. Washington, DC: International City Managers Association.

Rolf, M. 1982: Alarms: Intrusion detection systems. In *Handbook of loss prevention and crime prevention,* ed. L. J. Fennelly, 225–43. Boston: Butterworths.

Sacco, V. F., and L. W. Kennedy. 1996. *The criminal event.* Belmont, CA: Wadsworth.

Wright, R. T., and S. H. Decker. 1994. *Burglars on the job: Street life and residential burglary.* Boston: Northeastern Press.

CHAPTER 3

Private Security and the Community Policing Connection

CHAPTER OUTLINE

OBJECTIVES

After completing this chapter, you will be able to:

- Describe community policing.
- Identify the three core components of community policing.
- Describe the connection between private security and community policing.
- Explain the importance of private security partnerships with the community.
- Explain the importance of private security partnerships with law enforcement.
- Discuss challenges of the private security enterprise.
- Describe the broken windows theory.
- List the possible signs of terrorist activity.
- Discuss the problem-solving process and how it can be applied in private security operations.
- Identify each stage in the SARA problem-solving model.

In the 1990s, we introduced Boston's community policing strategy. We reversed the tide of violent crime that threatened our city, and we established a national model for preventing and fighting crime.

—*Thomas Menino, Mayor, City of Boston*

Students who have taken a college course in criminal justice have most likely been introduced to the strategy of community policing. Many colleges now offer a full course on community policing, and many textbooks address this strategy. In addition, you may have read or heard about the community policing activities of the police department in the city where you live. The community policing strategy is almost always associated with public law enforcement organizations. Much of the material in this chapter represents exciting possibilities about how community policing can be adapted by private security organizations. There is little literature that guides or, for that matter, describes how the community policing strategy can benefit private security operations.

As we pointed out in Chapter 1, the Bureau of Justice Statistics indicates that there are 16,661 state, local, and county law enforcement agencies in the United States, and they employ a total of 677,933 sworn officers. Studies on private security staffing indicate that there may be as many as 10,000 private security agencies employing slightly less than 2 million private security officers in the United States. It is reasonable to assume that, with the private security industry employing well over 1 million more security personnel than public police departments, a great many citizens will have contact with a representative from the private security industry.

It seems that private security officers are everywhere. They can be seen patrolling shopping malls, workplaces, apartment buildings, large supermarkets, condominiums, and neighborhoods. The growth of large private shopping malls, along with the steady shrinkage of public shopping streets, means that the public is more likely to encounter private security than a police officer on a daily basis. Think about this: The next time you visit your bank, take a look around—chances are that you will see a uniformed security officer standing conspicuously in the bank lobby. The private security officer may be the first person who greets you when you enter the bank. And the next time you visit your favorite shopping mall, you will probably see private security officers patrolling the shops and stores. You may also have had contact with a private security officer at your place of employment, especially if you work in a large manufacturing company. Most large manufacturing plants contract with a security agency to provide security for the plant. In some cases the security force is employed by the manufacturer.

The likelihood that citizens will have contact with a private security officer creates an ideal environment for private security personnel to practice community policing strategies. In many respects, private security and community policing seem to go hand in hand. Both private security and the community policing strategy emphasize crime prevention and increased community contact. This chapter has two objectives. The first is to provide students and private security practitioners with an overview of community policing, and the second is to present community policing as a viable strategy for private security operations.

WHAT IS COMMUNITY POLICING?

Community policing is a philosophy based on the concept that the police and citizens working together in creative ways can solve contemporary community problems related to crime, fear of crime, social and physical disorder, and general neighborhood conditions. The philosophy is founded on the belief that achieving these goals requires the police to develop a new relationship with citizens, allowing them the power to set local police priorities and involving them in efforts to improve the overall quality of life in their community. Community policing shifts the focus of police work from just handling crime calls to addressing community concerns. It has grown from a few small foot patrol projects to the preeminent reform agenda of modern policing.

Community policing is not a program; it is a philosophy or strategy, a way all department members from the top to bottom, sworn and nonsworn, view their job. We prefer to use the term *strategy*. Some police officers despise community policing efforts. They simply think it means being soft on crime. This belief could not be further from the truth. Some studies have found that community policing is very effective not only in reducing crime but also in decreasing the fear of crime among citizens. For community policing to be effective, it must permeate the entire organization, local government, and community, not just a group of specialized community policing officers, for example. It requires police officers to identify and respond to a broad array of problems, including crime, disorder, and fear of crime, drug use, urban decay, and other neighborhood concerns. Professor Robert Friedmann offers a comprehensive definition of community policing:

> Community policing is a policy and a strategy aimed at achieving more effective and efficient crime control, reduced fear of crime, improved quality of life, improved police services and police legitimacy, through a proactive reliance on community resources that seeks to change crime causing conditions. This assumes a need for greater accountability of police, greater public share in decision making, and greater concern for civil rights and liberties (Friedmann 1992, 4).

Put another way, community policing is a philosophy of policing based on the concept that the police and citizens working together in creative ways can solve contemporary community problems related to crime, fear of crime, social and physical disorder, and general neighborhood conditions. The philosophy is founded on the belief that achieving these goals requires the police to develop a new relationship with citizens, allowing them the power to set local police priorities and involving them in efforts to improve the overall quality of life in their community. Community policing shifts the focus of police work from just handling crime calls to addressing community concerns.

Since the federal Crime Act of 1994 set community policing in motion, two-thirds of U.S. police agencies and 62 percent of sheriff's offices have full-time personnel performing community policing (National Institute of Justice 2004). Community policing is presented as constituting a viable way to prevent crime as well as being applied with the goals of organizational change (Palmiotto, Birzer, and Unnithan 2000). It is an approach to law enforcement designed to reduce and prevent crime by increasing interaction and cooperation between local law enforcement agencies and the people and neighborhoods they serve. It represents a new era of police

Community policing: A strategy, and how all department members from top to bottom, sworn and nonsworn, view their job. The strategy must permeate the entire organization, local government, and the community, not just the community policing officers or the patrol division. Community policing entails problem solving, community partnerships, and organizational change.

Traditional Versus Contemporary Community Policing

Question	Traditional Policing	Community Policing
Who are the police?	A government agency principally responsible for law enforcement.	Police are the public; the public are the police; the police officers are those who are paid to give full-time attention to the duties of every citizen.
What is the relationship of the police force to other public-service departments?	Priorities often conflict.	The police are one department among many responsible for improving the quality of life.
What is the role of the police?	Focus on solving crimes.	A broader problem-solving approach.
How is police efficiency measured?	By detection and arrest rates.	By the absence of crime and disorder.
What are the highest priorities?	Crimes that are high value (e.g., bank robberies) and those involving violence.	Whatever problems disturb the community most.
What, specifically, do police deal with?	Incidents.	Citizens' problems and concerns.
What determines the effectiveness of police?	Response times.	Public cooperation.
What view do police take of service calls?	They deal with them only if there is no police work to do.	They are a vital function and a great opportunity.
What is police professionalism?	Swift, effective response to serious crime.	Keeping close to the community.
What kind of intelligence is most important?	Crime intelligence (study of particular crimes or series of crimes).	Criminal intelligence (information about the activities of individuals or groups).
What is the essential nature of police accountability?	Highly centralized; governed by rules, regulations, and policy directives; accountability to the law.	Emphasis on local accountability to community needs.
What is the role of headquarters?	To provide necessary rules and policy directives.	To preach organizational values.
What is the role of the liaison department?	To keep the "heat" off operational officers so they can get on with the job.	To coordinate an essential channel of communication with the community.
How do the police regard prosecutions?	As an important goal.	As one tool among many.

Source: M. K. Sparrow, *Implementing community policing* (Washington, DC: U.S. Department of Justice, National Institute of Justice, 1998), 8–9.

services in which the government asks the public to help in resolving crime-related problems (Thurman and Reisig 1996). Community policing typically entails three important core components: community partnerships, problem solving, and organizational change (Note: We will discuss organizational change in Chapter 4).

Community Partnerships

Community partnerships are based on the premise that the police and the community work together to solve crime-related problems. The term *community* as used in community policing is broad and may include any private or governmental resource that may be beneficial in solving a problem. Partnerships may involve the police, security professionals, the community, the government body, service agencies, and the criminal justice system working together as a team to solve community problems (Peak and Gleansor 1999). Effective partnerships recognize the value of activities that contribute to the orderliness and well-being of a neighborhood. These activities may include helping accident or crime victims; helping resolve domestic and neighborhood conflicts such as family violence, landlord–tenant disputes, or racial harassment; working with residents and local businesses to improve neighborhood conditions; controlling automobile and pedestrian traffic; providing emergency social services and referrals to those at risk (e.g., adolescent runaways, the homeless, the intoxicated, and the mentally ill); protecting the exercise of constitutional rights (guaranteeing a person's right to speak, protecting lawful assemblies from disruption); and providing a model of citizenship (helpfulness, respect for others, honesty, and fairness).

Community partnerships: The premise that the police and the community work together to solve community crime- and disorder-related problems.

Problem Solving

Problem-solving strategies are utilized by the police when they attempt to resolve the underlying cause of a problem. For instance, in the case of a neighborhood that has been the target of recent vandalisms, assessment may reveal that the area is not well lighted after dark. Simply encouraging neighborhood residents to turn their lights on at night may resolve the vandalism problem. Many police agencies have adopted systematic problem-solving models that can be utilized by police officers. One of the most popular models is known as *SARA,* an acronym for Scan, Analysis, Response, and Assess. Later in this chapter we will apply a problem-solving scenario to security operations.

Problem solving: The systematic identification and analysis of the actual and potential causes of crime and conflict within the community, with the results guiding development of measures to address the problems in the short, medium, and long term. Problem solving also involves conflict resolution and other creative methods to address service delivery and police–community relations problems.

- *Scanning* identifies a problem through a variety of sources of information, such as calls for service and citizen surveys. For this phase to succeed, citizens must consider the problem important.
- *Analysis* requires examination of the nature of the problem. Input from police and residents about the problem is important, as well as the collection of data the department may have about the frequency, location, and other significant characteristics of the problem.
- *Response* fashions one or more preferred solutions to the problem. This step, as well as the preceding analysis step, benefits from creative deliberation, or "thinking outside the box." Input clearly should come from police personnel, but also from residents, experts, and other individuals who can address the problem thoughtfully.
- *Assessment* evaluates the effectiveness of the expected solution. Agencies must evaluate the solution as objectively as possible, because this step speaks to end products, the key theme in problem-solving initiatives.

THE LINK BETWEEN PRIVATE SECURITY AND COMMUNITY POLICING

How do you think community policing pertains to private security operations? Can the security industry adapt principles from community policing into their operations? The short answer is yes. The following sections will examine how community policing strategies can be adapted by private security organizations, and how many of the components of community policing seem to be a natural fit with security operations.

Community Partnerships and Private Security

Just as community policing requires the police to forge partnerships with many community resources, so too must security personnel. Community policing, with its call to establish partnerships, requires cooperative efforts, including partnerships especially between private security and law enforcement. In the past, private security personnel and police officers have had strained relationships. Some police authorities have held private security in low regard and do not appreciate the important role they perform in the prevention of crime.

A recent report by the Department of Justice indicated that some corporate security directors have felt that the police were uninterested in or incapable of addressing many of their concerns, such as high-tech crime, white-collar crime, and terrorism (Connors et al. 2000). One Midwestern police officer was overheard saying that he goes out of his way to issue traffic citations to private security officers who are detected committing traffic infractions. Several other police officers were overheard saying that private security officers are "wannabe cops." "Wannabe" is a term that is sometimes used among police officers to refer to a person who wants to be a police officer but for some reason cannot be. This type of attitude by police toward private security is wrong, archaic, unprofessional, and should be discontinued. Police supervisors and commanders have a responsibility to put a stop to the use of such terms by any police officers about the private security industry. Because of the emergent security issues that our nation faces, the police and private security do not have time for petty turf battles, and they should work together. Fortunately, the trend in recent years has been toward a working partnership.

You may ask, what are the actual benefits of a private security and public law enforcement partnership? The benefits are many and may include networking and the personal touch, collaboration on specific projects (urban quality-of-life issues, high-tech crime), increased crime prevention and public safety, community policing, and the use of technology.

In a post-9/11/01 era that presents a host of new challenges for private security and public law enforcement, cooperation between the two entities has never been more critical. Public law enforcement agencies can prepare private security to assist in emergencies (in many cases, security officers are the first responders); coordinate efforts to safeguard the nation's critical infrastructure, the vast majority of which is owned by the private sector or protected by private security; obtain free training and services; gain additional personnel resources and expertise; benefit from private-sector knowledge specialization in cyber crime, for example, and advanced technology; gather better knowledge of incidents through reporting by security staff; obtain intelligence; and reduce the number of calls for police service.

The private security industry also has much to gain from this cooperation. This segment can coordinate its plans with the public sector, in advance, regarding evacuation, transportation, food, and other emergency issues; gain information from law enforcement personnel regarding threats and crime trends; develop relationships so that practitioners know whom to contact when they need help or want to report

Operation Cooperation

Operation Cooperation represents a major national initiative to encourage partnerships between law enforcement and private security professionals. Operation Cooperation is funded by the Bureau of Justice Assistance and supported by the American Society for Industrial Security, the International Association of Chiefs of Police, and the National Sheriff's Association. Operation Cooperation attempts to persuade police, sheriffs, and security professionals to talk and work together. The driving force behind it is a passion among practitioners who see the great benefits to be gained from public–private teamwork. The initiative is expressed at first through a guideline document, a video, a collection of partnership profiles, and a literature review, which together serve as a road map or guide for those who wish to establish productive partnerships. The fullest expression of Operation Cooperation will be an increase in collaboration between public law enforcement and private security efforts across the country.

information; build law enforcement's understanding of corporate needs such as confidentiality; and boost law enforcement's respect for the security field.

Partnerships between private security and law enforcement may also be beneficial for homeland security. The simple fact is that law enforcement's capacity to provide homeland security may be more limited than is generally acknowledged. For the most part, the public sector tends to have the threat information, while the private sector tends to have control over the vulnerable sites. Therefore, homeland security, including protection of the nation's critical infrastructure, depends partly on the competence of private security practitioners. Thus, building partnerships and cooperation is essential for effective homeland security. This is discussed in greater detail in Chapter 4.

Some other factors that increase the importance of public law enforcement and private security cooperation include information-age crime (computer and high-tech crime), private security performing many traditional law enforcement roles, the globalization of business, increased international operations by law enforcement authorities, and the interdependence of critical infrastructures.

Although private security and public law enforcement partnerships are of vital importance, private security authorities should also forge partnerships with other community resources. Private security officials must recognize that they are interdependent with the community. An active outreach to the community provides the private security industry with a better flow of information and a more accurate understanding of the problems and expectations of their customer base. Continual interaction between security personnel and citizens can serve as a catalyst in mobilizing them to protect themselves. Private security and citizen interaction can also result in the identification of resources that can assist in problem-solving endeavors.

Neighborhood Associations

Private security authorities should be familiar with neighborhood associations in areas where they provide security services. Neighborhood associations are groups of citizens that form and meet periodically for the purpose of disseminating relevant information regarding a specific neighborhood. Likewise, neighborhood associations provide an avenue to build and strengthen bonds through socialization at neighborhood meetings. In other words, neighborhood residents get to know one another. Neighborhood associations often start grass-roots anticrime programs and youth programs.

Neighborhood associations:
Groups of citizens that form
and meet periodically for the
purpose of disseminating
relevant information
regarding a specific
neighborhood. Neighborhood
associations promote
programs, services, and
activities aimed at
encouraging connections
between neighbors and
fostering civic involvement in
the community.

A few years ago, the Brighton Beach Neighborhood Association in Brooklyn, New York, started an impressive initiative aimed at youth. The Brighton Beach Neighborhood Association houses its youth department in a storefront office located snugly within the neighborhood. Services include after-school programs, antitruancy counseling, and "second-chance" summer school. Many young people visit the storefront office after school to discuss daily problems. Nearly 500 youngsters have found a place off the streets and safe in the after-school center, and since its inception over 1500 students have been promoted to the next grade because of the "second chance" summer school. Further, the youth in the program give back to their community. During one year alone they collected books for a book sale that raised hundreds of dollars for the library in Brighton. The program also organized about forty youth to clean up and plant flowers in a local park (Brighton Beach Neighborhood Association 2008).

Homeowners' Associations

It is very common for security companies to contract services with housing developments, condominium communities, and apartment complexes, many of which have formed homeowners' associations. Homeowners' associations are usually the governance function of a common-interest development. This governance, most often created by the real estate developer, is given the authority to enforce covenants and manage the common amenities of the development. Most homeowners' associations are nonprofit corporations and are subject to state statutes that govern nonprofit corporations. The fastest-growing form of housing in the United States is common-interest developments, a category that includes planned developments of single-family homes and condominiums, and cooperative apartments.

Homeowners' associations:
Organizations formed to
maintain, enhance, and
protect the common areas
and interests of an
association (also called a
subdivision or
neighborhood). The transfer
deeds to houses in new
developments almost
always include limitations on
how the property can be
used. Usually these
limitations, called covenants,
conditions, or restrictions,
put decision-making rights
into the hands of the
homeowners' association.
Some associations enforce
every rule, while others are
run in a more relaxed way.
Most associations try to make
decisions that will enhance
the value of the homes.

The primary purpose of a homeowners' association is to maintain, enhance, and protect the common areas of a subdivision or neighborhood. This may allow an individual homeowner access to an amenity (pond, pool, clubhouse, etc.) that he or she may not be able to afford alone. Each member of a homeowners' association pays *assessments*. The assessments are used to pay the common expenses of the community. Some examples are entrance monuments, landscaping for the common area, amenities such as clubhouses, tennis courts, or walking trails, insurance for commonly owned structures and areas, mailing costs for newsletters or other correspondence, a management company or on-site manager, or any other need delineated in the governing documents or agreed to by the board of directors. Community enhancements such as these give the impression that residents care about their neighborhood, and this is an important crime-prevention tool. The simple appearance of a neighborhood can go a long way in preventing crime and disorder. Professors George L. Kelling and James Q. Wilson point this out in their classic *broken windows theory.*

Broken Windows Theory

Kelling and Wilson (1982) presented their *broken windows theory* to explain the warning signs of a neighborhood that may nurture criminal activity. The theory suggests that there is a sequence of events that can be expected in deteriorating neighborhoods. For example, evidence of decay (i.e., accumulated trash, broken windows, deteriorated building exteriors, abandoned cars) that remains in a neighborhood for a long period of time is part of the sequence of events that can be expected in deteriorating

Neighborhood deterioration; trash in yard; cars parked in front yard; tree limbs down.

neighborhoods. Many neighborhoods where drug dealing is prevalent show evidence of this sequence of events. If you are a security officer reading this book, think about this for a moment. Recall the last time you were in an area where there is known to be a significant amount of drug dealing. It is more than likely that the neighborhood as a whole shows signs of deterioration. Citizens who live and work in the area feel vulnerable and are more likely to withdraw. Citizens become less willing to intervene to maintain public order or to address physical signs of deterioration. The *broken windows theory* suggests that neighborhood order strategies such as the ones listed below may help to deter and reduce neighborhood-related crime. Private security authorities should be mindful of these strategies.

Broken windows theory:
This theory uses the analogy that if a few broken windows on a vacant residence are left unrepaired, the tendency is for vandals to break more windows. Eventually, they may even break into the building and possibly take up residence in the building or light fires inside. The idea is that small disorder problems should be addressed promptly, or they may lead to more serious crime problems.

- Replace broken windows on vacant homes or buildings.
- Quickly remove abandoned vehicles from the street.
- Promptly clean up illegally dumped items, litter, and spilled garbage.
- Quickly remove or paint over graffiti.
- Find (or build) better places for teens to gather than street corners.
- Apply fresh paint to buildings.
- Clean up sidewalks and street gutters.
- Keep grass and weeds cut in vacant lots.

Security personnel should make it a point to establish regular contact with homeowners' association members for the purpose of discovering information about problems or concerns that the community may be experiencing. One security officer operating in the Midwest related that he is invited to all of the homeowners' association meetings in the neighborhoods for which he provides security. The security officer related that it is a great way to discover information about the neighborhood that he would have otherwise not known—not to mention a good way to meet the citizens living in the area.

Neighborhood Watch

Neighborhood Watch:
A citizens' organization
devoted to preventing
crime and vandalism in
their neighborhood.

Most private security professionals recognize that a Neighborhood Watch initiative is one of the most effective ways to prevent crime, address the safety of children and the elderly, and reduce fear and isolation. Unfortunately, private security officers historically have not been very involved with Neighborhood Watch associations, although they should be. Neighborhood Watch fosters civic involvement, collaborative problem solving, and mutual commitments, which have all helped communities and neighborhoods reduce crime by significant numbers. A Neighborhood Watch is a citizens' organization devoted to crime prevention within their neighborhood. The Neighborhood Watch concept is one of the oldest crime prevention programs in the United States. It is important for security officers to recognize that Neighborhood Watch is not a vigilante organization—members are not expected to intervene directly in criminal activity. Rather, Neighborhood Watch members are to stay alert to unusual activity and contact the authorities when they see it.

Neighborhood Watch is one of the most effective and least costly ways to prevent crime and reduce neighborhood fear. Neighborhood Watch organizations learn how to make their homes more secure, working with security organizations and the police department. Neighbors watch out for each other by reporting suspicious activities to the authorities. Neighborhood Watch meetings are usually held at residents' homes and are sometimes facilitated by a police officer.

Neighborhood Watch forges strong bonds among residents. Watch groups create a sense of community and pride by forming a unified group of citizens dedicated to improving their neighborhood. Partnering with security organizations, citizens become their eyes and ears. Neighborhood Watch groups also serve as an empowering outlet for victims of crime. They give victims a greater sense of control, ensuring that what happened to them will be less likely to happen to others. A Neighborhood Watch program is often a springboard for many other efforts to address the causes of crime, reduce crime, and improve neighborhood conditions, including youth recreation, child care, economic development, senior citizens' activities, and community beautification.

Private security officers who work in neighborhoods or other developed housing areas should be encouraged to work with local police in identifying those areas that do not have a Neighborhood Watch organization and would benefit from having one. Security officers should be familiar with Neighborhood Watch groups within their contracted areas. Security officers should regularly attend Neighborhood Watch meetings. This is an ideal way to get to know the citizens living in the area (customers) and vention to become more knowledgeable about their concerns. The National Crime Prevention Institute recommends the following two-phases strategy for establishing Neighborhood Watch programs.

Phase One: Getting Started—Meetings, Block Captains, and Maps

- Form a small planning committee of neighbors to discuss needs, the level of interest, possible challenges, and the Watch concept.
- Contact the local police or sheriff's department, or local crime prevention organization, to discuss Neighborhood Watch and local crime problems. Invite a law enforcement officer to attend your meeting.
- Publicize your meeting at least one week in advance with door-to-door fliers, and follow up with phone calls the day before.

"Hispanic family hammers Neighborhood Watch sign on their front lawn, Los Angeles, CA."

- Select a meeting place that is accessible to people with disabilities.
- Hold an initial meeting to gauge neighbors' interest; establish the purpose of the program; and begin to identify issues that need to be addressed. Stress that a Watch group is an association of neighbors who look out for each others' families and property, alert the police to any suspicious activities or crime in progress, and work together to make their community a safer and better place to live.

Phase Two: When the Neighborhood Decides to Adopt the Watch Idea

- Elect a chairperson.
- Ask for block captain volunteers, who will be responsible for relaying information to members on their block, keeping up-to-date information on residents, and making special efforts to involve the elderly, working parents, and young people. Block captains also can serve as liaisons between the neighborhood and the police and can communicate information about meetings and crime incidents to all residents.
- Establish a regular means of communicating with Watch members—e.g., newsletter, telephone tree, e-mall, fax, etc.
- Prepare a neighborhood map showing names, addresses, and phone numbers of participating households and distribute it to members. Block captains keep this map up to date, contacting newcomers to the neighborhood and rechecking occasionally with ongoing participants.

- With guidance from a law enforcement agency, the Watch trains its members in home security techniques, observation skills, and crime reporting. Residents also learn about the types of crime that affect the area.
- If you are ready to post Neighborhood Watch signs, check with law enforcement to see if they have such eligibility requirements as number of houses that participate in the program. Law enforcement officers may also be able to provide your program with signs. If not, they can probably tell you where you can order them.
- Organizers and block captains must emphasize that Watch groups are not vigilantes and do not assume the role of the police. They only ask neighbors to be alert, observant, and caring—and to report suspicious activity or crimes immediately to the police.
- The Watch concept is adaptable. There are Park Watches, Apartment Watches, Window Watches, Boat Watches, School Watches, Realtor Watches, Utility Watches, and Business Watches. A Watch can be organized around any geographic unit.

Landlord Associations

Security professionals should be familiar with landlord associations. This is especially true for security operations that service a large number of rental properties such as apartments and duplexes. Landlord associations are designed to promote positive and responsible partnerships among landlords, tenants, security professionals, and law enforcement officers. This partnership is vital to effectively preventing drug dealing and other illegal activities at rental properties. Because security officers in many cases are the first to encounter problems such as drug dealing in an apartment complex, the security officer is in an advantageous position to assist law enforcement in resolving this problem.

If there is drug dealing in an apartment complex, part of the solution may lie in proper maintenance of the property. The security officer may wish to make some simple suggestions to the landlord association. By responsibly maintaining their properties, landlords foster pride in the community and show respect for all residents of the community. It is also important to point out that these functions are carried out not by a specialized crime prevention unit but rather by the security officer in the field. Specifically, the security officer may provide information to landlords pertaining to:

- Preparing a rental property
- Screening applicants
- Rental agreements
- Active management
- Problem solving
- Recognizing illegal drug activity in the neighborhood
- Recognizing gang activity

National Night Out

Security authorities who engage in contract work in neighborhoods should make it a point to become fully involved in the National Night Out program. The National Association of Town Watch's annual National Night Out program, which is held on the first Tuesday each August, has been successful in promoting involvement in crime prevention activities, strengthening police–community relations, and encouraging

Area Police/Private Security Liaison

Area Police/Private Security Liaison (APPL) was founded by New York Police Department (NYPD) commanders and prominent security directors in New York City in 1986 to enhance public–private cooperation in protecting people and property, to exchange information, and to help eliminate the credibility gap between police and private security. Starting with only thirty private security organizations, it now includes more than 1000.

APPL is the largest local cooperative program between police and private security in the nation. The chief of the NYPD is APPL's chair, and a staff officer in the chief's office is assigned to coordinate the program. APPL's executive committee consists of five senior security executives, representing both corporate and contract security organizations. APPL's lengthy activity list includes the following:

- Monthly and annual meetings
- An inventory of private-sector closed-circuit television installations for use in criminal investigations
- A specialized business crime squad in midtown Manhattan
- Training for security supervisors
- A radio network for doormen
- Monitoring of security-related legislation

neighborhood camaraderie as part of the fight for safer streets. National Night Out has grown to involve over 34 million people from more than 10,000 communities. The program has grown to include cities and law enforcement agencies from all fifty states, U.S. territories, Canada, and U.S. military bases around the world.

Along with the traditional porch sitting and "lights on," areas hold locally tailored events such as block parties, cookouts, parades, rallies, marches, and visits from law enforcement personnel. National Night Out is a popular and effective strategy for heightening awareness, enhancing private security–community relations, and bolstering volunteer morale. Security officers should increasingly become involved in this annual event.

Collaborative Programs Between Law Enforcement and Private Security

Networking

- Breakfast and lunch meetings to discuss common problems and help each side understand the pressures, motivations, and constraints on the other
- Lectures by private security professionals during police recruit training
- Speeches by practitioners in one field at conferences of the other field.
- Sponsorship by security organizations of law enforcement appreciation functions and scholarships
- Directories of local law enforcement and private security contacts
- Honors and awards (from private security to law enforcement and vice versa)

Information Sharing

- Information (provided by law enforcement to the private sector) on criminal convictions (if authorized by law), local crime trends, *modus operandi*, and incidents, shared via email trees, Web pages, mailed newsletters, fax alerts, or telephone calls
- Information (provided by the private sector to law enforcement) on business crime and employees

Crime Prevention

- Joint participation in security and safety for business improvement districts
- Consultation on crime prevention through environmental design and community policing
- Special joint efforts on local concerns, such as check fraud, video piracy, graffiti, or false alarms
- Joint public–private support of Neighborhood Watch programs
- Joint participation in National Night Out

(continued)

Collaborative Programs Between Law Enforcement and Private Security (*continued*)

Resource Sharing

- Lending of expertise (technical, language, etc.)
- Lending of "buy" money or goods
- Lending of computer equipment needed for specific investigations
- Donation of computer equipment, cellular telephones, etc.
- Donation of security devices to protect public spaces
- Creation of a booklet that makes it easier for law enforcement to borrow equipment and resources from private security, listing specific contact information for using auditoriums, classrooms, conference rooms, firing ranges, four-wheel-drive vehicles, helicopter landing areas, indoor swimming pools, lecturers on security, open areas for personnel deployment, printing services, and vans or trucks

Training

- Hosting speakers on topics of joint interest (terrorism, school violence, crime trends, etc.).
- Exchange of training and expertise (corporations offer management training to police; private security trains law enforcement in security measures; law enforcement teaches security officers how to be good witnesses or gather

evidence in accordance with prosecutorial standards)
- Police training of corporate employees on such topics as sexual assault, burglary prevention, family Internet safety, drug and alcohol abuse, traffic safety, and vacation safety

Legislation

- Drafting and supporting laws and ordinances on such topics as security officer standards and licensing, alarms, and computer crime
- Tracking of legislation of importance to law enforcement and security operations

Operations

- Investigations (of complex financial frauds or computer crimes)
- Critical-incident planning (for natural disasters, school shootings, and workplace violence)
- Joint sting operations (cargo theft)

Research and Guidelines

- Review of, distribution of, and action on research papers and protocols regarding false alarms, workplace drug crimes, workplace violence, product tampering, mobile security devices, nonsworn alarm responders, closed-circuit television, security personnel standards, etc.

Source: Bureau of Justice Assistance, *Operation cooperation: Guidelines for partnerships between law enforcement and private security organizations* (Washington, DC: U.S. Department of Justice, 2000).

THE ROLE OF PRIVATE SECURITY IN CRIME PREVENTION

The private security industry plays a critical role in the prevention of crime. In fact, private security may be in a better position to prevent crime than the police, simply because the police don't have sufficient time and resources compared to private security. A significant part of public police resources is spent on reacting to crime and other service-related activities. Private security operations, however, put a vast amount of resources toward the prevention of crime. In fact, if you think about it for a moment, private security operations are almost exclusively orientated toward the prevention of crime. Consider, for example, the sophisticated video security system in a large shopping mall, the plain-clothes loss prevention officer walking around a major supermarket, the security alarm expert installing a state-of-the-art residential alarm system, or the security officer patrolling in a marked security vehicle and checking buildings. These activates are all related to the prevention of crime.

In the spirit of community policing, security authorities should work closely with public safety activists, police precincts, community members, neighborhood associations, state agencies, city bureaus, businesses, and local service providers to address crime and quality-of-life issues. Security operations should also focus on other aspects of crime prevention, including preserving public safety and enhancing neighborhood livability to meet the needs of each neighborhood or business area. This might include assisting residents and the police in problem-solving projects related to issues such as drug houses, youth gangs, graffiti, street drug dealing, prostitution, problem parks, problem liquor outlets, and neighborhood "hot spots." Following are some suggestions for private security organizations when engaging the community as part of a comprehensive crime prevention program.

- Help to create community networks and partnerships.
- Support community outreach functions, such as newsletters and Web pages, facilitate and attend community meetings, provide notification to neighbors, conduct community surveys, and provide other outreach materials.
- Assist residents, businesses, police, and other partners in problem-solving efforts to address crime and quality-of-life issues.

THE CHANGING SECURITY ENVIRONMENT

On September 11, 2001, a commercial airliner plowed into the North Tower of the World Trade Center in Lower Manhattan. A few moments later, a second airliner hit the South Tower. The Twin Towers, where up to 50,000 people worked each day, both collapsed less than 90 minutes later. That same morning, a third airliner slammed into the Pentagon, and a short time later, a fourth airliner crashed in a field in southern Pennsylvania. It had been aimed at the United States Capitol or the White House, and was forced down by heroic passengers armed with the knowledge that America was under attack. More than 2600 people died at the World Trade Center; 125 died at the Pentagon; 256 died on the four planes.

A high jacked airplane, United Airlines flight 175 crashes into the south tower of the World Trade Center during the September 11 terrorist attacks in New York.

According to the 9/11/01 Commission Report, the attacks were carried out by nineteen young Arab men acting at the behest of Islamist extremists based in Afghanistan. Some had been in the United States for more than a year, mixing with the rest of the population. Though four had training as pilots, most were not well educated. Most spoke English poorly, some hardly at all. In groups of four or five, carrying with them only small knives, box cutters, and cans of Mace or pepper spray, they had hijacked the four planes and turned them into deadly guided missiles.

The 9/11/01 terrorist attacks left the nation struggling for answers. The attacks changed the state of law enforcement and security operations drastically. Not only must security authorities continue to focus on the prevention of traditional crimes, they are now increasingly involved in recognition and prevention of terrorism. That's right: Security personnel are not exempt from this important mandate. Like police officers, many private security officers are in the field and may have the occasion to observe persons, places, or events that may be terrorism related.

Since the terrorist attacks in the United States, many in the public law enforcement and private security fields have become somewhat narrow in how they view the perpetrators of terrorism. Although in some respects this may be justified, it is important to recognize that other groups may also present potential security risks. Certainly, radical Islamic factions such as Al Qaida pose a real threat to our safety and well-being, but it is important to remain aware of the potential for other domestic terrorism, such as the Oklahoma City bombing of 1995. As you may recall, on April 19, 1995, terrorists bombed the Alfred P. Murrah Federal Building, a U.S. government office complex in downtown Oklahoma City. The attack claimed 168 lives and left over 800 injured. Until September 11, 2001, it was the deadliest act of terrorism on United States soil. Timothy McVeigh and Terry Nichols were arrested and convicted for their roles in the bombing. Investigators determined that McVeigh and Nichols were sympathizers of an antigovernment militia movement and that their motive was to avenge the government's handling of the Waco and Ruby Ridge incidents.

Federal law enforcement authorities were criticized for their handling of both the Ruby Ridge and Waco incidents. The Ruby Ridge incident unfolded on August 21, 1992, when U.S. marshals attempted to arrest Randy Weaver on a federal warrant for possession of an illegal firearm. When the marshals attempted to arrest Weaver at his cabin in Ruby Ridge, Idaho, a gunfight erupted between the marshals and Weaver's son. During the gunfight, the marshals killed Weaver's son as he was retreating back into the cabin. Randy Weaver, along with his wife, two daughters, and a family friend, then barricaded themselves in the cabin. The next day an FBI sniper wounded Weaver and the family friend, and killed Weaver's wife. Weaver eventually surrendered, after an 11-day standoff. Many militia groups praised the Weavers as martyrs. During subsequent U.S. Senate hearings on the incident, both the FBI and the U.S. Marshals Service were criticized for their handling of the incident.

On February 28, 1983, agents of the U.S. Bureau of Alcohol, Tobacco and Firearms attempted to execute a search warrant for illegal weapons and explosives on a religious group known as the Branch Davidians at their ranch located near Waco, Texas. The group was named after their founder and leader, David Koresh. During the attempted search, a gunfight between agents and members of the Branch Davidians resulted in the deaths of four agents and six members of the Davidian group. The FBI was summoned and took control of the standoff that followed. The standoff ended

51 days later. Fire destroyed the compound. Seventy-six people, including David Koresh, died during the fire. Some critics alleged that the several fires were started after the FBI improperly fired tear gas into the compound.

The following paragraphs provide a brief overview of the signs of terrorism that private security officials should be aware of in the post-9/11/01 era. A thorough discussion of terrorism is included in Chapter 6.

Indicators of Terrorism

SURVEILLANCE   In many cases, the first sign of planned terrorism is someone trying to monitor or record activities. If terrorists are targeting a specific area, they will most likely be observed in that area during the planning phase of the operation. Terrorists will attempt to determine the strengths, weaknesses, and number of personnel who may respond to an incident. Routes to and from the target are usually established during the surveillance phase. It is important to note suspicious actions such as someone using a camera (still or video), drawing diagrams or making annotations on maps, using vision-enhancing devices, and being in possession of floor plans or blueprints of places such as high-tech firms, financial institutions, or government/military facilities. Security authorities should be aware that any of these surveillance acts may indicate that something is not right and should be reported immediately to the appropriate local, state, or federal authority.

SUSPICIOUS PERSONS AND VEHICLES   Terrorists use vehicles for many purposes, from surveillance to planting bombs. Vehicles may be parked for an unusual length of time, sometimes in no-parking areas. Explosives can be heavy, so cars and vans may sit abnormally low on their suspensions. They may have expired registrations or have false or missing plates.

Another preincident indicator is observing suspicious people who just don't belong. This includes suspicious border crossings, stowaways aboard a ship, or people jumping ship in a port. It could be people in a workplace, building, neighborhood, or business establishment who don't fit in because of their demeanor or unusual questions they are asking, or a statement they make. This does not suggest that security officers should profile individuals, but it does mean that they should profile behaviors.

SUSPICIOUS ACCOMMODATION NEEDS   The way terrorists use, rent, and buy accommodations is often suspicious. This might mean someone purchasing or stealing explosives, weapons, or ammunition. It might be unusual purchasing or storing of fertilizer or harmful chemicals. Terrorists may also find it useful to acquire law enforcement equipment and identification, military uniforms and decals, as well as flight passes, badges, or even flight manuals. Terrorists often use false or stolen identification documents, including passports and driver's licenses. They may try to produce counterfeit identification by photocopying. Any of these items may make it easier to gain entrance to secured or usually prohibited areas. Anyone wearing a uniform should have the proper identification. Fertilizer is a widely available product that has been used in many terrorist bombs. For example, one of the clues in the Oklahoma City bombing was a receipt for 2 tons of fertilizer.

A New Role for Mall Guards

In a shopping mall outside Hartford, Connecticut, past the Abercrombie & Fitch and the cell phone kiosks, tucked away by the Barnes & Noble, security guards in a conference room are learning how to spot suicide bombers. They are being taught blast patterns and behavior profiles, how a bomb is packaged, and how a bomber is recruited. Suburban shopping mall security guards, whose job usually consists of watching for shoplifters and shooing away loitering teenagers, are receiving the type of training that just a few years ago was reserved for the Israeli police and the U.S. military.

"If they're carrying a bag, look for that white-knuckle grip. . . . They're carrying that package and they're holding onto it for dear life," Patrick Chagnon, a Connecticut State Police detective and national counterterrorism instructor, tells his class of ten students as the Shoppes at Buckland Hills mall bustles with holiday shoppers carrying bags and boxes of all sizes.

Chagnon's students are also told to watch for people wearing oversized clothes, and they are instructed to make eye contact with shoppers and look for either extremely focused people or those who won't return a look. Another tipoff: Terrorists often ritualistically shave their bodies before carrying out a suicide bombing, he says.

Around the country, enrollment in these suicide bombing classes has increased in recent years, and the students include not just elite SWAT team members but also local patrol officers and private security forces.

Source: Mall guards get terrorism tips, *Desert News* (Salt Lake City, Utah), December 3, 2004.

THINGS THAT JUST DON'T ADD UP   While planning an attack, terrorists may lead lives that appear unusual or suspicious. The 9/11/01 terrorists are classic examples: they wanted to learn to fly, but not how to land. The leader of that group also paid cash for many large purchases such as flight training, accommodations, vehicles, and airfare.

FALSE OR MULTIPLE IDENTITIES   Terrorists often use false or stolen documents, including passports and driver's licenses. They can also have several identities and may give conflicting details to those they come in contact with.

INQUIRIES   Terrorists often attempt to gain information through inquiries. This includes anyone attempting to gain information about a place, person, or operation. Elicitation attempts can be made by mail, fax, telephone, or in person. An example is someone inquiring about critical infrastructure such as a power plant, water reservoir, or a maritime port. Terrorists may attempt to research bridge and tunnel usage, make unusual inquiries concerning shipments, or look into how a facility such as a hospital operates. They may also attempt to place "key" people in sensitive work locations to gain intelligence.

Cybercrime:
Criminal offenses carried out using computers. Financial crimes, cyber pornography, sale of illegal articles, online gambling, intellectual property crimes, email spoofing, cyber defamation, and cyber stalking are all examples of cyber crimes.

Cybercrime

Cybercrime presents a serious threat to the infrastructure of a wide range of businesses and governmental organizations. *Cybercrime* is a term used broadly to describe activity in which computers or networks are a tool, a target, or a place of criminal activity. There is much evidence suggesting that computer crime is increasing rapidly. Because of the increasing use of computers and other forms of technology in the commission of crimes, security professionals, especially those employed in corporate or financial security, are increasingly coming into contact with computer-related crimes.

Computer crimes include the unauthorized use of a computer, which might involve stealing a username and/or password, and creating or releasing a malicious computer program. For example, releasing computer viruses and computer worms can be disastrous and costly to literately thousands of computers users, who might innocently open an email contaminated with the virus or worm. Other types of cyber crimes include financial crimes, cyber pornography, sale of illegal articles, online gambling, intellectual property crimes, email spoofing, forgery, cyber defamation, and cyber stalking. Consider the case of an Ohio man who was recently indicted for illegally transmitting over $3 million in electronic funds from various banks to AMERITRADE and E*TRADE. The indictment charged that the man devised a scheme to defraud AMERITRADE and E*TRADE, and to obtain money, funds, credits, assets, and other property by means of false and fraudulent pretenses, representations, and promises. The accused was also indicted for aggravated identity theft for using the personal identifier information of others during and in relation to the wire-fraud offenses. See Chapter 8 for a thorough discussion of computer and network security issues.

REACTIVE, PROACTIVE, AND COACTIVE SECURITY

Reactive Security

Reactive security occurs when security officers respond to a specific request from an individual or group in the community, which involves an immediate response to a crime that has been committed. For example, a business is broken into and the security company is notified and responds with the police to the location. In other words, reactive security is a security officer's response *after* a crime has been attempted or committed.

Reactive security: When security officers respond for security purposes after a crime has been attempted or committed.

Proactive Security

Proactive security involves the security enterprise acting on its own initiative and developing information about crime and strategies for its prevention. In essence, proactive security occurs when a security officer *prevents* a crime. This could be as simple as physically checking buildings at a busy shopping center or conducting a home security survey for the purpose of making the residence more crime-resistant. Preventing crime in a proactive manner sometimes involves using intelligence information. It is through credible intelligence that threats can be identified and appropriate countermeasures taken. Intelligence information does not always come from the general public; the intelligence may also come from law enforcement. For example, narcotics units, vice units, and gang units may gather intelligence information from surveillance and from informants who are sometimes involved in criminal activity. Law enforcement and security companies may then share information about the criminal activity, which may result in more effective response to crime and disorder problems.

Proactive security: When security organizations work to prevent crime.

Coactive Security

Coactive security is similar to proactive security. In coactive security, the security company involves citizens and other community resources to solve crime-related problems. Suppose, for example, that a security officer has been providing security for the same shopping strip mall for several years. The security officer prides himself on knowing

Coactive security: When security organizations, police, the community, and other public and private resources work together to solve crime and community problems.

"Hispanic young female reporter interviews Black middle-aged female college security officer on Los Angeles High School campus, Los Angeles, CA."

most of the mall employees. Within the past month, there have been several burglaries at businesses in the strip mall. After the police have taken the necessary reports, the security officer inspects the businesses where the burglaries occurred. He notes a similar pattern. Entry into the businesses was made by either a rear door or window. He also discovers that in all of burglary cases, the rear doors and windows are not visual from an adjacent street because of the overgrowth of bush and shrubbery, and because of several large commercial trash containers that are located near the window and consequently blocks the view from the street. The security officer believes that the overgrowth of bushes and shrubbery, and the commercial trash containers that have been placed near the rear windows and doors, make the business in the strip mall vulnerable to break-ins.

Now suppose that the security officer contacts the business owners and recommends that they hire a company to trim or remove the bushes and shrubbery from the rear of the buildings. The security officer also contacts the sanitation company and requests having the trash containers moved away from the windows and doors. In addition, the security officer contacts the police investigators who have been assigned to the case and informs them of the actions that are being taken. In this case the security officer is being coactive by working with other resources (the business owners, the landscape maintenance company, and the sanitation company) to correct conditions that may nurture criminal activity.

The coactive approach presented has also resulted in target hardening. *Target hardening* is a process whereby a building is made into a more difficult or less attractive target to would-be criminals. Removing shrubbery and trees from around the rear windows, and moving the commercial trash containers away from the windows and doors, may make the location less attractive to burglars because the doors and windows can be more easily viewed from the adjacent street. For a complete discussion of target hardening, refer back to Chapter 2.

Coactive Security	
• Coactive security is preventing crime and disorder. • Coactive security works to identify problems that affect quality of life in the community. • Coactive security is based on the security company and other public and private resources	working together to prevent crime and disorder problems. • The aim of coactive security is to identify conditions that need to be addressed to prevent crime. • Coactive security is a natural fit with community policing and problem-solving strategies.

PUTTING PROBLEM SOLVING INTO PRACTICE

Problem solving is an important component of community policing. Recall that community policing is a collaborative effort between a police department and community that identifies problems of crime and disorder and involves all elements of the community in the search for solutions to identified problems. Private security can also play a pivotal role in problem solving. Problem-solving techniques can easily be adapted to private security operations.

Many of the problems that security officers encounter can be resolved or minimized by eradicating the underlying cause to the problem. For example, suppose there have been a number of incidents of vandalism in a neighborhood that contracts services with a security company. It has been determined that the vandalisms all occurred after dark. It may be learned after a thorough analysis of the problem that several street lights in the neighborhood are burned out. The private security officer can then work with the police to contact the appropriate resource to replace the burned-out street lights. Problem solving involves gathering as much data as possible about a particular problem and then applying a systematic problem-solving model such as SARA, as discussed earlier in the chapter.

Scanning

Continuing the example of the neighborhood that has experienced numerous vandalisms, security officers can apply the SARA problem-solving model. Scanning allows incidents to be grouped into clusters or problems. These problems typically comprise similar, related, or recurring incidents, and are identified from police data, intelligence reports, and calls from members of the community. In the scanning phase, the security officer collects all available data from the police department and any other possible sources. Pertinent information that will be useful in the scanning phase may include time of the incidents, which properties were vandalized, what was the traffic pattern—both foot and vehicle (if known)—around the time of the incidents, whether there were witnesses, whether there are suspects, whether the vandalism appears to be random, whether there appears to be a pattern, whether the vandalism was in the form of graffiti, and if so, whether the graffiti appeared to gang-related.

Much of the information on crime that is reported to police is public information, so private security officers should be able to obtain much of the information. Of course, if the security officer has an established rapport with police officers who work in the affected neighborhood, this all the more advantageous and could save the security officer a trip to the police station. With this said, it is wise for the security officer to approach the reporting police officer and talk to him or her directly, and perhaps collaborate on the problem-solving process. Both the private security company and the police have a stake in the neighborhood. The police have a stake because they are ultimately responsible for the investigation of the vandalism and the identification and apprehension of the perpetrators. The security company has a stake because it was hired by the neighborhood association to provide security in the area.

Analysis

During the analysis stage, the security officer identifies the conditions that give rise to the vandalism and examines the characteristics and impact of the problem. Scanning might have revealed that there were numerous vandalisms in a particular area, but the analysis will provide more definitive information, such as the location, time, days, or months that the vandalisms occurred. Analysis also involves collecting information about offenders and victims, the time of occurrence, locations and any other details of the physical environment, the history of the current problem, the motivations, gains and losses of involved parties, and any apparent and hidden causes.

Response

The response is the action taken to try to address the problem. A response may entail the security officer advising people about what they should or should not be doing, or may involve a more complex response, such as involving the community to set up a project to educate youth about the potential consequences of vandalism. In the analysis phase the main objective is to identify or isolate the element that can most easily be tackled. Often, responses combine actions to tackle more than one aspect of the problem identified during the analysis phase. In the vandalism case, it is discovered that several city street lights have been burned out for several months. The security officer may be convinced that this element is a critical part of the problem. The security officer responds by alerting the police and the city public works department. The objective is to get the street lights replaced. The security officer believes that if the street lights are operable, then the vandalisms may be reduced or resolved.

Assess

In the "assess" phase, security officers review attempts to deal with the vandalisms and evaluate how successful they have been. There are several major reasons why the assessment stage is very important. First, the security officer must find out whether the particular problem of poor lighting still exists and requires continuing attention. Assessment can also be important because it gives security officers the opportunity to improve their problem-solving skills by finding out what seems to work in differing circumstances and how to avoid "reinventing the wheel." An assessment that concludes the vandalisms have been dealt with successfully does not always mean that the problem has been eliminated. Success can be defined a number of ways. For example:

1. The poor lighting and its impact (vandalism) remain the same, but the volume of police and private security effort to respond to it may be reduced.
2. The harm to the public may be reduced even though the number of incidents remains the same. The number of vandalism incidents in the particular neigh-

borhood may be reduced, but the location of the vandalisms may have simply moved from private premises to bridge overpasses or the like.

3. The vandalism may be eliminated entirely. This is the best-case scenario.

Problem solving as a component of community policing is an approach that produces long-term solutions to problems of crime or decay in communities. Private security, public police, residents, and other agencies work together to identify and find the causes for neighborhood crime problems, then develop responses to the problems based on the causes of the problems.

In many cases, responses are not cookie-cutter, procedure-driven, or a one-response-fits-all. Responses may not just include police and private security responses but may also include responses developed through joint community actions, which also involve participation by agencies such as the public city works department, fire department, code enforcement, youth services, waste management, park and recreation, and others.

Summary

- The private security enterprise in the United States is significantly larger than public law enforcement. Private security officers can be found virtually everywhere. Most citizens will have more contact with private security officers than with public police officers.
- Community policing is a strategy that many public police agencies have adapted. Since the 1994 Crime Act set community policing in motion, two-thirds of U.S. police agencies and 62 percent of sheriff's offices have full-time personnel performing community policing.
- Community policing is collaboration between the police and the community that identifies and solves community problems. It has also been described as a philosophy based on the concept that the police and citizens, working together in creative ways, can solve contemporary community problems related to crime, fear of crime, social and physical disorder, and general neighborhood conditions.
- Community policing consists of three core components: community partnerships, problem solving, and organizational change. Community partnerships entail the police working with a wide range of public and private resources to solve crime and community disorder problems.
- Problem solving involves the use of a systematic approach such as the SARA problem-solving model to identify and solve crime-related problems.

- Community policing is almost always associated with law enforcement organizations. Private security operations seem to go hand in hand with community policing strategies. Both focus on proactive crime prevention. It is believed that private security can adapt many of the principles of community policing.
- A significant part of public police resources is spent on reacting to crime and other service-related activities. Private security operations, however, put a vast amount of resources toward the prevention of crime.
- It is imperative that private security and the public police form partnerships and work together. The private security enterprise performs an invaluable function in society, carrying out many tasks that public police would otherwise be burdened with. Public police agencies can prepare private security to assist in a host of emergency situations.
- Private security organizations should also form partnerships with many other organizations, including Neighborhood Watch groups, homeowners' associations, landlord associations, and the like.
- Post-9/11/01 society has presented new challenges for private security operations. Private security is increasingly being asked by government to be alert to sign of terrorist activities.
- Cybercrime refers to activities in which computers or networks are a tool, a target, or a

place of criminal activity. As technology advances, so too will crimes that are committed using computers.

- Private security authorities, especially those involved in corporate and financial security, should tailor programs aimed to prevent and detect cyber crime within their organizations.
- Reactive security occurs when security officers respond to specific requests from individuals or groups in the community that results in an immediate response to a crime that has been attempted or committed.
- Proactive security occurs when security operations actively attempt to prevent crime.
- Coactive security occurs when private security organizations work with community groups and a variety of other resources to prevent crime and solve problems.

Review Questions

1. What are the three core components of community policing?
2. Discuss how private security organizations can adapt the strategy of community policing into their operations.
3. What are reactive, proactive, and coactive security?
4. What is the SARA problem-solving model? Discuss each element of the model.
5. Discuss the importance of cooperation between private security and public law enforcement.
6. Identify and discuss various crime prevention programs. How can private security become more involved in these programs?
7. Identify and discuss indicators of terrorism.

Class Exercises

1. Discuss how community policing and the SARA problem-solving strategy can be adapted into private security operations.
2. In small groups, list at least five reasons why the public police and private security enterprise must cooperate with one another. Then compare your list with those of other groups in class.
3. In small groups, discuss the role that private security plays in preventing terrorism, and in community policing and problem solving.
4. In small groups, identify a real community-related problem that security officials are experiencing. Use the SARA model to develop a tentative solution. Your instructor may also pose a hypothetical problem for you.

References

Brighton Beach Neighborhood Association. 2008. Brighton Beach youth services, www.brightonbeach.org.

Connors, E., W. Cunningham, W. Ohlhausen, L. Oliver, and C. Van Meter. 2000. *Operation cooperation: Guidelines for partnerships between law enforcement and private security.* Washington, DC: U.S. Department of Justice, Bureau of Justice Administration.

Friedmann, R. R. 1992. *Community policing: Comparative perspectives and prospects.* New York: St. Martin's Press.

Kelling, G. L., and J. Q. Wilson 1982. Broken windows. *Atlantic Monthly,* March, 29–38.

National Institute of Justice. 2004. *Community policing beyond the big cities.* Washington, DC: U.S. Department of Justice.

Palmiotto, M. J., M. L. Birzer, and N. P. Unnithan. 2000. Training in community policing: A suggested curriculum. *Policing: An International Journal of Police Strategies and Management* 23: 8–21.

Peak, K. J., and R. W. Glensor. 1999. *Community policing and problem solving: Strategies and practices,* 2nd ed. Upper Saddle River, NJ: Prentice Hall.

Sparrow, M. K. 1998. *Implementing community policing.* Washington, DC: U.S. Department of Justice, National Institute of Justice.

Thurman, Q. C., and M. D. Reisig. 1996. Community-oriented research in an era of community-oriented policing. *American Behavioral Scientist* 39: 570–86.

CHAPTER 4

Security Management

CHAPTER OUTLINE

OBJECTIVES

After completing this chapter, you will be able to:

- Discuss the purpose of an organization.
- Indentify and discuss major organizational management theories.
- Compare and contrast management and leadership.
- Describe the organizational design of a security organization.
- Identify and define organizational terminology.
- Identity the various types of organizational plans.
- Identify and discuss the strategic planning process.
- Discuss the importance of organizational change.
- Describe the learning organization.

> *The supervisor is selected by management, he derives his official authority from the spirit of cooperation that he is able to gain from his own subordinates. He is expected to represent management's issues to the workers, and their interests to management.*
>
> —*N. F. Iannone and M. P. Iannone (2001, 4)*

T he management of a private security organization is a complex process involving human resources from varying levels within the organization. Security organizations, like many other organizations, are simply organizations that are managed by administrators. Within any security organization there are persons, usually the chief of security or the owner of the security company, deputy security chief, and perhaps other top-level managers who have specific administrative responsibilities. These responsibilities encompass ensuring that the resources of the organization are so managed that its objectives are achieved economically and effectively. In addition, personnel in middle management carry out specific responsibilities to support the mission and goals of the organization and those directives passed down from top administration. Men and women at the supervisory level supervise the day-to-day activities of security officers who provide services to customers. The primary focus of this chapter is on security management. We do, however, provide brief coverage of leadership early in the chapter.

Whether a security company is small and employs a dozen or fewer employees or is large and employs hundreds of employees, managing human resources can be a daunting task for even the most competent and experienced manager. What is seemingly stable within the organization one day may turn to total chaos the next, requiring management to take effective action. Organizations are said to be "a deliberate arrangement of people to accomplish some specific purpose" (Robbins and Coulter 1999, 4.). Within the security operation, managers organize security personnel with the primary objective of providing effective security to safeguard life, property, and community. This chapter provides a sketch of the management function in security organizations.

The material in this chapter is presented in generic fashion so that security officials can benefit from the discussion regardless of the size of the organization they manage. The chapter provides an overview of some key principles that should be considered when managing employees. Much of the material is presented in a way that security managers can adapt the principles to their own organization. Likewise, early in the chapter we discuss the fundamental differences between managing and supervising, and how often in smaller organizations these two distinct functions merge with one another. In other words, in some organizations, security managers both manage and supervise operations. The chapter concludes with a brief sketch of the critical components of the planning process. We caution the reader that everything there is to know about supervising or managing a security organization cannot possibly be provided in one chapter. With this in mind, we suggest to the reader who desires to know more about the supervision and management function to consult one of the many textbooks devoted entirely to the subject.

THE PURPOSE OF AN ORGANIZATION

Organization:
An entity that has a deliberate structure and includes organized groups of people working toward a common purpose and objective.

Examples of organizations are everywhere. A private security company is an organization; so are churches, police departments, colleges and universities, sports teams, the military, hospitals, the local utility company, even your favorite neighborhood grocery store. They are all organizations because they share three common elements: a distinct purpose, a deliberate structure, and a group of people working together to accomplish a desired goal. An *organization* is a structure through which people work as a group (Iannone and Iannone 2001).

Private security organizations serve many purposes. Security officers may work in a busy shopping mall, walking around in uniform with the goal of preventing theft and other disruptive behavior; they may be under contract to provide security services at large community events, where their role is to prevent and respond to unruly behavior; they may patrol in a certain part of a community for which they have been contracted to provide security services for businesses, apartment complexes, or even neighborhoods. In fact, security companies, much like public police departments, are organizations that you can call anytime and be assured of a response.

Many security organizations express their distinct purpose in the form of goals that the organization wishes to accomplish, a goal being an unmet objective that usually has some measurable characteristic (Schuler 1995). Suppose, for instance, that a top-level manager of a security company believes that the most important goal at present is to reduce the number burglaries that are occurring in a business district for which the company is contacted to provide security services. To accomplish this goal, the manager arranges for a massive education campaign and aggressive security checks of buildings. The security checks have virtually tripled because of an increased incidence of break-ins. This goal can then be evaluated at some future time to see if education and aggressive security checks of buildings actually reduce the number break-ins. We can say, then, that an organization has a distinct purpose to work toward accomplishing some unmet objective.

Security organizations also have a deliberate structure so that the organization's members can perform their tasks. An organizational structure is the formal framework by which jobs are divided, grouped, and coordinated (Robbins and Coulter 1999). The organizational structure may be open and flexible, allowing for much problem solving and self-direction, or it may be a more traditional structure, setting out carefully defined rules, regulations, standard operating procedures, and job descriptions.

A security organization also has to have some kind of organizing function whose purpose is to make the best use of the organization's resources to achieve organizational goals. Formalization, the extent to which the units of the organization are explicitly defined and its policies, procedures, goals, and objectives are clearly stated, is an important aspect of structure. The official organizational structure is conceived and created by security managers, and this formal organization can be seen and represented in a chart, which displays the organization's structure and shows job titles, lines of authority, and the relationships among divisions.

Organization Terminology

- *Goal:* Unmet objective toward which effort is directed.
- *Policy:* Broad statement of principle.
- *Procedure:* Method of operation. A procedure is more specific than a goal or a policy but still allows some flexibility (within limits). Instructional materials or manuals are composed largely of procedural directives.
- *Rule or regulation:* Authoritative order dealing with situations in which no deviations or excep-
tions are acceptable, making it more restrictive than a policy or procedure.
- *Police manual:* Booklet containing statements of goals, permanent policies, procedures, and rules or regulations. Police employees usually receive a copy during recruit training or new-employee orientation.
- *Fiscal plan:* Information on matters such as budget preparation and use or control of funds allotted for personnel, equipment, and supplies.

MANAGEMENT AND LEADERSHIP

Manager:
A member of an organization who coordinates the work of others through planning, organizing, directing, budgeting, and controlling.

Managers perform four essential functions in every organization; organizing, leading, planning, and controlling. The function of *organizing* includes making decisions about the purpose, structure, job design, and allocation of resources. *Leading* is the function of motivating others to perform those tasks that are necessary to accomplishment of the agency's goals and objectives. *Planning* involves preparing for the future by setting goals and objectives and formulating courses of action to accomplish the goals and objectives. Planning includes conducting research, identifying strategies and methods, developing courses of action, and formulating policies and budgets. *Controlling* includes the ongoing assessment of how organizational systems and services are meeting established goals and objectives. Controlling does not mean assigning blame and punishment, but improving operations consistent with established plans.

Leadership has two different meanings in our society. First, it refers to the process that helps direct and mobilize people or their ideas. Second, it refers to individuals in formal positions where leadership is expected—for example, the security manager. In this chapter, leadership is used in the first sense, meaning the process that helps direct and mobilize people and or their ideas.

Leadership and management are not interchangeable terms. They are alike in that both involve deciding what needs to be done, creating networks that can accomplish an agenda, and then trying to ensure that the job gets done. Although both are complete action systems, neither is simply one aspect of the other. To differentiate between leadership and management, we use the distinction developed by John Kotter, a professor of organizational behavior at the Harvard Business School. Kotter (1990) defines the functions of management as

- Planning and budgeting
- Organizing and staffing
- Controlling and problem solving.

On the other hand, Kotter defines the process of leadership as

- Establishing direction
- Aligning people, and motivating and inspiring

As you will note from the above comments, leadership and management are distinct processes. For example, the planning and budgeting processes of management tend to focus on time frames, on details, on instrumental rationality, and on eliminating risks. Leadership processes often focuses on longer time frames, the big picture, strategies that take calculated risks, and people's values. Controlling and problem solving (management) usually focus on containment, control, and predictability, whereas motivating and inspiring (leadership) focuses on empowerment, expansion, and creating that occasional surprise that energies people (Kotter 1990).

Leadership and management also differ in terms of their primary function. Leadership can produce useful change. Management can create orderly results

Chief of security (standing) of a large security company—giving a debriefing on previous month's profit and the number of new security clients. Top Management staff looks on.

that keep something working efficiently. This does not mean that management is never associated with change, nor does it mean that leadership is never associated with order.

The differences in function and form between leadership and management can create conflict. Strong leadership can disrupt an orderly planning system and undermine management hierarchy. Strong management may discourage risk taking and enthusiasm needed for leadership. An organization needs both strong leadership and management. If either is weak or nonexistent, the organization is like a rudderless ship. Both need to be strong. Strong management and weak leadership may create a

Leadership:
The ability to lead others to accomplish the mission, goals, and objectives of an organization.

Characteristics of Managers and Leaders

Managers	Leaders
Focus on stability	Focus on change
Coordinate effort	Inspire achievement
Focus on doing things right	Focus on doing right things
Tend to be reactive	Tend to be proactive
Minimize risks	Take risks
Have subordinates	Have followers
Depend on the system for success	Rely on people for success
Plan, budget, and establish timetables	Create a vision and sells others on that vision
Assign subordinates to perform tasks	Empower and develop personnel

bureaucratic and stifling environment, producing order for order's sake. Strong leadership and weak management can create an organization that is cultlike and producing change for the sake of change.

MANAGEMENT THEORIES

Modern management practices are the result of significant increases in large, complex organizations that arose in the twentieth century. The management philosophies discussed in the following sections were developed by inventors and other pioneers, who were trying to produce consistent results on key dimensions expected by customers, employees, and other organizational constituencies, despite the complexity caused by large size, modern technologies, and geographic dispersion. They created management to help keep a complex organization on time and on budget.

Scientific Management

Frederick W. Taylor was the central figure in the development of scientific management. *Scientific management* was one of the first models of organizational and management behavior developed (McCalman and Paton 1992). Many security organizations, especially large ones with hundreds of employees, still operate under the many tenets of Taylor's scientific management principles.

Scientific management focuses on worker and machine relationships. In this theory, it is thought that organizational productivity can be raised by increasing the efficiency of production processes; this efficiency perspective is concerned with creating jobs that economize on time, human energy, and other productive resources. Jobs are designed so that each worker has a specific, well-controlled task that can be performed as instructed. Specified procedures and methods for each job must be followed, with no exceptions. Taylor concluded that supervision should be divided according to tasks, and that a subordinate should report to a number of different supervisors, each of whom is responsible for the various tasks

Frederick Taylor, the Father of Scientific Management.

that subordinates perform. For example, in a security company, a security officer may be responsible for patrolling an assigned area and checking clients' businesses; a security supervisor supervises security officers who are in the field performing the primary security objective; a mid-level security manager may be responsible for establishing security goals and objectives, and marketing the security company in an attempt to gain new clients.

The scientific management approach strives to achieve these five objectives:

1. Replace rules of thumb with science (organized knowledge).
2. Obtain harmony rather than discord in group actions.
3. Achieve the cooperation of human beings rather than cultivate chaotic individualism.
4. Work for maximum output rather than restricted output.
5. Develop all workers' capabilities to the fullest extent possible for their company's highest prosperity. (Koontz, O'Donnell, and Weihrich 1986, 10)

Administrative Management Theory

Administrative management theory is based on the work of Luther Gulick and Lyndall Urwick and is concerned with the organizational problems of the departmental division of work and coordination. While Frederick Taylor's scientific management theory was more concerned with operations at the bottom of the organizational hierarchy, the administrative management theorists were more concerned with operations at the middle and upper levels of the structure. Gulick coined the acronym POSDCORB to describe the functions of management. The POSDCORB description has become a classic in the administration and management literature:

1. *P (planning):* Working out in broad outline the things that need to be done and the methods for doing them to accomplish the purpose set for the enterprise
2. *O (organizing):* Establishing the formal structure of authority through which work subdivisions are arranged, defined, and coordinated for the defined objective
3. *S (staffing):* Bringing in and training staff and maintaining favorable conditions of work
4. *D (directing):* The continuous task of making decisions and embodying them in specific and general orders and instructions and serving as the leader of the enterprise
5. *CO (coordinating):* The all-important duty of interrelating the various parts of the work
6. *R (reporting):* Keeping those to whom the executive is responsible informed as to what is going on, which thus includes keeping himself and his subordinates informed through records, research, and inspections
7. *B (budgeting):* Overseeing all that goes with budgeting, including fiscal planning, accounting, and control (Gulick 1969, 13)

Bureaucratic Management

German sociologist Max Weber is credited with being the first person to outline the principles of organization. Weber studied the army and the church in an attempt to understand why those organizations were effective. The main purpose of a

Max Weber, a German sociologist wrote extensively about the ideal organization which he called bureaucracy.

bureaucracy is to develop lines authority, to delineate divisions of labor, and to create productive workers and job efficiency. Analysts today speak of a "Weberian bureaucracy," meaning one that fits his ideal type closely. Weber did not see bureaucracy in the negative light we tend to see today. Weber saw it as the most logical and rational form of organizational structure for large organizations. Bureaucracies are founded on legal or rational authority, which is based on law, procedures, rules, and so on. Management expert Warren Bennis described the basic principles of a bureaucracy as

1. A division of labor by functional specialization
2. A well-defined hierarchy of authority
3. A system of rules covering the rights and duties of employees
4. A system of procedures for dealing with work situations
5. Impersonal relations between people
6. Promotion and selection based on technical competence (Bennis 1966, 5)

The environment in which many security organizations operate is unique, composed of economic and social forces. Some large security organizations operate under a hierarchical structure characterized by several layers of management bureaucracy. A large security organization, for example, is likely to have several clear layers of authority: the executive of the agency (security executive, security company owner, etc.) top managers, line supervisors, and line staff (security officers).

In many security organizations, the executive and top managers make the decisions and middle managers develop procedures for implementing those decisions. Line supervisors strive to ensure consistency of the line staff who actually do the work involved.

An important feature about many security organizations is that bureaucratic characteristics, such as rules, division of labor, written records, hierarchy of authority, and impersonal procedures, become important as the agency grows large and complex. Bureaucracy is a logical form of organizing that lets the executive use resources efficiently. However, bureaucracies are not very responsive to their customers, and this is a serious limitation in the profit environment of the security industry. This is due in large part to the layers one must go through to get a message communicated to the top. Many large security organizations have attempted to decentralize authority, flatten organization structure, reduce rules and written records, and subdivide into small divisions in an effort to be more responsive to their clients. The rule in the security business, like many other businesses, is that they are there to make a profit and to keep the customer happy. Security executives and top managers should strive to reduce bureaucracy whenever possible. Because the security industry for the most operates in the private sector and not the government sector, it is much easier to reduce unnecessary bureaucracy.

Administrative Management

Henry Fayol was a key figure in the turn-of-the-century Classical School of management theory. He is often described as the founding father of the Administration School. Fayol spoke of "Administrative Science" and identified five functions of management:

1. Forecast and plan ("prevoyance"): Examine the future and draw up plans of action.
2. Organize: Build up the structure, material and human, of the undertaking.
3. Command: Maintain activity among the personnel.
4. Coordinate: Bind together, unify, and harmonize activity and effort.
5. Control: Ensure that everything occurs in conformity with policy and practice.

Most of these activities are very task-oriented rather than people-oriented. This is consistent with the philosophies of Frederick Taylor and the ideology of scientific management. It is important to point, however, that Fayol's focus was directed at the activities of all managers, while Taylor was more concerned with management at the shop level (Robbins and Coulter 1999).

Fayol identified fourteen principles of management that are common to all organizations seeking to work constructively. He laid down the following principles of organization (he called them principles of management):

1. *Specialization of labor.* Specializing encourages continuous improvement in skills and the development of improvements in methods.
2. *Authority.* The right to give orders and the power to exact obedience.
3. *Discipline.* No slacking, no bending of rules.
4. *Unity of command.* Each employee has one and only one boss.
5. *Unity of direction.* A single mind generates a single plan, and all play their part in that plan.
6. *Subordination of individual interests.* When at work, only work things should be pursued or thought about.
7. *Remuneration.* Employees receive fair payment for services, not what the company can get away with.
8. *Centralization.* Consolidation of management functions. Decisions are made from the top.
9. *Scalar chain (line of authority).* A formal chain of command running from top to bottom of the organization, as in the military.
10. *Order.* All materials and personnel have a prescribed place, and they must remain there.

11. *Equity.* Equality of treatment (but not necessarily identical treatment).
12. *Personnel tenure.* Limited turnover of personnel. Lifetime employment for good workers.
13. *Initiative.* Think out a plan and then do what it takes to make it happen.
14. *Esprit de corps.* Harmony, cohesion among personnel. (Fayol 1949)

Human Relations Management

The human relations movement stemmed from the studies of Elton Mayo and Fritz Roethlisberger at Western Electric's Hawthorne Works plant near Chicago during the 1920s and 1930s. Where the scientific management theory focuses on efficiency, the human relations model focuses on the humanistic approach and in particular on group behavior and relations among group members and management (Wren 1994). The human relations approach considers the security managers as team leaders who create a cooperative effort among security officers through the use of management teams. Obviously, this approach will be more conducive in larger security companies.

As a bit of background on Mayo's work in human relations theory, he guided a series of experiments known as the Hawthorne Studies. These studies grew out of pre-liminary experiments at the Western Electric Hawthorne plant from 1924 to 1927 on the effect of light on productivity. Those experiments showed no connection between productivity and the amount of illumination. But as a result of this work, researchers began to wonder what kind of changes *would* influence output. The work of Mayo and his research colleagues contributed to organization development in terms of human relations and motivation theory.

In one of the studies, Mayo wanted to find out what effect fatigue had on the productivity of workers. He took five women from the telephone relay assembly line, segregated them from the rest of the factory, and made frequent changes to their working conditions. Mayo changed the hours in the work week, the hours in the work day, the number of rest periods, and the time of their lunch break. On occasion, the workers were returned to their original, harder working conditions. Throughout the experiments, an observer recorded the actions of the workers and informed them about the experiment.

The results of the experiments showed that even when the conditions changed unfavorably, production increased. Rest periods were given and taken away, yet the production of telephone relays continued to rise gradually. Mayo and his colleagues concluded that the workers exercised a freedom that they did not have on the factory floor. They had formed a social environment that also included the observer who tracked their productivity. They socialized both at work and eventually outside the workplace. In short, when they were allowed to have a friendly relationship with their supervisor, they felt happier at work. When they were allowed to discuss changes prior to them occurring, they felt part of a team and became extremely loyal to the plant (Roethlisberger and Dickson 1939).

Imagine for a moment that security supervisor James Tough supervises a team of eight security officers for a local security company. He supervises the team on the midnight shift. The primary responsibility of the team is to check several busi-nesses throughout the night and to patrol eight apartment complexes with which the security company contracts. Supervisor Tough is a retired police officer who spent thirty years on the force, and he has been in the private security field for the past five years. He is known for his no-nonsense approach to work. His favorite advice to his officers is "Keep your nose down, ask me first before you make a decision, do your job, and don't let me get any complaints on you, or else." Supervisor Tough is adamant about his security officers not making decisions without consulting him first. He requires his security officers to keep detailed time sheets of their activities, including when they take a break and where. Supervisor Tough is under the impression that if he doesn't constantly stay on his security officers, they will goof off, not do their jobs, and get into mischief. Do you think that you would like to work for this supervisor?

Employed at the same security company is another supervisor who supervises eight security officers on the opposite side of the city. His name is Supervisor John Fun. Supervisor Fun is considerably younger than his counterpart James Tough, and Fun has been with the security company for about seven years. He came directly after graduating from college with a degree in criminal justice and an emphasis on security management to initiate a career in security services. His upbeat and dynamic personality shows that he loves his job. He is considered by many to be on the fast track in the security company, and rumor has it that he is being groomed for a top management position within just a few years. He is well liked by the security officers he supervises. He insists that they be involved in decision making and encourages them to look for ways to continuously improve security services for their clients. He regularly holds focus groups and chat sessions with his security officers, with the objective of soliciting feedback on security operations and how they can be improved. His security officers feel very comfortable talking with him, and he is also popular with the company's clients.

How do we explain these two contrasting supervisory styles and their view of workers and work? Based on the information provided above, most of you would probably want to work for Supervisor John Fun. We would be willing to bet that many of you reading this book have come across a supervisor like James Tough, and you may have worked for one like him. Chances are that the times you spent working for Tough were stressful and demotivating. Some theories out of the behavioral science model have addressed these two contrasting views of workers.

The Humanistic model is based primarily on the work of Abraham Maslow. Maslow developed his theory of a hierarchy of human needs in the early 1940s. According to this theory, the needs that motivate people fall into a hierarchy, with lower-level needs (physical and safety needs) at the bottom of the hierarchy and higher-level needs (esteem and self-actualization) at the top (Maslow 1998). Douglas McGregor, in his book, *The Human Side of enterprise* (1960), examined theories on the behaviors of individuals in the workplace and developed the concept of Theory X and Theory Y, which make basic assumptions regarding human behavior. Theory X presents a very negative view of people. Theory X assumes that employees are lazy, have little ambition, dislike work, and must be coerced in order to perform satisfactorily. On the other hand, Theory Y managers have a positive view of people. They assume that people will be creative and work in a self-directed manner. Theory Y assumes that people do not inherently dislike work, and if they are properly rewarded, they will perform well on the job (McGregor 1960).

Theory X:
A management approach predicated on a negative view of people. Theory X managers assume that employees inherently dislike work, are lazy, and will avoid responsibility. Managers who subscribe to this view most likely supervise and direct employees closely to ensure that they get the job done. They have little trust in employees.

Theory Y:
A management approach predicated on a positive view of people. Managers who subscribe to this assumption may empower employees to be creative. In turn, employees seek additional responsibility and exercise much self-direction.

Theory X and Theory Y Assumptions

Theory X	Theory Y
Because people inherently dislike work, they must be closely supervised and controlled.	Employees like work. They will perform their job as naturally as rest or play.
Employees must be threatened with punishment to achieve desired goals.	Control and punishment is not the only way to make employees work. Employees will direct themselves if they are committed to the organization's objectives.
The average worker prefers to be directed and will shirk responsibility whenever possible.	The average worker will accept and even seek out responsibility.
Most workers place security as a priority and will display little ambition.	Ingenuity and creativity can be used by a large number of employees to solve work-related problems.
Theory X gives rise to the tough management approaches that are in place in many organizations today.	

Systems Theory

Systems theory is based on the concept that all parts of a system are interrelated and interdependent to form the whole. The system is composed of elements or subelements that are related and dependent on one another. When the subsystems interact with one another, they form a whole. Managers must be aware of the actions of other subsystems and that any changes they make in their own subunits will have an effect on other subunits (Luthans 1976). Systems may be viewed as "open" or "closed" systems. A system is open if it interacts with its environment and closed if it does not. The concept of open and closed systems is not an absolute but a relative matter, because all systems interact with the environment to various degrees.

Contingency Theory

Contingency theory is based on the concept that there is no single form of organizational structure or style that is appropriate for all situations. Both systems theory and contingency theory recognize the importance of the interrelationships between the parts of the organization and between the organization and the environment, systems theory is more abstract and does not attempt to define these relationships. Contingency theory developed as researchers discovered that certain methods and practices that were effective in one situation might not be in another situation. Accordingly, contingency theorists contend that there are no universal principles that can be applied in all circumstances. The task for managers is to determine which methods are more effective in their special situations.

This theory may have particular relevance in the security field. The level and type of security will certainly vary in different areas of the community. In addition, security manager must be willing to take into account clients' special needs, thus being flexible, or allow for a contingency approach when providing security services. One business that has a state-of-the art security monitoring system and is located in an area of the community that has a low break-in rate probably won't require the same security tactics as a business on the opposite side of the community that does not have a security monitoring system and that has been the target of two burglaries and

Protocol for Effective Management by Objectives

1. The security supervisor should start with a few well-chosen overriding objectives that the security company wishes to accomplish.
2. The security supervisor then sets subordinates "security officers" objectives that fit in with the company's overriding objectives.
3. Finally, the security supervisor should allow security officers to set their own key results to enable them to meet their objectives.

one attempted burglary within the past year. The security manager in this case will develop specific plans to deal with the level and quality of security of each client.

Human Resources Model

The *human resources model,* like the behavioral sciences model, recognizes the importance of human resources in security management. In this section we briefly describe two current management philosophies that were developed by corporate management and have been used by some security firms in the United States: Management by Objectives (MBO) and Total Quality Management (TQM).

Management by Objectives aims to increase organizational performance by aligning goals and subordinate objectives throughout the organization. Ideally, security officers will get strong input to identify their objectives, and time lines for completion of these objectives. MBO includes ongoing tracking and feedback in the process to reach objectives. MBO is based on the concept that the best way to ensure success is through planning. For example, security management and security officers first agree as to the goals to be achieved. One goal might be how to increase burglary prevention education among clients by 25 percent in the coming year. Then emphasis is placed on planning how to achieve this goal.

MBO is more concerned with general organizational planning than the other two philosophies. It also deemphasizes the role of specific personnel in the planning process. It is critical that managers of the various units or subunits, or divisions of a security company, know not only the objectives of their unit but also participate actively in setting these objectives and hold responsibility for them.

Total Quality Management is a method by which management and employees can become involved in the continuous improvement of the production of goods and services (Deming 1986). It is a combination of quality and management tools aimed at increasing business and reducing losses due to wasteful practices. The TQM philosophy is given credit for turning the Japanese from a low-tech, substandard industrial nation to one of the world's industrial leaders (Deming 1986). TQM attempts to create a culture that encompasses feedback from all levels of the organization, cooperative teamwork, and treats customers as critical considerations in the organizational enterprise. It is customer-oriented and sees the production system as a supplier–customer chain. It involves proactive problem seeking and the concentration on work process control and improvement (George and Weimerskirch 1998). In other words, the organization must constantly examine both internal operations as well as external operations in a effort to continuously improve the quality of the services provided.

Management by Objectives (MBO):
A systematic and organized approach that allows management to focus on achievable goals and to attain the best possible results from available resources.

TQM seems to be a natural fit with a profit-based security business. It only makes sense that if the company is offering good service to its customers, it will get renewed service contracts, and perhaps additional business once the word gets out. Under TQM, it is recognized that customer satisfaction can only be obtained by providing a high-quality product, and continuous improvement of the quality of the product is seen as the only way to maintain a high level of customer satisfaction.

According to Deming (1986), a core concept in implementing TQM is fourteen points that foster a set of management practices with the goal to help companies increase their quality and productivity:

1. Create constancy of purpose for improving products and services.
2. Adopt the new philosophy.
3. Cease dependence on inspection to achieve quality.
4. End the practice of awarding business on price alone; instead, minimize total cost by working with a single supplier.
5. Improve constantly and forever every process for planning, production, and service.
6. Institute training on the job.
7. Adopt and institute leadership.
8. Drive out fear.
9. Break down barriers between staff areas.
10. Eliminate slogans, exhortations, and targets for the workforce.
11. Eliminate numerical quotas for the workforce and numerical goals for management.
12. Remove barriers that rob people of pride of workmanship, and eliminate the annual rating or merit system.
13. Institute a vigorous program of education and self-improvement for everyone.
14. Put everybody in the company to work accomplishing the transformation.

ORGANIZATIONAL FEATURES

Many large private security organizations tend to be not only bureaucratic but are also modeled loosely after the military style of organization. *Paramilitary* means that the enterprise has borrowed certain aspects from the military and applied them to the security organization. In other words, security organizations are modeled similar to the military. For example, some security organizations use military-style rank designations, such as security officer, sergeant, lieutenant, captain, and chief of security. Many security officers wear identifiable uniforms similar to those of the military. A few of the characteristics borrowed from the military and present in many security organizations include:

- Centralized command structure with a chain of command
- Rules and regulations
- Frequent use of commands or orders
- Clearly marked lines of communication
- Strict discipline
- Differentiation between ranks or positions
- Authoritarian leadership
- Distinguishing uniform

- Armed with firearms or other defensive equipment (in some cases)
- Professional jargon

The operational units within a private security organization are also very similarly classified to the military units of line, staff, and auxiliary units. Public police organizations are usually modeled in this same manner. There is much discussion in some of the management literature suggesting that agencies move away from the paramilitary system.

Levels of Management and Supervision

Security organizations have various levels of supervision and management. The layers of supervision and management are determined largely by the size of the security organization. In a small security company, a supervisor may perform many of the duties that a mid- or top-level manager performs in a large company. Like other organizations, security organizations often have three layers of supervision and management: (1) top management, (2) middle management, and (3) line-level supervision.

TOP MANAGEMENT LEVEL   At the top of the organizational structure are those security managers who are involved primarily in administration. Top managers spend most of their time on the functions of planning and organizing. The top management team determines the mission and sets the goals for the organization. Likewise, their primary function is long-range planning. Top management is accountable for the overall management of the organization. Security managers have the responsibility for planning the organization's mission, implementing programs, planning how the department will carry out programs, budgeting and procuring funds, and planning and directing the organization's future. If the security organization uses military rank terminology, top-level management generally consists of chief of security, deputy chief of security, and majors.

MIDDLE MANAGEMENT   Middle management implements top management's goals. In large security organizations (if they subscribe to the paramilitary system), those in middle management usually hold the rank of captain or lieutenant (if they subscribe to military terminology). In smaller security organizations the rank of sergeant may be included in middle management. Those security personnel in middle management positions have the responsibility of commanding bureaus or divisions. For example, in some large security organizations the captain may be a field security division commander and a lieutenant security watch commander. A lieutenant would be responsible for field security activities in a specific geographic area, for example, during second watch.

The captain, on the other hand, is responsible for managing the entire field security division. This usually includes developing goals and objectives for the division, budgeting, and ensuring that the mission and directives passed down from the chief of security or the owner of the security company are carried out. The security captain manages all activities within the field security division. In some security companies, captains contract for building security details, retail store security, shopping mall security, and special activity security such as sporting events. There may be a captain who oversees each of these areas.

LINE-LEVEL SUPERVISION   Supervisors are those persons who direct and control the work of employees in order to achieve the organization's goals. They are the only level of management that manages nonmanagers. Thus, most of the supervisor's time is allocated to the functions of directing and controlling security officers in the field. Supervisors usually hold the rank of sergeant. Sergeants are the front-line supervisors in most security organizations. The job of security sergeant differs from that of security officer in that while they perform essentially the same security duties, the security sergeant has full supervisory responsibility for subordinates and is responsible for assisting management with the development and implementation of specialized security programs designed to secure and attract a larger customer base.

Security supervisors have the most day-to-day contact with the men and women performing the security function. In one sense it can be said that they hold one of the most important positions in the organization. It is usually through a supervisor that orders and directives are given to those security officers at the bottom of the hierarchy. The supervisor plays an instrumental role in gaining the support of officers to carry out the chief of security or owner's programs, mission and goals set for the company.

Security supervisors are usually responsible for preparing written performance evaluations of subordinates, recommending commendations and disciplinary action when appropriate, responding to grievances at the first level, training new security offices, and observing officers' performance in the field. In addition, they may make critical decisions in emergency situations.

Chain of Command

In security organizations, there are sergeants who directly supervise security operations in the field. Lieutenants may also supervise security activities in the field, or they may serve as mid-level managers. Mid-level managers usually hold the rank of lieutenant. Sometimes security organizations borrow the term "watch commander," which is commonly used in police departments. The watch commander or director, usually a lieutenant or captain, oversees all security operations during a specific shift. The chain of command normally dictates that a sergeant answers directly to a lieutenant, the lieutenant answers directly to a captain, and the captain answers directly to the chief executive officer or chief of security. The chain of command will vary from one security organization to the next and is dependent on such factors as the size of the organization and the organizational structure. A steep hierarchal organizational structure will generally have more levels in the chain of command, whereas a horizontal structure will tend to have fewer levels.

Chain of command:
The line of authority and responsibility in an organization along which orders are passed.

If a security organization operates under a paramilitary system, then most interagency communication operates on the chain-of-command principle. For example, if a sergeant desires to communicate with a captain, he or she first has to go through the lieutenant. If the lieutenant wishes to communicate with the chief of security, he or she must go through the chain of command (i.e., captain, major, deputy chief of security, and then the chief of security).

The chain-of-command principle is important in situations where large numbers of security officer are deployed. In these situations it is critical that all security officers know who they answer to. Suppose that numerous security officers are providing security for a large sporting event, say, a baseball game. Suppose that in front of the

Paramilitary Terminology Used in Some Security Organizations

- **Span of control:** The number of persons that one person can effectively supervise.
- **Unity of command:** The principle under which subordinates report to one and only one supervisor.
- **Division of labor:** Work specialization—the degree to which tasks in an organization are divided into separate jobs.
- **Bureau:** Typically the largest unit within a security organization.
- **Division:** A subdivision of a bureau.
- **Section:** A subdivision of a division.

- **Unit:** A subdivision of a section.
- **Watch or shift:** A time division of the day for purposes of security officer assignment.
- **Hierarchy of authority:** The progressive concentration of control over subordinate units in successively higher levels of authority in an organization's vertical command structure. Generally, most security organizations are organized in successively higher levels of authority in a vertical command structure with the chief of security at the apex.

entrance to the baseball stadium a large group has gathered and is protesting steroid use among baseball players. The protesters are attempting to turn away fans. After the protesters see security officers arriving at the gates to the ballpark, they become unruly. Some of the protesters begin to yell epithets at the security officers. The situation is volatile and could erupt at any minute. The sergeant soon arrives at the scene and takes command. In other words, all officers at the scene take orders from the sergeant. A few moments later, a lieutenant arrives at the scene. The lieutenant assumes command at the scene. Every security officer at the scene, including the sergeant, now answers to the lieutenant. In situations like these, it is imperative that all security personnel know exactly who they answer to. This principle is called the *unity of command*.

Unity of Command

Unity of command means that all organizational personnel operate under a single commander with the requisite authority to direct all personnel employed in pursuit of a common purpose. The unity-of-command principle also ensures that conflicting orders are not issued to the same security officers by several supervisors.

Unity of command: A principle that states that all organizational personnel operate under a single commander with the requisite authority to direct personnel employed in pursuit of a common purpose.

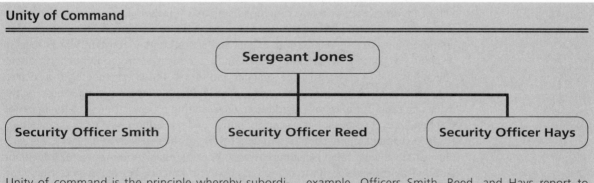

Unity of Command

Sergeant Jones

Security Officer Smith | Security Officer Reed | Security Officer Hays

Unity of command is the principle whereby subordinates report to one and only one supervisor. In this example, Officers Smith, Reed, and Hays report to Sergeant Jones.

Span of Control

Span of control refers to the number of persons that one person can effectively supervise. The span of control is often limited unknowingly by administrators and supervisors who are trying to control too much of the work or are trying to supervise too many people. Two factors may cause administrators to make this kind of error: (1) overestimation of their own ability, and (2) inability or unwillingness to delegate authority because of a desire or real need to exercise close control over operations. Efficiency is supposed to be enhanced by limiting the number of subordinates who report directly to one supervisor to a small number.

The principle of span of control is routinely taught in management schools and is widely employed in large organizations such as the military, security organizations, government agencies including police departments, and educational institutions. As a general rule, the span of control is usually three to five at the top level of the organization, and often broader at the lower levels, depending on factors such as the capacity of the supervisor and those persons supervised, the time needed to perform the tasks, and the types of persons served (Iannone and Iannone 2001). Within a security organization, the more levels there are in the pyramid, generally the smaller is the span of control.

Organizational Clarification

To prevent internal conflict, members of a security organization need to understand their duties and the duties and assignments of others. Two devices commonly used to demonstrate the structure of an organization, and inform members of the organization of their duties and assignments, are organizational charts and position descriptions.

Organizational charts are pictorial representations of the agency that map lines of authority for the entire organization. One major limitation of organizational charts is that they fail to delineate the informal structure that exists in every organization. Each position within a security organization normally has a position description. The position description should include basic job functions and their relationship to others.

PLANNING

Planning provides a framework for action and a mechanism to accomplish the organization's goals and objectives. Planning lets private security managers and others within the organization assess situations similarly, discuss alternatives in a common language, and decide on actions based on shared understandings. Planning provides an opportunity to adjust to current events and actions, either constantly or at least on an annual basis. This is extremely important in the security profession to serve clients effectively and to stay abreast of changes and threats in the community. If a security organization plans effectively, this may correlate with a larger customer base, which means larger profit margins. In addition, the planning process allows for the improvement and reevaluation of basic security policy and procedure.

Security planning should include a review of the research in the field. Research plays an invaluable role in shaping the way security organizations operate. It is important that a protocol for the transition of theory to practice be established. Marketing research can shed light on many other important issues for security authorities, including perceived security threats, the nature and amount of crime in a specific area, how often clients report unusual situations to the police or security, and what other competition the security organization has.

Types of Plans

Various types of plans are used in security organizations. Typically these plans are either strategic plans or operational plans. Strategic plans (which we discuss in detail in the following section) apply to the entire organization and establish the primary objectives. Operational plans, on the other hand, give direction as to how the overall objectives are to be achieved. Strategic plans tend to cover an extended time span, usually three years or more. Thus, the most specific way to describe organizational plans is by their latitude. Most security organizations have strategic and operational plans in place. In addition, security organizations use plans that are based on a specific time frame (e.g., short term versus long term), and sometimes use plans that are labeled "single-use" plans. Operational plans usually cover shorter periods of time.

Some security organizations have standard operating procedures in place that provide direction to officers in a given situation. For example, standard operating procedures may dictate private security's response to given field situations such as a burglary scene, a building alarm, a shoplifter, checking buildings, and the like.

Standard operating procedures:
A written and codified manual of a security organization—a roadmap that guides officers in the field.

Security organizations may use single-use plans for specific events. For example, suppose that a security company has been awarded a one-time contract with the city to provide security at the state high school basketball tournament, which is expected to attract thousands of spectators over a weekend. Single-use plans are developed to provide specific direction and assignments for security officers assigned to provide security at the basketball tournament.

Single-use plan:
A plan developed for a specific one-time event, such as a large sporting event.

Chief of security of a major security company explains security plans for the forthcoming quarter.

Strategic Planning

Planning has been presented in many different wasys in the literature. Many definitions present the notion that planning is a process of anticipatory decision making, and a process that involves deciding on appropriate responses before action is taken. However, the process of strategic planning may offer security organizations a more effective way to meet the demands of the twenty-first century. *Strategic planning* has been defined as "the process by which the guiding members of an organization envision its future and develop the necessary procedures and operations to achieve that future" (Goodstein, Nolan, and Pfeiffer 1993, 3).

Strategic planning:
Organization-wide plans to establish overall objectives and position the organization in terms of the internal and external environment.

Strategic planning presents an opportunity for the security organization to envision and anticipate the future. This is in contrast to organizations that just do short- and long-term planning. Short- and long-term planning is primarily an extrapolation of current trends. On the other hand, strategic planning is a process designed to anticipate future trends. Strategic planning is the process of determining what your organization intends to accomplish and how you will direct the organization and its resources toward accomplishing these goals in the future.

Applied Strategic Planning Model

The applied strategic planning model presented by Goodstein, Nolan, and Pfeiffer (1993) is an excellent guide for anyone preparing for applied strategic planning. The model provides a comprehensive look at the crucial steps involved in the strategic planning process. The authors presented a nine-step model that includes: planning to plan, values scan, mission formation, strategic business modeling, performance audit, gap analysis, integrating action plans, contingency planning, and implementation.

PLANNING TO PLAN   The stage of planning to plan involves the strategic planning team evaluating and answering various questions as well as making some important decisions before initiating the planning process. The following questions should be asked at this stage:

- How much commitment to the planning process is present?
- Who should be involved?
- How will we involve the absent stakeholders?
- How does the organization's fiscal year fit the planning process?
- How long will it take?
- What information is needed in order to plan successfully?
- Who needs to develop the data? (Goodstein et al. 1993, 9)

These questions set the tone for the planning process. Commitment levels within the security organization should be established before initiating the strategic planning process. Once commitment by management is secured, then the strategic planning team should be formed. It is recommended that the planning team should not exceed ten twelve permanent members who broadly represent the security organization.

VALUES SCAN   The values scan is an examination of not only the values of the organization but also those of the members of the planning team. *Values* are an enduring belief that a specific mode of conduct or end state of existence is personally or socially preferable to an opposite or converse mode of conduct or end state of existence (Rokeach 1973). Values are expressions of the organization through the actions of the employees. Values are what the organization believes in and is committed to. Values describe attitudes and behavior toward the operation of the security business and its relationship with customers, the local community, employees, and other stakeholders (Charney 2006). A values statement by a security organization may include providing high-quality and courteous security services to our customers. All employees should be involved in the identification of organizational values.

When values scanning is initiated, the organization's purpose, philosophy, and assumptions should be clearly identified. Ideally, during the values scan the planning team moves from individual focus to broader examination of the organization. Organizational values will be adapted in the future behavior of the organization. Furthermore, values represent a shared sense of purpose for all within the security organization.

MISSION FORMATION   *Formation of the mission* is the process of defining the nature of the business, the purpose of the organization, and how matters are conducted on a day-to-day basis (Charney 2006). The security organization needs a mission that defines why it is in business. The mission statement is a concise definition of the purpose the organization is attempting to fulfill. It is through the mission statement that management ensures the overall goals and objectives of the organization are being worked toward. According to Goodstein et al. (1993, 17–18), the mission statement should answer four primary questions:

1. What function(s) does the organization perform?
2. For whom does the organization perform this function?
3. How does the organization go about filling this function?
4. Why does the organization exist?

STRATEGIC BUSINESS MODELING   *Strategic business modeling* is the path by which the police organization will accomplish its mission. This is a fairly succinct process, which should spell out the specific direction of the organization. The planning team may be asked to examine and analyze several possible future scenarios. The planning team should also address the steps necessary to achieve those scenarios, who will be responsible for the various steps involved, and when the steps can be accomplished.

The strategic business model should reflect the mission, goals, and objectives of the organization. For example, the security organization may be considering a new surveillance technology. The steps to implement this strategy should be identified. The quantifiable organizational objectives are established during the strategic business modeling. One objective, for example, might be to have all security officers trained in the new technology within two years.

PERFORMANCE AUDIT   A *performance audit* is an examination of the organization's current performance. Questions asked include what the organization currently does and how it does it. During this stage, internal (within the organization) strengths and weakness are examined and the external operating environment (outside of the organization) is also examined. During the examination of the external environment, strengths, weaknesses, opportunities, and threats (SWOT) should be identified. Strengths and weaknesses are essentially external to an organization and relate to matters concerning resources, programs, and organization in key areas. Opportunities and threats tend to be external, from competing organizations, global trends, and other environmental factors (Charney 2006). Internally, it is important to examine the recent performance of the organization in terms of staffing patterns, technology, tactical considerations, budget considerations, and service quality. As part of examining the external environment, the planning team may want to ask the following questions:

1. Is the current vision being realized? If not, why not?
2. How has the company's focus changed over the past few years? Why have changes occurred (or why not)? Identity primary reasons and categorize them as either internal or external.
3. What strategies have been followed over the past few years with respect to products/services, operations, finance, marketing, technology, management, etc? Critically examine each strategy statement by questioning activities and actions in key functional areas. (Charney 2006, 154)

In addition to asking questions about the internal environment, getting information about the external environment is crucial. Charney (2006, 155–6) suggests looking at similar organizations to compare best practices as well as strengths and weaknesses. He offers the following:

1. Look beyond your industry at organizations in different industries that have similar processes.
2. Meet with your customers to find out:
   • What you do that makes them loyal to you
   • What frustrates them when they deal with you
   • How user-friendly your customer services are
   • What policies prevent people from doing their best
3. Collect information on the outside forces that will influence you, including:
   • What's happening with our main competitors (their strengths and weaknesses)
   • Current or future changes in legislation that may affect your industry
   • Economic trends that will have an impact on your revenues and costs
   • New technologies that might revolutionize how you do business

GAP ANALYSIS   *Gap analysis* is the process of examining the gaps between the current performance of the organization and the desired performance specified in the strategic business model. Gaps that may prohibit the successful obtainment of goals and objectives are identified during this stage. Gap analysis compares the data generated during the performance audit with what is necessary execute its strategic plan. Specific strategies should be tailored to close any gap identified. Gap analysis in a security organization, for example, may identify gaps in implementing new surveillance technology. If for some reason the gap cannot be closed, the planning team must return to the strategic business modeling stage and rework the model until the gap can be closed.

INTEGRATING ACTION PLANS   Once the gaps discovered in the gap analysis stage have been closed, two important issues remain:

1. A grand strategy or master business plan must be developed for each of line of business (services the organization offers).
2. The various units of the organization need to develop detailed operational plans based on the overall organizational plan. These unit plans must reflect the grand strategy and must include budgets and timetables. (Goodstein et al. 1998, 29)

Action plans should be written to reflect the mission of the organization. For example, if the security organization is planning for the implementation of new surveillance technology, then each division within the organization should write operational plans to reflect the change in technology and how it will affect retail security, event security, and general security of businesses.

CONTINGENCY PLANNING   Security planners should develop a specific set of contingency plans. Contingency planning is based on the assumption that the ability to forecast accurately significant factors in the environment is somewhat limited, especially in terms of variations in those factors. For example, external threats to the organization may involve a number of factors. There are many factors in the external operating environment that may affect the applied strategic planning model. One example might be the current or projected unemployment in a community, which might spark more crime-related activities, which in turn might result in more demand for security services. This might require the security organization to hire and train additional security personnel.

IMPLEMENTATION   Implementation of the strategic plan involves the concurrent initiation of several operational plans designed at the functional level. In addition, implementation involves monitoring the strategic plan at the operational level. It is important that all divisions within the security organization know that the strategic plan has been initiated. Thus, all divisions and personnel in the security organization should begin to integrate the strategic plan into daily operations. The strategic plan becomes a living and breathing document. Decisions that are made at all levels of the organization should reflect the strategic plan. When this occurs, the strategic plan truly assimilates into the organizational culture.

ORGANIZATIONAL CHANGE

Organizational change involves substantial administrative issues that are beyond the scope of this book and is therefore covered only briefly here. Recall from Chapter 3 that organizational change is an important component of implementing community policing. Public police agencies continue to grapple with the best way to foster organizational change. Security company management should periodically examine their organizational structure and processes to ensure that they are not an impediment to carrying out the mission and objectives of the organization. In other words, it is important to ensure that the organization can support change in the way the security organization does business.

Organizational change:
Sometimes referred to as
organizational reengineering.
Organizational change may
include changes in policy and
procedures, organizational
values, organizational
structure, management,
and leadership.

Organizational change is necessary to make way for community policing strategies. Most discussions of organizational change and community policing spotlight primarily police agencies, because they are typically bureaucratic and hierarchal in nature, with a clear succession of paramilitary authority. Private security organizations may be at a distinct advantage because they are not government organizations with steep bureaucracies. The concept of organizational change usually entails organization-wide change, as opposed to smaller changes such as adding new officers or modifying a program. Organizational change may include a change in mission, restructuring operations, new technologies, mergers, major collaborations, "rightsizing," and new security programs.

Private security organizations are profit-driven and a steeply layered bureaucratic organizational design may adversely affect profit. The key to organizational efficiency and effectiveness in the private sector is to stay as close to the customer as possible. Thus, the trend in the private security industry is to eliminate bureaucracy and, increasingly, to have horizontal organizational structures. Some conclude that the steep hierarchical structure found in some security organizations often makes them dysfunctional and that the organization should be restructured or flattened in order to become more efficient, more effective, and more responsive to the community. However, there are a few advantages to the line organization: Quick decisions can be made because of the direct lines of authority; and each member in the organization knows to whom he or she is accountable.

The advantages of a leaner and more horizontal structure are clear. A few of these advantages are that communication is enhanced because orders don't have to move through several levels of command; morale may improve because of the enhanced communication; the organization can be more flexible to respond to changing environments; employees in the field providing services to customers are more empowered; and the organization is more adaptable for problem-solving endeavors.

The Learning Organization

Learning organization:
An organizations where
people continually expand
their capacity to create the
results they truly desire,
where new and expansive
patterns of thinking are
nurtured, where collective
aspiration is set free, and
where people are continually
learning to see the whole
together (Senge 1990).

One mechanism to foster organizational change that has been presented in the management and human resource development literature is the concept of the *learning organization*. A brief introduction to the concept is given here. For private security officers and students who desire to learn more about the learning organization, we recommend that you review the excellent work of Peter Senge. Senge (1990, 3) describes the learning organization as one "where people continually expand their capacity to create the results they truly desire, where new and expansive patterns of thinking are nurtured, where collective aspiration is set free, and where people are continually learning how to learn together." He proposes a systems approach to doing business, one that encourages a continuing flow of feedback from the external environment and through and among organizational units to promote the learning necessary for the organization to adapt to changing conditions.

A system is a collection of parts that interact with each other to function as a whole (Kauffman 1980). Managers should focus on the system or organization as a whole but often are deterred from doing so successfully by workplace learning disabilities, such as the natural tendency for territoriality in the workplace and the tendency to put the blame on nonexistent third parties for things amiss (Senge, 1997).

A learning organization is one that is able to adapt and respond to change, which empowers employees because they acquire and share knowledge and then apply this learning to decision making and because they are pooling collective intelligence and stimulating creative thought to improve performance. Supervisors facilitate learning by sharing and aligning the organization's vision for the future and sustaining a sense of community and strong culture. The challenge issued by the learning organization is to use knowledge as a basis for its strategy and to use organizational learning as bedrock for its ability to be proactive. According to one author, learning organizations possess several characteristics:

> Learning organizations are skilled at five main activities: systematic problem solving, experimentation with new approaches, learning from the experiences and best practices of others, and transferring knowledge quickly and efficiently throughout the organization. Many companies practice these activities to some degree. But few are consistently successful because they rely largely on happenstance and isolated examples. By creating systems and processes that support these activities and in integrating them into the fabric of daily operations, companies can manage their learning more effectively. (Garvin 1993)

A learning culture may enable the security organization to adapt more effectively in a changing environment. For example, the idea that security organizations establish a research and development unit that actually performs research will allow the management to make more informed and fiscally responsible decisions. In order to provide more effective service to customers, a loss prevention organization should know whether there is a relationship between new detection techniques and decreases in, for example, employee thefts. Security executives may desire to know the level of customer satisfaction or fear of crime in various areas when innovative security patrol methods or crime prevention techniques are employed.

Imagine a security organization that allows guards and officers the opportunity to participate in group processes with the objective of identifying new and improved methodologies aimed at improving security services. This is a stark deviation from the traditional bureaucratic organizational environment, in which most decisions are made at the top of the organizational pyramid and filter down to employees in the bottom ranks. Line-level security officers deal with problems on a daily basis and are in the best position to offer solutions and recommend new or improved procedures to adapt to the ever-changing environment.

Summary

- Modern security operation in the United States is the result of various organizational management approaches that have been tried and tested over the last century.
- The terms management and leadership are often used interchangeably, but management and leadership are not the same. Management is an operational function used to guide an organization. Management involves adherence to established practices to get the job done. Leadership is a people-oriented concept that operates outside and beyond the perimeters of rules and policies.

Leadership permeates all levels of an organization from the line staff to the chief executive. It has nothing to do with job titles and everything to do with relationships.

- Modern management practices are the result of significant increases in large, complex organizations that arose in the twentieth century.

- Management philosophies were developed by inventors and other pioneers, who were trying to produce consistent results on key dimensions expected by customers, employees, and other organizational constituencies, despite the complexity caused by large size, modern technologies, and geographic dispersion.

- Frederick Winslow Taylor (1856–1915) is considered the father of scientific management. Under scientific management theory, it is thought that organizational productivity can be raised by increasing the efficiency of production processes. This efficiency perspective is concerned with creating jobs that economize on time, human energy, and other productive resources.

- Max Weber was the first to observe and write on bureaucracies that developed in Germany during the nineteenth century. Weber is considered the father of bureaucratic management. He considered bureaucracies to be efficient, rational, and honest, a big improvement over the haphazard administration they replaced.

- One criticism of bureaucracies is that they are not very responsive to their customers, and this is a serious limitation in the profit environment of the security industry. This is due in large part to the layers one must go through to get a message communicated to the top.

- The human relations movement stemmed from the studies of Elton Mayo and Fritz Roethlisberger at Western Electric's Hawthorne plant near Chicago. Whereas scientific management theory focuses on efficiency, the human relations model focuses on the humanistic approach and in particular on group behavior and relations among group members and management.

- Total Quality Management (TQM), developed by W. Edward Deming, is a set of management practices enforced throughout the organization, geared to ensure that the organization consistently meets or exceeds customer requirements. TQM places strong focus on process measurement and controls as means of continuous improvement.

- Management by Objectives (MBO) is a systematic and organized approach that allows management to focus on achievable goals and to attain the best possible results from available resources. It aims to increase organizational performance by aligning goals and subordinate objectives throughout the organization.

- Douglas McGregor, in his book, *The Human Side of Enterprise* (1960), examined theories on behavior of individuals at work, and he formulated two models that he calls Theory X and Theory Y. These assumptions are based on social science research and demonstrate the potential that is present in people and that organizations should recognize to become more effective.

- Systems theory is based on the concept that all parts of a system are interrelated and interdependent to form the whole. The system is composed of elements or subelements that are related and dependent on one another.

- Security organizations typically have three layers managing human resources: top management, middle management, and line-level supervision.

- Many security organizations are paramilitary in structure. They borrow traits from the military such as the wearing of uniforms, chain of command, military rank, and military organizational jargon.

- Planning is a critical part of a security manager's job. Planning provides a framework for action and a mechanism to accomplish the organization's goals and objectives. Planning allows private security managers and others in the organization to assess situations similarly, discuss alternatives in a common language, and decide on actions based on shared understandings.

- Plans vary in scope and purpose. For example, security organizations use both long- and short-term planning, single-use plans, contingency planning, and strategic planning.

- Strategic planning is a time-consuming and complex task, but a very necessary one. Strategic planning is the process by which the guiding members of an organization envision its future and develop the necessary procedures and operations to achieve that future.

- Organizational change is the process of ensuring that the organization is prepared to adapt a community policing strategy. Organizational change may include, leadership, organizational structure, and ensuring that line-level personnel are empowered to make decisions that affect community problems of crime and disorder.
- Peter Senge describes the learning organization as one where people continually expand their

capacity to create the results they truly desire, where new and expansive patterns of thinking are nurtured, where collective aspiration is set free, and where people are continually learning how to learn together.

- A private security organization that has adapted principles of the learning organization as part of organization change may be able to adapt and respond to change more effectively. Security officers are more empowered because they acquire and share knowledge and then apply this learning to decision making.

Review Questions

1. What is the difference between management and leadership?
2. Describe the scientific management approach.
3. What are the characteristics of bureaucracies?
4. What is meant by the term *paramilitary?*
5. Identify and define some of the military jargon that is used in some security organizations.
6. Discuss Theory X and Theory Y organizations. Which one would you rather work in? Why?
7. What is the purpose of standard operating procedures?
8. Identify and discuss elements of strategic planning.
9. Identify and discuss the questions that the mission statement should answer.
10. What is a learning organization?

Class Exercises

1. Interview a security professional working for a large security company and ask him or her what some of the organizational problems are. Discuss this in your next class meeting.
2. Contact a local security company and ask if they have a mission statement. Request a copy and discuss it in class.
3. In small groups, discuss times (if any) when Theory X management approaches are appropriate. Do the same for Theory Y approaches.
4. In small groups, write a mission statement for a hypothetical security company. Discuss it in class.

References

Bennis, W. 1966. *Beyond bureaucracy: Essays on the development and evolution of human organization.* New York: McGraw-Hill.

Charney, C. 2006. *The leaders tool kit.* New York: American Management Institute.

Deming, W. E. 1986. *Out of crisis.* Cambridge, MA: Massachusetts Institute of Technology.

Fayol, H. 1949. *General and industrial management.* Trans. Constance Storrs. London: Sir Isaac Pitman.

Garvin, D. 1993. Building a learning organization. *Harvard Business Review,* August, 78–91.

George, S., and A. Weimerskirch. 1998. *Total quality management: Strategies and techniques proven at today's most successful companies.* Hoboken, NJ: John Wiley & Sons.

Goodstein, L. D., T. M. Nolan, and J. W. Pfeiffer. 1993. *Applied strategic planning: A comprehensive guide.* New York: McGraw-Hill.

Gulick, L. 1969. Notes on the theory of organization. In *Papers in the science of administration,* edited by L. Gulick and L. Urik. New York: August M. Kelly.

Iannone, N. F., and M. P. Iannone. 2001. *Supervision of police personnel,* 6th ed. Upper Saddle River, NJ: Prentice Hall.

Kauffman, D. L. 1980. *Systems I: An introduction of systems thinking.* Minneapolis: S. A. Carlton.

Koontz, H., C. O'Donnell, and H. Weihrich, H. 1986. *Essentials of management,* 4th ed. New York: McGraw-Hill.

Kotter, J. P. 1990. *A force for change.* New York: Free Press.

Luthans, F. 1976. *Introduction to management: A contingency approach.* New York: McGraw-Hill.

Maslow, A. H. 1998. *Maslow on management.* New York: John Wiley & Sons.

McCalman, J., and R. A. Paton. 1992. *Change management: A guide to effective implementation.* London: Paul Chapman.

McGregor, D. 1960. *The human side of enterprise.* New York: McGraw-Hill.

Robbins, S. P., and M. Coulter, M. 1999. *Management,* 6th ed. Upper Saddle River, NJ: Prentice Hall.

Roethlisberger, F. J., and W. J. Dickson. 1939. *Management and the worker.* Cambridge, MA: Harvard University Press, 1939.

Rokeach, M. 1973. *The nature of human values.* New York: Free Press.

Schuler, R. S. 1995. *Managing human resources,* 5th ed. Minneapolis/St. Paul: West Publishing.

Senge, P. M. 1990. *The fifth discipline: The art and practice of the learning organization.* New York: Doubleday.

Senge, P. M. 1997. All systems are go: The model of the learning organization integrates psychological realism in understanding and modify the organization. *Management Today,* November, 137–138.

Wren, D. A. 1994. *The evolution of management thought,* 4th ed. New York: John Wiley & Sons.

CHAPTER 5

Retail and Business Security

CHAPTER OUTLINE

OBJECTIVES

After completing this chapter, you will be able to:

- Discuss the nature of employee theft.
- Identify problems associated with detecting employee theft.
- Discuss how differential association theory explains internal business theft.
- Identify common indicators of internal business theft.
- Explain ways to reduce internal business theft.
- List the types of questionable employee conduct.
- Discuss important considerations in investigating employee misconduct.
- Discuss the issues involved in uniformed security versus plain-clothes security.
- Identify types of check crimes.
- Describe the methods of operation of shoplifters.
- Identify the different types of shoplifters.
- List techniques that can be used to deter and prevent shoplifting.
- Discuss the problem of robbery.

- Describe procedures that security professionals should train retail and business employees to follow in the event they are robbed.
- Describe embezzlement.

He who holds the ladder is as bad as the thief.

—German proverb

After studying crime prevention methods and the criminal justice system for more years than we care to remember, two things have become apparent: First, it is easier and cheaper to prevent crime than to deal with its consequences; and second, a great many crimes against businesses are committed by employees, not by strangers. Many business failures can be attributed directly to employee crime. Employee misconduct takes many forms, from the employee who sells information on pending customer orders to a competitor to the individual who steals company time by reading paperback novels on the job. One of the biggest problems with regard to employee misconduct is the reluctance of employers to believe that long-term, trusted employees can be dishonest or involved in misconduct.

Not only do employee crime and misconduct take its toll on businesses, external thefts do too. External thefts such as shoplifting, robbery, check fraud, and the like present pressing problems for retail and businesses security. The National Association for Shoplifting Prevention reports that more than $25 million worth of merchandise is stolen from retailers each day in the United States. Likewise, recent years have witnessed increases in check fraud and other financial crime schemes, while at the same time robberies of retail stores and gas stations have increasingly become more violent (National Check Fraud Center 2007).

This first half of this chapter provides an overview of the various types of crimes and misconduct that may be committed by employees. The second half of the chapter focuses on retail and business shoplifting, check crimes, and robbery.

THEFT BY EMPLOYEES

The extent of employee theft is unknown, but estimates have it exceeding $30 billion a year. Approximately 2 percent of all employees are caught stealing each year. Many employee thefts continue for years before they are discovered. Consider the department store that discovered its employees had established a barter system using the store's inventory; for example, the manager of the men's wear department was trading men's clothes to the manager of the housewares department for pots and pans. Both managers then juggled their inventories to hide the losses.

All industries are affected by employee theft. Documented employee thefts range from petty cash to railroad boxcars. Many studies indicate that 60 percent of all employee thefts are of noncash items. Employers have a natural tendency to watch cash registers; however, they often do not show the same degree of concern for the security of their property and merchandise. Although small, useful consumer items may be and are more easily stolen, it is the theft of larger and more expensive items that causes serious problems for most businesses with employee theft problems.

Problems in Detecting Employee Theft

The following factors and concepts prevent business owners and managers from realizing the extent of employee theft in their businesses.

1. It is difficult to distinguish employee theft from customer theft. The general tendency is to assume that inventory "shrinkage" is due to shoplifting, although most studies indicate that the major cause of shrinkage is employee theft.

2. In many cases, employees fail to report thefts by their fellow workers. This failure may occur because the observer is also a thief. For example, "I don't worry that Fred will report me; I've seen him steal too many times." In addition, nobody in our society wants to be considered a "rat" by fellow employees.

3. Employers are reluctant to suspect employees, especially long-term employees, of dishonesty. Long-term employees usually hold positions of trust and are familiar with the checks and controls instituted by the company. In addition, employers tend to assume that employees in positions of high responsibility are highly responsible. Note, however, that managers and supervisors have greater opportunity to steal than do other employers.

4. Many otherwise honest employees consider theft a form of job enrichment.

5. In some instances, employees are permitted to steal company cash or property in lieu of a raise. In one case, an employer determined that his office manager was stealing several thousand dollars a year from the petty cash fund but decided not to take corrective action because it would cost more than the loss to hire and train a new manager.

6. It may be cheaper to allow employee thefts than to prevent them. For example, if employees are stealing $200 a month, it is less costly to allow them to continue to steal that amount than to pay $250 a month to prevent the thefts.

7. Employees are encouraged to steal by observing thefts by their managers or supervisors. Management personnel should be made aware that they are role models and that their conduct on the job establishes the employees' norms and values in many situations.

8. An employee will steal not only for material enrichment but because his or her job is boring and theft creates excitement. In many cases, the employee gives away the merchandise after it is stolen from the company. As one researcher noted, "Theft serves as a safety valve for employee frustration in many situations."

9. Some employees steal to get even with the company for not giving them a promised raise or one they feel they deserve.

10. Businesses with few controls and a trusting and casual attitude regarding the use of company resources make employee theft easy and in many cases encourage it. Research indicates that attitude plays a significant role in creating a favorable climate for employee theft.

11. Most employees do not condone thefts, but those who do steal justify their actions with statements such as "I'm not stealing, just getting even for what's due me"; "Everybody's doing it, it's considered part of the wages"; or "This job is boring, beating the system adds excitement."

12. Many times the hardest workers, the eager beavers, those who arrive early, never take breaks, and stay late are the ones stealing from the company.

13. Beginners start with basic tactics and small amounts, and then graduate to more sophisticated means and larger amounts. Normally, when an employee is caught stealing from the company, he or she has been at it for an average of eight months.

14. When a thief is caught, he or she will never admit to the true value of his or her thefts. As a rule of thumb, always triple the amount of the theft that the person admits to for a more accurate estimation of the amount stolen.

The Employment Environment

Criminologists list four workplace factors that contribute to employee theft: opportunity, differential association, managerial dishonesty, and low job satisfaction.

OPPORTUNITY   Many companies, because of lack of controls and a casual attitude toward employee theft, provide an inviting opportunity for an employee who has a tendency to steal. In many cases, employees, provided with a wealth of opportunities to steal, consider company property as their own.

DIFFERENTIAL ASSOCIATION   Differential association is a criminal behavior causation theory that contends that the influence of those persons with whom we associate determines to a great extent our own behavior. Thus, if our associates either directly or indirectly encourage theft from the company, we are likely to be influenced by them to steal. This explains why, when employee theft is discovered, many employees are often involved. Under this theory, if the majority of employees steal from a company, then a new employee is also likely to steal from the company.

Differential association theory:
A theory developed by Edwin Sutherland during the 1930s and 1940s that proposes that criminal behavior is learned through interaction with others.

The differential association theory was developed by the late Edwin Sutherland of the University of Chicago, considered by many to be the dean of American criminology. His crime causation theory is probably the most widely accepted criminal causation theory today in the United States.

Differential association theory is based on the laws of learning—that is, we learn to commit thefts in much the same way we learn to drive a car or play basketball. Sutherland's principles include:

1. The processes that result in systematic criminal behavior, such as stealing from an employer, are learned the same way we learn other things. For example, an employee learns to steal in much the same way that he learns the other aspects of his or her job.

2. Systematic criminal behavior is learned by the same process of association with those who commit criminal conduct as lawful behavior is learned by the process of association with those who do not commit criminal behavior.

3. Whether a person will commit certain criminal behavior such as theft generally is determined by the frequency and consistency of that person's contacts with fellow workers who steal. If a person observes acts of stealing, the chances are far greater that she or he will also steal.

4. We learn to commit criminal behavior. Criminals are not born. A person does not inherit criminal tendencies. Such tendencies are acquired in a series of learning experiences that establish accepted norms of behavior. The effects of differential association vary according to the frequency, duration, priority, and intensity of the association because of the individual physical, psychological, and social differences among people.

5. Criminal behavior is learned during interactions with others. According to this theory, television and other passive forms of communication are not that important in our learning process; rather, it is interactions with others that forms our behavioral tendencies.

6. Our most influential learning occurs within small, intimate, personal groups. Accordingly, the employee thief learns to steal from other employees within his or her close personal group. Close personal contacts or associations are the key factors in shaping our value system or developing tendencies toward or away from criminal behavior.

Sutherland's theory is valid to the extent that criminal behavior has an almost contagious nature to it. Many criminologists state that, although to a large extent criminal behavior is learned, differences in biological and constitutional makeup explain why some employees resist the learning processes favoring criminal behavior.

MANAGERIAL DISHONESTY   Managerial dishonesty is closely associated with the differential association theory as a causative factor in employee thefts. If managerial-level employees set a bad example by misusing company property, other employees are encouraged to take company property. Both managerial dishonesty and differential association establish that theft of company property is an acceptable behavior norm.

LOW JOB SATISFACTION   Low job satisfaction is the least understood of the job-related influences on employee theft. In many cases, the employee uses controlled thefts as a means of job enrichment. Employee job dissatisfaction also leads to vandalism. Although it often is difficult to increase job satisfaction, any steps taken in that direction will tend to reduce the incidence of employee theft.

Motives

In one study of over 1000 cases of employee theft, the researchers assigned four general motives for stealing: (1) to allow the employee to live beyond his or her means; (2) to pay gambling debts; (3) to support drug abuse habits; and (4) to pay for an extended illness of the employee or of a member of his or her immediate family.

The most common motive was to allow the employee to live beyond his or her means. In most of these cases, no apparent effort was made by the stealing employees to live within their salary limits. These people apparently prefer to steal rather than curb their desires.

Theft Indicators

Be alert for indications that thefts of company property are occurring. Some of the most common indicators are

1. Mistakes in shipping and receiving records
2. Inaccurate accounting records
3. Shortages in inventory records
4. Merchandise and supplies missing or found in inappropriate places
5. Security devices inoperative
6. Doors and windows left unlocked at closing time
7. Employees who seem sensitive when questioned about their duties

8. Customers who demand to be waited on by a particular employee
9. Employees who are always the last to leave the storage areas
10. Employees who regularly come in early
11. Employees hanging around areas where they are not required to be
12. Employees who are living beyond their incomes
13. Shortages or overages in the cash registers
14. Increases in the amount of raw materials needed to complete products

Theft of Cash

There are numerous methods of stealing from an employer, and more are being discovered each year. Some of the most common methods of stealing cash from an employer are listed below. Check your own operation to see if you are vulnerable.

1. Ringing up sales but not giving the customer a sales receipt, pocketing the extra money
2. Failing to register sales and pocketing the money
3. Ringing up "no sale" in a cash sale transaction and then keeping the money
4. Pocketing cash from a common register drawer
5. Overcharging or shortchanging customers and keeping the difference
6. Cashing worthless checks presented by accomplices
7. Giving fraudulent refunds to accomplices
8. Keeping checks made payable to "Cash"
9. Paying invoices twice and keeping the second check
10. Failing to record returned purchases, reselling the goods, and keeping the money
11. Issuing checks for returned merchandise that was not in fact returned
12. Decreasing the amount on invoices after they have been paid and keeping the extra money
13. Receiving kickbacks from supplies and vendors
14. Keeping collections made on accounts that were considered uncollectible
15. Increasing the amount payable on checks that have been cashed and keeping the extra money
16. Keeping incoming cash payments
17. Padding payrolls as to time worked or number of employees
18. Stealing unclaimed wages
19. Submitting false expense claims

Theft of Products and Supplies

Just as there are many ways to steal cash, there also are numerous ways to steal products and supplies from an employer. Retail and other business security officials should assess how many of the following methods their company is vulnerable to.

1. Slipping out stolen goods in the trash. This appears to be a very popular method to get goods out, because no one wants to inspect the trash.
2. Shoplifting during off-duty times. Off-duty employees are in a good position to know how to shoplift without being caught.
3. Hiding goods in employee lockers or other areas for later removal from the premises.

4. Giving extra merchandise to delivery persons who are working as accomplices.
5. Padding inventories to prevent the discovery of shortages.
6. Keeping returned goods.
7. Shipping goods to the clerk's own post office box.
8. Picking up discarded sales receipts and using them to walk out with similar merchandise.
9. Giving employee or other discounts to friends.
10. Putting on jewelry, watches, and so forth and wearing them home.
11. Stealing "package passes" to be used later.
12. Putting address labels on packages received and sending them to the employee's own home.
13. Using the postage meter or postage stamps for personal mail.

Expense Account Scams

Employer should keep historical records of all employee expense claims, comparing them to other claims submitted by that employee as well as those submitted by other employees. Following are some common methods employees use to pad their expense accounts.

1. *Airline tickets:* Employees purchase full-fare tickets, keep the receipts, then turn the tickets in for discount-fare tickets and claim the full fare using the full-fare receipts. To avoid this, you can purchase the tickets on a company account and obtain the lowest fares to start with. This not only reduces the opportunity for theft, it also saves the company money in the form of reduced fares.
2. *Car rentals:* The employee rents a car using a personal credit card. When the car is returned, the employee claims to have lost the original contract. A new one is issued and charged to the employee's personal credit card. The employee then takes the original contract and completes it with excess miles and charges. You can prevent this by requiring employees to have the rental company bill the company directly or by requiring employees to submit both the rental contract and their evidence of payment (charge receipt).
3. *Ground transportation:* Employees charge their meals to their hotel bill and then claim meal expenses. To prevent this, require itemized hotel bills. Also check for meals that are included in seminar fees or provided without charge to ensure that a separate expense is not being charged for them.
4. *Double payments for meals:* Employees charge their meals to their hotel bill and then claim meal expenses. To prevent this, require itemized hotel bills. Also check for meals that are included in seminar fees or provided without charge to ensure that a separate expense is not being charged for them.

Most companies do not check travel expenses under a certain amount. Establish a policy of selectively auditing these smaller amounts and keep employees informed of the possibility of an audit of all expense claims. Do not allow employees to know what travel expenses are claimed by other employees on similar trips. If an employee does not know what other employees submit, he or she is more likely to submit a conservative claim.

Custodial and Maintenance Personnel

Custodians, because of the nature of their duties, are very familiar with the operations of the company and the layout of the premises. They normally can justify being in any part of the premises at any time. Thus, they are in a position to observe the alarm systems and other protective devices. In addition, janitors are in most cases low-paid and semipermanent employees. Because of these conditions, they are in an excellent position to steal company property, and you must closely monitor their activities and never permit janitors to be left unobserved in company areas.

To prevent disruption of business, many companies require janitors to clean the offices during times when other workers are off. This is inviting the custodians to steal. Although a company normally cannot afford to hire persons to watch the custodians, the mere presence of other workers tends to discourage theft.

Preventing Employee Theft

EMPLOYEE LOCKERS   If lockers are provided for employees, security officials should encourage retail and business managers to retain copies of the keys and get signed statements from the employees that reserve the right to make unscheduled inspections of the lockers without their further permission. Do not locate employee lockers in an area close to supplies or easily stolen company products. Have a printed policy on the use of the lockers that precludes the storage of company property in them. This policy should be posted on company bulletin boards. In addition, policy should be in place for handling cases if you find company property in employee lockers.

PERIMETER SECURITY   Perimeter security can be established in many companies without disrupting the company's activities. If this is so in your case, evaluate perimeter security. Most companies fail to realize the need to look at perimeter security from the aspect of preventing removal of stolen property from the company premises. Perimeter security must be cost-effective, but it should, if possible, reduce the number of exits and entrances to the premises. Perimeter security acts as a psychological deterrent to employees who are thinking about stealing company property.

EMPLOYEE PARKING   An important factor in reducing employee theft is to reduce the opportunity for theft. With this in mind, examine designated employee parking areas. Where do they park? Is it easy for employees to put company supplies or equipment in their cars without being observed? If practical, employee parking should be located in an area where anyone taking anything to his or her car will be observed. In addition, institute a procedure that requires preauthorization before employees can remove any company equipment for legitimate purposes.

ALARM SYSTEM CHECKS   If the business has an alarm system and it is one that requires that an employee call in after opening the door, ensure that employees are not calling in to have the alarm turned off during unusual hours. Have the alarm company keep a record of all employee openings at other than normal business hours and provide you with a monthly report.

Security officials and retail and business managers should examine the following checklist, which aims at reducing employee theft.

1. Carefully screen job applicants to weed out potential problem employees and thieves.
2. Provide close supervision of employees who have personal problems.
3. Monitor employees who either arrive early or leave late.
4. Establish an internal audit system to spot potential critical areas.
5. Do not allow employees to make sales to themselves, their friends, or family members.
6. Establish a control system for employee packages.
7. Make employees check out and sign for all tools and equipment issued to them.
8. Do not allow employees free access to storerooms.
9. Have at least two persons check all deliveries received.
10. Conduct inventories at specific intervals and investigate all significant shortages.
11. Establish a merchandise return system with checks and balances.
12. Change locks and combinations when employees with access to keys leave or are transferred to a different department.
13. Do not fall to the temptation of attributing inventory shortages to shoplifting.
14. Lock cash registers so that employees cannot read the totals.
15. Keep a control on all sales books and company invoices.
16. Monitor the petty cash account.
17. Have the mail opened by someone other than the cashier and in the presence of another person.
18. Audit the reconciliation of bank statements. This should be done by someone other than the person who is writing the checks.
19. Provide a sales drawer for each person and keep records of cash shortages and overages. Keep the employees informed daily of shortages and overages. Note that overages as well as shortages can be an indication of theft of cash. Overages can mean that customers were short-changed, which will have an adverse affect on repeat customer sales.
20. Restrict employee exits to as few as feasible.
21. Investigate all losses even minor ones, because most embezzlers and thieves start with small amounts.
22. If a loss occurs, remember that management might also be involved.

THEFT OF COMPANY TIME

Many employers do not consider theft of time as a theft of company resources. Many researchers, however, contend that employees waste more company resources by misusing time for which they are paid to work than by any other form of misconduct. When employees misuse time for which they are paid to work, they are stealing company resources just as if they were taking home company property. Security officials should work with retail management in the development of comprehensive plans that not only prevent theft of company time but also detect it.

Time Clocks

Time clocks have been used for years to monitor employees' working time. Time clocks, however, can cause more problems than they solve, especially in small companies. In dealing with small companies, one of the authors has noticed that employees resent the use of time clocks. Other problems associated with time clocks are that employees can clock in for fellow employees and that clocks can be set back, punched in, and then reset. Most businesses either are small enough or divided into small enough groups to monitor an employee's work time without using a time clock. In addition, time clocks are expensive.

EMPLOYEE ABSENTEEISM

At least 50 percent of all employee absenteeism is not caused by a bona-fide illness or other acceptable reason, according to a book on employee misconduct research. In other words, one-half of all employee absences are avoidable. All employers have a problem with employee absenteeism. Absenteeism as used here refers only to unapproved employee absences and approved absences in cases where approval was based on false information submitted by the employee.

A review of absenteeism research reveals that there is a general lack of systematic attempts to find the underlying causes for absenteeism; thus, the reports have little to offer in the form of explaining absenteeism.

Research does indicate that absenteeism is a very complex, subtle, and elusive concept. In many cases, it may be symptomatic of a deeper illness or personal problem. For example, alcoholics tend to be absent on Mondays and Fridays, late for work, and take long lunch breaks. It is also difficult to determine which absences are preventable and which are not.

Reducing Absenteeism

Following are steps that security officials can take together with management to reduce short-term, discretionary employee absences. Not all of these steps are feasible for every situation.

1. Realize that proper job placement is critical to reducing absenteeism. Included in proper job placement is the employee selection process. When screening job applicants, check their attendance records at school and with previous employers, if possible. Make sure the employee is suitable and qualified for the position. If an employee cannot handle a position or is overqualified for it, it is more likely that he or she will be dissatisfied and thus have a high rate of absenteeism.
2. Institute job training programs so that employees are properly trained for their position.
3. Maintain clear and concise policies on attendance. The policies should be published and communicated directly to employees, especially new employees. Attendance policies should be consistent and make provisions for progressive discipline for absenteeism, rewards for attendance, minimization of managerial discretion regarding absenteeism, and equal enforcement of rules.
4. Give bonuses for perfect attendance. Bonuses for attendance achievements have, in those cases studied, decreased the absentee rates of the companies that have used them properly. For example, one nonprofit corporation gives four hours extra pay for each four weeks worked without an absence. The corporation's absentee rate has been reduced by 50 percent.
5. Modify the unwritten contract with employees as to how much absenteeism you will accept. If your attendance policies, discussed above, are clear and concise, they should modify the unwritten contract.
6. Improve job satisfaction. Employees now expect more from their jobs than fair pay. Many companies are using counseling, in-house educational programs, and employee goal setting to improve job satisfaction. Increasing the employee's self-respect increases job satisfaction and attendance and reduces absenteeism.

7. Provide educational programs on stress reduction, personal finance, and substance abuse.
8. Use "flex time" or a four-day work week. These options have reduced the absentee rate in most companies that have adopted them.
9. Follow up on an employee's absence in a nonthreatening manner by letting the employee know that he or she was missed. Ask the employee how he or she feels.
10. Keep detailed records of employee absences. The records should include reasons for the absence provided by the employee. There is a major difference between the employee who is absent for twenty days for major surgery and the employee who is absent twenty unconnected days for a variety reasons. Detailed records help identify patterns of absences by specific employees. One firm noted a 25 percent reduction in absenteeism after installing a better recording-keeping system and informing the employees of that system.

INVESTIGATING EMPLOYEE MISCONDUCT

Once an employee is suspected of misconduct, security officials should check his or her background, including former employers and acquaintances. Find out as much as possible about the employee before interviewing him or her.

If possible, find an information source in the same department where the suspect works. Ask if the information source knows or can find out anything regarding the activities of the suspect. Be careful that the information source is neither involved in the criminal activity nor a close friend of the suspect.

The Interview

Talk to the suspect in a nonthreatening environment. Because private security officials are not law enforcement agents, they are not required to give the individual any warnings regarding possible prosecution or to advise the employee of his or her right to counsel.

Avoid confrontation and accusations. If possible, get the suspect to admit to the thefts or other misconduct by implying that you know more than you do and have inside information. Avoid direct threats and promises of leniency. Ask the employee to return any merchandise that has been taken. If any is brought in, mark it and keep it for evidence. If the suspect names other employees, talk to them before they have a chance to get together.

Arresting Employees

In most states, private security officers may arrest an employee who is caught committing a crime. Because the private security officer is not a law enforcement agent, such an arrest is called a citizen's arrest. Security officials are advised to contact their local district attorney or county prosecutor's office to obtain the local rules regarding citizen's arrest powers. The general rule is that, if you see another person commit a crime, you can arrest the criminal and hold him or her until police authorities arrive.

If you cannot arrest an employee under the authority of a citizen's arrest, then you normally have no authority to arrest the employee. When you arrest an employee without authority, you could possibly be sued for false imprisonment. Remember, we live in a litigious society and it could happen.

PLAIN-CLOTHES VERSUS UNIFORMED SECURITY

Security management must decide whether security personnel working in retail or other business establishments should be in plain clothes or wear a security uniform. There is little published literature that offers guidance in this area. This answer depends largely on the security objective. Uniformed security personnel can probably do more to prevent and deter criminal activities in a business or retail store. The uniform is a sign of authority. Security uniforms resemble a police uniform. Security officers carry much of the same equipment that police officers carry. One of the authors recently observed a security officer who was dressed in what is typically considered a SWAT or military tactical uniform. The security officer was dressed in a black battle-dress uniform, and on the back of the shirt it read "SECURITY" in big yellow letters. The security officer in uniform, walking around and making his or her presence known in a retail store, will have an impact on deterring and preventing potential criminal activity.

There has been a trend in recent years for security companies to dress their officers in military battle-dress uniforms (BDUs). BDUs are typically black in color or sometimes camouflage. This attire is usually worn with black gloves and in some cases a black military-style combat helmet. Public police have also begun to use BDUs in the field. There are some drawbacks to wearing BDUs, which mirror military battle uniforms. Paul and Birzer (2004) argue that the modern militarized police uniform (with its emphasis on camouflage and/or black colors) is a force of symbolic violence that may actually distance the community from the police. The removal of traditional police uniforms is a symbolic act used to distance outsiders (e.g., the community) from the practice of policing.

Security officer watches busy shopping area.

A crisp blue security uniform that is conspicuously identifiable to the public conveys a sense of pride and professionalism. The presence of a uniformed security guard is one of the best deterrents a store manager can have. A potential shoplifter will probably not steal anything if he sees a security guard standing and walking around the store. However, let's assume that security has received a tip that there is going to be a major shoplifting attempt at a certain time of the day. It may make sense to have a plain-clothes security officer walking the store for the purpose of detecting and apprehending those responsible for the shoplifting. Note, however, that actually confronting a suspect can be dangerous, and any contact with an offender should be conducted with the utmost officer safety techniques, and the public police authorities should be summoned immediately.

The objective of the plain-clothes security officer may not to be to prevent criminal activity as much as it is to detect and apprehend shoplifters and other criminals. The plain-clothes officer is just that, in plain clothes, and a possible thief will have no idea that he or she is in the store. So the plain-clothes officer has a better change of detecting and arresting a shoplifter or other violator.

For security personnel who work with management in a retail store or other business, it is most appropriate that he or she wear plain clothes, usually a jacket and tie.

SHOPLIFTING

Shoplifting is a form of theft that has become one of the most prevalent crimes in the United States. However, it remains one of the most understudied crimes (Cromwell, Parker, and Mobley 2006). Shoplifting entails stealing merchandise from retail establishments. Shoplifters cost businesses a great deal of money in terms of lost inventory. Some estimates have the national shoplifting loss at $10 billion annually in the United States. As a result, retailers charge higher prices to recover the money they lose through shoplifting, so you and your family are paying for the items that shoplifters take. Sometimes, retailers lose so much that they are forced to go out of business.

Shoplifting:
The theft of merchandise from a commercial business establishment. In street slang referred to as "five-finger discount." Most shoplifting is committed by amateurs, who use unorganized and sometimes haphazard methods. Professional shoplifters are methodical and sophisticated in their methods. Professional shoplifters are sometimes referred to as "boosters."

There is no typical shoplifter. Persons of every sex, age, race, and social and economic background shoplift. Teenagers make up a large percentage of shoplifters. According to the National Crime Prevention Council, about a quarter of all the people who get caught shoplifting are between the ages of thirteen and seventeen. According to the Small Business Association, petty shoplifting may not seem like a major crime, but to the small business fighting for survival, it can add up to devastating losses. To bring the problem of shoplifting into perspective, think about this. Just to cover a yearly loss of $1000 in thefts, a retailer has to sell each day over 900 candy bars, 130 packs of cigarettes, or 380 cans of soup. Faced with such unreasonable selling volumes, most small businesspeople are forced instead to raise their prices and lower their ability to compete.

A shoplifter is anyone who deliberately takes merchandise from a store without paying for it, whether the theft is large or small, premeditated or impulsive. There are about 550,000 shoplifting incidents per day in the United States, resulting in more than $10 billion worth of goods stolen from retailers annually. Shoplifters present significant problems, especially for retail businesses. Loss from shoplifting has become a

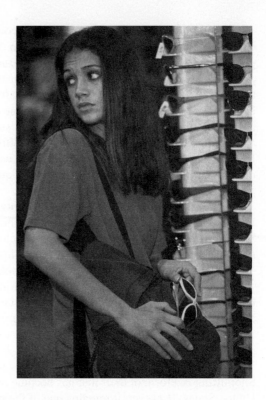

Women shoplifting some sunglasses.

major source of shrinkage. *Shrinkage* refers to a reduction in inventory due to shoplifting, employee theft, paperwork errors, and supplier fraud.

The Investigator's Warning Signs

Shoplifters have an arsenal of professional tools. Articles as innocent as bulky packages, pocketbooks, baby carriages, knitting bags, shopping bags, umbrellas, newspapers, and magazines can be used to carry stolen goods. Even an oversized arm sling can help a shoplifter conceal merchandise. Specially constructed devices, such as coats or capes with hidden pockets and zippered hiding places, are used by more experienced shoplifters. Some thieves use "booster boxes" (large boxes with a hinged end, top, or bottom). Booster boxes can even be gift-wrapped to frustrate detection. It may not be possible to detect every single shoplifting technique, but the following are potential warning signs:

- *Packages:* A great many packages; empty or open paper bags; clumsy, crumpled, homemade, untidy, obviously used, poorly tied packages; unusual packages; knitting bags, hat boxes, zipper bags, briefcases, brown bags with no store name on them; newspapers, magazines, school books, folded tissue paper
- *Clothing:* A coat or cape worn over the shoulder or arm; a coat with slit pockets; ill-fitting, loose, bulging, unreasonable, or unseasonable clothing
- *Actions:* Unusual actions of any kind; extreme nervousness; a strained look; aimless walking up and down the aisles; leaving the store but returning in a few

minutes; walking around holding merchandise; handling many articles in a short time; dropping articles on the floor; making rapid purchases; securing empty bags or boxes; entering elevators at the last moment or changing mind and letting the elevator go; excessive concealing of merchandise behind a purse or package; placing packages, a coat, or a purse over merchandise; using stairways; loitering in vestibules

- *Eyes:* Glancing without moving the head; looking from beneath a hat brim; studying customers instead of merchandise; looking in mirrors; quickly glancing up from merchandise from time to time; glancing from left to right in cross aisles
- *Hands:* Closing hands completely over merchandise; palming; concealing or destroying a ticket; folding merchandise; holding identical pieces for comparison; working merchandise up sleeve and lowering arm in pocket; concealing a ticket while trying on merchandise; trying on jewelry and leaving it on; crumpling merchandise
- *At counters:* Taking merchandise from the counter but returning it repeatedly; taking merchandise to another counter or to a mirror; standing behind a crowd and taking merchandise from a counter; placing merchandise near the exit counter; starting to examine merchandise, then leaving the counter and returning to it; holding merchandise below counter level; handling a lot of merchandise at different counters; standing a long time at a counter
- *In fitting rooms:* Entering with merchandise but without a salesperson; using a fitting room before it has been cleared; removing hangers before entering with packages; taking in identical items of various sizes or obviously wrong sizes; gathering merchandise hastily, without examining it, and going into the fitting room
- *In departments:* Sending clerks away for more merchandise; standing too close to dress racks or cases; placing a shopping bag on the floor between racks; refusing a salesperson's help
- *Miscellaneous:* Requesting a questionable refund; acting in concert, separating and meeting, setting up lookouts, swapping packages, following a companion into a fitting room without a salesperson (Fischer 1987, 286–7)

Types of Shoplifters

Shoplifters can be divided into several types, including juveniles, professionals, vagrants and drug addicts, kleptomaniacs, and amateurs.

JUVENILES   Young people account for about 50 percent of all shoplifting. Juveniles often steal on impulse. They may steal on a dare or simply for kicks. Often they expect store owners and courts to go easy on them because of their youth. They may enter stores in gangs in an attempt to intimidate management. Shoplifting is usually the first type of theft attempted by juveniles, and it may lead to more serious crimes. Their lack of sophistication and their shoplifting techniques are often clumsy (Palmiotto 1998). Juvenile theft should be pursued and prosecuted through the proper legal channels.

PROFESSIONALS   The professional shoplifter is in the business of theft, so he or she is usually highly skilled and hard to spot. The professional is trained in shoplifting techniques and is clever, alert, and well disguised (Palmiotto 1998). Professionals generally steal items that will quickly be resold to an established fence. They tend to concentrate on expensive and high-demand, easily resold consumer goods such as televisions, stereos, and other small appliances. The professional, or "booster," may case a store or department well in advance of the actual theft.

VAGRANTS   Vagrants are commonly classified as career criminals who shoplift time after time. Security officials should use due caution when trying to detain such persons. They may offer violent physical resistance may even be carrying a weapon. Vagrant as shoplifters most often use the *grab and run* technique. They typically do not try to conceal the crime.

DRUG ADDICTS   Drug addicts shoplift to support their drug habits. In one study, over 60 percent of addicts shoplifted for resale purposes, and only 33 percent reported stealing items for their own use (Klemke 1992). An urgent physical need can drive people to theft, as well as to other crimes. Addicts are often clumsy or erratic in their behavior and may be easier than other types of shoplifters to detect. Retail store managers should keep in mind that people under the influence of drugs or with an obsessive physical need may be violent and/or armed. It is best to leave the handling of such people to trained security professionals or the police. Refer to Chapter 13 for a comprehensive discussion on the alcohol, drugs, and related issues in the security industry.

KLEPTOMANIACS   Kleptomaniacs are actually the smallest threat to retailers and are rarely encountered by security professionals (Sennewald and Christman 1992). Kleptomania is a serious mental disorder that can be described as a repeated failure to resist the urge to steal items and articles not needed for monetary value and personal gain (Palmiotto 1998). People who suffer from kleptomania have a driving psychological need that leads to shoplifting. Kleptomaniacs have a compulsion to steal. They usually have little or no actual use for the items they steal and in many cases could well afford to pay for them. When a kleptomaniac is arrested for shoplifting and the family is notified, the family usually arranges to pay for the stolen merchandise (Sennewald and Christman 1992).

AMATEURS   The amateur shoplifter usually steals on impulse. The most important motive for this type of shoplifter is a simple desire for the item itself. Food, clothing, and other items that the shoplifter can actually use are items of choice. The main difference between the amateur and the professional shoplifter is the motivation for the theft. Recall that the professional steals and may fence (sell) the stolen goods quickly, whereas the amateur keeps the stolen items for personal use. Thefts by amateur shoplifters account for the largest number of incidents but not necessarily the largest percentage of financial losses (Sennewald and Christman 1992). Juveniles, drug addicts, or those suffering from kleptomania are most likely amateur shoplifters.

Shoplifting Prevention and Detection

TWO-WAY MIRRORS   Two-way mirrors have been around for some time. They are placed strategically throughout the business establishment and allow security officials to maintain constant surveillance. So how do two-way mirrors actually work? Consider a suspected shopper in a large retail store. On the sales floor, which is generally kept well lit, the glass looks like a mirror. In the security room, where the lighting is kept dim so there is very little light to transmit through the glass, the glass looks like a window. On the sales floor side, the shoplifter sees his or her own reflection. On the security officers' side, the large amount of light coming from the shoplifter's side is what they see. Thus, the shoplifter cannot see the security officer on the other side of the glass, but the security officer can see the shoplifter. If the lights on the retail store floor side were suddenly dimmed, it would be possible to see through the glass. Persons on both sides of the glass would be able to see each other. Likewise, if the room where the security officer is monitoring the sales floor were suddenly brightly lit, the two-way mirror would become a glass and people on both sides would be able to see each other.

VIDEO MONITORING   The tremendous advances in technology have made video surveillance more flexible and easy to use. Security systems using Internet Protocol cameras are easy to install and maintain, and are almost infinitely customizable, allowing businesses to create a security system based on their specific needs. Video monitors placed at strategic locations throughout a business can alert security officials of not only shoplifting but also other crimes. For example, recently in Overland Park, Kansas, a 26-year-old man was arrested and charged with the murder of 18-year-old women after a Target store video surveillance camera showed the suspect forcing the victim into her car. The victim's body was found in a wooded area in Missouri a few days later. The Target video that captured the abduction was instrumental in identifying the suspect, which led to his arrest.

SECURITY OFFICER PRESENCE   As discussed previously, having properly trained security officers on site is invaluable. The specific needs of the retail store or business will dictate whether uniformed or plain-clothes security officers are employed. It is important that security officers be thoroughly trained in shoplifting techniques, what to do when encountering and apprehending a shoplifter, and use of force and restraint issues.

Photo of security video monitoring system near the entrance to commercial/retail store

If uniformed security officers are utilized, their role must be more than simply standing at the front of the store and greeting customers. Uniformed security officers should walk around and make their presence known in all areas of the store or business. The objective is to maximize physical presence as a deterrent to shoplifting. They should not follow a routine when walking around the store. In other words, don't do it at the same time each day, or follow the same pattern of movement. This will prevent a shoplifter from learning the security officer's routine.

If plain-clothes security officers are utilized, their role will be different from that of uniformed officers. Plain-clothes security officers are concerned primarily with detecting shoplifters in the act. They must blend in with other shoppers and assume an "undercover" role. They need to look inconspicuous. In other words, a plain-clothes security officer should not wear apparel that resembles police or security attire, which might reveal their undercover role. Their role may include patrolling stores looking for shoplifters, arresting and searching suspects, sharing information with local police, keeping detailed notes and writing reports, and keeping store management informed on the latest shoplifting trends.

TRAINING STORE EMPLOYEES   Training store employees in antishoplifting techniques is important. The last thing a shoplifter wants is to be noticed. Having sales staff make contact with customers in their areas can go a long way in preventing shoplifting. A simple "Can I help you?" or, if the sales clerk is busy with another customer, saying something like "I'll be with you in just a moment" can deter a potential shoplifter. Training sales staff always to be alert to the indicators of shoplifting is wise. For example, they should be trained to watch for customers carrying the concealment devices discussed earlier in this section, or walking with short or unnatural steps because items are concealed between their legs.

If store employees observe shoplifting, they should be cautioned against attempting to apprehend the suspect. This could result in bodily harm to the store employee and customers. Store employees should quickly notify store security officers or the police.

MONITORING FITTING ROOMS   Unsupervised fitting rooms offer excellent opportunities for shoplifters. Shoplifters simply pile on layers of clothing, or they may exchange new items for the clothes they were wearing and return their own clothes to the rack. Fitting rooms should be carefully monitored. For example, policy should be developed that limits the number of items a person can take into a fitting room. The ideal situation is for a store clerk to be assigned to the fitting-room area. This will allow the clerk to keep track of the amount of clothing that customers take into fitting rooms.

Auditable signaling devices installed on each fitting-room door are recommended. These devices alert a clerk that someone has entered the fitting room. Keep in mind that the last thing a shoplifter wants to do is to attract attention.

MERCHANDISE TRACKING   There are several ways to identify merchandise as having been legitimately paid for. One way is to instruct store cashiers to staple receipts to the outside of packages. Similarly, electronic tags that trigger alarms at the business's exits may be attached to soft articles such as clothing; these tags can be removed only by a cashier using special shears.

OTHER DETERRENCE TECHNIQUES   The Small Business Administration recommends the following shoplifting deterrence techniques:

- Attach noise alarms to unlocked exits.
- Close and block off unused checkout aisles.
- If you are involved in store design, plan to have entrances and exits in a common vestibule.
- Plan store layout with deterrence in mind. Maintain adequate lighting in all areas of the store. Keep protruding wings and displays low, not more than two or three feet high. Set display cases in broken sequences.
- Keep small items of high value (film, cigarettes, small appliances) behind a counter or in a locked case with a salesclerk on duty.
- Keep displays neat; it is easier to spot an item missing from an orderly array.

CHECK FRAUD

Check fraud is a significant challenge facing businesses. Literally thousands of checks are written daily to businesses as payment for goods and services. Unfortunately, hundreds of these checks are not honored when processed at the bank. Check fraud can be perpetrated as easily as someone stealing a blank check from your home or vehicle during a burglary, searching for a canceled or old check in the garbage, or removing a check you have mailed to pay a bill from the mailbox. The three types of check fraud that security officials need to be particularly aware of are check kiting, check forgery, and nonsufficient funds.

Fraud:
The unlawful deception of another, intended to wrongfully obtain money or property from the reliance of another on the deceptive statements or acts, believing them to be true.

Check Kiting

Check kiting is a systematic pattern of depositing nonsufficient funds checks between two or more banks. This can result in the books and records of those banks showing inflated balances that permit the nonsufficient checks to be honored rather than returned unpaid (Turner and Albrecht 1993). For example, a person with checking accounts at two banks can create an illusion of money in either account. A check drawn on the first bank is deposited with the second bank. Before the check reaches the first bank for payment, a check drawn on the second bank is deposited to the first bank. Because check kiting can be difficult to detect, security officials should work closely with financial institutions. Often, by the time a check kiting scheme is identified, it is too late in the sense that the kiter has already cashed a large amount of money. Turner and Albrecht (1993) offer the following methods that are helpful in the detection of check kiters:

Check kiting:
The practice of issuing a check from an account for which the endorser knows sufficient funds are not available to cover the encumbrance, but with the faith that funds will become available to pay the amount by the time the check clears. It is essentially a fraudulent method of obtaining credit by kiting (Falcone 2005).

- Area abnormalities (many out-of-area checks)
- Frequent deposits, check writing, and balance inquiries
- Escalating balances
- Bank abnormalities (deposited checks are usually drawn on the same banks)
- Average length of time money remains in account is short
- Nonsufficient funds is a frequent problem
- Kiters commonly keep banks from recognizing the frequency of transactions by using ATM, night-drop, drive-up, and other branches for deposits and withdrawals.

Picture of store clerk who suspects a check forgery.

Forgery of Checks

Forgery:
The process of making or counterfeiting objects, documents, or personal signatures with the intent to defraud.

Forgery is the making or the material altering of a document with the intent to defraud. A person's signature that is written without the person's consent and without the person otherwise authorizing it is forgery. The forgery of checks is no different. Check forgery has always been a concern of retail and business security officials. Check forgery is committed by a person who, with intent to defraud, knowingly makes or utters (passes, offers, or puts in circulation) a false writing that apparently imposes a legal liability on another or affects his legal right or liability to his prejudice (O'Hara and O'Hara 2003).

THEFT FORGERY   In theft forgery, the forger may steal blank checks from an office by posing as a salesman, telephone repair worker, window cleaner, or other worker. The forger may await an opportunity to steal a number of checks from the back of a check book. Another method is to pilfer mail and thus obtain cashed or uncashed checks (O'Hara and O'Hara 2003).

PRINTING FORGERY   A second type of check forgery, printing forgery, occurs when the offender uses a stolen check as a model. For example, the forger may print facsimiles. Alternatively, he or she may print a check bearing the name of a fictitious company (O'Hara and O'Hara 2003).

SIMULATED AND FREEHAND FORGERY   A *simulated forgery* is produced by a writer who learns to mimic a genuine signature; it may or may not be possible to identify the forger, depending on the extent to which the suspect's normal handwriting characteristics remain in the signature (Swanson, Chamelin, and Territo 1996). A *freehand forgery* occurs when the suspect makes no attempt to mimic a genuine signature. This signature represents the suspect's normal handwriting.

RESPONDING TO FORGERY   Once it has been determined that a forgery has occurred, retail security officials should try to have the following information available for police authorities:

- The identity of the clerk who accepted the check, and his or her name, address, and phone number.
- The register at which the check was accepted, and the date and time the check was accepted.
- Whether the forger received merchandise, cash, or both when he or she passed the check.
- Any identifying information about the suspect that may assist police in apprehension (sex, race, height and weight, clothing worn, visible scars, marks or tattoos).
- The original check that was forged.

Nonsufficient Funds

Checks are an important part of our lives in the sense that we all probably write several at the end of the month in order to pay utility bills, credit card bills, the rent, or the car and mortgage payments. Unfortunately, too many times checks are not honored by the bank upon processing because of insufficient funds, no account, payment stopped, or some other reason. The problem of nonpayment usually lies with the issuer of the check and not with the bank that denies payment.

Nonsufficient funds, or giving a worthless check, bounced check, or bad check, is the term for demand for payment of a check that cannot be honored because the account on which the check was drawn has insufficient funds. In other words, the offender knowingly writes a check when he or she knows there are insufficient funds in the checking account to cover payment.

Preventing Nonsufficient Funds

Many businesses no longer accept personal checks from consumers because of the problem of nonsufficient funds. Some businesses put nonsufficient-funds checks and the identity of the offender on public display. Businesses should be mindful that if prudent precautions are not taken when accepting checks, they could eventually end up eating the loss.

Keeping a file of the names of persons who have passed nonsufficient-funds checks in the past is a wise business and security practice. Many businesses share their lists with other businesses in the area. For example, one of the authors knows that several grocery stores share their bad check lists with three other stores in the immediate area. Each time a check is written by a customer, it is checked against the name file or database. If the name appears in the file, the manager or security officer should be notified. Management or security should in turn inform the customer that his or her check will not be accepted by the business.

In the age of sophisticated computer technology, the name list can be tracked in a computer database. The employee simply runs the name through the computer. If the name results in a "hit," management or security should be called. Many times the check writer will become very upset that the business has refused to accept a check. One of the authors knows of several cases where the check writer got so upset at the manager for not accepting his check that he attempted to assault him. In another case, the rejected check writer kicked in the front glass of the exit door before leaving the premises. Fortunately, the police had been called, and he was arrested several blocks away while leaving the area in his vehicle.

Another technique that may help reduce a business's losses from nonnsufficient-funds checks is to develop a comprehensive policy that accepts only cash or a bank debit card. Debit cards present a viable option for business owners to ensure that they are paid for their services or goods. Debit cards can be substituted for writing a check and offer the advantage of immediate electronic payment from the cardholder's account. Debit cards are linked directly to a cardholder's checking account, and money is withdrawn electronically. For the business owner, this means avoiding the problem of nonsufficient funds that written checks pose. Debit cards also offer consumers an alternative to carrying a checkbook or cash. It is estimated that 60 million Americans have a debit card. Debit cards increasingly rival cash and checks as a form of payment. Debit cards look like credit cards or ATM (automated teller machine) cards, but operate like cash or a personal check. Debit cards are accepted at many locations, including grocery stores, retail stores, gasoline stations, and restaurants.

GUIDELINES FOR ACCEPTING CHECKS   The Maricopa County [Arizona] Attorney Office (2007) has published a comprehensive guide for retailers regarding accepting checks. This guide can be useful in a wide variety of retail settings. Early detection is the key to eliminating many hardships that result from accepting a bad check. Retailers should be aware of techniques that may prevent a great many check crimes. These guidelines may also reduce losses and increase the chances of full recovery:

1. Look at the check number: Be cautious of checks that have low check numbers or no printed check numbers. Nearly 90 percent of bad checks are drawn on accounts less than one year old.
2. Check the date for accuracy: Eliminate the possibility of receiving a postdated check. A postdated check may be a defense to prosecution and full restitution.
3. Compare the amount written on the check: Make sure that the numeric dollar amount matches the written dollar amount. A valid check for $35.50 should be written as "Thirty-five and fifty/100 dollars" or "Thirty-five and 50/100 dollars."
4. Demand identification and write it on the check: Verify the identity of the check writer by requesting picture identification, and write the information on the face of the check yourself. This protects against the check writer providing false numbers. Also important, the presence of your handwriting is another way to identify the check if required for prosecution.
5. Examine the printing on the check: A check that appears to be altered, or uses two or more type sets, may be a forgery. Check the numerals and words to compare for consistency. Review for crowded letters. Check for contrasts in ink color or density. Inconsistencies are keys to catching forgeries.

Types of Checks

- *Personal check.* A check that is written and signed by the individual offering it. The individual makes it out to you or your business.
- *Two-party check.* Issued by one person, the maker, to a second person, who endorses it so that it may be cashed by a third person. This type of check lends itself to fraud because, for one thing, the maker can stop payment at the bank.
- *Payroll check.* Issued to an employee for wages earned. Usually the name of the employer is printed on the check. In most instances, "Payroll" is also printed on the check. The employee's name is printed by a check-writing machine or typed. You should not cash a payroll check that is hand-printed, rubber-stamped, or typewritten, even if it appears to be issued by a local business and drawn on a local bank, unless you are in a small community where you know the company officials and the employee personally.
- *Government check.* Issued by the federal government, a state, a county, or a local government. Such checks cover salaries, tax refunds, pensions, welfare allotments, and veterans' benefits, to mention a few examples. You should be particularly cautious with government checks. Often they are stolen and the endorsement has been forged. In some areas, such thievery is so great

that some banks refuse to cash Social Security, welfare, relief, or Internal Revenue Service checks unless the customer has an account with the bank. You should follow this procedure also. In short, know your endorser.
- *Blank check.* Sometimes known as a universal check, no longer acceptable to most banks because of Federal Reserve Board regulations that prohibit standard processing without the encoded characters. This universal check may be used, but it requires a special collection process by the bank and incurs a special cost.
- *Counter check.* Still used by a few banks and issued to depositors when they are withdrawing funds from their accounts. It is not good anywhere else. Sometimes a store has its own counter checks for the convenience of its customers. A counter check is not negotiable and is so marked.
- *Traveler's check.* A check sold with a preprinted amount (usually in round figures) to travelers who do not want to carry large amounts of cash. The traveler signs the check at the time of purchase and countersigns it in the presence of the person who cashes it.

Source: U.S. Small Business Administration, www.sba.gov/library/pubs/cp-2.txt, accessed July 24, 2007.

6. Look at the name of the payee: Changes or additions to the name indicate a possible forgery. If the color, density, or writing of the name appears different, or if the check appears payable to two or more payees (for example, "AB or CD"), there may have been an alteration.

ROBBERY

Imagine that late one evening you are working your job at the convenience store. About fifteen minutes before midnight, when you will close the store, two men walk in wearing ski masks and gloves and carrying what appear to be semiautomatic handguns. One of the robbers jumps clumsily behind the counter and shoves you violently to the floor, yelling for you to open the cash register. Your heart is racing and you are shaking. You get up off the floor and open the cash register drawer as the robbers requested. Upon seeing the cash drawer open, the second robber jumps over the counter and begins frantically removing cash from the register and placing it in a paper bag. You smell alcohol on his breath. You think to yourself that the way the robbers are acting, they may be under the influence of an illegal drug as well. As the robbers turn to leave, one of them yells, "Don't call the police for ten minutes or we'll come back and kill you!" To show he means it, he hits you in the head with the gun.

Robbery:
The unlawful taking of another's property by force or threat of force.

This fictional scenario is all too real for many convenience store clerks. Security officials have to take robberies dead serious. The Uniform Crime Report defines *robbery* as the taking or attempted taking of anything of value from the care, custody, or control of a person or persons by force or threat of force or violence and/or by putting the victim in fear. Robbery is a violent crime. Robbery involves not only the loss of property but also the threat or use of violence. Unlike victims of other personal assaults, robbery victims seldom know their assailants. Victims know their robbers in only about 26 percent of robberies. Of all violent crimes, robbery is the most likely to be committed by more than one offender.

According to data from the 2004 Uniform Crime Report (the most recent available), robbers relied on strong-arm tactics in 41.1 percent of robberies, and they employed firearms in 40.6 percent of robberies. Robbery offenders used knives or other cutting instruments in 8.9 percent of these crimes. In the remaining 9.4 percent of robberies, the offenders used some other type of weapons.

The Uniform Crime Report indicates that the annual loss to robberies is an estimated $525 million. The average loss per robbery is about $1308, and the average dollar losses were highest for banks, which lost $4221 per offense. Gas and service stations lost an average of $1749. Commercial houses, which include supermarkets, department stores, and restaurants, had average losses of $1529. An average of $1488 was taken from residences; individuals lost an average $923 from robberies on streets and highways. An average of $653 per robbery was taken at convenience stores. An average of $1682 per robbery was taken in all other types.

There are essentially two types of robberies, planned and unplanned. In planned robberies, the offender considers not only the victim of the robbery but also such operational facts as the number of accomplices necessary to successfully complete the crime, the weapons selected, the number of persons likely to be present during the robbery, and the escape route. In unplanned robberies, the offender does not plan the robbery and usually acts on impulse. The offender often selects a weapon based on its availability, and then cruises an area without a specific victim in mind but in haphazard search of a victim (Weston and Wells 1997, 257).

Business establishments such as convenience stores, gas stations, and other retail stores typically have large amounts money on hand near closing time, making them especially vulnerable to robbery. The best advice that security professionals can give to store employees who find themselves the victim of a robbery is to remain calm and listen to the robber's demands. The safety and welfare of the employee is paramount. Listen closely to what the robber says, and do not argue with him or her. Try to remember the exact words spoken by the robber, as this may help the police investigation. Store employees and unarmed security officers should not resist the robber, nor should they try to disarm or attack the robber. The chance of successfully disarming a robber is small and not worth the potential risk. If possible, employees should activate the silent alarm system, pay close attention to the description of the robber, and get a description of the getaway vehicle.

ACTIVATE THE SILENT ALARM SYSTEM   If a business has a silent alarm system, employees should activate it immediately if they can do so. If it is too risky to activate the silent alarm during the robbery, it should be done as soon as the robber leaves the business. It is important to avoid any overt motion that might anger the robbers or cause them to panic. This may jeopardize employees and customers who happen to be in the business during the robbery.

OBTAIN A PHYSICAL DESCRIPTION OF THE ROBBER   Security officials should train business employees on how to get a proper physical description of a robber. Obtaining a good physical description of the robber can greatly assist law enforcement in identifying a suspect. If there are more than two robbers, get a description of the closest one. The physical description should include such distinguishing characteristics as race, approximate age, weight, height, type of complexion, color of hair and eyes, clothing worn (head to foot), build, speech (accent), and any noticeable scars, marks, or deformities. Some business have a height strip placed by the entrance and exit doors. This assists business employees in estimating a suspect's height. Attention should be given to the robbers' method of operation, and try to remember exactly what they said. Many robberies are committed by more than one person. The accomplice(s) may be outside in a getaway car or in another section of the business. If this is the case, make a conscious effort to look for an accomplice, but don't be too obvious.

If the robber(s) has a weapon, pay close attention and try to obtain as much information as possible. For example, what color is the weapon? Is it blue steel, chrome, or stainless steel in appearance? Is it a pistol or a long gun? If it is a pistol, is it a semiautomatic or a revolver? If it is a shotgun, is it double-barrel or single-barrel? Security officials can train employees who may not be familiar with the various types of weapons by showing them photographs of different firearms.

DESCRIPTION OF GETAWAY VEHICLE   If possible, the employee should obtain a description of the getaway vehicle. The description should include the color, make, model, and year of the vehicle. If you are not familiar with car style by year, try to note some distinguishing style characteristic, such as tail light design, hood ornament, or front grill design. Try to write down the license plate number. Was a tail light burned out? Were there any dents in the fenders? Security officials should caution store employees not to run out of the building to get a look at the getaway vehicle. This is dangerous and should be avoided. Your observation of the getaway vehicle should be done from inside the store looking out the window and only if you can do so in an inconspicuous manner.

WHAT TO DO AFTER THE ROBBERY   After the robber(s) has left the business, the police should be notified immediately. Initial information that can be provided to the police is crucial. Be prepared to inform the police of the address, with an exact location in the building; as complete a description as possible of the robber(s); whether or not a weapon was implied or used; and a vehicle description with number of occupants and direction of travel. Employees should not chase the robber(s) on foot or in a vehicle. The sooner the police are notified and given pertinent information, the better are the chances for an apprehension.

While waiting for the police to arrive, lock the doors and do not touch anything. Keep everyone away from the hold-up area and guard anything that may have been touched by the robber(s). Save anything left behind by the robber(s), such as a note, weapon, bag, or clothing. Do not handle any of these items, because they are physical evidence that can be contaminated if handled improperly. While waiting for the police, do not discuss the crime with other witnesses. All those involved should make individual notes of the information they have while it is fresh in their minds.

It would be virtually impossible to eliminate all commercial robberies; however, security professionals can recommend the following robbery deterrence steps:

- Keep the exterior and interior of the business well lit.
- Keep the rear and side doors locked at all times.
- Maintain a clear view into the building from the street.
- Display signs without blocking view of the counter.
- Record, serial number and series, some "bait" money to be kept in the cash register and given to a robber.
- Don't keep large bills in the cash drawer.
- Keep as little cash on the premises as possible.
- Keep checks separate from cash.
- Acknowledge all customers and make eye contact.
- Don't allow unauthorized persons behind the counter.
- Increase staffing during high-risk times.
- Maintain alarm or video surveillance systems.
- Install mirrors and keep store shelves low as to not obstruct view.

EMBEZZLEMENT

Embezzlement:
The fraudulent appropriation by a person to his or her own use of property or money entrusted to that person's care but owned by someone else, including an employee who steals assets or funds of a company.

Embezzlement accounts for a substantial amount of business losses suffered by employers. The chances are great that corporate security officials may encounter embezzlement. *Embezzlement* is the fraudulent appropriation by a person to his or her own use of property or money entrusted to that person's care but owned by someone else. For example, a bank clerk or cashier may embezzle money from his or her employer, or a civil servant may embezzle funds from the treasury.

One embezzling employee can quickly bankrupt a company. In one three-month period, three major U.S. banks discovered that they had been the victims of embezzlements by senior executives of $21.3 million, $20 million, and $17 million. In one case, the bank executive was known for his flamboyant lifestyle. Instead of suspecting him of embezzlement, his employers assumed that he had a secret partner who was financing his business ventures.

According to the Bureau of Crime Statistics, each year, employers lose three times as much from employee embezzlement as they do from robberies and burglaries. The average robbery nets the robber under $4000, the average burglary under $500, whereas the average embezzlement loss exceeds $50,000. In addition, most employers who would not hesitate to prosecute a robber or burglar are reluctant to prosecute an embezzler.

Although management should always be alert for embezzlement, the following are some indicators that you should watch for in employees with positions of financial trust:

- Excessive drinking, or gambling in any form
- Carrying unusual amounts of cash, or other acts indicating an abundance of money

- Borrowing money from other employees (even small amounts)
- Refusing to allow others to have custody of the records
- Rewriting records with the excuse that they need to be neater
- Working overtime regularly
- Personal checks being returned for a variety of reasons
- Inability to answer routine questions regarding duties or the records without getting angry
- Excessive criticism of others
- Being too busy to take a vacation
- Turning down a promotion
- Explaining a higher standard of living as a sudden inheritance
- Appearance of collectors or creditors trying to collect personal debts of the employee
- Having an unusually large bank balance

Larceny entails the illegal taking and carrying away of personal property belonging to another person with the purpose of depriving the owner of its possession. For example, you leave your lawn mower sitting on in your front yard overnight, only to wake in the morning and find it missing. Embezzlement differs from larceny in two ways. First, in embezzlement, an actual conversion must occur; second, the original taking must not be trespassory. In other words, the embezzler must have had the right to possess the item, and used that position of trust to convert the property. Embezzlement may range from the very minor, involving only a very small amount, to immense, involving very large sums and very sophisticated schemes. Newman (2006) offers nine steps for businesses to guard against embezzlement. Security professionals should work to educate their clients on the following points:

1. Don't leave cash lying around in an unprotected spot. It can easily disappear, and you don't want to tempt people by being careless.
2. Don't use signature stamps for checks. They are too easy to misuse. Sign the checks yourself with a pen.
3. Minimize the number of employees who have signature authority on your bank account. Too many hands in the pot can lead to disaster.
4. Make deposits nightly, so that excess funds are not left on-site.
5. Do cross-training so that multiple people know multiple functions. This means that multiple people will have the ability to do audits on each others' work to ensure that processes are followed. It also minimizes the chance of theft. You may also want to pull in your outside accountant to do spot checks from time to time.
6. Have separate check cards for each individual, if you choose to authorize check cards. You want to know exactly who is spending what. Remember, embezzlement is not just about taking cash. Employees could misuse the cards to purchase personal items.
7. Bond with the employees who will be handling the money. Having a close relationship with the boss offers some protection for your company, because it may dissuade people from stealing—they won't want to hurt someone they care about.

8. Do a background check on your employees when hiring them to see if they have had financial problems in the past. That may be a sign that they are struggling financially and might be tempted to take resources from the business to smooth out personal financial problems.
9. Institute a proper division of functions. The following functions should be assigned to different people to help provide a checks-and-balance function at your company:
   - Prepare checks for payments.
   - Receive payments from customers.
   - Make bank deposits.
   - Sign checks.
   - Bank reconciliation.

Inadequate attention to detail by managers provides the opportunity for persons under their supervision to embezzle. Managers, therefore, should not continually leave all details to subordinates without occasionally checking on them. A system of random checks will create the general feeling that all aspects of every financial transaction are subject to verification.

In addition to reducing the opportunity to embezzle, you should be alerted by employees who are living above their apparent income or who have a record of financial problems. As a rule, persons who embezzle do not hide the money in a secret account; they tend to spend the money as soon as they embezzle it. They normally use it to support a living standard beyond their apparent means or to solve present financial problems.

Requiring key employees to submit full financial disclosure statements on an annual basis may help detect embezzlement. You can compare annual statements to detect sudden changes in net worth. In most cases, a negative change in the personal estate of a key employee is a danger flag. The employee who appears to manage his or her personal estate adequately is not normally an embezzler. Note that some state and local statutes may prohibit employers from requiring employees to submit personal financial statements. Check with your attorney before instituting this requirement. The federal government requires its key employees to submit annual personal financial statements to check on possible conflicts of interests. A similar check could reveal signs of embezzlement by an employee.

Carefully screen aspiring applicants for positions of financial trust, especially if they have a history of frequent job changes, vice, or serious financial indebtedness. Be suspicious of employees who refuse to take vacations or days off or who refuse promotions. Require that all employees take scheduled vacations. At least once a year, during the bookkeeper's vacation, have someone else send out the monthly statements.

Negotiable instruments should be under the control of at least two persons. Require two signatures on every check, and require that both persons review the documentation for each payment. Checks should never be presigned. The person who computes the payroll should not be the same employee who distributes the checks to the employees. The person who writes the checks for the payment of bills should not be the person who mails them.

Summary

- Internal employee theft accounts for significant losses to business each year in the United States. It is difficult to determine the extent of employee theft, but some estimate it be $30 billion a year.
- All industries are affected by employee theft. Documented employee thefts range from petty cash to railroad boxcars. Many studies indicate that 60 percent of all employee thefts are of noncash items. There are numerous methods of stealing from an employer, and more are discovered each year.
- Employee misconduct such as theft of company time, absenteeism, and drug and alcohol use present problems for businesses that could result in significant economic losses.
- Once an employee is suspected of misconduct, security officials should conduct a thorough investigation into his or her background, including former employers and acquaintances. The goal is to find out as much as possible about the employee before interviewing him or her.
- The suspected employee should be interviewed in a nonthreatening manner. It is always best to avoid a confrontation during the interview. The objective is to get the suspected employee to admit to the theft or other misconduct.
- Security management must decide whether security personnel working in retail or other business establishments should be in plain clothes or wear a security uniform. The answer depends largely on the objective of security. If the objective is to prevent criminal acts, then a security officer in uniform is probably the best choice. On the other hand, if the objective is to detect crimes, then a plain-clothes security officer is a better choice. It is recommended that the security uniform resemble the standard blue police uniform and that security companies avoid, if possible, wearing military-style uniforms, which can create a warrior-like image and detract from the security service role.
- Shoplifting is one of the most prevalent and costly crimes in the United States today.

- Retailers suffer huge losses each year as a result of shoplifting. Just to cover a yearly loss of $1000 in thefts, a retailer would have to sell each day over 900 candy bars, 130 packs of cigarettes, or 380 cans of soup.
- Shoplifters can be divided into several types, including juveniles, professionals, vagrants and drug addicts, kleptomaniacs, and amateurs.
- There are many ways in which shoplifters carry out their crimes. Articles as innocent as bulky packages, pocketbooks, baby carriages, knitting bags, shopping bags, umbrellas, newspapers, and magazines can be used to carry stolen goods. Constructed devices, such as coats or capes with hidden pockets and zippered hiding places, are used by more experienced shoplifters.
- Security officials should stay abreast with the latest intelligence trends pertaining to the method of operation of shoplifters.
- Check fraud is one of the largest challenges facing businesses, especially financial institutions, today. There are three types of check fraud that security officials should be particularly aware of.
- Technology has made it increasingly easy for criminals, either independently or in organized gangs, to create realistic counterfeit and fictitious checks as well as false identification that can be used to defraud financial institutions.
- Fraud schemes involving checks take many forms. Checks may be altered, either as to the payee or the amount; counterfeited; forged, either as to signature or endorsement; drawn on closed accounts; written off an account with insufficient funds, and check kited.
- Robbery is a violent crime that involves the taking or attempted taking of anything of value from the care, custody, or control of a person or persons by force or threat of force or violence and/or by putting the victim in fear.
- There are essentially two types of robberies, planned and unplanned. The robber may go to great extremes to plan the robbery, such as casing the business for days or weeks, taking notes

on how many employees are present at particular times, and noting when the business is busiest with customers. The unplanned robber may rob on a sudden impulse.

- Security officials should train business employees on what to do if they become the victim of a robbery, and the techniques for obtaining a proper description of a suspect(s).

Review Questions

1. Discuss how differential association theory explains internal business theft.
2. Identify some of the common indicators of internal employee theft.
3. What is a major cause of inventory shrinkage?
4. Identify and discuss a minimum of three ways to prevent employee theft.
5. Are there advantages to uniform security versus plain-clothes security in a retail store environment? If so, what are they?
6. Identify and discuss at least three warning signs of a shoplifter.
7. What is the difference between a freehand and a simulated forgery?
8. What is check kiting?
9. What is fraud?
10. Define and discuss kleptomania.

Class Exercises

1. Visit a local retail store and interview the manager about his or her perceptions of employee theft. Be sure and ask whether he or she has encountered employee theft and to what extent he or she thinks it occurs. Discuss your finding with the class.
2. List two types of employee misconduct and write a policy on how you would handle it if you were a business owner.
3. Interview a business security professional about the problem of internal employee theft and other misconduct. Ask the security officer how he or she deals with the various forms of employee misconduct. Report your findings to the class.
4. Examine the local newspaper for one week. Make a list of all incidents of retail store robberies that occurred. Pay attention to loss. Discuss your findings in class.
5. Visit several large department stores in your area and take notes on the presence of security officers. What did the officers' uniforms look like? Where were they standing? Did they walk around the store? Did they greet customers? Report to the class and compare your notes with those of others.
6. In small groups, write a fictitious scenario for a check kiting scheme.
7. In small groups, write a protocol that retail store clerks should follow in the event they are robbed.

References

Cromwell, P., L. Parker, and S. Mobley. 2006. The five finger discount: An analysis of motivations of shoplifting. In *In their own words: Crime and criminals on crime*, 4th ed., ed. P. Cromwell, 113–26. Los Angeles: Roxbury.

Falcone, D. N. 2005. *Dictionary of American criminal justice, criminology, and criminal law*. Upper Saddle River, NJ: Pearson–Prentice Hall.

Fischer, R. J. 1987. *Introduction to security,* 4th ed. Boston, MA: Butterworths.

Klemke, L. W. 1992. *The sociology of shoplifting: Boosters and snitches today*. West Port, CT: Praeger.

Maricopa County [Arizona] Attorney's Office. 2007. *Check enforcement guide*. www.maricopacountyattorney.org, retrieved July 28, 2007.

National Check Fraud Center. 2007. *Check fraud prevention.* www.ckfraud.org/ckfraud.html, retrieved July 28, 2007.

Newman, P. 2006. Protecting your business against embezzlement. www.entraupreneur.com, retrieved July 24, 2007.

O'Hara, C. E., and G. L. O'Hara. 2003. *Criminal investigation,* 7th ed. Springfield, IL: Charles C Thomas.

Palmiotto, M. J. 1998. *Criminal investigation,* 2nd ed. San Francisco: Austin & Winfield.

Paul, J., and M. L. Birzer. 2004. Images of power: A critical analysis of the militarization of police uniforms and messages of service. *Free Inquiry in Creative Sociology* 32: 121–8.

Sennewald, C. A., and J. H. Christman. 1992. *Shoplifting.* Boston: Butterworths-Heinemann.

Swanson, C. R., N. C. Chamelin, and L. Territo. 1996. *Criminal investigation,* 6th ed. New York: McGraw-Hill.

Turner, J. S., and S. W. Albrecht, 1993. Check kiting: Detection, apprehension, and prosecution. *The F.B.I. Law Enforcement Bulletin,* 62: 12–6.

Weston, P. B., and K. M. Wells. 1997. *Criminal investigation: Basic perspectives.* Upper Saddle River, NJ: Prentice Hall.

CHAPTER 6

Terrorism and Natural Disasters

CHAPTER OUTLINE

OBJECTIVES

After completing this chapter, you will be able to:

- Discuss what constitutes terrorism.
- Explain the role of private security personnel when a natural disaster or terrorist activity occurs.
- Describe how to handle suspicious mail.
- Explain the concept of threat assessment.
- Explain the Department of Homeland Security's mission and structure.
- Describe the importance of establishing formal partnerships between police and private security organizations.
- Describe the history and current status of cooperation between the police and private security.

- List the obstacles that keep law enforcement from working with private security.
- Define the potential organisms for bioterrorism.
- Explain why the food supply is a target for terrorist activity.
- List the lessons learned from 9/11/01.
- Explain the "two hat" problem.
- Discuss the psychological issues in terrorist attacks.

In New York on 9/11, over 70 police officers died, yet so did 35 private security staff.

> *The record shows that neither public law enforcement nor firefighters were the first to respond to the attack on the Twin Towers in 2001; private security personnel stationed in the two buildings and nearby facilities rapidly and selflessly became the first responders.*

> —*U.S. Department of Justice, Bureau of Justice Assistance (2005)*

The terrorist attacks of September 11, 2001, altered the security roles and responsibilities of the private sector. The use of commercial aircraft as missiles against the World Trade Center and the Pentagon, and statements by al-Qaeda leaders declaring their intention to "fill [American] hearts with terror and target [America's] economic lifeline," made it clear that the critical infrastructures that support our society and economy—including transportation, oil and gas, electricity, water, chemicals, telecommunications, computers, and the food supply—are potential targets of future terrorist attacks. Because about 85 percent of that infrastructure is owned and/or operated by the private sector, U.S. businesses must be part of any national effort to confront the threat of catastrophic terrorism (Flynn and Prieto 2006, 21–2).

In many ways, preparedness for potential terrorist acts and for natural disasters overlap. In August 2005, Hurricane Katrina hit the Gulf Coast region of the United States. At least 1836 people lost their lives during the storm and the subsequent floods, making it the deadliest U.S. hurricane since the 1928 Okeechobee hurricane. The storm is estimated to have been responsible for $81.2 billion in damage, making it the costliest natural disaster in U.S. history. The disaster recovery efforts in New Orleans and surrounding communities suffered many of the same problems that were experienced after 9/11/01 in New York.

In June 2007, a person suspected of being infected with a potentially deadly, drug-resistant strain of tuberculosis could have exposed hundreds of fellow travelers. The person first flew from New York to Paris in mid-May, and then returned to the United States via Montreal two weeks later. He was allowed to cross the Canadian border into the United States by a customs agent who was aware that the individual was on a restricted list. The customs agent stated that "He didn't look sick." Had this individual started an epidemic, it probably would have been more deadly than the 9/11/01 acts. It also raised the possibility that a terrorist group could provide a person who is infected with a deadly disease and send that individual an all-expense-paid vacation to a major U.S. city. This would be a relatively inexpensive method of financing a terroristic event.

Paramedics transfer a patient to the care of personnel in protective suits at a decontamination station after a chemical spill.

National critical infrastructure and key assets:
The infrastructure and assets vital to a nation's security, governance, public health and safety, economy, and public confidence. They include telecommunications, electrical power systems, gas and oil distribution and storage, water supply systems, banking and finance, transportation, emergency services, industrial assets, information systems, and continuity of government operations.

In this chapter we will explore the role of private security in homeland security and during natural disasters. As noted during the national summit on law enforcement and private security cooperation discussed later in this chapter, private security is a key element in protecting our homeland from terrorist acts. Why? Because the private sector owns and protects 85 percent of the nation's infrastructure. While local law enforcement may possess information regarding threats to infrastructure, law enforcement–private security partnerships can put vital information into the hands of the people who need it. The summit concluded that to protect the nation's infrastructure effectively, law enforcement and private security must work collaboratively, because neither possesses the necessary resources to do the job alone.

Private security individuals and organizations have three distinct roles in combating terrorism:

1. Information gathering and sharing, to provide early warnings of terrorist threats or natural disaster.
2. Acting as first responders. Note that when the planes struck the twin towers, private security individuals were the first on the scene—and thirty-five of them died that day.
3. Providing assistance and aid after a terrorist attack or natural disaster.

Biochemicals:
The chemicals that make up or are produced by living things.

While 9/11/01 was a horrible example of the ability of international terrorist groups to cause mass casualties on U.S. soil and to disrupt our lives, we need to be careful not to consider 9/11/01 as the sole criterion for antiterrorist planning. The 1995 Oklahoma City bombing and the 2001 anthrax incidents demonstrate that threats can come from domestic terrorist sources as easily as foreign ones, and that these acts or threats can significantly impact business and government. Security managers must prepare for potential terrorist attacks not only from well-financed terrorist groups on an international crusade but also from a wide range of radical or fringe elements of our own society who seek to gain attention or to further their agendas through acts of terrorism.

Not only can terrorists groups attack targets at almost any location, the attacks potentially can come in a wide range of forms, depending on the means and objectives of the group responsible. For example, the attacks on the World Trade Center in 1993 and in Oklahoma City in 1995 involved truck bombs utilizing conventional explosives. And the 9/11/01 hijackers turned commercial airplanes into deadly unconventional weapons for a destructive, mass-casualty attack (Metro Atlanta Homeland Security Advisory Group, 2004).

The Metro Atlanta Homeland Security Advisory Group (MAHSAG) (2004) notes that security managers must focus on the potential targets for terrorist activities (e.g., overt, covert, explosive, biological, chemical, or cyber) and develop systematic plans and procedures for workplace response; companies cannot rely solely on law enforcement agencies to protect them from such attacks. Company managers must incorporate into their business practices steps to increase awareness of, monitoring for, and security against terrorism and must develop response plans in case an attack occurs at the workplace.

Biological weapons:
The intentional use of biological agents as weapons to kill or injure humans, animals, or plants, or to damage equipment.

Antiterrorism:
Defensive measures used to reduce the vulnerability of individuals and property to terrorist acts, to include limited response and containment by local military forces.

DEFINING TERRORISM

Terrorism is simply a psychological weapon aimed at both its immediate victims as well as a much wider audience, in the hope of obtaining some sort of behavior change from that audience. (Hanser 2007, 4)

Defining terrorism is difficult. The first general use of the term *terrorism* is considered to have occurred in France during the French Revolution (1792–1794). To many individuals, terrorism is the systematic application of violence to promote or maintain a political or religious system. Although a rape victim probably feels that she is the victim of an act of terrorism, that type of violent act is not included in the general definition of terrorism. Most definitions of terrorism exclude acts of violence in which the terror component is incidental or secondary to some other primary objectives. For example, kidnapping for the purpose of obtaining money for personal use is not considered a terrorist act. Labeling someone a terrorist does not preclude also considering that individual to be a criminal, madman, or murderer.

Alex Scmid contends that a definition of terrorism should have two general characteristics: first, an individual being threatened; and second, the meaning of the terrorist act derives from the choice of targets and victims. Scmid (1983, 107–9) concludes that certain elements are common among the different definitions of terrorism:

Terrorism:
A violent act or an act that is dangerous to human life, in violation of the criminal laws of the United States or any segment thereof, to intimidate or coerce a government, the civilian population, or any segment thereof, in furtherance of political or social objectives (U.S. Department of Justice, FBI National Security Division 1996).

- Terrorism is an abstract concept with no essence.
- A single definition does not account for all the possible uses of the term.
- Many different definitions share common elements.
- The meaning of terrorism derives its classification from the victim or target.

The FBI uses the definition of terrorism that is set forth in the Code of Federal Regulations. According to that definition, terrorism is the unlawful use of force and violence against persons or property to intimidate or coerce a government, the civilian population, or any segment thereof, in furtherance of political or social objectives (28 CFR Sec. 0.85).

According to a Department of Homeland Security definition, terrorism is the use of force or violence against persons or property in violation of the criminal laws of the United States for purposes of intimidation, coercion, or ransom. The U.S. Code, Title 22, Section 2656f(d), provides that the term *terrorism* means premeditated, politically motivated violence perpetrated against noncombatant targets by subnational groups or clandestine agents, usually intended to influence an audience. The U.S. Code also describes *international terrorism* as terrorism involving citizens or the territory of more than one country, and *terrorist group* as any group that practices or that has significant subgroups that practice international terrorism.

Because there is a lack of definitional consistency, it is important to mention some important characteristics of terrorism:

- Terrorist groups adapt as times change.
- The majority of terrorist groups are unsuccessful in their long-term goals.
- Terrorist groups network and pool resources.
- Terrorist groups work with other organizations, including organized crime groups, to finance activities and mobilize resources.
- Terrorist groups are creative in their tactics and leave open the possibility that anything can happen.

Handling Suspicious Mail

It is relatively easy to send biological agents through the mail (e.g., the anthrax incidents), so businesses need to develop specific procedures for managing suspicious packages. Employees should be educated about recognizing suspicious packages and the procedures to follow if they receive such a package. Emphasis should be on minimizing exposure (unprotected contact between employees and the suspicious package) and timely notification of security managers. The U.S. Postal Service lists the following warning signs of mail and packages that might indicate a terrorist or bioterrorist parcel:

- Unexpected mail or mail from someone unfamiliar to you
- Addressed to someone no longer with your organization or otherwise outdated
- Excessive postage
- Handwritten or poorly typed addresses
- Incorrect titles
- Title, but no name
- Misspellings of common words
- Oily stains, discolorations, or strange odors
- No return address, or a return address that cannot be identified as legitimate
- A city or state in the postmark that does not match the return address
- Restrictive endorsements, such as "Personal" or "Confidential"
- Oddly shaped, or an unusual weight for its size
- Protruding wires, or dripping powders or liquids

If a parcel appears suspicious (i.e., it might contain biological, chemical, or explosive agents), the following are some important steps to take:

- Handle the parcel with care.
- Isolate the parcel.
- Do not open, smell, or shake the parcel.
- Call the police.

THREAT ASSESSMENT

The term *threat assessment* is commonly used in counterterrorism. Threat assessment refers to the assessment of a potential terrorist act as to whether it will happen, where it will happen, and expected damage or injuries if it happens. Threat assessment is a developing field pioneered by the U.S. Department of the Treasury's U.S. Secret Service, which is charged with protecting the President of the United States and other U.S. and foreign leaders. With the creation of the Department of Homeland Security, threat assessment became one of its major duties. Threat assessment measures involve investigation and analysis of situations and individuals that may pose threats to the public.

THE HOMELAND SECURITY ACT

> *The enemies of freedom have no regard for the innocent, no concept of the just and no desire for peace. They will stop at nothing to destroy our way of life, and we, on the other hand, we stop at nothing to defend it.*
>
> —*Secretary Tom Ridge, Department of Homeland Security, Remarks celebrating the 213th birthday of the United States Coast Guard [As reported in Remarks by Secretary of Homeland Security Tom Ridge at the American Association of Port Authorities Spring Conference, Washington, D.C., at the American Association of Port Authorities (AAPA) Spring Conference, March 23, 2004].*

In January 2003, the Department of Homeland Security (DHS) became the nation's fifteenth and newest Cabinet department, consolidating twenty-two previously

Biological weapons agents:
Living organisms or the chemical compounds derived from them that cause disease or disrupt physiological activity in humans, animals, or plants, or that cause deterioration of material. Biological agents may be dispersed as liquid droplets, aerosols, or dry powders.

Counterterrorism:
Operations that include the offensive measures taken to prevent, deter, preempt, and respond to terrorism.

Emergency telephone operators at work before rows of computer terminals facing a video screen in a dimly lit room.

disparate agencies under one unified organization. Prior to the establishment of the DHS, no single federal department had homeland security as its primary objective. The most important mission of the DHS is to protect the American people and our way of life from terrorism. It is expected that the DHS, through partnerships with state, local, and tribal governments and the private sector, will work to ensure the highest level of protection and preparedness for the country and the citizens it serves.

The Homeland Security Act (HLS), passed in 2002, was a direct result of the terrorist acts of 9/11/01. The act was perhaps the biggest "change management" challenge since the establishment of the U.S. Constitution. The primary mission of the HLS, as set forth in Section 102(a) of the act, is to: prevent terrorist attacks within the United States; reduce the vulnerability of the United States to terrorism; and minimize the damage, and assist in the recovery, from terrorist attacks that do occur within the United States.

The Department of Homeland Security absorbed many different law enforcement resources and organizations, including customs enforcement, the Federal Law Enforcement Training Center (FLETC), the Federal Protective Service, immigration-related law enforcement and the Border Patrol, maritime enforcement, and drug interdiction.

PRIVATE SECURITY'S ROLE AS A FIRST RESPONDER

When the first responder is a private security professional rather than a police officer or public emergency employee, the private individual does not have the authority to take certain actions. He or she can take still take certain steps to assist in the mitigation of the consequences of a catastrophic event—for example, shutting off gas lines and assisting in restoring basic services such as water, communications, and transport. The first responder can also assist in obtaining from private businesses needed materials, logistics, and know-how to provide relief. For instance, private companies can marshal heavy-lifting equipment and cutting torches to assist in urban search and rescue.

The private security professional does have the authority to make a "citizen's arrest," which is discussed in Chapter 12. The private professional, however, must be aware that a false arrest can incur civil liability. Probably the main function of the security professional when he or she arrives at the scene is to protect people and property until the police or public authority arrives on the scene.

PARTNERSHIPS BETWEEN POLICE AND PRIVATE SECURITY

The majority of studies involving the role of private security in preventing and responding to terrorism see the need for law enforcement–private security partnerships. Yet, years after 9/11/01, there are few jurisdictions with such partnerships. Instead, the agencies are focusing on crime prevention partnerships. Some of the principles observed in these crime prevention-driven partnerships are also transferable to homeland security-driven partnerships, and they are interrelated and inseparable from them. Many of the present partnerships that do exist were formed prior to 9/11/01 (U.S. Department of Justice, Bureau of Justice Assistance 2005).

Potential Organisms for Bioterrorism

High-priority agents classified as Category A pose a risk to national security because they:

- Can be easily disseminated or transmitted from person to person
- Result in high death rates and have the potential for major public health impacts
- Might cause public panic and social disruption
- Require special action for public health preparedness

Category A

Anthrax (*Bacillus anthracis*)

Botulism (*Clostridium botulinum* toxin)

Plague (*Yersinia pestis*)

Smallpox (*Variola major*)

Tularemia (*Francisella tularensis*)

Viral hemorrhagic fevers (filoviruses [e.g., Ebola, Marburg] and arenaviruses [e.g., Lassa, Machupo])

Source: Centers for Disease Control and Prevention, Atlanta, GA.

BUILDING PARTNERSHIPS

In 2004, the U.S. Department of Justice Office of Community Oriented Policing Services (COPS), in partnership with the International Association of Chiefs of Police (IACP) and a broad-based group of private-sector/law enforcement professionals, released a comprehensive policy paper titled *Private Security/Public Policing Partnerships*. This comprehensive report outlined a national strategy to establish partnerships between private security and public law enforcement agencies to create action plans for responding to terrorism.

The report was based on the findings of a national policy summit that took place January 26–27, 2004, in Arlington, Virginia. The policy summit was sponsored by the IACP, the American Society of Industrial Security International (ASIS), the International Security Management Association (ISMA), the National Association of Security Companies (NASCO), and the Security Industry Association (SIA). Participants included:

- Law enforcement: municipal, county, and tribal police chiefs; sheriffs; state police executives; and representatives of federal and special law enforcement agencies (such as transit police)
- Private security: CEOs of security firms, major corporate security directors and chief security officers, security consultants, and representatives of security service and technology companies
- Professional organizations: representatives of ASIS International, IACP, International Security Management Association, Joint Council on Information Age Crime, Major Cities Chiefs Association, National Association of Security Companies, National Sheriffs' Association, Police Executive Research Forum, and Security Industry Association
- Academic institutions: representatives from John Jay College of Criminal Justice, Michigan State University, Northeastern University, and the University of Washington

Bioterrorism:
The illicit use of biological agents (e.g., bacteria, viruses, and parasites or their by-products) to cause illness and spread fear.

- Federal government: representatives from the Department of Defense, Department of Justice, Department of Homeland Security, Federal Bureau of Investigation, U.S. Secret Service, and Sandia National Laboratories

In its report, the summit concluded:

Since September 11, 2001, law enforcement agencies have been under tremendous pressure to conduct their traditional crime prevention and response activities, plus a large quantum of homeland security work, in a time of tight city, county, and state budgets. Private security organizations have been under similar pressure to perform their traditional activities to protect people, property, and information, plus contribute to the nation-wide effort to protect the homeland from external and internal threats, all while minding the profitability of the businesses they serve.

Despite their similar interests in protecting the people of the United States, the two fields have rarely collaborated. In fact, through the practice of community policing, law enforcement agencies have collaborated extensively with practically every group but private security. By some estimates, 85 percent of the country's critical infrastructure is protected by private security. The need for complex coordination, extra staffing, and special resources after a terror attack, coupled with the significant demands of crime prevention and response, absolutely requires boost.

Policy Recommendations

The summit participants made five major recommendations. The first four are national-level, long-term efforts. The fifth recommendation relates to local and regional efforts. The summit noted that existing cooperative efforts have been limited by the lack of a coordinating entity. The participants concluded that the first four recommendations (regarding national coordination) will support the fifth recommendation (local and regional efforts).

- Leaders of the major law enforcement and private security organizations should make a formal commitment to cooperate.
- The Department of Homeland Security and/or Department of Justice should fund research and training on relevant legislation, private security, and law enforcement–private security cooperation. The appropriate body should conduct both baseline and ongoing research and should encourage training.
- The Department of Homeland Security and/or Department of Justice should create an advisory council composed of nationally prominent law enforcement and private security professionals to oversee the day-to-day implementation issues of law enforcement–private security partnerships. The advisory council would work to institutionalize partnerships, address tactical issues and intelligence sharing, improve selection and training guidelines and standards of private security personnel, market the concept of law enforcement–private security partnership, and create a national partnership information center.
- The Department of Homeland Security and/or Department of Justice, along with relevant membership organizations, should convene key practitioners to

move this agenda forward in the future. It should do so by organizing future summits on issues in law enforcement–private security cooperation.

- Local partnerships should set priorities and address key problems as identified by the summit.

Examples of local and regional activities that can and should be undertaken immediately included the following:

- Improve joint response to critical incidents.
- Coordinate infrastructure protection.
- Improve communications and data interoperability.
- Bolster information and intelligence sharing.
- Prevent and investigate high-tech crime.
- Devise responses to workplace violence.

The participants opined that the execution of their recommendations should benefit all concerned:

- Law enforcement agencies will be better able to carry out their traditional crime-fighting duties and their additional homeland security duties by using the many private security resources in the community. Public–private cooperation is an important aspect—indeed, a potent technique—of community policing.
- Private security organizations will be better able to carry out their mission of protecting their companies' or clients' people, property, and information, while at the same time serving the homeland security objectives of their communities.
- The nation as a whole will benefit from the heightened effectiveness of law enforcement agencies and private security organizations.

The group noted that preparing for terrorism and public disorder has taxed the nation's law enforcement agencies. The agencies have held tabletop emergency response exercises, coordinated emergency radio communication with fire and emergency medical services, developed multijurisdictional incident command centers, and increased staffing and overtime in response to elevated terror alerts. Responding to actual terror events would tax law enforcement agencies even further. This workload sits atop law enforcement's already enormous task of crime prevention and response.

The group also noted that private security operations have also been busy planning their responses to such events. These private-sector organizations have staged evacuation drills, secured their computer networks, and increased protection around critical infrastructure assets. Private security practitioners are adding their antiterror efforts to the already demanding requirement to protect the interests and assets of their organizations and clients.

For the most part, the public sector tends to have the threat information, and the private sector tends to have control over the vulnerable sites. Law enforcement's capacity to provide homeland security may be more limited than is generally acknowledged. Clearly, the need for public-sector law enforcement agencies and private-sector security organizations to work together is great. Each side can and will benefit from the capabilities of the other.

Crisis management:
Measures to identify, acquire, and plan the use of resources needed to anticipate, prevent, and/or resolve a threat or an act of terrorism. Crisis management is predominantly a law enforcement response, most often executed under federal law.

Some positive outcomes of the summit included the following.

- The Philadelphia Police Foundation decided to adopt public–private cooperation—an aspect of the report's Recommendation 5—as its central project.
- The Regional Community Policing Institutes (RCPIs), funded by the COPS Office, are expanding their training outreach to private-security practitioners. Participating in co-located courses will teach both private security and law enforcement a little more about each other's needs, concerns, and capabilities and will also provide opportunities for relationship building. Additionally, there is talk of developing new courses in the RCPIs regarding public–private cooperation.

Descriptions and Relations of Law Enforcement and Private Security

The participants in the national policy summit concluded that although private security and law enforcement possess certain similarities and are in many ways complementary, law enforcement and private security differ in some key respects. Training of law enforcement officers is substantially more rigorous than that of security officers. Standards and certification are also more demanding in law enforcement than in security. Of course, law enforcement has legal powers far exceeding those of private security. On the other hand, private security has the resources to develop specializations beyond the capacity of most law enforcement agencies, such as the protection of computer networks, chemical plants, financial institutions, health care facilities, and retail establishments.

The participants noted that in several respects, the line between public law enforcement and private security is blurred. Many retired law enforcement officials at the federal, state, and local levels migrate to positions in private security. Some

---

Major Organizations Involved in the National Policy Summit

ASIS International
1625 Prince Street
Alexandria, VA 22314
(703) 519-6200
www.asisonline.org

International Association of Chiefs of Police
515 North Washington Street
Alexandria, VA 22314
(703) 836-6767
www.theiacp.org

International Security Management Association
P.O. Box 623
Buffalo, IA 52728
(800) 368-1894
www.ismanet.com

National Association of Security Companies
1625 Prince Street
Alexandria, VA 22314
(703) 518-1477
www.nasco.org

Office of Community Oriented Policing Services
U.S. Department of Justice
1100 Vermont Avenue, NW
Washington, DC 20530
(202) 307-1480
www.cops.usdoj.gov

Security Industry Association
635 Slaters Lane, Suite 110
Alexandria, VA 22314
(703) 683-2075
www.siaonline.org

agencies themselves straddle the line. For example, the Amtrak Police Department is a private-sector police force with over 300 sworn officers. Many college campuses, too, have private-sector, sworn police agencies. In addition, many law enforcement officers work as private security officers in their off-hours.

The participants in the summit concluded that relations between law enforcement and private security vary considerably. Although the groups have much to offer each other, they are not always confident in each other. For example:

- Some police lament the lack of preemployment screening, training, standards, certification, and regulation of security officers.
- Some police feel that security officers receive insufficient training (particularly those who carry weapons).
- Some police view security officers as individuals who sought a career in law enforcement but were unable to obtain a position.
- Some police see private security as a threat to their domain.
- Police generally have little understanding of the broad range of private security functions, capabilities, expertise, and resources and therefore fail to appreciate the role of private security.
- Some private security practitioners view police as elitists.
- Some private security practitioners feel that law enforcement professionals do not care about private security until they are considering a job in that field.

History and Current Status of Cooperation

The participants in the national policy summit concluded that informal private security–law enforcement cooperation may have begun with the advent of modern policing, but there is little in the literature to document it. Certainly, formal cooperation has long taken place between the federal government and security practitioners in the defense industry. In fact, that interaction led to the creation of the American Society for Industrial Security (now called ASIS International) in 1955.

Later, when aircraft hijacking became a threat, police began to staff airport security checkpoints. When the staffing burden became too great, they handed the responsibility over to private security. The two groups remained in contact so that law enforcement could respond quickly to threats identified by private security.

From 1972 to 1977, the Law Enforcement Assistance Administration of the U.S. Department of Justice chartered the Private Security Advisory Council "to improve the crime prevention capabilities of private security and reduce crime in public and private places by reviewing the relationship between private security systems and public law enforcement agencies, and by developing programs and policies regarding private protection services that are appropriate and consistent with the public interest" (Hall 2003, 1).

In the early 1980s, the Washington Law Enforcement Executive Forum was formed to address problems facing both law enforcement and the business community in that state. In 1983, the Dallas Police/Private Security Joint Information Committee was formed. In 1986, the public sector–private sector liaison committees of the National Sheriffs' Association, IACP, and ASIS International formed the Joint Council of Law Enforcement and Private Security Associations. By 1989, the Detroit area had at least four formal cooperative programs.

In the early 1990s, the Federal Law Enforcement Training Center's Operation Partnership brought together representatives of law enforcement and private security operations from particular jurisdictions for three-day training courses. Upon returning home, they were asked to submit quarterly reports on the progress of their cooperative programs.

In 1999, the Bureau of Justice Assistance funded Operation Cooperation, which consisted of guidelines, a video, a literature review, and a set of partnership profiles, all designed to foster partnerships between private security and public law enforcement. The project identified the benefits of collaboration and described key elements of successful partnerships.

Incident management:
A national comprehensive approach to preventing, preparing for, responding to, and recovering from terrorist attacks, major disasters, and other emergencies. Incident management includes measures and activities performed at the local, state, and national levels and includes both crisis and consequence management activities.

In that same year, the Office of Justice Programs in the Department of Justice funded Michigan State University to study public–private partnerships for critical-incident planning and response. That project produced a best practices guide, *Critical Incident Protocol: A Public and Private Partnership* (Connors et al. 2000). With funding from the Department of Homeland Security, the university conducts programs across the nation at which representatives of public and private-sector organizations meet to develop mutual emergency response plans suited to their local communities. Through this Critical Incident Protocol/Community Facilitation Program (CIP/CFP), research is also being conducted on the elements of successful partnerships and associated partnership dynamics.

Currently, public–private cooperation takes many forms and occurs at many levels, ranging from national-level, mainly information-sharing programs (such as the federal Information Sharing and Analysis Centers, or ISACs) to local-level, operational partnerships (such as the approximately 1200 business improvement districts).

Cooperation may include:

- Informal, ad-hoc collaboration
- Formal partnerships to maintain good relations, share information, or solve specific problems
- Contractual arrangements in which government agencies contract with private security for services traditionally performed by law enforcement agencies
- Employment of off-duty law enforcement officers by private security agencies

Law enforcement–private security partnerships may be

- Encouraged or mandated
- Led by private security, law enforcement, or both
- Strategic or tactical
- Nonprofit organizations
- Local, regional, statewide, or organized in some other geographic fashion
- Well or poorly supplied with resources
- Supplied with their own paid staff, served by the staff of another organization, or operated entirely by volunteers

What Obstacles Keep Law Enforcement from Working with Private Security?

The national policy summit participants concluded that information sharing is difficult. Corporations do not feel they receive timely information from police, and they also fear that information they give to the police may end up in the newspaper. Police fear that the corporate sector may not treat law enforcement information discreetly. Other issues include respect (that is, law enforcement's lack of respect for security), trust, training differentials, and competition. A further obstacle is that the two sides may not realize the extent of their common goals.

Law enforcement executives know too little about private security. For example, when they speak about first responders, they refer to themselves, firefighters, and emergency medical technicians. Why not mention private security? In many emergencies, security officers are in fact the first on the scene. In many cases, security professionals are at the scene first and can show police and fire responders where to go. There is a lack of awareness of what private security is and what it does. Partly this is due to an absence of cohesion in security. For example, security is not always organized as a functional group within an organization, and security organizations tend not to train in mutual aid and usually lack communications interoperability. Sometimes conflicts between the law enforcement chief executives of neighboring jurisdictions prevent multijurisdictional public–private partnerships from forming.

What Would Help Eliminate the Obstacles to Cooperation?

According to the national policy summit conclusions, both parties have a responsibility for improved partnership. Law enforcement conferences host sessions on many of the same topics covered at security conferences: investigation of cyber crime, privacy rights, civil liberties, and so on. Presenters from law enforcement should speak at security conferences, and presenters from security should speak at law enforcement conferences. Aside from the cross-training benefits, the interaction would itself be another form of cooperation.

Law enforcement executives should learn what the private sector has to offer. For ex-ample, one summit participant reported that financial giant Merrill Lynch lent numerous computer staffers to the New York City Police Department to help with COMSTAT (an acronym for COMmand STATus Policing Method).

Security professionals should take the initiative to set up face-to-face meetings with law enforcement executives before a crisis occurs. Such meetings can help build personal relationships and trust. Police sometimes look askance at private security, yet in their off-duty employment they may be part of that occupation.

Each side should educate the other about its capabilities before a crisis, so that each will know when to call on the other and what help to expect (and to offer). Integrated training may break down some barriers.

The national professional associations may be able to present some models of cooperation. On the other hand, it may be best to let experiments be done throughout the country and see what works.

In a hypothetical case, twice a week a huge tanker comes through the port of a major U.S. city. As it stops to load up on liquefied natural gas, the government provides armed police, frogmen, helicopters, and other high-end protection against terrorism. However, when the ship is not there, the plant itself is protected by unarmed guards because the company is afraid of liability resulting from an accidental shooting. What is needed is a way to balance the competing interests—between the risk of one person being shot accidentally and the risk of a terrorist blowing up the plant and destroying several neighborhoods.

National Security Emergency: *Events include nuclear, conventional, chemical, biological warfare, civil disorder, terrorism, and/or energy shortages.*

What Is Going Well?

The national policy summit participants concluded that there may be more cooperation than people realize. The United States is home to more than 1200 business improvement districts (BIDs), which are a form of public–private cooperation. Law enforcement has shaped private security, in that many corporate security directors formerly worked in law enforcement. Some jurisdictions have public safety coordinating councils, in which businesses and law enforcement (state police, sheriff, local police, fire, emergency medical services) discuss solutions to crime problems.

EARLY PARTNERSHIPS

Discussed in this section are a few of the local, state, or federal partnerships that existed before 9/11/01. These early partnerships have served as the basis for the numerous programs that have been formed since 9/11/01.

New York City's Area Police/Private Security Liaison

The Area Police/Private Security Liaison (APPL) in New York City was formed in 1986. Its goals were to protect persons and property, encourage the exchange of information between the police and private security, and eliminate issues of credibility and misperception. In 1986 there were only thirty private security organizations involved. By 2007 the number of organizations had increased to over 1000. The APPL is linked with the Crime Prevention and Recruit Training sections (RTS) of the New York Police Department (NYPD). The mission of the RTS is to provide crime prevention services and programs to the citizens and businesses of the city, including, but not limited to, conducting security surveys, giving lectures, administering crime reduction programs, and providing various forms of outreach.

Since 9/11/01, APPL's mandate has widened and taken on new importance. Because New York is presumed to be a high-priority target for terrorist activities, both the NYPD and the APPL operate under a heightened state of awareness. Lessons learned from the partnership include:

- Security personnel need to pay special attention to employee and visitor identification, suspicious packages, and all entrances and exits, particularly those that are not commonly used.
- Give careful scrutiny to all vehicles entering the facilities and those parked in the immediate area.
- Review building evacuation plans to ensure they are up to date.
- Remind security directors not to hesitate to call 911 if they encounter suspicious packages, automobiles, or trucks.

The Law Enforcement and Private Security Council of Northeast Florida

The Law Enforcement and Private Security Council of Northeast Florida was started in St. Johns County in 1996. The council now includes organizations and jurisdictions throughout the greater Jacksonville area. The council was expanded dramatically after 9/11/01 and shifted its focus from private security companies to all individuals who serve in a security function. The other major change since 9/11/01 has been the present focus on information exchange among the members.

The council has established a council website and expanded its fax notification system so that messages are shared as quickly as possible. Council representatives now participate in the Local Domestic Security Task Force.

North Texas Regional Law Enforcement and Private Security

North Texas Regional Law Enforcement and Private Security (LEAPS) was founded in 1983 but lasted only a few years. In 1993 it was revived and has been active ever since. LEAPS offers workshops for the training academy and for in-service officers. Once a private security individual has completed the core training, the officer receives a badge that indicates the officer has received the training. LEAPS graduates can be "activated" in situations where the police need additional people. LEAPS partners have shown a propensity to share information, which has led to a number of arrests. Board meetings are open, so that any issue can be brought to the table immediately.

Awareness of National Security Issues and Response Program

The Awareness of National Security Issues and Response Program (ANSIR) began in the 1970s as the FBI worked to reduce the "vulnerability of United States persons, corporations, and institutions to intelligence and terrorist activities" (FBI 2007). ANSIR was originally designed to protect classified government information, property, and personnel. In the 1990s it was expanded to include a focus on private-sector proprietary economic information. After 9/11/01, it was expanded to reach nongovernmental organizations and their infrastructure. ANSIR programs provide services, including information sharing.

Overseas Security Advisory Council

The Overseas Security Advisory Council (OSAC) was created in 1985 by the federal government as a joint venture between government and nongovernmental organizations. One of its missions is to develop and maintain effective security communications and information sharing between the federal government and private-sector enterprises overseas, including private security organizations. Today, the OSAC consists of thirty private-sector and four public-sector organizations and has an additional 2300 affiliated U.S. companies and organizations, all of which are involved with information sharing. Currently, the OSAC has four major committees:

- Transnational Crime and Terrorism
- Protection of Information and Technology
- Security Awareness and Education
- Country Council Support

The OSAC's website (www.ds-osac.org) provides member organizations with unclassified information issued by the U.S. Department of State on security-related new articles, terrorist group profiles, significant anniversary dates, general crime information for cities and countries, locations of and contacts at U.S. posts overseas, and updates on new or unusual situations. OSAC also provides publications on all aspects of security.

THE NATION'S FOOD SUPPLY AS A TARGET

[The material in this section is adapted from National Institute of Justice Report NCJ 214752, "Agroterrorism—Why We're Not Ready: A Look at the Role of Law Enforcement (Rockville, MD: National Institute of Justice, 2006).]

In May 2006, the National Institute of Justice (NIJ) held a regional planning meeting on preventing and responding to a bioterrorism attack on the nation's agriculture industry. The meeting—which grew out of the NIJ's research project, "Defining the Role of Law Enforcement in Protecting American Agriculture from Bioterrorism"—brought together key law enforcement, animal health, and homeland security officials from nine Midwestern states.

Officials rated their state's preparedness in preventing an agroterrorism attack and discussed ways to improve the response, should an attack occur. One of the most vital topics concerned coordination among law enforcement and veterinary and animal health authorities, within the state and across state borders.

A New Security Paradigm

The paradigm for protecting the nation's food supply changed after 9/11/01, focusing attention on areas that require greater security measures. Research funded by the NIJ recommends that, to protect the nation's 2.1 million farms, the U.S. Department of Agriculture (USDA), the U.S. Department of Homeland Security, and other agencies work with local and state law enforcement and the livestock industry to develop a national plan to prevent, respond to, and ultimately recover from an incident of agroterrorism.

Terrorists seeking to strike a blow at the U.S. economy need look no further than the nation's heartland for a "soft" target. An agroterrorist attack could dramatically affect many aspects of U.S. life, including local law enforcement, which—especially in rural areas—is financially and strategically unprepared to respond.

Agricultural experts say that today they are most concerned about the intentional introduction of foot-and-mouth disease (FMD) into the food supply. Twenty times more infectious than smallpox, FMD causes painful blisters on the tongues, hooves, and teats of cloven-hoofed animals (such as cows, pigs, goats, and deer), rendering them unable to walk, be milked, eat, and drink. Although people generally cannot contract FMD, they can carry the virus in their lungs for up to 48 hours and transmit it to animals. The animal-to-animal airborne-transmission range of FMD is 50 miles.

The introduction of FMD in the United States—with its generally open and difficult-to-protect farms, fields, and feedlots—would require the mass slaughter of animals and the disposal of potentially millions of animal carcasses. It could halt the domestic and international sale of meat and meat products for months or even years. Based on the FMD outbreak in the United Kingdom in 2001, researchers estimate that an attack against the U.S. livestock industry could cost taxpayers up to $60 billion.

Because terrorists rely on a lack of preparedness, farm businesses should develop a plan for preventing an agroterrorism attack. The best way to prevent an agroterrorism attack—and the only way to contain one—must be created among local farmers, truckers, feedlot owners, and other critical members of the food supply chain. A working relationship between criminal investigators and veterinarians and animal and plant health inspectors must be established.

LESSONS LEARNED FROM 9/11/01

The Executive Session on Domestic Preparedness (ESDP), a standing task force of leading practitioners and academic specialists, in a joint study sponsored by the John F. Kennedy School of Government, Harvard University, and the U.S. Department of Justice, prepared a report on the role of the private sector in preparedness planning (Kayyem and Chang 2002). Part of the findings of the study concentrated on the reaction of the private sector immediately after 9/11/01. Findings from the study as reported by Kayyem and Chang (2002) are included in this section. A security manager designing security program for his or her private employer should consider what happened that morning.

Corporations near Ground Zero (such as Merrill Lynch, American Express, Morgan Stanley, Dean Witter, and Lehman Brothers) worked frantically in the first few hours after the attack to locate their dispersed employees. These corporations also attempted to return to business by relocating to satellite office spaces, pulling up backup files, and trying to stem the loss of revenues. Some companies that were affected by the attacks performed an extensive reevaluation of their employee safety strategies, facilities strategies, communication strategies, information technology strategies, and insurance coverage in the weeks following the attacks. Some of the things they learned are listed as follows.

- *Communications.* Communications plans should be in place in order to reassure, give instructions, and share information. Good communication is needed

One of the twin towers of the World Trade Center, in the background, before the terrorist attack of 9/11/01.

to prevent rumors and misinformation. New technology has made it possible for telecommunications to be an alternative for conducting business, bypassing the necessity of face-to-face interaction.

- *Leadership.* Management needs to review its emergency planning and practice executing decisions before a crisis occurs. Learning how to handle a disaster effectively is a management responsibility; consequently, leadership should familiarize itself with how to declare a disaster and how to appropriate necessary resources in response.
- *Transportation.* Many employees were stranded or unable to work after 9/11/01. Businesses that rely on transportation for critical functions were paralyzed: Overnight shipping was postponed, paychecks went undelivered. Commuting to recovery sites was in some cases difficult or impossible.
- *Geographic location.* Many companies affected by the attachs have chosen to diversify their geographic locations. According to TenantWise.com, an online real estate broker, only 17 percent of the 137,919 employees displaced by the attacks have returned to the area. Some Wall Street firms—Lehman Brothers Holdings, Cantor Fitzgerald, and Fiduciary Trust, among others—have relocated to midtown Manhattan. In all, firms based in downtown New York have moved 30 percent of their employees outside the city, many of them permanently.
- *Personnel backup.* Few companies had thought about succession planning, and those that hade, focused primarily on the potential replacement of top executives. Cantor Fitzgerald experienced one of the worst losses, with 700 employees killed as a result of the terrorist attacks.
- *Database backup.* Companies have learned that some redundancy in operations and processing is helpful. With the destruction of desktops, laptops, local-area networks (LANs), and other technology and data support systems, managers realized that paper files remain an important means of information storage and maintenance for work in progress.
- *Key dependencies.* Companies should understand their dependencies on key vendors. The reliance on extended enterprise such as suppliers and service providers became a problem especially when the shipment of supplies was delayed and manufacturing cycles were disrupted. Understanding dependencies can help to minimize the risk of a supply chain or service breakdown.
- *Security.* Both physical and logical security efforts should be reviewed, and the right amount of preparedness should be chosen. This includes, but is not limited to, the physical security of buildings as well as the security of IT systems.

These ideas about improving business continuity plans were mostly, if not completely, focused internally, neglecting how the government might guide or assist in contingency planning. Instead of collaborating with the government to assess risks, determine protection needs, select and implement cost-effective policies and controls, and initiate program tests, businesses made their security and emergency preparedness decisions individually. In other words, businesses concentrated solely on improving their own particular response when addressing safety concerns, mirroring how the government focuses on its own agenda for homeland security.

The study group characterizes the private sector response as follows: "The private sector people dealt like the government people, for instance, by putting more security in their lobbies. . . . But more needs to be done on the front of preparedness . . . and with coordinating with the government."

THE "TWO HAT" PROBLEM

If you were the security manager for a large company and tasked with designing an emergency preparedness plan for the company, would you consider the possibility that some of your key employees hold positions as volunteer firefighters or are members on the National Guard? Denlinger and Gonzenbach (2002) reported that the Executive Session on Domestic Preparedness, held at Harvard University in 2002, considered the problems involved when key personnel in private companies' readiness plans held an assignment in public service, such as being a volunteer firefighter.

The panel noted that whenever a large-scale emergency occurs, there is a corresponding surge in the number of activities requiring the services of first-responder agencies, a vast group that includes police, fire, emergency medical services (EMS), 911 communications, public health, emergency management, and sheriffs' agencies. Many first responders are public safety employees, but a significant number are private providers, especially in EMS and police services. Emergencies that cause a surge lasting days, weeks, even months or years are unusual, but they have now become more likely with the rising incidence of terrorism and the threat of deadlier, more powerful attacks. Thus, in order to deliver and sustain operations at an increased level of service, first-responder employers must have a "surge capacity" of personnel who may respond to such events.

Many public first-responder employers have developed call-up plans designed to increase the number of personnel available to perform the agency's mission during a disaster. Call-up plans generally assume that off-duty personnel will report to work when contacted, in order to expand the agency's capability. However, many emergency workers, particularly fire and rescue employees, work at more than one first-responder agency or are key members in their private employers' disaster preparedness plan. The panel describes this as the "two hat syndrome."

In a large-scale emergency, these workers might be called on to perform both jobs, that is, to wear both hats. Calling them in means they would have to abandon assigned duties at private ambulance services, local hospitals, or neighboring fire departments. Thus it narrows the pool of personnel for nearby volunteer fire departments, because in reality, each employee would be able to fill only one position.

First-responder agencies must therefore identify which employees wear more than one hat, gauge how critical each of those hats is to each employer, and consequently assess the region's ability to manage a disaster. In order to manage personnel successfully during a disaster, leaders of first-responder agencies must gather and share this information. This information is crucial to a reliable call-up plan, which must be tested and implemented. The recommendations of the panel thus included the following:

1. Assess off-duty commitments.
2. Determine impact on call-up personnel.
3. Share information across borders.
4. Develop alternative personnel solutions.
5. Test and implement.

The panel recommended that first-responder agencies and employers conduct a survey of their workers to reveal how many have secondary employment at another first-responder agency. Of particular concern is that extended breaks between long shifts have allowed many first responders, especially firefighters and EMS personnel, to make significant commitments to more than one agency. The "secondary" employer is likely to depend on the employee as much as the "primary" employer.

PSYCHOLOGICAL ISSUES IN TERRORIST ATTACKS

Terrorism is a preeminent mode of psychological propaganda warfare.

—*Robert D. Hanser (2007, 5)*

Fear management:
Comprises the programs that reduce the incidence of adverse psychological effects following a disaster.

History suggests that there may be even more psychological victims than physical victims in a terrorist attack. The Sarin attacks in the Tokyo subway system in 1995 engendered thousands of psychological casualties, in addition to a dozen fatalities and hundreds of injuries. Although the 9/11/01 attacks on the World Trade Center and the Pentagon resulted in thousands of deaths and physical injuries, the psychological casualties numbered in the tens to hundreds of thousands. An attack using a weapon of mass destruction (WMD)—a biological, chemical, nuclear, or radiological device—might produce even more extreme numbers (Pangi 2002).

Fear management comprises the programs that reduce the incidence of adverse psychological effects following a disaster. Fear management is, technically, "the mitigation of panic and the management of public response following a WMD or other mass casualty incident" (Connolly 2003), but should not be limited to waiting for the next attack. Effective fear management is built on an understanding of the potential psychological effects of a WMD terrorist attack. It is critical to anticipate victims' reactions so that first responders can plan accordingly. In other words, panic and shock would affect response operations and must be anticipated.

Many emergency management plans currently lack well-developed mental health components. There is a lack of comprehensive response plans for fear management. This translates to a gap in preparedness on the part of federal, state, and local governments. The psychological impact of a terrorist event need not cripple the community. The deleterious psychological effects of terrorism can be ameliorated if a well-defined mental health plan is incorporated into emergency response plans. Such a plan should include all the tools of fear management (Pangi 2002).

Recommendations on fear management of the Executive Session on Domestic Preparedness, Harvard University, include:

1. Address the fear.
2. Minimize convergence at the scene.
3. Cross-train.
4. Strengthen state and local resources.
5. Craft roles for victims and bystanders.
6. Intervene early and widely.
7. Broaden the definition of at-risk individuals. (Pangi 2002, 121)

VICTIM IMPACT OF NATURAL DISASTERS AND TERRORIST ATTACKS

The Office for Victims of Crime (OVC) of the U.S. Department of Justice and the American Red Cross conducted a research project on victim impact for both natural disasters and terrorist attacks. The information in this section was taken from their report (Office for Victims of Crime 2007). They concluded that many types of natural disasters, such as floods, tornadoes, and hurricanes, follow regional and seasonal patterns. These patterns provide some degree of familiarity and predictability for community victims, emergency responders, and disaster relief workers. When a major disaster is caused by deliberate human acts, sudden and unexpected threat, horror, and destruction inevitably affect innocent and unsuspecting people in the course of their daily routines. The resulting deaths and property destruction become reminders to many of their own vulnerability and their inability to keep their loved ones out of harm's way. When fostering terror is the goal, the threat of attack at any time and in any public setting is implicit and intended. Some of the impacts on victims of natural disasters and acts of terror are compared in the following.

THE FEDERAL EMERGENCY MANAGEMENT AGENCY

The Federal Emergency Management Agency (FEMA) has as its primary mission to reduce the loss of life and property and protect the nation from all hazards, including natural disasters, acts of terrorism, and other man-made disasters, by leading and supporting the nation in a risk-based, comprehensive emergency management system of preparedness, protection, response, recovery, and mitigation. For those who live in the Gulf Coast region of the United States, experiences with FEMA's rapid responses to natural disasters was unfortunately not the best. During Hurricanes Rita and Katrina,

The front page of *The Call Chronicle Examiner* newspaper in San Francisco on April 19, 1906: "Earthquake and Fire: San Francisco in Ruins."

Comparison of Natural Disasters and Acts of Terrorism and Mass Violence Crimes

Psychological Impact

Natural disaster: Separation from family members, trauma, evacuation, lack of warning, threat to life, and loss of irreplaceable items and homes contribute to disaster stress reactions. Property loss and damage are often primary results of a disaster; reactions are related to loss, relocation, financial stress, and daily challenges. Traumatic stress from a disaster is typically resolved in eighteen months unless the number of fatalities and serious injuries was high.

Terrorist attack: Mass casualties, threat to life, exposure to trauma, and prolonged recovery efforts may result in significant and long-term physical and emotional reactions. Higher rates of posttraumatic stress disorder (PTSD), depression, anxiety, and traumatic bereavement that can last a long time.

World View/Basic Assumptions

Natural disaster: Spiritual beliefs may be shaken ("How could God allow this destruction?"). Lost sense of security in "terra firma"—no longer believe the earth is solid and dependable. Loss of all illusion of invulnerability—realization that everyone is vulnerable to random acts of nature.

Terrorist attack: Assumptions about humanity change—that the world is secure, just, orderly, and that danger can be kept out. Survivors confronted with the reality that evil things can happen to good people. Resulting distrust and fear of people or being "out in the world," may cause withdrawal and isolation. Loss of the illusion of invulnerability—realizing that anyone can be in the wrong place at the wrong time.

Stigmatization of Victims

Natural disaster: Disasters tend to have greater impact on people with fewer economic resources because they live in more vulnerable, lower-cost residences that are less structurally sound and located in higher-risk areas. Certain groups, including survivors from specific cultural, racial, and ethnic groups, single-parent families, people with disabilities, and the elderly on fixed incomes experience greater barriers to recovery, causing double jeopardy and potential stigma.

Terrorist attack: Some victims may come to feel humiliation, responsibility for others' deaths, survivor guilt, self-blame, and unworthy of assistance—thus assigning stigma to themselves. The larger community, associates, friends, and even family may become distant to avoid facing the fact that crime victimization could happen to anyone. Well-meaning loved ones may urge victims and those bereaved to "move on," causing them to feel rejected and wrong for continuing to suffer. Hate crimes reinforce the discrimination and stigma that targeted groups may already experience.

Secondary Injury Impact

Natural disaster: Disaster relief and assistance agencies and bureaucratic procedures can be seen as inefficient, fraught with stressors, and impersonal. Disillusionment can set in when the gap between losses, needs, and available resources is realized. Victims rarely feel that they have been "made whole" through relief efforts.

Terrorist attack: Victims' needs may conflict with necessary steps in the criminal justice process. Steps required to obtain crime victim benefits and compensation can seem confusing, frustrating, and bureaucratic, triggering feelings of helplessness. Bias-crime victims may suffer prejudice and blame. Victims often feel that the remedy ordered or the punishment imposed on the criminal is inadequate compared to the crime and their losses.

Response Teams Involvement

Natural disaster: Local government emergency management agency leads the response activities; other agencies lend needed support.

Terrorist attack: Response environment often more complex, intense, demanding, chaotic, and stressful. Disaster impact area is a crime scene, which may limit the movements of responders.

Subjective Experience

Natural disaster: Expectations defined by disaster type. Awe expressed about the power and destruction of nature. Disasters with warnings increase feelings of predictability and controllability. Recurring disasters pose ongoing threat. Anger and blame are directed toward agencies/individuals responsible for prevention, mitigation, and disaster relief.

Terrorist attack: Victims suddenly caught unaware in a dangerous, life-threatening situation. Many experience terror, fear, horror, helplessness, betrayal, and violation. The event seems incomprehensible and senseless. Some view the disaster as uncontrollable and unpredictable, while others view it as preventable. Outrage, blaming the responsible individual or group, desire for revenge, and demand for justice are common.

many of the first responders were private security professionals. It is expected that in the event of a similar natural disaster or terrorist attack, private security professionals will play significant roles. Following are some steps that FEMA recommends for particular situations.

Evacuation Plans

When community evacuations become necessary, local officials provide information to the public through the media. In some circumstances, other warning methods, such

Disaster Alert

If you have advance warning:

- People come first. Provide assistance. Note needs of people with disabilities.
- Move or secure vital records/high-priority items if it can be done safely.
- Screw plywood over windows or use tape to reduce shattering. (Note: Taping windows to prevent flying glass is not recommended.)
- Verify master switch shut-off (water, gas, electricity) by trained staff.
- Move items away from windows and below-ground storage into water-resistant areas:
  - Flooding: Move items to higher floors.
  - Hurricane: Avoid areas under roof.
- Wrap shelves, cabinets, other storage units in heavy plastic sealed with waterproof tape.
- Move outdoor objects indoors or secure.
- Take with you lists of staff, institutional/public officials, insurance and financial data, inventory, emergency plan, and supplies.
- Appoint a staff contact to give instructions on returning to work.

After a Flood

- Listen for news reports to learn whether the community's water supply is safe to drink.
- Avoid floodwaters; water may be contaminated by oil, gasoline, or raw sewage. Water may also be electrically charged from underground or downed power lines.
- Avoid moving water.
- Be aware of areas where floodwaters have receded. Roads may have weakened and could collapse under the weight of a car.
- Stay away from downed power lines, and report them to the power company.
- Return home only when authorities indicate it is safe.
- Stay out of any building if it is surrounded by floodwaters.
- Use extreme caution when entering buildings; there may be hidden damage, particularly in foundations.
- Service damaged septic tanks, cesspools, pits, and leaching systems as soon as possible. Damaged sewage systems are serious health hazards.

(continued)

- Clean and disinfect everything that got wet. Mud left from floodwater can contain sewage and chemicals.

What to Do During a Fire

If your clothes catch on fire, you should:

- Stop, drop, and roll— until the fire is extinguished. Running only makes the fire burn faster.

To escape a fire, you should:

- Check closed doors for heat before you open them. If you are escaping through a closed door, use the back of your hand to feel the top of the door, the doorknob, and the crack between the door and door frame before you open it. Never use the palm of your hand or fingers to test for heat—burning those areas could impair your ability to escape a fire (i.e., use ladders or crawl).

Hot Door	Cool Door
Do not open. Escape through a window. If you cannot escape, hang a white or light-colored sheet outside the window to alertg fire fighters to your presence.	Open slowly and ensure that fire and/or smoke is not blocking your escape route. If your escape route is blocked, shut the door immediately and use an alternate escape route, such as a window. If it is clear, leave immediately through the door and close it behind you. Be prepared to crawl. Smoke and heat rise. The air is clearer and cooler near the floor.

- Crawl low under any smoke to your exit—heavy smoke and poisonous gases collect first along the ceiling.

- Close doors behind you as you escape, to delay the spread of the fire.
- Stay out once you are safely out. Do not reenter. Call 9-1-1.

THE GREAT FIRE AT CHICAGO OCT. 9TH 1871. VIEW FROM THE WEST SIDE.

The Great Fire of Chicago, October 9, 1871. Panicked residents flee from the burning buildings of Chicago.

What to Do After a Fire

- *If you are with burn victims, or are a burn victim yourself,* call 9-1-1; cool and cover burns to reduce chance of further injury or infection.
- *If you detect heat or smoke* when entering a damaged building, evacuate immediately.
- *If you are a tenant,* contact the landlord.
- *If you have a safe or strong box,* do not try to open it. It can hold intense heat for several hours. If the door is opened before the box has cooled, the contents could burst into flames.
- *If you must leave your home* because a building inspector says the building is unsafe, ask someone you trust to watch the property during your absence.

Before a Hurricane

- Make plans to secure your property. Permanent storm shutters offer the best protection for windows. A second option is to board up windows with 5/8-inch marine plywood, cut to fit and ready to install. Tape does not prevent windows from breaking.
- Install straps or additional clips to securely fasten your roof to the frame structure. This will reduce roof damage.
- Be sure trees and shrubs around your home are well trimmed.
- Clear loose and clogged rain gutters and downspouts.
- Determine how and where to secure your boat.
- Consider building a safe room.

as sirens or telephone calls, also are used. Additionally, there may be circumstances under which you and your family feel threatened or endangered and you need to leave your home, school, or workplace to avoid these situations.

The amount of time you have to leave will depend on the hazard. If the event is a weather condition, such as a hurricane that can be monitored, you might have a day or two to get ready. However, many disasters allow no time for people to gather even the most basic necessities, which is why planning ahead is essential.

EVACUATION: MORE COMMON THAN YOU REALIZE   Evacuations are more common than many people realize. Hundreds of times each year, transportation and industrial accidents release harmful substances, forcing thousands of people to leave their homes. Fires and floods cause evacuations even more frequently. Almost every year, people along the Gulf and Atlantic Coasts evacuate in the face of approaching hurricanes.

Ask local authorities about emergency evacuation routes and see if maps are available with evacuation routes marked.

During a Hurricane

If a hurricane is likely in your area, you should:

- Listen to the radio or TV for information.
- Secure your home, close storm shutters, and secure outdoor objects or bring them indoors.
- Turn off utilities if instructed to do so. Otherwise, turn the refrigerator thermostat to its coldest setting and keep its doors closed.
- Turn off propane tanks. Avoid using the phone, except for serious emergencies.
- Moor your boat if time permits.

ALWAYS EVACUATION GUIDELINES

Keep a full tank of gas in your car if an evacuation seems likely. Gas stations may be closed during emergencies and unable to pump gas during power outages. Plan to take one car per family to reduce congestion and delay.

Make transportation arrangements with friends or your local government if you do not own a car.

Listen to a battery-powered radio and follow local evacuation instructions.

Gather your family and go if you are instructed to evacuate immediately.

Leave early enough to avoid being trapped by severe weather.

Follow recommended evacuation routes. Do not take shortcuts; they may be blocked.

Be alert for washed-out roads and bridges. Do not drive into flooded areas.

Stay away from downed power lines.

IF TIME PERMITS

Gather your disaster supplies kit.

Wear sturdy shoes and clothing that provides some protection, such as long pants, long-sleeved shirts, and a cap.

Secure your home:
   Close and lock doors and windows.
   Unplug electrical equipment, such as radios and televisions, and small appliances, such as toasters and microwaves. Leave freezers and refrigerators plugged in unless there is a risk of flooding.

Let others know where you are going.

- Ensure a supply of water for sanitary purposes such as cleaning and flushing toilets. Fill the bathtub and other large containers with water.

You should evacuate under the following conditions:

- If you are directed by local authorities to do so. Be sure to follow their instructions.
- If you live in a mobile home or temporary structure—such shelters are particularly hazardous during hurricanes, no matter how well fastened to the ground.
- If you live in a high-rise building—hurricane winds are stronger at higher elevations.
- If you live on the coast, on a floodplain, near a river, or on an inland waterway.
- If you feel you are in danger.

If you are unable to evacuate, go to your safe room. If you do not have one, follow these guidelines:

- Stay indoors during the hurricane and away from windows and glass doors.
- Close all interior doors—secure and brace external doors.
- Keep curtains and blinds closed. Do not be fooled if there is a lull; it could be the eye of the storm—winds will pick up again.
- Take refuge in a small interior room, closet, or hallway on the lowest level.
- Lie on the floor under a table or another sturdy object.

What to Do After a Hazardous Materials Incident

The following are guidelines for the period following a hazardous materials incident:

- Return home only when authorities say it is safe. Open windows and vents and turn on fans to provide ventilation.
- Act quickly if you have come in to contact with or have been exposed to hazardous chemicals. Do the following:
  - Follow decontamination instructions from local authorities. You may be advised to take a thorough shower, or you may be advised to stay away from water and follow another procedure.
  - Seek medical treatment for unusual symptoms as soon as possible.
  - Place exposed clothing and shoes in tightly sealed containers. Do not allow them to contact other materials. Call local authorities to find out about proper disposal.
  - Advise everyone who comes in to contact with you that you may have been exposed to a toxic substance.
- Find out from local authorities how to clean up your land and property.
- Report any lingering vapors or other hazards to your local emergency services office.

Hazardous material (HAZMAT):
Any substance or material in a quantity or form that may be harmful or injurious to humans, domestic animals, wildlife, economic crops, or property when released into the environment. The four traditional classes are chemical, biological, radiological, and explosive.

Summary

- Terrorism is a difficult concept to explain.
- The first responders to the 9/11/01 terrorist attack in New York City were private security individuals. At least thirty-five of them died that day.
- Terrorism is a psychological weapon that is aimed at its immediate victim and also a wider audience, with the goal of creating a behavior change from that audience.
- Any definition of terrorism includes two general characteristics: the individual being threatened, and the meaning of the act is derived from the choice of target and victim.
- Special precautions should be taken when handling suspicious mail.
- Threat assessment refers to an assessment of a potential terrorist act as to whether it will happen, where it will happen, and expected damages and injuries if it does happen.
- The Department of Homeland Security was organized to protect the country from terrorist acts and to minimize the damage of a terrorists attack or natural disaster.
- The Department of Homeland Security absorbed many different law enforcement resources and organizations.

- The private security individual's role as a first responder is more limited than the role of the first police officer or other public authority on the scene.
- There appears to be a definite need for law enforcement agencies to build formal partnerships with private security organizations.
- The relationships between law enforcement and private security vary considerably.
- Although both groups have much to offer each other, they are not always confident in each other.
- Public–private cooperation takes many forms and occurs at many levels. Cooperation may consist of informal, ad-hoc collaboration, formal partnerships, or contractual agreements.
- Obstacles that tend to keep law enforcement from working with private security include:
  - Private security agencies feel that they do not always receive timely information from the police.
  - Police fear that private security organizations may not treat information as discreetly as needed.
  - Law enforcement individuals feel that private security individuals are not adequately trained.

- Law enforcement officials do not understand the functions of private security.
- The food supply is a potential terrorist target.
- Many lessons were learned from the 9/11/01 terrorist attacks.
- One problem in planning for disaster recovery is that many individuals holding key positions in private security or major companies also hold reserve positions with the police, fire departments, or National Guard.

- The psychological issues involved in terrorist attacks are significant. There are generally more psychological victims than physical victims.
- The impact on victims of natural disasters and terrorist attacks is different, and care should be taken to treat the victims accordingly.
- FEMA has the mission to assist in the recovery after a natural disaster or terrorist attack.

Review Questions

1. Why is it difficult for police and private security to form partnerships for homeland security?
2. What are the primary duties of a first responder?
3. What differences does it make in duties if the first responder is not a police officer?

4. What can be done to promote better police and private security partnerships?
5. What is FEMA's primary mission?
6. What should you do if you are the first to arrive at the scene of a fire?

Class Exercises

1. Have the class participate in a disaster recovery drill.
2. Have the class discuss how FEMA could better improve its response to disasters.

3. Have students make a list of potential terrorist targets in the community and discuss how to harden those targets.

References

Building partnerships between private sector security and public sector police. 2003. *The Police Chief* 70(3), 19–21.

Connolly, Charles P. 2003. *Journal of Homeland Security,* July, www.homelandsecurity.org, retrieved May 6, 2007.

Connors, E., W. Cunningham, P. Ohlhausen, L. Oliver, and C. Van Meter. 2000. Operation Cooperation: Guidelines for partnerships between law enforcement and private security organizations. Washington, DC: Bureau of Justice Assistance, www.ilj.org/securitypartners/Operation_Cooperation.PDF, retrieved July 6, 2005.

Denlinger, Rebecca F., with Kristin Gonzenbach. 2002. The "two-hat syndrome": Determining response capabilities and mutual aid limitations. In Beyond the beltway: Focusing on hometown security: Recommendations for state and local domestic preparedness planning a year after 9/11. Report of the Executive Session on Domestic Preparedness, Harvard University.

FBI. 2007. www.fbi.gov/hq/ci/ansir/ansirhome,htm, retrieved May 23, 2007.

Flynn, Stephen E., and Daniel B. Prieto. 2006. *Neglected defense: Mobilizing the private sector to support homeland security.* Washington, DC: Council on Foreign Relations.

Hall, Mimi. 2003. Private security guards—Homeland defense's weak link." *USA Today,* January 23, p. 1.

Hanser, Robert D. 2007. Psychological warfare and terrorism. *Professional Issues in Criminal Justice* (1): 3–9.

Kayyem, Juliette N., and Patricia E. Chang. 2002. Beyond business continuity: The role of the private sector in preparedness planning. *Perspectives on Preparedness No. 6.* Boston: Belfer Center for Science and International Affairs, Harvard University.

Metro Atlanta Homeland Security Advisory Group (MAHSAG). 2004. *Company primer on preparedness and response planning for terrorist and bioterrorist attacks*. Atlanta: Business Executives for National Security, Metro Atlanta Region.

National Institute of Justice (NIJ). 2006. Agroterrorism—Why we're not ready: A look at the role of law enforcement, NCJ 214752. Rockville, MD: National Institute of Justice.

Office for Victims of Crime, U.S. Department of Justice. 2007. Responding to victims of terrorism and mass violence crimes: Coordination and collaboration between American Red Cross Workers and crime victim service providers, NCJ 209681. Washington, DC: U.S. Government Printing Office.

Pangi, Robyn. 2002. After the attack: The psychological consequences of terrorism. In Beyond the beltway: Focusing on hometown security: Recommendations for state and local domestic preparedness planning a year after 9/11. Report of the Executive Session on Domestic Preparedness, Harvard University.

Scmid, Alex P. 1983. *Political terrorism.* Cincinnati: Anderson, 107–9.

U.S. Department of Justice, Bureau of Justice Assistance. 2005. Engaging the private sector to promote homeland security: Law enforcement–private security partnerships, NCJ 210678. Washington, DC: U.S. Government Printing Office.

U.S. Department of Justice, FBI National Security Division. 1996. *Report on terrorism in the United States 1995.* Washington, DC: U.S. Department of Justice.

U.S. Department of Justice, Office of Community Oriented Policing Services (COPS) and International Association of Chiefs of Police (IACP). 2004. Policy paper: Private security/public policing partnerships. Washington, DC: IACP.

CHAPTER 7

Investigating Crime

CHAPTER OUTLINE

OBJECTIVES

After completing this chapter, you will be able to:

- Explain the role of private security at the crime scene.
- Describe proper detention and handcuffing and suspect search procedures.
- Discuss issues concerning the use by force for private security officers.
- Describe the use of force continuum.
- Describe positional and restraint asphyxia.
- Discuss the role of private security in the investigation of crime.
- Explain the differences between gang graffiti and tagger graffiti.
- Discuss the protocol for security officers at the scene of a violent crime.
- Identify and describe the types of evidence.

> *With all these technological advances, the basic activities of the investigator have remained unchanged. He will construct the investigation around the establishment of the elements of the offense.*
>
> —*Charles E. O'Hara*
> *Gregory L. O'Hara*
> *Fundamentals of Criminal Investigation, 7th ed.*

S ecurity Officer Steve McGruff is employed by a local private security firm that contracts security services with several businesses and housing developments. Officer McGruff is assigned to the midnight shift. He is four hours into his shift when he pulls into the driveway of a business that he is assigned to check. Building checks are such a routine matter that McGruff can do them in his sleep. The routine goes something like this: Walk around the building checking windows and doors for signs of a break-in, check the building for graffiti or other vandalism, check the property for suspicious persons, and walk through the interior of the building making sure everything appears to be ok.

The business he is about to check, a computer software company, is located about fifty yards from the street and is well lit. The building is large, and it usually takes McGruff about fifteen minutes to walk around the entire outer perimeter. He has checked this business on countless evenings over the course of his three-year employment as a security officer.

As he parks his marked private security car in front of the business, he suddenly notices a reflection coming from the front door area of the business. He has a gut feeling that something is wrong. As he walks closer, shining his flashlight in the direction of the entrance, he sees the reflection once again, but this time the reflection is coming from the ground. He soon realizes that broken glass is lying all over the ground. The glass front door to the business has been broken out. Closer examination reveals that someone made entry into the building. Officer McGruff illuminates with his flashlight the front office that serves as a reception area. The front office is in total disarray. Desk drawers have been pulled out and emptied onto the floor, file cabinets have been opened and their contents scattered about. An eerie feeling comes over McGruff. He wonders whether the suspects are still inside of the building. Maybe he has interrupted a burglary in progress. He calls the security dispatcher from his hand-held portable radio and advises her to notify the police that he has discovered a burglary.

Because the potential is great for security officers to discover crimes or even interrupt a crime in progress, it is important that they know some fundamental investigative techniques, including how to preserve a crime scene. This chapter provides an overview of the role the private security industry plays in crime scene investigation, including suspect apprehension and use of force issues. Once a crime has been discovered, private security authorities usually relinquish an investigation to public police authorities. With this in mind, basic information is presented in the chapter about the role of private security at the crime scene. The chapter does not discuss advanced investigative procedures that will most likely be handled by the police investigators.

THE ROLE OF PRIVATE SECURITY AT A CRIME SCENE

A crime scene is a highly important source of physical evidence. The crime scene is usually also where forensic science investigations begin. Once it has been established that a private security officer has discovered a crime, several things should be done without delay.

The personal safety of security officers is of the upmost importance. If security officers are armed and feels that a suspect(s) is still present on the scene, they should unholster their weapon and retreat to a safe location where they can make constant visual contact with the crime scene, and then wait for the police to arrive. Police authorities should be called as soon as possible. Many security firms have communication dispatching centers similar to those of police departments. Security dispatchers should be kept apprised of the on-scene security officer's activities and observations so that they can relay the information to the police dispatcher. Security officers should relay to incoming police officers their exact location at the crime scene. Responding police officers should also be informed if the security officer is in plain clothes (without a clearly visible security uniform). This may prevent a security officer from being ordered to the ground at gunpoint by the police. If security officers move to another location before the police arrive, they should advise the security dispatcher or the police dispatcher. For safety, it is best for security officers to wait for the police before the suspect(s) is taken into custody. If security officers are in plain clothes (not wearing an identifiable security uniform), they should inform the police dispatcher of this and provide a description of what they are wearing. This will prevent incoming police units from mistaking security officers for the bad guys.

Security officers should record the time, date, and weather conditions when they arrived at the crime scene. This information should be written in the security officer's report and passed on to police officials.

Administering medical assistance to any victims at the crime scene is a priority, although any unauthorized access must be disallowed, because any individual present poses a risk of contaminating or destroying physical evidence. While waiting for the police to arrive, security officers should record all movements at the scene and any items that are moved or touched. Until the police arrive, security officers should take any action necessary to preserve and secure the crime scene. Once the scene has been secured, investigating police authorities will evaluate the scene and decide on the system for examination to be employed by the crime-scene investigators. This is discussed in further detail later in the chapter.

Evidence:
Anything that assists in proving or disproving a fact. Any object that can establish that a crime has been committed, or any object that can link a suspect to a crime, or can provide a link between the victim and a crime. The weapon used in a homicide is considered evidence that can assist in proving the crime of murder.

When a crime has been committed, all efforts are directed at recording the facts of the crime, identification of the offender(s), and their apprehension and arrest. The primary responsibility of security officers is to report the incident and secure the area until they are relieved by law enforcement authorities. Because security officers may be the first to discover a crime scene, they play an irreplaceable role in ensuring that potential evidence is not destroyed or contaminated.

Security officers must ensure that no personal harm can result from a hidden suspect. If it is determined that the suspect is still present at the scene and that immediate action is required before the police arrive, security officers should detain and remove the suspect as soon as possible. The search and arrest of the suspect must be done in a manner as not to destroy physical evidence that may link the suspect to the crime scene. If the suspect is apprehended in the area near the crime scene, he or she should not be returned to the crime scene. This will prevent potential contamination of the scene, and may prevent an altercation with a victim, a victim's family, or others who may be still present at the crime scene.

Security officers present at the crime scene boundaries should not smoke, chew tobacco, use the bathroom, eat or drink, move any items including weapons (unless necessary for the safety and well-being of persons at the scene), adjust the thermostat, or open windows or doors. The crime scene should be maintained as it was found. Items at the crime scene should not be touched unnecessarily. If a security officer

Crime scene tape is used to secure scene.

moves or repositions an item, this fact should be documented and reported to the responding police authorities.

Some security companies issue barricade tape to their officers. If this is the case, while waiting for law enforcement to arrive at the crime scene, security officers should place barricade tape around the crime scene to keep people away from the crime scene. The police can always replace the tape when they arrive if they don't like the way it was put up. Barricade tape is used for a variety of reasons and is designed to protect and identify above-ground hazardous areas or elements such as construction sites, work areas, crime scenes, crowd control scenes, and any potentially dangerous areas. Barricade tape used in security and police work is usually reflective bright yellow and plastic, with a large black legend printed continuously across the tape that reads, "POLICE LINE—DO NOT CROSS."

APPREHENDING AND DETAINING SUSPECTS

Security officers may discover a crime scene where the suspect is still present. As highlighted throughout this book, the safety of the security officer is paramount. There are times when a security officer will be required to detain a suspect for police authorities. This can be a potentially dangerous situation, especially in light of the fact that many security officers do not carry firearms.

When no other alternatives exist, and the security officer has to detain a suspect, it is best to obtain voluntary compliance from the suspect. In reality, however, it is impossible to predetermine suspects' reactions to being detained. They may submit peacefully, or they may fight violently for their freedom. They may even fake sickness or resort to other trickery, in the hope that they can escape from custody. If suspects realize that private security officers are detaining them, they may resist and attempt to escape, thinking that the punishment will be less than for resisting a police officer. This critical period from the time suspects are first handcuffed and restrained until they are safely turned over to law enforcement requires increased vigilance on the part of security officers. This is the time when suspects have the opportunity to decide what action to pursue, and they may attempt to escape or violently attack the security officer. Some basic guidelines for apprehending an offender are

- If possible, wait for the police to arrive and let them take the suspect into custody.
- Remain alert at all times.
- Always expect the worst.
- Evaluate the suspect's demeanor and physical conditioning.
- Maintain a safe distance during the initial contact.
- Give clear verbal commands to suspects. Tell them exactly what you want them to do: "Get down on the ground." "Place your hands behind your back."
- If you are carrying a firearm, stand with your gun side away from the suspect.
- After suspects have been handcuffed, advise them that they are being detained for law enforcement authorities.
- When placing suspects in custody, do it quickly.
- Remove suspects to a safe but secure place as soon as possible to avoid bystander interference.
- Notify the police dispatcher that suspects are in custody.

Handcuffing and Search

When handcuffing suspects, security officers should always expect the unexpected. For tactical reasons, security officers should handcuff suspects before searching them for weapons. This reduces the chances that suspects may attempt to grab the security officer's firearm or resist commands. Suspects' hands should always be handcuffed behind their backs unless a serious handicap or condition would make handcuffing painful or impossible for the suspect. Handcuffing suspects in the front increases the chances that they could obtain a potential weapon and perhaps inflict serious bodily harm. The more quickly suspects can be handcuffed, the less likely is a physical confrontation between the suspect and the security officer. Handcuffed suspects will find it much more difficult to put up a fight with their hands cuffed behind their back. After the suspects have been handcuffed, they should be told why they are being detained and that law enforcement authorities will be arriving shortly.

If security officers think that suspects may be armed, the suspects should be searched. Anything that can be used as a weapon should be taken away from the suspect. In addition to the usual assortment of guns, knives, and other weapons, pencils, pens, heavy buckles, and similar items should be removed. Some guidelines when handcuffing and searching offenders are:

- Handcuff first and search second.
- Maintain a balanced position at all times.
- Keep the suspect off-balance.
- Watch the suspect's head and shoulders for signs of movement.
- Keep verbal commands brief and clear (suspects have to understand what you want them to do).

Officer leading handcuffed shoplifting suspect to temporary security holding cell.

- Keep a tight grip on the handcuffs during the entire handcuffing procedure.
- Always expect the unexpected (be prepared for the worst).
- Check the snugness of the handcuffs to sure that prisoner can't get their hands out of them.
- Never handcuff yourself to a prisoner. This is a good way to get seriously injured or killed.
- Double-lock the handcuffs so that they won't tighten up on the prisoner.
- Place the handcuffs on the prisoner snuggly, but not so tightly that they cause pain or leave visible marks on the prisoner's wrists.

Security officers are responsible for the safety of any suspects until they are turned over to police authorities. Special care in handling suspects should always be used. Proper handcuffing procedures should be used to protect from positional or restraint asphyxia. *Positional asphyxia* occurs when the head and neck are turned or situated so as to obstruct the upper airway (interfering with the ability to breathe), and the reflex drive to right the head is dulled by alcohol, drugs, injury, or disease. This can result in death.

Restraint asphyxia occurs when one or more individuals restrain another, impairing the subject's ability to breathe. Mechanical impairment of respiration can occur in a prone (face-down) restrained position, or in other positions, by restriction of chest and abdominal movements necessary for proper breathing. Restraints in such situations may include a combination of handcuffing hands and feet behind the back

Positional asphyxia:
Most simply defined as death that occurs because the position of a person's body interferes with respiration (breathing), and the person cannot get out of that position. Death occurs because of the person's inability to breath. A body position that obstructs the airway or that interferes with the muscular or mechanical means of getting air into and out of the body will result in a positional asphyxia death, if the person cannot get out of it.

Restraint asphyxia:
Restraining an offender in a
manner that physically
restricts the body's
movement. The factor that
distinguishes a restraint
asphyxia death from a
positional asphyxia death is
that some form of restraint is
the reason the victim could
not escape the asphyxiating
position.

and with pressure applied to the torso, or laying a suspect prone for any length of time. These can interfere with respiration and result in an asphyxia death. Exertion and drugs can be additive factors in such situations. Security officers should use additional restraints as needed in the case of a combative offender.

USE OF FORCE

If at all possible, security officers should avoid confronting a potentially dangerous suspect. The best practice is to call the police, and move to a position where you can observe and report. Although security officers may encounter situation where they have to use legal force to take a suspect into custody, they typically have more limited authority than police and other law enforcement officers. Specific powers vary by jurisdiction, but they generally correspond to the police authority of private citizens. In most states, citizens may make arrests only when a crime is committed in their presence; suspicion that a crime has taken place is not enough. In some states, citizens may make arrests only for felonies, and then must immediately turn the suspect over to a police officer. It is wise for security officers who do see felonies in progress to arrest with caution. Unlike police officers, private security officers who accidentally take innocent suspects into custody are liable for false arrest.

It should also be pointed out that security officers may face further limitations to their police power according to individual state licensing or other regulation, where it exists. For example, the following authorities are listed in California's security officer training manual:

- As an agent of the employer, a security guard can question an individual on the employer's property and may prevent entry to the property by standing in the individual's way.
- Although a security guard has the power of citizen's arrest, a guard is not obligated by law to make arrests.
- A security guard should never touch a criminal suspect except for self-defense, or when necessary to use reasonable force in an arrest.
- If a security guard believes an arrested person is armed, the guard may search for weapons only. A suspect may not be legally searched for weapons unless he or she is actually arrested.
- A security guard cannot legally carry a firearm or baton without a state permit and a valid security guard license. (State of California Bureau of Security and Investigative Services 2002)

Reasonable Force

Private security officers can use the amount of force that is reasonable and necessary to detain and/or take a person into custody. You may ask, what is reasonable and necessary force? The amount of force depends on the specific situation. Suppose that a security officer is working in a busy shopping mall and is called to a clothing store to investigate the report of a rowdy customer. The security officer makes contact with the customer, who is upset over the clothing store's return policy. In a rage, the customer knocks over a display case and begins to walk away. The security officer tackles the upset customer and then begins to strike the unresisting customer several times in the head and neck with a baton. The customer begs the security officer to stop. After the customer is handcuffed and led away to await the arrival of the police, the security officer delivers several more baton strikes to the customer. Was the force used by the security officer reasonable and necessary? The short answer is no. The absolute guideline in the use of force is that only the minimal amount of force necessary to make an arrest or defuse a situation should be used. In the above fictional account, the customer was unresisting, and after the security officer handcuffed the suspect, he was no longer a threat. Thus, the additional baton blows were unnecessary.

So how do security officers know how much force to use? When the use of force is reasonable and necessary, private security authorities should, to the extent possible, use an escalating scale of options and not employ more forceful means unless it is determined that a lower level of force would not be, or has not been, adequate. For some time, police academies have trained police officers in what is referred to as the *use of force continuum*. The use of force continuum can serve as a guide for private security officials. Generally, the use of force continuum consists of six levels: (1) physical appearance, (2) verbalization, (3) weaponless strategies, (4) CAP-STUN (pepper spray), (5) impact weapons, and (6) lethal force. The use of force continuum provides a guide as to how much force should be used in a given situation.

The use of force continuum represents an escalation in force from the preceding level when a situation warrants such escalation. Each situation that an officer encounters is unique. Good judgment and the circumstances of each situation will dictate the level on the continuum of force at which an officer will start. Depending on the circumstances, officers may find it necessary to escalate or deescalate the use of force by progressing up or down the force continuum.

The officer does not have to enter at the lowest option on the use of force continuum. The officer can enter at the level that is reasonable to defuse the situation. If a suspect approaches the security officer with a deadly weapon, let's say a knife; the officer should meet this force by drawing his or her weapon and ordering the suspect to drop the knife. If the suspect fails to drop the knife and makes an aggressive move toward the officer, the officer is justified in using lethal force. It is important to point out that the objective is to approach each situation on the lowest level of the continuum as possible, in order to achieve the best resolution to the problem.

Pepper Spray

Many security officers carry nonlethal pepper spray as a defensive device. Pepper spray has for the most part replaced a type of tear gas referred to as Mace. Mace was once the choice of private security and law enforcement as a defensive technique; however, it has largely been replaced with pepper spray.

Pepper spray, oleoresin capsicum (OC), is a natural substance derived from the oily resins found in cayenne and other varieties of pepper. When a person is sprayed with OC mist, it induces an immediate and intense burning sensation of the skin but especially affects the eyes, causing them to slam shut, burn, tear, and swell. The mucous membranes of the nose, throat, and sinuses burn, swell, and make breathing difficult. Pepper spray has proven to be more effective compared to tear gas sprays. Once a suspect has been sprayed with pepper spray, it usually takes only a few seconds to work. The effects of pepper spray can last between fifteen and sixty minutes,

Use of Force Continuum

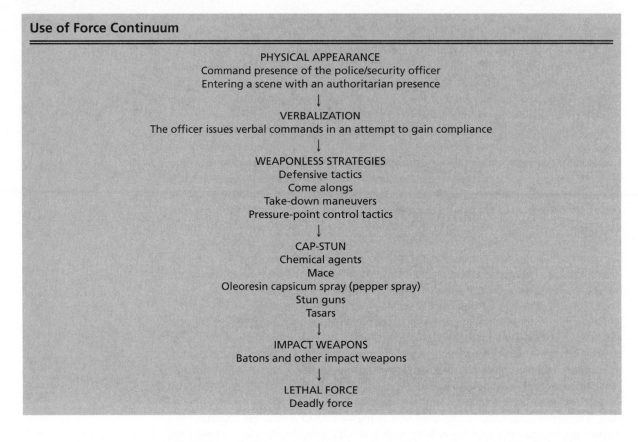

PHYSICAL APPEARANCE
Command presence of the police/security officer
Entering a scene with an authoritarian presence

↓

VERBALIZATION
The officer issues verbal commands in an attempt to gain compliance

↓

WEAPONLESS STRATEGIES
Defensive tactics
Come alongs
Take-down maneuvers
Pressure-point control tactics

↓

CAP-STUN
Chemical agents
Mace
Oleoresin capsicum spray (pepper spray)
Stun guns
Tasars

↓

IMPACT WEAPONS
Batons and other impact weapons

↓

LETHAL FORCE
Deadly force

depending on the concentration. Once suspects have been sprayed and taken into custody, their eyes and skin should be rinsed with water. If security officers carry pepper spray, it is important that they be trained in its proper use. Many law enforcement agencies require during training that officers be sprayed with pepper spray. The purpose is to demonstrate the effects that it will have on a suspect.

Tasers

Some security professionals have begun to carry Tasers as a defensive device. Many police agencies carry the Taser. There is some debate by police authorities as to whether electric Tasers should be placed in the use of force continuum. Some propose that Tasers should not be placed before weaponless strategies on the continuum because officers may get into the habit of using them on every suspect who resists, regardless of the severity of the resisting actions. In other words, there is some argument that Tasers should not be used as a compliance tool—for example, using a Taser on suspects who are running away or do not follow commands to raise their hands, turn around, or simply lie on the ground. On the other hand, there is some thought that as a matter of officer safety, the Taser should be placed directly after verbalization on the continuum. The thought here is that it will prevent an officer from having to engage suspects physically until they are in complete compliance. Nevertheless, Taser weapons are touted by many authorities as a safe, nonlethal alternative to using a firearm in a violent confrontation.

The Taser Gun at a Glance

The electric Taser is a handgun-sized weapon that can deliver 50,000 volts to an unruly suspect from distances up to eighteen to thirty feet away. Tasers fire small dartlike electrodes that stick to the suspect. The electrical voltage can then be administered by the officers. Newer versions of the Taser allow for neuro-muscular disruption without needing metal prongs penetrating the skin. Use of the device allows police to deal with unruly suspects from a relatively safe distance without having to resort to deadly force. There has been some concern over allegations of the effect that Taser guns may have on people with heart problems, as well as their potential use as torture devices and their effect on people under the influence on drugs. These concerns, along with a lack of independent studies on the dangers of the Taser gun, has led many agencies to allow it to be used only by special units or by supervisors.

Electric Taser guns are a relatively new defensive weapon. Because they are new, one problem is the lack of objective empirical data on the potential harm a Taser can cause a suspect. Most of the evaluations have been done by Taser manufactures and should be viewed with caution. Private security executives should make informed decisions when equipping their personnel with Tasers.

OFFICER SAFETY

Officer safety cannot be overemphasized. Security officers who find themselves in the middle of a crime scene where a suspect is still on the scene must always remember basic officer safety techniques. Controlling individuals at the crime scene is an important function of security officers. Like the public policing profession, private security work can be a hazardous profession. Private security professionals put themselves into potentially dangerous situations every time they check a building, apprehend a shoplifter, or encounter a suspicious person. Security officers must educate themselves about the dangers they might face and how to minimize those risks.

Security officers must be prepared to deal with a potentially dangerous situation as well as being prepared to defend themselves and the public from a suspect who may still be present at the scene. If there is a likelihood that a suspect is still on the scene, security officers should notify law enforcement without delay. Security officers should anticipate potential threats while waiting for the arrival of law enforcement. Will a victim's relatives turn in anger on the emergency responders? What kind of hazards can you expect? What is the anticipated time of arrival of the police? How big is the crowd that has gathered? What is the most immediate threat? Has the suspect indicated that he or she has a weapon? These and other questions must be considered and hasty contingencies developed that may allow the officer to overcome any potential threat that presents itself (Gardner 2005). Security officers can enhance safety by learning and practicing good tactics and techniques. The following are a few basic tips for security officer safety:

- Always expect the worst.
- Use your senses (site, smell, sound) to anticipate potential hazards.
- Secure your equipment when checking a building so that you do not announce your presence or give away your position to a suspect.

- Take up a secure position so that you can observe the crime scene. Don't engage a suspect unless absolutely necessary.
- If a suspect is still on the scene and immediate action is necessary, handcuff the suspect immediately in order to maintain control.
- If a weapon is taken from a suspect, lock it in the trunk of your security vehicle or in some other secure location until the arrival of the police, and then promptly turn it over to the police.
- If working in teams of two security officers, always coordinate your moves with your partner and keep him or her in sight at all times.
- If you carry a firearm, always stand in a bladed position when talking to a suspect. Your gun side should be bladed in the direction opposite the suspect.
- If you have to enter a darkened building, always be on the lookout for cover in the event you need to take up a defensive position quickly.
- Don't stand in front of doors. Never stand directly in front of the door when opening closets and store rooms. Open them in a position so that the least amount of your body is exposed.
- Use extreme caution when walking up stairs. Stairways present extraordinary dangers for the security officers. It should always be remembered that a desperate suspect has a distinct advantage when hiding at the top of a stairway. If the security officer needs to take cover immediately, there is only two ways to move, up the stairs or down the stairs.
- Move slowly and cautiously down hallways. If you need to take cover quickly when moving down a hallway, drop to a prone or kneeling position and retreat slowly.

THE ROLE OF PRIVATE SECURITY IN THE INVESTIGATION OF CRIME

The goal of any crime scene investigation is to identify, preserve, document, and collect evidence with the objective of identifying and providing enough evidence to successfully prosecute the perpetrator. The investigation may be as simple as a burglary investigation or as complicated as a multiple homicide investigation. Regardless of the nature of the crime, the methods for processing the crime scene generally remain the same.

Each crime has elements that must be met to establish how the crime was committed. The goal of the crime scene investigator is to identify the evidence at the crime scene that helps identify these elements and the suspect(s). Each crime has its own unique evidence to be looked for in the scene. The collection of this crime scene evidence varies, and specialty equipment may be necessary. The method for documenting the crime is the same in every case.

The role of private security in the investigation of crime is primarily to ensure that the crime scene is preserved as well as possible prior to the police arriving on the scene. In most cases, the public police have the mandate to investigate crime. Thus, the focus here is on the role of the crime scene once it has been discovered. What are some key objectives early on in the investigation or before the police arrive to take over the scene? Security officials need to be aware that simple little mistakes made early on in the investigation or after the crime is discovered can destroy evidence. Simply avoiding an unnecessary walk through the crime scene or keeping spectators from walking through the scene is of utmost importance in crime scene preservation.

As has been pointed out several times in this chapter, it is not uncommon for a security officer to discover a crime scene or interrupt a crime in progress. In the case of corporate security, investigators may, as a matter of routine, investigate crimes that occur within the corporate structure. For example, employee thefts and computer crimes are two such crimes that may be investigated by security personnel who are employed in the corporate sector. We address computer crimes in Chapter 8 and employee thefts in greater detail in Chapter 5.

The actions taken at the outset of an investigation at a crime scene can play a critical role in the successful resolution of a case. The treatment and preservation of the crime scene is vital to the identification and ultimate prosecution of the perpetrators. A crime scene that is handled in a haphazard manner can be detrimental to the successful resolution of the case, not to mention the security company's reputation. In the private security industry, reputation is important because it can mean the securing of additional contracts with businesses.

It should be pointed out that just because a crime remains unsolved does not indicate a deficiency in the investigation, nor does a conviction of the accused necessarily mean that the investigation was conducted in an intelligent manner (O'Hara and O'Hara 2003). "An investigation can be considered a success if all the available information relevant and material to the issues or allegations of the case are uncovered" (O'Hara and O'Hara 2003, 6). Many cases go unsolved simply because of a lack of evidence.

PROPERTY CRIMES

Property crimes include such offenses as burglary, larceny-theft, motor vehicle theft, and arson. The objective of a crime of theft is the taking of money or property, but there is no force or threat of force against the victims. Thefts that are classified as property crimes are committed outside the victim's presence. For example, a lawn mower that was left in the front yard overnight is stolen. A suspect breaks into a storage shed and takes items. A group of juveniles vandalizes a park bathroom by spray-painting graffiti on the walls. These are examples of property crimes. Security professionals are likely to discover property crimes. Security officers checking buildings may come across a break-in at a business or residence or a thefts of such items as lumber and equipment from a construction site. In the following sections we discuss briefly a few property crimes that security professionals may be likely to come across in the performance of their duties.

Burglary

The average citizen in the United States has about a one-in-four chance of being the victim of a burglary at some time. According to the FBI, the average property loss in a burglary exceeds $1000. Most burglars know that the key to success is planning.

According to the Burglary Prevention Council (a national organization dedicated to preventing residential burglaries), there are in general three different types of burglars: professionals, semiprofessionals, and amateurs (Burglary Prevention Council 2008). Although the average homeowner will probably not have to face a professional thief who focuses on extremely valuable items, security professionals should educate their clients and themselves about semiprofessional and amateur burglars.

Burglary:
The unlawful entry of a structure with the intent to commit a felony or theft.

A semiprofessional burglar may scout a neighborhood for up to a week, whereas an amateur burglar will spend only a few hours "casing" a residence. After selecting a target, the burglar spends just a few minutes burglarizing it. Wright and Decker (2006) found that the decision to commit a residential burglary is usually prompted by a perceived need for cash. In their study, ninety-five offenders reported that they committed residential burglaries primarily for financial reasons, and forty-three reported that they used the cash to purchase various status items. The most popular item was clothing; thirty-nine of the forty-three said that they bought clothes with the proceeds of their crimes.

Security officials should be aware that there are different types of burglary offenders, some not so experienced and others who have learned by their experience. Marilyn Walsh, in her classic work, *The Fence* (1977), set forth a typology of burglary offenders from the most adept to the least organized. The following is a listing of Walsh typologies:

- *The professionals.* These are skilled burglars who exhibit the characteristics of career criminals. These offenders plan their crimes and concentrate on lucrative targets because they earn their living by engaging in burglaries.
- *Known burglars.* These are not as skilled as the professionals, nor are they as successful. They may plan their crimes, but they are not as adept as the professionals. Their name comes from the fact that they are known to the police because of prior arrests.
- *Young burglars.* These are usually offenders in their late teens or early twenties. They do not plan as well as known or professional burglars.
- *Juvenile burglars.* These criminals are under the age of sixteen. They confine themselves to local neighborhoods, which are chosen by chance. Many times these juvenile burglars operate at the direction of an older fence or burglar.
- *Junkies.* These burglars are the least organized offenders. They wait for opportunities and quickly dispose of any stolen property to feed their drug habit.

Residential burglars are often young males who live near their targets. They are opportunists who look for easy targets. If the risk of detection is too high, the average burglar will not attempt to enter a home.

If security officers discover a possible burglary scene, for example, a door or window ajar, they should call the police without delay. Unless absolutely necessary, security officers should not enter the building until the police arrive, nor should they attempt to detain the burglar, as he or she may be armed. If security officers are in a position where they have to detain a suspect, remember that reasonable force must be used to make the detention and all safety precautions discussed earlier in this chapter should be followed. While you wait for the police to arrive, don't touch anything or attempt to clean up the mess. You may ruin or destroy important evidence.

Larceny-Theft

Theft:
The wrongful taking of someone else's property without that person's willful consent.

Theft is generally defined as taking without authority the personal property of another with the intent to deprive the other of the property permanently. Theft is carried out without the use of force, excluding theft during burglary or motor vehicle theft. Theft covers anything from picking a pocket to stealing a car radio to taking off with a bike left unattended. The terms *theft* and *larceny* are often used interchangeably.

Property crime rates appear to act as a kind of indicator of economic cycles. The National Crime Victimization Survey peaked the year before the two recessions of the early 1980s and rose again as the 1990–1991 recession ended, dropping steadily thereafter in the more prosperous economy of the 1990s. The FBI Property Crime Index peaked between the two recessions in the 1980s and immediately after the recession of 1990 and 1991. The index ticked up two points between 2000 and 2001 as the economy stuttered a little, with motor vehicle theft leading the charge. In 2006 property crimes decreased slightly, about 1.9 percent. Data are not yet available for 2007 or 2008.

The National Crime Prevention Council (2008) recommends the following to improve home safety and prevent thefts. Security professionals should educate their clients about these comprehensive theft prevention techniques.

- Organize neighborhood clean-up days to send the message that your community is closed to thieves, vandals, and loiterers.
- Ask the police to increase patrols of your neighborhood.
- Sponsor a Neighborhood Watch.
- Be sure the outside doors of your home or business have strong deadbolt locks.
- Keep spare keys with a trusted neighbor or nearby shopkeeper, not under a doormat or planter, on a ledge, or in the mailbox.
- Lock gates, garage doors, and shed doors after every use.
- Illuminate or eliminate places an intruder might hide: the spaces between trees or shrubbery, stairwells, alleys, hallways, and entryways.
- Set timers on lights when you are away from home or your business is closed so it appears to be occupied.
- Keep your bike and sports equipment inside the house when they are not in use.
- Avoid confrontations with burglars.

Vandalism

Vandalism is the intentional destruction of property. It includes but is not limited to breaking windows, slashing tires, spray-painting a wall with graffiti, and destroying a computer system through the use of a computer virus. Vandalism is a malicious act and may reflect personal ill will, although the perpetrators need not know their victim to commit vandalism.

Vandalism:
Malicious and intentional destruction or defacing of property.

In recent years, vandalism in the form of graffiti has become an increasing problem. Chances are that you have observed this trend in your community. Many neighborhoods are literally plagued by graffiti. Graffiti can have a disastrous effect on a community. Nationwide, it is estimated that graffiti clean-up costs upwards of $12 billion annually (Weisel 2002). This figure, however, likely underestimates the true cost of graffiti, because it does not include indirect costs such as "lost revenue associated with reduced ridership on transit systems, reduced retail sales and declines in property values" (Weisel 2002, 2). The costs associated with police investigations are not included in this figure either.

Graffiti can devalue property and can make citizens feel unsafe in their neighborhoods. Graffiti may be the result of idle juveniles out for a night of fun who decide to spray-paint graffiti on the side of the building. In other cases graffiti may be the work of gangs, which leave their mark on a neighborhood and provoke rival

Graffiti:
Illegal or unauthorized defacing of a building, wall, or other structure or object by painting, drawing, or otherwise marking it with words, pictures, or symbols. Graffiti is often painted on property by gang members, who use it as a means to mark their territory and communicate with rival gang members.

sets into a violent confrontation. Graffiti is how gangs identify and claim their "turf." A U.S. Department of Justice report indicates that 44 percent of graffiti vandals are under age eighteen, and of those, 88 percent are male. According to this report, the race of perpetrators generally correlates with their representation in the general population (Stahl 2000).

Gangs typically leave their mark in the form of graffiti on fences, buildings, sidewalks, and at times even homes. Graffiti can offer important insight and intelligence information about a gang. Graffiti may spell out a gang name, their geographic area, or a numeric identifier. It can sometimes show an entire list of gang nicknames, called a "roll call" or "roster." Gang graffiti serves several purposes, all of which are understood by other "gang bangers," even members of rival sets. Graffiti has been called the "newspaper of the streets" and communicates many messages, including violent challenges, warnings, as well as bragging about crimes that have been committed. Graffiti can also be used to show disrespect for a rival gang. For example, Blood sets may refer to Crip sets as "Crabs," and Crip sets may use "Slobs" in their graffiti as an insult to Blood sets.

Graffiti presents a rather perplexing problem for security officers. Security officers must discern whether the graffiti represents gang graffiti or "tagger" graffiti. The security officer should be able to recognize the differences between the two.

Tagger graffiti differs from street gang graffiti in that it is generally more intricate and more "artistic" than street gang graffiti (Gomez 1993). Taggers see graffiti as an art. The lettering may be entwined and turned upside down or sideways, to the point of looking more like a maze than letters. The graffiti that taggers paint on walls usually is done in several colors and may include caricatures of animals or humans. On the other hand, street gang members put up graffiti to increase

Walls in skateboarding area covered in graffiti.

their visibility, threaten rivals, and intimidate residents in the area. Their graffiti is usually much more primitive and sometimes more easily read than graffiti done by taggers.

If it is determined that the graffiti is gang-related, security officers should contact police authorities. It may be helpful for the security officer to attempt to interpret the meaning of the graffiti so that this information can be relayed to law enforcement. If graffiti is suspected of being a gang communication, don't allow the graffiti to be painted over or cleaned up until the police have had an opportunity to view it.

Sometimes gang graffiti is the first sign of a future act of gang violence, such as one gang invading another's territory. Security officers are often in a good position to recognize this and can take proactive action working with the police. Gang graffiti should be removed as soon as possible. The authors recommend that security officers develop sound working relationships with members of police gang units who they (security officers) can call and exchange intelligence information with on a regular basis.

Some gang graffiti can communicate grave messages. Gang graffiti that includes "187" indicates a threat to kill. "187" is the California penal code for homicide, and when used in street graffiti, tells rival gangs that those who painted the graffiti intend to kill them. Hispanic gangs often use the number "13." The "13" may be represented as "XIII," "X3," "13," or with the word "trece." Hispanic gangs tend to use the number "13" because the thirteenth letter of the alphabet is "M." This is significant because the "M" refers to the Mexican Mafia, and may also be used to designate Mexico, the homeland.

Tagger Language

Battle: A contest between crews

Bomb: Multicolored tag in large bubble letters

Buff: To remove graffiti

Crew: A group of individuals that tag together

Caps (fat/skinny): Spray can nozzles used to vary the style and width of paint

Fade: To blend colors

Fresh: *Really good graffiti*

Get up: To put up a large amount of graffiti tags

Graf: Graffiti

Heavens: High, hard-to-reach areas such as freeway signs and the tops/upper floors of buildings

Hit/hit up: To tag

Landmark: A prime location where graffiti won't quickly be erased

Mob: A whole crew doing graffiti on a wall at the same time

Piece book: A tagger's sketch book

Rack: To steal from off a store rack

Streak: Short for mean streak, a solid paint stick that looks like chalk and is used on dark surfaces

Tag banging: To use violence to defend a tag

Toy: A new, inexperienced writer

Throw up: One layer of spray paint filling in bubble letters that are outlined in another color

Wild style: A complicated piece constructed with interlocking letters

Yard/train yard: Gathering place

Zine: Short for magazine

Source: Birzer, M. L., and C. Roberson, 2008. *Police field operations: Theory meets practice.* Boston: Pearson—Allyn & Bacon.

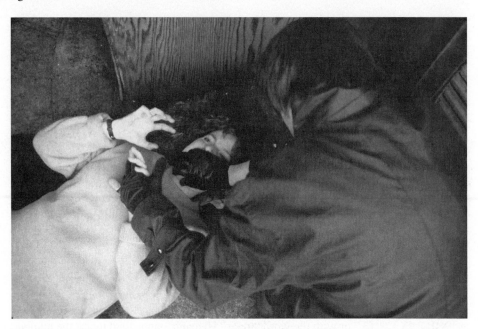

A woman being mugged.

VIOLENT CRIMES

Imagine for a moment that you are a security officer assigned to patrol several apartment complexes in your community. You have just left one apartment complex and are driving to the next complex. As you pull into the apartment complex, you suddenly hear screaming and see a young women running toward your security car. She begins frantically to tell you that her husband has been beating her. You notice that her eye is bruised and swollen and that her lip is bleeding. It seems clear that you have driven up on a domestic violence situation. In a matter of seconds, the victim's husband comes out of the apartment building and begins to walk toward you. What would you do?

Private security officers should be prepared for the worst while on security patrol. It is not uncommon for a crime victim to flag down a private security officer to report a violent crime. You may be surprised to know that often citizens don't distinguish between a private security officer and a police officer. They simply see the marked security vehicle or the uniform. Violent crimes are crimes in which the perpetrator accosts the victim and in some cases inflict bodily harm on the victim. Murder, robbery, domestic violence, and assault and battery are considered violent crimes.

It would be virtually impossible to provide a protocol for every violent crime that a security officer might encounter while on duty. In the following sections we provide an overview of standard operating procedures that should be adhered to regardless of the type or severity of the violent crime. As you will note, some of this protocol is the same as for property crimes as discussed earlier in the chapter.

Control and Secure the Crime Scene

One of the most important responsibilities of private security officers who encounter a violent crime is to protect the crime scene until they are relieved by the police. If a suspect is still on the scene, he or she should be detained. Handcuff the suspect and place him or her in the security vehicle or somewhere other than the crime scene. The arrest of the suspect must be done in a way that does not destroy physical evidence that may link the suspect to the crime scene. If the suspect is apprehended in the area near the crime scene, never return him or her to the crime scene, and notify the police of the location where you are holding the suspect. This practice will prevent potentially contaminating the scene, or an altercation with a victim, a victim's family, or others who may be still present at the crime scene.

Once the security officer has ensured that the suspect is no longer on the scene and that there is not a need to administer first aid, the crime scene should be secured. The security officer is responsible for scene protection until relieved by the responding public police units. Names and contact information should be obtained from anyone present at the crime scene. This will ensure that the police can follow up with these potential witnesses if they should leave the scene before the police arrive.

Persons present within the crime scene boundaries should not smoke, chew tobacco, use the bathroom, eat or drink, move any items including weapons (unless necessary for the safety and well-being of persons at the scene), adjust the thermostat, or open windows or doors. The scene should be maintained as it was found. No item(s) at the crime scene should be touched unnecessarily. If the security officer does move or reposition an item or touch something, that fact should be documented.

If a witness or another person at the crime scene turns evidence over to the security officer, all pertinent information should be obtained. Pertinent information includes what was turned over to the security officer as well as the name and contact information of the person who turned the item over to the security officer. The security officer should turn the evidence over to the police as soon as they arrive at the scene. The security officer should record the name of the police officer to whom the item was given, and the time. Following these steps when collecting or receiving evidence protects the integrity of the chain of custody. *Chain of custody* is a legal term that refers to the ability to guarantee the identity and integrity of evidence, from collection through to reporting of test results. It is a process that documents the chronological history of evidence from the time it was collected to the time it was tested in the crime lab.

The basics of taking violent suspects into custody:

1. Check for weapons. If any are present, remember to be aware of safety and that they are evidence. Firearms need to be recorded and unloaded (don't handle or dry-fire them!)
2. Remove from the scene and isolate the suspect. If necessary, stay with suspect while using any restroom facilities.
3. Do not let the suspect return to the scene.
4. Document the condition of the suspect—describe, photograph, etc.
5. Document the behavior of the suspect and record any spontaneous statements made by the suspect.
6. Document any injuries of the suspect and record the condition of the suspect's clothing. (Lee 2001, 53)

First Responding Security Officer(s) Duties at a Glance

- Immediately take control of the crime scene.
- Notify public police authorities.
- Detain suspect if still at the crime scene.
- Administer first aid as needed.
- Remove all persons from the crime scene.
- Determine the extent to which the scene has been protected. Obtain information from personnel who have knowledge of its original condition.
- Establish a perimeter to protect the scene.

- Continue to take extensive notes.
- Keep out unauthorized personnel. (When personnel who have no bona fide need to be on the scene insist on entering, record their names and the times they were on the scene, for court purposes.)
- Record all persons who enter and leave the crime scene.
- Maintain control of the scene until relieved by public police authorities.

Render First Aid

After the suspect has been detained, first aid should be administered to victim(s) or suspect(s). Emergency medical services should be called. All precautions should be taken when rendering aid to a person who is bleeding. If the security officer has been issued protective latex gloves, they should be worn when administering first aid. Wearing protective gloves will minimize the risk of direct skin-to-skin contact with blood or other body fluids and prevent exposure to a blood-borne pathogen.

If paramedics arrive before the police, they should be instructed not to clean up the crime scene and to avoid removing or altering items originating from the scene. The security officer should also record the names of all emergency paramedic personnel and turn this information over to the police.

Any changes or alterations to the crime scene that paramedics make should be carefully documented. Consideration must be given to the eventual reconstruction of the condition of the injured party before the administration of first aid. Security officers should point out potential physical evidence to paramedics and ask them to minimize contact with such evidence.

EVIDENCE

It is extremely important that private security officers not destroy or tamper with physical evidence. Often, it is through evidence that police are able to solve a crime. Physical evidence is any evidence in the form of a physical object. All physical evidence must be examined and closely evaluated for information that may assist in the identification of the suspect. The proper collection of physical evidence is required to confirm or disprove reasonable lines of inquiry in order to determine the causes of incidents. Physical evidence can prove a fact in issue based on its demonstrable physical characteristics, and it can conceivably include all or part of any object. In a murder case, for example, the physical evidence includes the body itself, the weapon used to commit the crime, pieces of carpet spattered with blood, and casts of footprints or tire prints found at the scene of the crime.

Class and Individual Characteristics

Evidence is typically considered to have class characteristics or individual character-istics. *Class characteristics* are traits or characteristics of evidence that cannot be traced back to a particular individual. Class characteristics are those characteristics that are common to a group of similar objects. For example, suppose you purchase a pair of New Balance model 767 running shoes. All New Balance model 767 running shoes have the same shape and the same tread design. These are considered class char-acteristics. Other examples of evidence with class characteristics include size, color, manufacturing patterns, or taxonomic classification (Gardner 2005). Glass fragments that are too small to be matched to broken edges and tool marks are also examples of class characteristics (Swanson, Chamelin, and Territo 1996).

Individual characteristics are those characteristics that are unique to a given object and set it apart from similar objects. Individual characteristics allow for the comparison of the evidence to a specific person. Put another way, evidence with indi-vidual characteristics can be identified as originating from a particular person. For example, suppose that for the past four months you have completed your daily three-mile run wearing your New Balance model 767 running shoes. Over the four months, your shoes have begun to show wear. The treads have begun to wear down, and they have developed pits, marks, and gouges. These pits, marks, and gouges are individual to your shoes, because no one else has walked over the exact same surfaces in the exact same way as you have in your New Balance running shoes. Other examples of individual characteristics may include but are not limited to fingerprints, palm prints, and footprints. No two fingerprints, palm prints, or footprints are the same.

Class characteristics:
Evidence that has characteristics that are common to a group of similar objects. Examples of evidence with class characteristics include soil, glass, and paint.

Individual characteristics:
Evidence that has characteristics that are unique to a given object and set it apart from similar objects. Examples of evidence with individual characteristics include fingerprints, palm prints, and footprints.

Associative Evidence

Associative evidence is any evidence that can connect a suspect to a crime (Horswell and Fowler 2004). For example, hair is associative evidence. Because hairs can be transferred during physical contact, their presence can associate a suspect to a victim or a suspect/victim to a crime scene. The types of hair recovered and the condition and number of hairs found all affect their value as evidence in a criminal investigation. Comparison of the microscopic characteristics of questioned hairs to known hair sam-ples helps determine whether a transfer may have occurred.

Associative evidence:
Any evidence that can link a suspect to a crime.

Tracing Evidence

Every person who is physically involved in a crime leaves some trace of his or her presence behind at the crime scene. This is called *tracing evidence*. No matter how much the suspect tries to clean up a crime scene, something is generally left behind. It may not always be detected, but it is difficult to take any kind of violent action with-out shedding something. Tracing evidence, though often insufficient on its own to make a case, may corroborate other evidence or even prompt a confession.

Tracing evidence:
Evidence that results from the transfer of small quantities of materials. Tracing evidence is usually in the form of small particles and includes such items as hair, paint, glass, and fibers.

Testimonial Evidence

Testimonial evidence is evidence obtained from individuals. Generally they are wit-nesses, survivors, or some other person at the scene who has knowledge of the crime. For example, a witness told a police officer that the suspect of a crime was observed wearing a red shirt with vertical blue stripes.

Testimonial evidence:
Evidence that may be presented by witnesses at a trial or other type of hearing. Generally, testimonial evidence is given by a witness to the crime or by an expert.

Fingerprint Evidence

Fingerprint evidence is one of the most common types of evidence that the investigator will collect from the crime scene. Fingerprint evidence can be in the form of a latent print (one that is invisible to the naked eye) or a visible print that you can readily see with an enhancement technique. Most fingerprints discovered at a crime scene will be found on paper, glass, metal, or other smooth-surfaced objects. Fingerprints collected at a crime scene, or on items of evidence from a crime scene, can be used in forensic science to identify suspects, victims, and other persons who touched a surface. However, the usefulness of fingerprints before any suspect is identified depends on two things: (1) the likelihood that the offender has prints on file (usually, the likelihood of prior arrest in the jurisdiction), and (2) the investigator's ability to search the files rapidly (Williams 2003).

DNA Evidence

Deoxyribonucleic acid analysis (DNA) represents a significant advance in scientific forensic evidence. DNA analysis allows scientists to compare genetic material from two different samples. It is important for security professionals and other public safety officials to keep abreast of these ever-changing techniques and methods in technology.

A significant variety of evidence can be analyzed for DNA. For example, genetic samples (physical evidence) such as blood, hair, tissue, saliva, and semen left by a perpetrator at the scene of a crime can potentially be analyzed using DNA techniques. Any type of organism can be identified by examining DNA sequences that are unique to that species. No two individuals (except identical twins) have exactly the same DNA sequence patterns, so if two samples (say, from a suspect and from physical evidence gathered at the scene of a crime) are identical, the suspect was definitely present at the scene. This is yet another reason why security professionals need to be especially careful to avoid leaving evidence of their own at the scene.

Summary

- Private security officers play an important role in the investigation of crimes. The primary role of private security in the investigation of crimes is to ensure that the crime scene is preserved as well as possible until the police arrive on the scene.
- By the nature of private security work, it is not uncommon for private security officers to discover a crime scene or to interrupt a crime in progress. Security officers should be well versed in the proper protocol to follow in these situations. Failing to follow protocol can result in injury or death to the security officers, the public, or the suspect, as well as contaminate crucial evidence.

- Security officers should record the time, date, and weather conditions when they arrived at the crime scene and any other pertinent information. This information should be passed on to law enforcement officials.
- It is important that any potential evidence at the crime scene not be touched or altered. If evidence or other items are altered, this fact should be documented and promptly reported to the police investigators. All persons should be removed from the crime scene as soon as possible to prevent the contamination of the scene or the destruction of evidence.
- If suspects are still present on the scene, security officers should restrain them by handcuffing

them behind their backs and securing them in the security vehicle or some other area, preferably outside the crime scene.

- First aid should be administered to injured parties, and emergency medical services should be called.
- Security officers must be prepared to deal with a potentially dangerous situation as well as be prepared to defend themselves and the public from a suspect who may still be present at the scene.
- If at all possible, security personnel should not approach a dangerous suspect and should wait for the police to arrive. The security officer should take up an observation point and observe the suspect's actions and promptly relay pertinent information to incoming police units. In some cases this may not be possible, and the security officer has to detain or arrest the suspect to prevent escape or to prevent injury to the suspect, victim, or public.
- When talking with or handcuffing suspects, security officers should practice good officer safety techniques and always expect the worst.
- Security officials should ensure that proper handcuffing procedures are followed to prevent positional or restraint asphyxia. Positional asphyxia occurs when the head and neck are turned or situated so as to obstruct the upper airway (interfering with the ability to breathe), and the reflex drive to right the head is dulled by alcohol, drugs, injury, or disease. Restraint asphyxia occurs when one or more individuals restrain another, impairing the subject's ability to breathe. Mechanical impairment of respiration can occur in a prone (face-down) restrained position, or in other positions, by restricting the chest and abdominal movements that are necessary for proper breathing.
- Only the necessary and reasonable amount of force necessary to restrain the suspect should be used. If Tasers or pepper spray, or some other defensive equipment, is used, it should be used in accordance to the policy of the security organization and in accordance with the officer's training.

- Security personnel can be held both criminally and civilly liable for using excessive force. Security officials should use the force continuum as a guide to how much force to use in a given situation. Security officers should be required to be trained on the use of force continuum. The force continuum presents guidelines to be followed on how much force is appropriate in a given situation.
- The protocol for securing and maintaining a crime scene until the arrival of the police is primarily the same regardless of the type of crime. Property crimes include burglary, vandalism, larceny-theft, shoplifting, and embezzlement. Violent crimes usually involve crimes against a person, including murder, domestic violence, assault and battery, and robbery.
- One form of vandalism that has increased in recent years is graffiti. Security officers should be able to determine whether graffiti represents gang graffiti or tagger graffiti. Security officers should be able to recognize the differences between the two.
- Tagger graffiti differs from street gang graffiti in that it is generally more intricate and more "artistic" than street gang graffiti. Taggers see graffiti as an art. The lettering may be entwined and turned upside down or sideways, to the point of looking more like a maze than letters. On the other hand, street gang members put up graffiti to increase their visibility, threaten rivals, and intimidate residents in the area.
- Evidence can be in many forms, such as associative, trace, fingerprint, and testimonial. Hair evidence is a type of associative evidence in that it can establish an association between a suspect and the crime. Tracing evidence is any evidence left behind by the suspect at the crime scene. Fingerprint evidence can be in the form of latent fingerprints or visible fingerprints. Testimonial evidence is evidence obtained from individuals. Generally, these are witnesses, survivors, or some other person at the scene who has knowledge of the crime.
- Evidence is typically considered to have class characteristics or individual characteristics. Class characteristics are traits or characteristics

of evidence that cannot be traced back to a particular individual.

- Individual characteristics are those characteristics that are unique to a given object and set it apart from similar objects. Individual characteristics allow for the comparison of the evidence to a specific person.

Review Questions

1. What is evidence?
2. What factors should dictate whether a security officer should take a suspect into custody at a crime scene?
3. Discuss the primary role of security officers at the crime scene.
4. Describe positional asphyxia and restraint asphyxia.
5. Describe and give examples of class characteristics and individual characteristics.
6. Identify the six elements of the use of force continuum.
7. Identify a few basic tips for security officer safety.
8. What do gangs use graffiti for?
9. Define trace evidence.
10. Define the crime of burglary.
11. What are the three types of burglars according to the Burglary Prevention Council?

Class Exercises

1. In small groups, using the use of force continuum as a guide, discuss the amount of force that private security officers can use if the suspect threatens them with a knife.
2. Taser weapons are increasingly being issued to both public law enforcement officers and private security officers. In small groups, discuss some of the problems that center on the Taser.
3. Drive to an area of your community that is known for graffiti. Can you distinguish tagger graffiti from gang graffiti? (Conduct this exercise safely. Remain in your car to observe the graffiti, and leave the area at the first sign of trouble.) Report your finding back to the class.
4. Interview one or more security officers in your community. Ask them about the amount of training they received on the use of force. Ask specifically about their training in avoiding positional and restraint asphyxia. Discuss your findings with other students in class.
5. Imagine that you are a security officer who has encountered a burglary in progress. In small groups, discuss what you would do.

References

Burglary Prevention Council. 2008. *Understanding the burglar.* Burglary Prevention Council, www.burglaryprevention.org.

Gardner, R. M. 2005. *Practical crime scene processing and investigation.* New York: CRC Press.

Gomez, M. 1993. The writing on our walls: Finding solutions from distinguishing graffiti art from graffiti vandalism. *University of Michigan Journal of Law Reform* 26: 633–708.

Horswell, J., and C. Fowler. 2004. Associative evidence: The Locard exchange principle. In *The practice of crime scene investigation,* ed. J. Horswell, 47–55. London: CRC Press.

Lee, H. C. 2001. *Henry Lee's crime scene handbook.* New York: Academic Press.

O'Hara, C. E., and G. L. O'Hara. 2003. *Criminal investigation,* 7th ed. Springfield, IL: Charles C. Thomas.

National Crime Prevention Council. 2008. *Home safety.* Arlington, VA: National Crime Prevention Council, www.ncpc.org.

Stahl, A. L. 2000. Juvenile vandalism. OJJDP factsheet. U.S. Department of Justice, www.ojjdp.usdoj.gov, retrieved November 12, 2007.

State of California Bureau of Security and Investigative Services 2002. *Power to arrest training manual.* West Sacramento, CA: State of California Bureau of Security and Investigative Services.

Swanson, C. R., N. C. Chamelin, and L. Territo. 1996. *Criminal investigation,* 6th ed. New York: McGraw-Hill.

Walsh, M. E. 1977. *The fence: A new look at the world of property theft.* Westport, CT: Greenwood Press.

Weisel, D. L. 2002. *Graffiti.* Problem-Oriented Guides for Police Series, No. 9. U.S. Department of Justice, www.cops.usdoj.gov, retrieved November 11, 2007.

Williams, G. L. 2003. Criminal investigations. In *Local government police management,* 4th ed., ed. W. A. Geller and D. W. Stephens, 169–205. Washington, DC: International City Managers Association.

Wright, R. T., and S. H. Decker. 2006. Deciding to commit a burglary. In *In their own words,* ed. P. Cromwell, 90–101. Los Angeles: Roxbury.

CHAPTER 8

Computer and Network Security

CHAPTER OUTLINE

OBJECTIVES

After completing this chapter, you will be able to:

- Identify and discuss the problems of keeping the information infrastructure secure.
- Discuss why the information infrastructure is a prime target for terrorism.
- Explain the necessary steps in establishing a data security system.
- Describe the rationale for using passwords and explain how to secure them.
- Discuss the importance of auditing data security systems.
- List the steps that should be taken before hardware is sent out for repair.
- Define cracking and explain why it is a problem.
- Discuss the essential steps involved in internal auditing of a data system.
- Explain why management needs to be involved in the security system.

In this chapter, we will explore the issues involved in keeping information infra-structures, which includes networks and computers, secure from unauthorized access and or modifications. In any present-day discussion of network and computer security, terrorist issues must be considered. Accordingly, there is some overlap between the discussion of terrorism in this chapter and that in Chapter 6. Our information infrastructures are an inviting target for terrorists. Most problems and attacks on business computers and networks, however, will probably arise from individuals trying to gain an unfair economic advantage, or a theft or malicious act, rather than a terrorist act. Whatever the motive, an attack from any source can create havoc in a company's information system.

According to the Institute for Information Infrastructure (2003), the information infrastructure, taken as a whole, is not an engineered system. It is the result of the entrepreneurial efforts and the collective genius of individuals and companies working to improve efficiency and provide new opportunities for themselves. The institute contends that security was not a significant consideration at its inception, and that even today, security concerns do not override market pressures for new uses of technology or innovation, despite the frequent incidents of hackers, criminals, and, increasingly, terrorists and nations using or planning to use the information infrastructure as a weapon to harm the United States.

The institute states that wireless technologies are increasingly crucial to enterprise systems and across critical infrastructure sectors. Their definition of wireless networks include not only wireless telecommunications but an increasingly diverse set of end devices, such as computers, sensors, process controllers, and information appliances for home and business users; in many cases, end devices also provide wireless telecommunications services.

In principle, many of the security concerns about wireless networks mirror those of the wired world; in practice, solutions developed for wired networks may not be viable in wireless environments. According to the institute, research is needed to make security a fundamental component of all wireless networks, develop the basic science of wireless security, develop security solutions that can be integrated into the wireless device itself, investigate the security implications of existing wireless protocols, integrate security mechanisms across all protocol layers, and integrate wireless security into larger systems and networks. In particular, the institute contends that research is needed into security situation awareness techniques for wireless networks and strategies to address distributed denial-of-service attacks.

COMPUTER-ASSISTED MISCONDUCT

Almost three-fourths of businesses responding to a BJS [Bureau of Justice Statistics] pilot survey said they had been victimized by cyber-crime. Computer virus infections were the most common form of attack (64 percent), followed by denial of service incidents (25 percent) and vandalism or sabotage (19 percent). Among the companies that detected a computer virus, less than 6 percent said they notified a law enforcement agency.

Department of Homeland Security (2007)

The computer has changed the capability of management to store, retrieve, and use data. It also has provided new opportunities to misuse that information. The types of misconduct accomplished using a computer are little different from those committed without the use of a computer. The computer, however, enhances a person's ability to commit misconduct a thousandfold. Most studies conclude that computer-assisted misconduct is the fastest-growing white-collar crime in business. In addition, careless employees can significantly damage a business by accidental destruction or erroneous input of data. In this section, we focus on how to prevent employee misconduct as well as careless errors in using computer systems.

Viruses:
Programs with the ability to replicate and install themselves, or infect, a computer without the computer user's knowledge or authorization.

Some of the innovations provided by computers are that the electronic information is not limited by physical distance and can be transmitted thousands of miles in a matter of milliseconds. In many cases the data also may be accessed without being physically present. The volume of data is enormous and can be contained on disks or tapes that can fit in small packages. For example, you can capture gigabytes of information on a flash drive, put it in your pocket, and carry it home without fear of detection. Another problem is that many transgressions into the system are invisible.

In establishing a security system, a total data and network security concept should be used, not just computer security. The total system should at least include physical security of the workplace, the hardware, the network, the data storage devices, and the software. The planning and implementation of a security system is a continuous process.

A high percentage of networks have been attacked in one form or another. Some companies experience attacks on their systems daily. Contrary to popular belief, many attacks are committed by employees rather than by outsiders. The abusers are motivated by personal gain, misguided playfulness, ignorance, or maliciousness or revenge. Most of the attempts or attacks are not publicly reported. Most are detected by accident rather than by security or audit personnel. A general concern by researchers in this area is that many abuses are not detected at all.

Criminal justice professionals traditionally have used profiles to help identify persons who may be prone to different types of misconduct. The most famous was the "skyjacker" profile used in the 1970s in an attempt to identify potential airplane skyjackers. One common problem with the use of profiles in detecting criminal misconduct is the tendency to place too much emphasis on them. They are at most guesses, and many times the criminal does not fit the profile or an innocent person does, a fact the Federal Aviation Administration discovered when a black male who was searched at an airport because he fit the profile of a skyjacker turned out to be a member of the U.S. Congress.

According to the profile, the typical computer criminal is well educated, has not been previously involved in criminal activity, is relatively young compared with fellow employees (average age is 29), has the knowledge and ability to grasp computer systems quickly, is willing to take risks, is a disgruntled employee who feels that he or she is not receiving his or her just due, is an employee with serious personal problems, or is an extremely ambitious person.

The above conclusions are the result of many studies dealing with computer-assisted misconduct. This profile should not be relied on as a guide as to which employees will commit misconduct when given the opportunity. Regarding the negligent employee, if he or she is careless in performing other job-related tasks, normally the same personal trait will be present when that employee is using the computer system.

DATA AND NETWORK SECURITY PROGRAMS

For a data and network security program to be successful, management must feel the need for it and have the desire to establish and continually monitor it. There is no room for apathy in security. Each member of the management team must be convinced that he or she has a vested interest in preventing computer-assisted misconduct in order for the program to work.

The variables in computer-assisted misconduct and employee negligence involved in a computer information system include the number of people who have access to the computer system, the number of entry or access terminals in the system, and the degree of security management imposed within the system. There are no easy solutions to security management, nor is any system safe from abuse.

Employees are the most critical link in any security management program. Accordingly, much depends on the integrity and morale of the persons involved with the system. For the program to be successful, any controls established must be adhered to by all persons involved.

The security program should provide the following:

1. Protection against unauthorized disclosure of sensitive data
2. Protection against unauthorized data destruction
3. Protection against misuse of data
4. Protection against data changes or movement
5. Protection against destruction, theft, or misuse of physical assets (hardware)
6. Contingency plans to ensure that backup procedures are available when abuses are discovered in the system or if the data are destroyed because of fire or other natural catastrophe
7. Fidelity bonding of personnel involved with the security management system, to reimburse the business for any losses sustained from computer-assisted misconduct. Bonding employees can be a psychological deterrent to misconduct. Employees should be told that they are bonded, that this is a privilege, and thus a badge of honor. Employees also should be advised of the problems that can occur if the bonding company is required to pay because of their misconduct.

Cyberterrorism:
Computer-based attack or threat of attack intended to intimidate or coerce government or societies in pursuit of goals that are political, religious, or ideological.

Data Security Management Personnel

Most businesses with in-house computer systems do not assign the duty of monitoring data security to a specific person. To deter computer-assisted misconduct, a data security manager should be assigned, at least on a part-time basis, as the data and network system security person. The more the data system security manager knows about the system, its procedures, hardware, the network, and data entry routines, the less vulnerable the system will be to misconduct. The security manager, however, should not be someone whose primary responsibility involves data management. The person who supervises the data system should never be the one trusted with monitoring its security. One proven key to a successful security program is division of responsibility.

The functions of a security manager are to evaluate the risks involved, develop policy to minimize those risks, and monitor adherence to the security policy. The security manager must be able to get along with associates, because he or she will in effect be looking over their shoulders. And because the program must be sold to fellow employees and managers, excellent communication skills also are essential.

Assignment of an alternate data security manager may also be appropriate. In addition, administrative or clerical personnel support must be made available to the data security manager; it is not cost-effective to have a manager performing routine administrative or clerical duties.

All personnel involved with data input and retrieval should be made aware that it is their duty to observe and point out any unusual activities to the data security manager. Data security responsibilities should be listed as a part of the job description of all employees associated with the system.

Cyberwars:
Disruption to the flow of information, principally through computer viruses that eat data or freeze up systems and logic bombs that force machines to try to do something they can't.

Organizing the Data Security System

The first phase of planning a security system should be directed toward determining its overall structure. The use of an organizational chart with dotted lines for data security management is highly recommended. If the data security program is to be successful, top management must be actively involved. Accordingly, top management should sign the company directives or policy statements that establish the data security system. Because no two companies are the same, the security system must be tailored for each specific company.

Plan the security program in phases. In the first phase, imagine a worst-case situation to determine what types of damages the business might suffer as the result of computer-assisted misconduct or employee negligence. This is the time to brainstorm and use your imagination to determine what a person could do to or with the data or system. For purposes of this phase, consider that any person involved in computer-assisted misconduct will be an expert, will know the system, and will be lucky. Also consider that a negligent employee will commit gross errors and will do everything wrong. For example on June 21, 2007, an employee of United Airlines, while performing a test, corrupted the company's computer system and shut down its flight operations for about two hours, which turned out to be very costly for the airline. Such scenarios will give you a true worst-possible-case situation and will provide the guidelines to use in determining the amount of effort and expense that should be spent to protect the information system.

In the second phase of planning the security system, determine the value of the data, information, and so on, to the organization, and the problems that will be encountered should this data be entered incorrectly, modified, damaged, erased, or deliberately manipulated. For example, how much damage will the company incur if data are made known to its closest competitor or to the public? What will be the financial loss to the company if the data are modified improperly? How much will it cost to retrieve the data if the files and records are destroyed or modified? What problems will be involved if the data is incorrectly entered, modified, or erased? Answering questions such as these will give you a good evaluation of the information system to use as a basis in determining how much time and effort to spend on protecting it.

The third phase of planning a data security system should be to indoctrinate all employees involved with the system, including top management. As noted earlier, to be successful, the security program must be supported by all. The natural resistance to change must be overcome. This resistance may be reduced by conducting discussions with key employees during the formulation phase of the data security program. The security indoctrination should include at minimum:

1. The sensitive nature of the data involved and the implications of misuse of that data
2. A description of the data security program and illustrations of its application
3. Alternatives for protection of the data and why the selected procedures were selected
4. An explanation of procedures for security of the data and the requirements to comply with the established rules
5. The necessity to report to the data security manager and to a supervisor any deviations observed by anyone

A recognition awards plan for employees who make useful recommendations for improving the program should be instituted and discussed with employees during the indoctrination phase.

The security program should include access control procedures that ensure that only designated persons have access to the use of a computer or to the use of specific data in the computer memory. The two most common methods to limit access are by the use of passwords and physical access controls.

Cryptography:
The art and science of "secret writing," through which the meanings of messages are concealed from unintended recipients. The actual method of concealing a message, or plaintext, as it is commonly referred to, is called enciphering or encryption.

Passwords

Most computer security systems use passwords for protection. The following steps should be followed when using a password system:

1. Personnel must be motivated to protect and not allow unauthorized persons to obtain the password. Employees are best motivated with positive training that stresses the need to prevent compromise of passwords.
2. Passwords should be modified at frequent intervals, at least once every three months.
3. Passwords should be easy to remember so that passwords users will not have to write them down. Password users should make up their own passwords so they mean something to them. In this latter regard, don't use obviously known words. Never use first names, initials, or names spelled backward as a password. Also, do not use curse words. Research has indicated that curse words are some of the first ones tried by people trying to break the code. Microsoft has a site where you can check the strength of a password (www.microsoft.com/protect/yourself/password/checker.mspx).
4. A record of the passwords is required in case of the unavailability of the principal user of the data. This record should be maintained only by top management and should be placed in an inviolable container to ensure that no unauthorized person has access to it unless approved by top management. Keep a record of any use of the password by other than the primary user.
5. Passwords should be entered without observation by unauthorized persons and should not be displayed on the terminal. Most computer software is designed to

blank out passwords. If your current programs do not do this, have them adapted or change software.

6. If feasible, use different passwords for the computer system and the database. If different databases reside on the same computer, use different passwords for each one, thus limiting its use to only the people who need to use it. If only one or two people enter data but others need to view it, make use of a special password for those people who are authorized to enter or modify the data.

7. Program the computer to record unsuccessful password attempts. This will alert you to possible unauthorized attempts to gain entry into the database. To prevent computer hackers from breaking the system with random attempts, the software should be programmed to shut down the computer after three unsuccessful attempts to enter the correct password.

8. Access to the password should depend on the degree of security needed for the data. There should be tighter control over the access passwords to company financial data than for a database containing less sensitive information.

9. Change passwords when personnel change. When sending out a new shared or system password, make sure the list you are sending it to is up to date (i.e., don't send the new password to the person who just left).

10. Change a password any time there is a question about whether it has been compromised.

11. Do not permit passwords to be taped to the sides of the terminals or in the back of the desk calendar. Security personnel should randomly inspect the desks of authorized users in an attempt to discover passwords. Such random inspections should be known to users. If users are aware that security personnel will attempt to discover their passwords, they normally will be more protective of them.

12. Passwords should have at least six characters. With only three characters, a professional computer criminal can solve the code in less than ten minutes. With six characters, the time required to try all possible combinations increases to five years. Passwords of alphanumeric characters should include at least one digit—for example, p8ssw4rd.

Hardware Protection

An important part of any security program is physical control of access to the computer hardware, that is, terminals. Computer devices should be located in a limited-access area. This can be a private area or an out-of-the-way area where personnel traffic is at a minimum. Employees should not be allowed to congregate in the area.

Locking devices are available for computer systems. These devices work like locks and require keys either to load a program or to modify one. The most popular one, Data Lock, can be set either to prevent a system from reading a program without the insertion of a special key or to prevent any entry of data without the key.

Encryptor devices that use a code system in transmitting or receiving data are also available. These devices prevent unauthorized users from understanding or copying your transmissions. These devices are expensive, however, making them impractical for most businesses.

Information Storage Devices

A security program should also include provisions for disposal of printed or recorded data, used computers, hard drives, and other items. Although disposal requirements are no different for computer records than for other types of company records, because of the ease with which printed records, floppy disks, cartridges, and so forth, can be reproduced with computers, special care must be taken to ensure that these items are disposed of properly. Experience has demonstrated clearly that the computer has not eliminated paper documents. Although some interoffice forms may have disappeared, they have been replaced by reams of computer printouts, which require the same degree of protection as other business records that contain important information.

When a machine is sent out for repair, it is important to monitor what is on that machine and who will be doing the repair.

Customer Complaints

Customer complaints are a valuable source of information about irregularities in a computer information system. Accordingly, businesses should channel customer complaints regarding financial accounts to the data security manager, not to someone in the data processing department. In addition, retain a record of all complaints and review them periodically. This will not only provide the manager with a better view of customer problems, it also will enable him or her to look for trends or other indicators of possible misconduct.

Incident Reports

Like customer complaints, incident reports or reports of errors, unusual events, and so forth, should be retained by the security manager and reviewed for possible patterns that might indicate misconduct or mistakes in the system.

Network Security Training

To be successful, a data and network security program must establish security awareness in all employees, including those who have no involvement with the computer system. The security awareness program should include:

- Employee security indoctrination (discussed earlier) and new employee orientation.
- Appropriate posting in conspicuous places such as bulletin boards or attention-getting posters. If the company has a newsletter, it should include an article regarding data and network security as a regular feature.
- Specialized training for the data security manager. Several good seminars on computer crime prevention, detection, and investigation are available. A good seminar will help the attendee understand the extent of computer crime vulnerabilities, methodology for risk assessment of the particular system being used by the company, key strategies for computer crime prevention, and a step-by-step approach to investigating computer crime.

Testing and Reviews

Test the security program thoroughly before implementing it to determine if there are any discrepancies in the system. Tests also help detect unexpected vulnerabilities in

Phishing:
Scam artists send emails that contain links to malicious websites to obtain personal information. Computer users follow the link, which directs them to a website designed to capture personal information. According to the FBI, phishing has become the leading type of Internet-based fraud, with financial institutions accounting for approximately 90 percent of all phishing attacks.

the system. Make unannounced retests and reviews of the system to ensure that employees are following prescribed procedures and that no unauthorized modifications have been made.

In most cases of computer-assisted misconduct, the offender is an authorized user of the system using it in an unauthorized manner. Unfortunately, such misconduct is the most difficult to detect. Random file and transaction monitoring is the best method for preventing this. Such monitoring should be publicized so that users are aware that their work is subject to review. A careful person may still be able to misuse the system, but the knowledge that it will be reviewed is a psychological deterrent to misuse.

Using random security tests to detect errors in or misuse of data is also an excellent method of deterring misconduct. One popular method used by security consultants is to insert dummy codes into the system to re-create or develop shortcomings in the system to detect possible weaknesses in the system.

Auditing

Auditing only those records that pertain to financial matters is a common mistake. All information in a database is subject to abuse or negligence and should be reviewed. In addition, many times unusual entries in nonfinancial data may be the key to discovering manipulation of financial data.

Internal Auditing

Make internal auditing a routine part of the security program. Include in the internal auditing a review of customer complaints and incident reports. A number of randomly selected transactions should be audited. The best method of auditing these transactions depends to a great extent on the type of information and the nature of the transactions. The recommended method in most cases is to follow a limited number of transactions completely through the system to detect any problems.

Employees should not be forewarned about audits. The report of the transactions audit, however, should be publicized. This will alert employees that their work is subject to random audit and thus will probably forestall some misconduct.

If it is impossible to select random transactions and trace them through the system, then the next best method appears to be audits of portions of the system, using a random method to select the portions to be audited. Employees should be made aware that any part of their work is subject to audit at all times.

Clues to computer-assisted misconduct uncovered by an internal audit include:

1. Unexplained or unusual activities regarding data
2. Entries made without supporting documents
3. Out-of-balance accounts
4. A high number of customer or vendor complaints
5. Incomplete or invalid data in files and records
6. Invalid codes, dates, or times
7. Same code for different entities or overuse of a catch-all code
8. Records input out of sequence
9. Erroneous batch totals

10. Missing document numbers
11. Improper job control language or job scripts (commands used by a computer operating system to instruct the system on how to run a job or start a process)

Routine Procedures to Reduce Misconduct

1. Maintain computer hardware and software. Keep them properly maintained and do not allow use of a system with known, uncorrected mechanical or electrical defects. Software with logical errors or other problems should not be used. A defective system or program may prevent the discovery of misconduct.
2. Prevent the intentional or accidental destruction of backup documents. Always store backup copies of software and data in secure off-site locations. Having backup copies readily available tends to encourage personnel to treat the original with less care. If, however, great effort is required to replace destroyed originals, employees will be forced to be more careful with them. In addition, this prevents the easy modification of both originals and backups in cases involving deliberate misconduct. An additional justification for the separation of documents is to prevent total chaos in case of accidental fire or other disaster.
3. Have all information verified by someone other than the person who entered the data into the system. Keep a log of all errors to help reduce design-induced errors and to detect possible misconduct. In this regard, the use of transaction logs is strongly recommended.
4. Schedule the processing of data for specific time periods. It is more difficult to prepare and input false data without detection when the data input is closely monitored.
5. If practical, prohibit data entry persons from working alone. If this is not practical, management personnel should be present when data are being entered or modified.
6. Install time meters on the computer equipment and require logs to account for the use of all computer system time.
7. Control and monitor computer supplies, special forms, and blank documents. This action also reduces employee thefts of such supplies.
8. If practical, rotate the duties and shifts of personnel. In this regard, require employees to take regular vacations. This will not only give an employee a needed rest but will also allow others to detect any irregularities with that employee's duties.
9. Establish a schedule of unannounced audits.
10. Control the use of personal computers that lack the security devices necessary to protect the confidential data of the company. Many companies are discovering that the growing use of desktop computers by management personnel is causing more problems than it solves. Problem areas include management getting so caught up in having the right data that they never get to the decision-making process and individual managers making decisions based on incomplete information available on their personal computer. Some companies require that only data generated from the main data system be used in decision making, so that all decisions are based on the same data. Restricting the use of desktop computers not only eliminates the above problems but also provides better control of the company's data.

Pharming:
A scheme whereby criminal crackers redirect Internet traffic from one website to a different, identical-looking site in order to trick the user into entering a username and password into the database on the fake site. Unbeknownst to the user, these crackers have hijacked the computer into going to the fake site or hijacked the DNS server on the intended site.

11. Never network more computer terminals than is absolutely necessary. Networking refers to sharing of some parts of a computer system, normally the CPU or storage devices.

12. Monitor adjustments to customer accounts. In the past this has been a popular method used to commit fraud. Designs the system so that adjustments to customer accounts are entered by persons other than those who entered the original data to the accounts.

Cracking

According to Senior IT Architect Kenn Roberson of IBM, the correct term to use is *cracking,* not *hacking.* According to Roberson, the media has latched on to "hacking," but that is a different, nonmalicious way of getting the most out of a system. Roberson says that, when thinking about security and computers, the following areas should be considered.

- *Physical security.* Keep the computers and equipment safe from malicious attacks and theft (both physical and of the information contained on the machine). Following are examples of areas to be mindful of when physically securing systems:

  - The explosion of jump, flash, or thumb drives have made it easy to either infect or steal data from a computer system. Consider keeping machines that handle extremely sensitive data or programs in "black rooms." A black room is a room that is shielded so that no electronic signals, not even a cell phone signal, can get out. Usually these rooms have no windows, to prevent observation of the machines and what is done on them, and all physical access to the room and the machines in them is logged.
  - With the increased use of laptop, tablet, and notebook computers, more care must be used to protect these from theft. Places with high people traffic and distractions are prime areas for your portable device to be taken. At airports, for example, when you go through security, you must take out laptops and place them in a separate container to go through the x-ray machine. The computer usually makes it through the checkpoint before you do. That exposure of time in a busy area makes it a prime target for theft.

  To help minimize this type of theft, the following are good ideas:

    - Do not put your machine through the x-ray machine until you are ready to go through the metal detector.
    - Use boot and hard drive passwords (these can usually be set in the BIOS Setup). These won't stop people from stealing the machine, but they will reduce theft of data from the stolen machine.
    - Cable lock systems can help impede the theft of a machine by tying it to a larger physical device (a table, bedpost, chair, etc.). These work on the same principle as bicycle locks do.
    - Sending machines out for repair can compromise the data contained in them. When a system is sent out to be repaired or upgraded, be careful: You are giving a third party complete access to all of the information on the system. According to interviews with people who perform computer repair,

there are some who do scan the hard drives to see what is there. For the most part, pictures and movies/clips of an exhibitionist nature are the targets, but it is just as easy to pull financial information, credit card numbers, proposals, and other confidential information from the machine. If you have to send out a machine, consider having the hard drive removed and, if available, replaced with a "clean" drive (one without sensitive information on it).

- *Backup, backups, and backups.* There is a constant need for backups to secure data against an act of God, poor programming, fire, or other cause. Arrangements should also be made for safekeeping of backups in an offsite location (away from the source) in case of fire or terrorist attack. Depending on the need for access to the information, redundant equipment, kept in synch at regular intervals, may be required.
- *Audit logs.* Keep track of who has had access to machines and systems, both physically and via software. These logs should keep track of what changes or activity the user has done on/to the system and when. Electronic badge access into a room can be used to monitor access.
- *Network security.* Firewalls are a must to keep people from connecting to your machines from the network. IP Forwarding should be accomplished by your router. The outside world talks directly to the router, and your router sends the data on to your machines. Some uses, say for a Web server, may require IP Forwarding to be bypassed for that system. Any access directly to the machine from the DMZ (demilitarized zone, a fancy term for the Internet beyond your business), should be carefully monitored and maintained.
- *Wireless security.* Roberson states that this is probably the biggest missed security opportunity for some businesses. All wireless routers support security methods that, by default, are turned off. Methods that may be used in securing wireless security include:

  - MAC (Media Access Control) addressing, by which you specify what physical machines can connect to the wireless network. All others will be kicked off. All network adapters, both internal and external, have a MAC address assigned by their manufacturer. The downside is that people can still "listen" to the data being sent (see "spoofing" below). MAC address control can be used in conjunction with other wireless security such as WEP or LEAP.
  - WEP (Wireless Encryption Protocol) allows only people who have the proper "password/encryption" key to connect. All data transferred is encrypted. Always use the highest level of security. The downside here is that anyone who has the password can get in.
  - LEAP (a bridging software) uses a user ID/password combination to connect to the wireless network. Data sent across the network is encrypted. The advantage over WEP encryption is that you know who is connected; there isn't just one password/encryption key for everyone.
  - None. According to Roberson, you are careless if you have an unsecured network. This is the easiest way for individuals to steal Internet access from you. Devices may be purchased that allow individuals to find unsecured networks. Most laptops now have software built into them to automatically try to access any wireless networks that are available.

- Another concern is with what people do with that stolen Internet access. If, for example, they use it to access child pornography, you may have a visit from the FBI as they show up at your home or work with warrants in hand. They can track down to the DSL or cable modem that feeds the wireless router/switch. At that point, they can confiscate all computers on the premises.

- *Software attacks security.* Always install some type of spyware monitor and virus detection software on your machines to help prevent virus and data theft.

Spyware can monitor what websites you visit and what activity is done on the machine. They can capture passwords and credit card numbers and transmit them to someone else.

Malware:
Short for malicious software, an umbrella term for any software that may be harmful to a computer user. Malware includes computer viruses, worms, Trojan horses, and also spyware, programming that gathers information about a computer user without permission.

Common software virus or *malware* are evil little programs written by people with too much time on their hands and no life. These programs are usually transmitted by downloading, viewing, executing, opening, or performing some action on an infected file. They can also access the email address book on a computer and forward themselves to others in the form of an email from someone the recipient knows. Some of the more frequently encountered virus types include:

- *DOS* (denial of service), by which a bunch of machines are set up to talk to your Web server. They flood the network so no one else can get to your site, or your site crashes.

- *Spoofing* refers to code/programs that are inserted between your browser and the website you are going to. It can take over and act like the site you are trying to access and steal your information. It can also record everything that you do on the network.

- *Phishing* refers to emails and Web addresses that look like they are from legitimate sites but are actually from someone else trying to get your information.

Keystroke logging (also known as key logging):
A diagnostic tool used in software development that captures the user's keystrokes. Keystroke logging can be useful. For instance, it is sometimes used to measure employee productivity on certain clerical tasks or for law enforcement. However, keystroke logging is also used by individuals to spy on computers by providing a means to obtain passwords or encryption keys. Unfortunately, keystroke loggers are widely available on the Internet.

- *Worms* are programs that consume parts of your machine and cause performance to drop. They can take up all free space on a hard drive or eat up available memory, not allowing any additional programs to be executed. They can also delete or corrupt existing files on the machine.

- A *Trojan horse* is a program that pretends to be innocuous file such as a game, picture, song, or movie. Once it is executed, listened to, or viewed, it installs the malicious part of itself on the system.

- *Spam* can be more dangerous than just the better mortgage rates and cheap pharmaceuticals they claim. They can contain some of the above-listed types of viruses in combination to infiltrate the machine they are accessed by. A good rule of thumb is that if you don't know who it is from or it look suspicious, treat it as such. If it is from someone you know but doesn't look right, call the person and confirm he or she sent it before you act on anything in the email. It is a good idea to set your email program not to load images in an email automatically.

Instant Messaging

According to Dan Ilett (2007), real-time communication software can undermine security efforts by permitting unlimited numbers of individuals to link directly to a company network. He notes that over 80 percent of companies employ some type of instant messaging (IM), as the tool has many business benefits, such as enhanced communication. Although many organizations utilize free, Internet-based IM software, a growing number of worms and viruses are invading the more prevalent software, and experts are unsure as to who is launching the attacks. The most frequent attack comes in the form of a message, which contains either a link to a virus-spreading website or a file attachment containing malicious code that can corrupt a computer and hijack it to launch other attacks, putting innocent workers on the line. To protect themselves, companies that convey information over a public network should either run their own closed system or use an encrypted, managed system. Ilett notes that companies need to be concerned with federal compliance issues, such as the Sarbanes-Oxley Act and its associated regulations, which require companies to regard IM conversations as documents subject to federal retention regulations, and therefore the conversations must be archived (see later). Ilett contends that because IM began as a form of social networking, the tool may make it harder for employees to keep intellectual property from leaving the office.

Spyware:
An umbrella term for any technology that gathers information about people or organizations without their knowledge. Advertisers or other interested parties often use spyware programming to gather and relay information.

Laptops

Laptops today have very similar computing capabilities as desktop computers. They are also convenient because you can take them with you when you travel or to your home in the evenings. Each year, thousands of laptops are stolen or lost. The problem with a stolen or lost laptop is the confidential information that may be stored on the laptop. Strict accountability for laptops is needed to prevent the disclosure of confidential data.

A 2005 survey by the Calgary Public Safety Committee, Calgary, Alberta, Canada, on laptop thefts included the following findings in its report:

- Multiple levels of physical and personnel security and procedures do work if properly applied.

Trojan horse:
A program that, unlike a virus, contains or installs a malicious program, sometimes called the payload or "trojan." A trojan horse can run autonomously, masquerading as a useful program, or it can hack into the code of an existing program and execute itself while that program runs.

Packing the laptop is part of the packing process for many individuals going on business-related travel. A high percentage of laptops is stolen from individuals who are on business trips.

Federal officials yesterday announced the recovery of computer equipment stolen from an employee of the Department of Veterans Affairs. They said that sensitive personal information of 26.5 million veterans and military personnel apparently had not been accessed. The laptop and external hard drive, stolen May 3 from a VA data analyst's home in Aspen Hill, contained the names, birth dates and Social Security numbers of millions of current and former service members. The theft was the largest information security breach in government history and raised fears of potential mass identity theft.

Source: The Washington Post, June 30, 2006, A1.

- The average loss per event is in excess of several thousand dollars. Rarely were stolen laptops recovered.
- Most victimized companies only spent money on security once several laptops were stolen.
- More important than the loss of equipment was the loss of morale and productivity of concerned employees of victimized companies.

SOFTWARE SECURITY

The majority of this the material in this section is summarized and excerpted from Department of Homeland Security, *Security in the Software Lifecycle: Making Software Development Processes—and Software Produced by Them—More Secure* [DHS 06], posted at Department of Homeland Security website https://buildsecurityin.us-cert.gov/daisy/bsi/547.html, (accessed on retrieved June 21, 2007.)

Bill Gates one of the key figures in starting the computer revolution.

National Cyber Security Division

Mission

The National Cyber Security Division (NCSD) works collaboratively with public, private, and international entities to secure cyberspace and America's cyber assets.

Strategic Objectives

To protect the cyber infrastructure, NCSD has identified two overarching objectives:

- To build and maintain an effective national cyberspace response system
- To implement a cyber-risk management program for protection of critical infrastructure

Organization and Functions

NCSD works to achieve its strategic objectives through the following programs:

National Cyberspace Response System

The National Cyber Security Division seeks to protect the critical cyber infrastructure 24 hours a day, 7 days a week. The National Cyberspace Response System coordinates the cyber leadership, processes, and protocols that will determine when and what action(s) need to be taken as cyber incidents arise. Examples of current cyber preparedness and response programs include:

- **Cyber Security Preparedness and the National Cyber Alert System.** Cyber threats are constantly changing. Both technical and non-technical computer users can stay prepared for these threats by receiving current information by signing up for the National Cyber Alert System.
- **US-CERT Operations.** US-CERT is responsible for analyzing and reducing cyber threats and vulnerabilities, disseminating cyber threat warning information, and coordinating incident response activities.
- **National Cyber Response Coordination Group.** Made up of 13 Federal agencies, this is the principal Federal agency mechanism for cyber incident response. In the event of a nationally significant cyber-related incident, the NCRCG will help to coordinate the Federal response, including US-CERT, law enforcement, and the intelligence community.
- **Cyber Cop Portal.** Coordination with law enforcement helps capture and convict those responsible for cyber attacks. The Cyber Cop Portal is an information sharing and collaboration tool accessed by over 5,300 investigators worldwide who are involved in electronic crimes cases.

Cyber-Risk Management Programs

Through Cyber Risk Management, the National Cyber Security Division seeks to assess risk, prioritize resources, and execute protective measures critical to securing our cyber infrastructure. Examples of current cyber risk management programs include:

- **Cyber Exercises: Cyber Storm.** Cyber Storm is a nationwide cyber security exercise that took place in early February 2006, to assess preparedness capabilities in response to a cyber incident of national significance. Cyber Storm was the Department of Homeland Security's first cyber exercise testing response across the private sector as well as international, Federal, and state governments.
- **National Outreach Awareness Month.** Every October the National Cyber Security Division coordinates with multiple states, universities and the private sector to produce National Cyber Security Awareness month.
- **Software Assurance Program.** This program seeks to reduce software vulnerabilities, minimize exploitation, and address ways to improve the routine development and deployment of trustworthy software products. Together, these activities will enable more secure and reliable software that supports mission requirements across enterprises and the critical infrastructure.

Source: www.dhs.gov/xabout/structure/editorial_0839.shtm. Retrieved March 20, 2008.

Build Security In

As part of the Software Assurance program, Build Security In (BSI) is a project of the Strategic Initiatives Branch of the National Cyber Security Division (NCSD) of the Department of Homeland Security (DHS). The Software Engineering Institute (SEI) was engaged by the NCSD to provide support in the Process and Technology focus areas of this initiative. The SEI team and other contributors develop and collect software assurance and software security information that helps software developers, architects, and security practitioners to create secure systems.

BSI content is based on the principle that software security is fundamentally a software engineering problem and must be addressed in a systematic way throughout the software development life cycle. BSI contains and links to a broad range of best practices, tools, guidelines, rules, principles, and other knowledge that can be used to build security into software in every phase of its development.

What makes it so easy for attackers to target software is the virtually guaranteed presence of vulnerabilities, which can be exploited to violate one or more of the software's security properties. The most successful attacks result from targeting and exploiting known, non-patched software vulnerabilities and insecure software configurations, many of which are introduced during design and code.

The President's Information Technology Advisory Committee summed up the problem of non-secure software as follows:

- Software development is not yet a science or a rigorous discipline, and the development process by and large is not controlled to minimize the vulnerabilities that attackers exploit. Today, as with cancer, vulnerable software can be invaded and modified to cause damage to previously healthy software, and infected software can replicate itself and be carried across networks to cause damage in other systems. Like cancer, these damaging processes may be invisible to the lay person even though experts recognize that their threat is growing. And as in cancer, both preventive actions and research are critical, the former to minimize damage today and the latter to establish a foundation of knowledge and capabilities that will assist the cyber security professionals of tomorrow reduce risk and minimize damage for the long term.
- The software development process offers opportunities to insert malicious code and to unintentionally design and build software with exploitable weaknesses. Security-enhanced processes and practices—and the skilled people to perform them—are required to build software that can be trusted not to increase risk exposure.

The objective of software security is to design, implement, configure, and support software systems in ways that enable them to

- Continue operating correctly in the presence of most attacks by either resisting the exploitation of faults or other weaknesses in the software by the attackers or tolerating the errors and failure that result from such exploits
- Isolate, contain, and limit the damage resulting from any failures caused by attack-triggered faults that the software was unable to resist or tolerate and recover as quickly as possible from those failures

Software security and secure software are often discussed in the context of software assurance. Software assurance is broader than software security, encompassing the additional disciplines of software safety and reliability.

A key objective of software assurance is to provide justifiable confidence that software is free of vulnerabilities. Another is to provide justifiable confidence that software functions in the "intended manner" and the intended manner does not compromise the security and other required properties of the software, its environment, or the information it handles.

A third objective of software assurance is the ability to trust, with justified confidence, that software will remain dependable under all circumstances. These include the presence of unintentional faults in the software and its environment exposure of the operational software to accidental events that threaten its dependability exposure of the software to intentional threats to its dependability, both in development and in operation.

COMPUTER- AND NETWORK-RELATED STATE STATUTES

As many court decisions have noted, technology advances faster than legal changes. The computer, like the photocopier in earlier decades, has forced both federal and state governments to change old statutes and add new ones.

All states have enacted statutes aimed at reducing computer-assisted misconduct. For example, California Penal Code §502(c)(7) prohibits unauthorized access to any computer, computer system, or computer network. The California statute is typical and provides, in part, that any person who intentionally accesses or causes to be accessed any computer system or network for the purposes of devising or executing any scheme to defraud or wrongfully obtain money, property, or services is guilty of a public offense. Conviction of any violation of this statute subjects a person to a fine and jail sentence.

New York State Penal Statute (2007)

§156.00. Offenses involving computers; definition of terms

The following definitions are applicable to this chapter except where different meanings are expressly specified:

1. "Computer" means a device or group of devices which, by manipulation of electronic, magnetic, optical or electrochemical impulses, pursuant to a computer program, can automatically perform arithmetic, logical, storage or retrieval operations with or on computer data, and includes any connected or directly related device, equipment or facility which enables such computer to store, retrieve or communicate to or from a person, another computer or another device the results of computer operations, computer programs or computer data.
2. "Computer program" is property and means an ordered set of data representing coded instructions or statements that, when executed by computer, cause the computer to process data or direct the computer to perform one or more computer operations or both and may be in any form, including magnetic storage media, punched cards, or stored internally in the memory of the computer.
3. "Computer data" is property and means a representation of information, knowledge, facts, concepts or instructions which are being processed, or have been processed in a computer and may be in any form, including magnetic storage media, punched cards, or stored internally in the memory of the computer.
4. "Computer service" means any and all services provided by or through the facilities of any computer communication system allowing the input, output, examination, or transfer, of computer data or computer programs from one computer to another.

(continued)

5. "Computer material" is property and means any computer data or computer program which:

   a. contains records of the medical history or medical treatment of an identified or readily identifiable individual or individuals. This term shall not apply to the gaining access to or duplication solely of the medical history or medical treatment records of a person by that person or by another specifically authorized by the person whose records are gained access to or duplicated; or

   b. contains records maintained by the state or any political subdivision thereof or any governmental instrumentality within the state which contains any information concerning a person, as defined in subdivision seven of section 10.00 of this chapter, which because of name, number, symbol, mark or other identifier, can be used to identify the person and which is otherwise prohibited by law from being disclosed. This term shall not apply to the gaining access to or duplication solely of records of a person by that person or by another specifically authorized by the person whose records are gained access to or duplicated; or

   c. is not and is not intended to be available to anyone other than the person or persons rightfully in possession thereof or selected persons having access thereto with his, her or their consent and which accords or may accord such rightful possessors an advantage over competitors or other persons who do not have knowledge or the benefit thereof.

6. "Computer network" means the interconnection of hardware or wireless communication lines with a computer through remote terminals, or a complex consisting of two or more interconnected computers.

7. "Access" means to instruct, communicate with, store data in, retrieve from, or otherwise make use of any resources of a computer, physically, directly or by electronic means.

8. "Without authorization" means to use or to access a computer, computer service or computer network without the permission of the owner or lessor or someone licensed or privileged by the owner or lessor where such person knew that his or her use or access was without permission or after actual notice to such person that such use or access was without permission. It shall also mean the access of a computer service by a person without permission where such person knew that such access was without permission or after actual notice to such person, that such access was without permission.

   Proof that such person used or accessed a computer, computer service or computer network through the knowing use of a set of instructions, code or computer program that bypasses, defrauds or otherwise circumvents a security measure installed or used with the user's authorization on the computer, computer service or computer network shall be presumptive evidence that such person used or accessed such computer, computer service or computer network without authorization.

9. "Felony" as used in this article means any felony defined in the laws of this state or any offense defined in the laws of any other jurisdiction for which a sentence to a term of imprisonment in excess of one year is authorized in this state.

The California statute, like the majority of state statutes, prohibits the malicious access, altering, deleting, damaging, or destroying of any computer system, computer network, computer program or data, and the accessing of data for the purpose of obtaining unauthorized information concerning the credit or confidential information of another person. The statute also prohibits the malicious entry of false data into an electronic information system that either damages or enhances a person's credit rating. "Malicious entry" as used in the statute includes not only deliberate and willful misconduct but also reckless conduct and acts committed without regard to the correctness of the information or results of the acts.

The regular penal statutes of a state, such as those involving theft and embezzlement, are also applicable to control computer-assisted misconduct.

COMPUTER-RELATED FEDERAL STATUTES

Several federal statutes have specific provisions dealing with the illegal use of computers.

Foreign Corrupt Practices Act of 1977

The Foreign Corrupt Practices Act of 1977 (15 U.S.C.S. §§78dd-1, 78dd-2), which amended the Securities and Exchange Act of 1934, has considerable impact on data information systems. The act, despite its title, affects all domestic and international public corporations and privately held businesses. The act states that any corporation, partnership, or sole proprietorship that has its principal place of business in the United States or that is organized under the laws of a state, territory, or possession of the United States must use uniform accounting standards. Failure to comply with the requirements of the act subjects violators to fines and jail sentences.

The act also requires that any business subject to the Securities Exchange Act of 1934 shall

1. Make and keep books, records, or accounts that in detail accurately reflect the transactions and dispositions of the assets of the company, and
2. Maintain a system of internal accounting controls sufficient to provide reasonable assurances that proper procedures are being used in the company in regard to its assets.

Computer Fraud and Abuse Act (CFAA)

The Computer Fraud and Abuse Act (CFAA) was originally enacted in 1984. The two principle sections of the act are:

18 U.S.C. §1030(a)(5)(A) provides that whoever "knowingly causes the transmission of a program, information, code, or command, and as a result of such conduct, intentionally causes damage without authorization, to a protected computer" is guilty of a crime (felony).

18 U.S.C. §1029 makes it a felony to use, sell, or transfer counterfeit access devices to data processing systems. This offense is punishable by a fine of $10,000 or twice the value obtained in using the device, whichever is greater, and imprisonment not to exceed twenty years.

The act makes it a crime to access without authorization any data processing system if the data processing system is involved in or used in relationship to interstate commerce. It is also a crime to use a public telephone system to access without authority any data processing system. The act also prohibits those who have the authority to access a data processing system from using the authority in an unauthorized manner. The act gives the Federal Bureau of Investigation and the Secret Service jurisdiction to investigate possible violations of this act.

The 1986 amendments also enlarged the scope of the CFAA by creating three new felony offenses: computer fraud, trafficking in network passwords, and hacking. The amendment also created a federal computer fraud offense, but Congress distinguished computer fraud from mail and wire fraud by mandating that using a computer was a requirement for criminal liability. The act was substantially modified again in 1994 and in 1996. It was rewritten to create two new offenses. The first offense covered intentional acts, which remained a felony, and the second created a misdemeanor crime for merely reckless acts. This misdemeanor crime was a departure from the 1986 act, which did not criminalize unintentional damage caused while accessing a system.

THE NATIONAL STRATEGY TO SECURE CYBERSPACE

[Excerpts from U.S. President's "Executive Summary," *The National Strategy to Secure Cyberspace,* (2003)].

Our Nation's critical infrastructures are composed of public and private institutions in the sectors of agriculture, food, water, public health, emergency services, government, defense industrial base, information and telecommunications, energy, transportation, banking and finance, chemicals and hazardous materials, and postal and shipping. Cyberspace is their nervous system—the control system of our country. Cyberspace is composed of hundreds of thousands of interconnected computers, servers, routers, switches, and fiber optic cables that allow our critical infrastructures to work. Thus, the healthy functioning of cyberspace is essential to our economy and our national security.

This National Strategy to Secure Cyberspace is part of our overall effort to protect the Nation. It is an implementing component of the National Strategy for Homeland Security and is complemented by a National Strategy for the Physical Protection of Critical Infrastructures and Key Assets. The purpose of this document is to engage and empower Americans to secure the portions of cyberspace that they own, operate, control, or with which they interact. Securing cyberspace is a difficult strategic challenge that requires coordinated and focused effort from our entire society—the federal government, state and local governments, the private sector, and the American people.

The National Strategy to Secure Cyberspace outlines an initial framework for both organizing and prioritizing efforts. It provides direction to the federal government departments and agencies that have roles in cyberspace security. It also identifies steps that state and local governments, private companies and organizations, and individual Americans can take to improve our collective cybersecurity. The Strategy highlights the role of public-private engagement. The document provides a framework for the contributions that we all can make to secure our parts of cyberspace. The dynamics of cyberspace will require adjustments and amendments to the Strategy over time.

The speed and anonymity of cyber attacks makes distinguishing among the actions of terrorists, criminals, and nation states difficult, a task which often occurs only after the fact, if at all. Therefore, the National Strategy to Secure Cyberspace helps reduce our Nation's vulnerability to debilitating attacks against our critical information infrastructures or the physical assets that support them.

Strategic Objectives

Consistent with the National Strategy for Homeland Security, the strategic objectives of this National Strategy to Secure Cyberspace are to:

- Prevent cyber attacks against America's critical infrastructures;
- Reduce national vulnerability to cyber attacks; and
- Minimize damage and recovery time from cyber attacks that do occur.

Threat and Vulnerability

Our economy and national security are fully dependent upon information technology and the information infrastructure. At the core of the information infrastructure upon which we depend is the Internet, a system originally designed to share unclassified research among scientists who were assumed to be uninterested in abusing the network. It is that same Internet that today connects millions of other computer networks making most of the nation's essential services and infrastructures work. These computer networks also control physical objects such as electrical transformers, trains, pipeline pumps, chemical vats, radars, and stock markets, all of which exist beyond cyberspace.

A spectrum of malicious actors can and do conduct attacks against our critical information infrastructures. Of primary concern is the threat of organized cyber attacks capable of causing debilitating disruption to our Nation's critical infrastructures, economy, or national security. The required technical sophistication to carry out such an attack is high—and partially explains the lack of a debilitating attack to date. We should not, however, be too sanguine. There have been instances where organized attackers have exploited vulnerabilities that may be indicative of more destructive capabilities.

Uncertainties exist as to the intent and full technical capabilities of several observed attacks. Enhanced cyber threat analysis is needed to address long-term trends related to threats and vulnerabilities. What is known is that the attack tools and methodologies are becoming widely available, and the technical capability and sophistication of users bent on causing havoc or disruption is improving.

In peacetime America's enemies may conduct espionage on our Government, university research centers, and private companies. They may also seek to prepare for cyber strikes during a confrontation by mapping U.S. information systems, identifying key targets, and lacing our infrastructure with back doors and other means of access. In wartime or crisis, adversaries may seek to intimidate the Nation's political leaders by attacking critical infrastructures and key economic functions or eroding public confidence in information systems.

Cyber attacks on United States information networks can have serious consequences such as disrupting critical operations, causing loss of revenue and intellectual property, or loss of life. Countering such attacks requires the development of robust capabilities where they do not exist today if we are to reduce vulnerabilities and deter those with the capabilities and intent to harm our critical infrastructures.

The Government Role in Securing Cyberspace

In general, the private sector is best equipped and structured to respond to an evolving cyber threat. There are specific instances, however, where federal government response is most appropriate and justified. Looking inward, providing continuity of government requires ensuring the safety of its own cyber infrastructure and those assets required for supporting its essential missions and services. Externally, a government role in cybersecurity is warranted in cases where high transaction costs or legal barriers lead to significant coordination problems; cases in which governments operate in the absence of private sector forces; resolution of incentive problems that lead to under provisioning of critical shared resources; and raising awareness.

Public–private engagement is a key component of our Strategy to secure cyberspace. This is true for several reasons. Public–private partnerships can usefully confront coordination problems. They can significantly enhance information exchange and cooperation. Public–private engagement will take a variety of forms and will address awareness, training, technological improvements, vulnerability remediation, and recovery operations.

A federal role in these and other cases is only justified when the benefits of intervention outweigh the associated costs. This standard is especially important in cases where there are viable private sector solutions for addressing any potential threat or vulnerability. For each case, consideration should be given to the broad-based costs and impacts of a given government action, versus other alternative actions, versus non-action, taking into account any existing or future private solutions.

Federal actions to secure cyberspace are warranted for purposes including: forensics and attack attribution, protection of networks and systems critical to national security, indications and warnings, and protection against organized attacks capable of inflicting debilitating damage to the economy. Federal activities should also support research and technology development that will enable the private sector to better secure privately-owned portions of the Nation's critical infrastructure.

Critical Priorities for Cyberspace Security

The National Strategy to Secure Cyberspace articulates five national priorities including:

    I. A National Cyberspace Security Response System;

    II. A National Cyberspace Security Threat and Vulnerability Reduction Program;

    III. A National Cyberspace Security Awareness and Training Program;

    IV. Securing Governments' Cyberspace; and

    V. National Security and International

Cyberspace Security Cooperation

The first priority focuses on improving our response to cyber incidents and reducing the potential damage from such events. The second, third, and fourth priorities aim to reduce threats from, and our vulnerabilities to, cyber attacks. The fifth priority is to prevent cyber attacks that could impact national security assets and to improve the international management of and response to such attacks.

PRIORITY I: A NATIONAL CYBERSPACE SECURITY RESPONSE SYSTEM Rapid identification, information exchange, and remediation can often mitigate the damage caused by malicious cyberspace activity. For those activities to be effective at a national level, the United States needs a partnership between government and industry to perform analyses, issue warnings, and coordinate response efforts. Privacy and civil liberties must be protected in the process. Because no cybersecurity plan can be impervious to concerted and intelligent attack, information systems must be able to operate while under attack and have the resilience to restore full operations quickly.

The National Strategy to Secure Cyberspace identifies the following major actions and initiatives for cyberspace security response:

1. Establish a public-private architecture for responding to national-level cyber incidents;
2. Provide for the development of tactical and strategic analysis of cyber attacks and vulnerability assessments;
3. Encourage the development of a private sector capability to share a synoptic view of the health of cyberspace;
4. Expand the Cyber Warning and Information Network to support the role of DHS in coordinating crisis management for cyberspace security;
5. Improve national incident management;
6. Coordinate processes for voluntary participation in the development of national public-private continuity and contingency plans;
7. Exercise cybersecurity continuity plans for federal systems; and
8. Improve and enhance public-private information sharing involving cyber attacks, threats, and vulnerabilities.
9. Enhance law enforcement's capabilities for preventing and prosecuting cyberspace attacks;
10. Create a process for national vulnerability assessments to better understand the potential consequences of threats and vulnerabilities;
11. Secure the mechanisms of the Internet by improving protocols and routing;
12. Foster the use of trusted digital control systems/supervisory control and data acquisition systems;
13. Reduce and remediate software vulnerabilities;
14. Understand infrastructure interdependencies and improve the physical security of cyber systems and telecommunications; and
15. Prioritize federal cybersecurity research and development agendas.

PRIORITY II: A NATIONAL CYBERSPACE SECURITY THREAT AND VULNERABILITY REDUCTION PROGRAM   By exploiting vulnerabilities in our cyber systems, an organized attack may endanger the security of our Nation's critical infrastructures. The vulnerabilities that most threaten cyberspace occur in the information assets of critical infrastructure enterprises themselves and their external supporting structures, such as the mechanisms of the Internet. Lesser-secured sites on the interconnected network of networks also present potentially significant exposures to cyber attacks. Vulnerabilities result from weaknesses in technology and because of improper implementation and oversight of technological products.

PRIORITY III: A NATIONAL CYBERSPACE SECURITY AWARENESS AND TRAINING PROGRAM   Many cyber vulnerabilities exist because of a lack of cybersecurity awareness on the part of computer users, systems administrators, technology developers, procurement officials, auditors, chief information officers (CIOs), chief executive officers, and corporate boards. Such awareness-based vulnerabilities present serious risks to critical infrastructures regardless of whether they exist within the infrastructure itself. A lack of trained personnel and the absence of widely accepted, multi-level certification programs for cybersecurity professionals complicate the task of addressing cyber vulnerabilities.

The National Strategy to Secure Cyberspace identifies four major actions and initiatives for awareness, education, and training:

1. Promote a comprehensive national awareness program to empower all Americans—businesses, the general workforce, and the general population— to secure their own parts of cyberspace;
2. Foster adequate training and education programs to support the Nation's cybersecurity needs;
3. Increase the efficiency of existing federal cybersecurity training programs; and
4. Promote private-sector support for well-coordinated, widely recognized professional cybersecurity certifications.

PRIORITY IV: SECURING GOVERNMENTS' CYBERSPACE   Although governments administer only a minority of the Nation's critical infrastructure computer systems, governments at all levels perform essential services in the agriculture, food, water, public health, emergency services, defense, social welfare, information and telecommunications, energy, transportation, banking and finance, chemicals, and postal and shipping sectors that depend upon cyberspace for their delivery. Governments can lead by example in cyberspace security, including fostering a marketplace for more secure technologies through their procurement.

The National Strategy to Secure Cyberspace identifies five major actions and initiatives for the securing of governments' cyberspace:

1. Continuously assess threats and vulnerabilities to federal cyber systems;
2. Authenticate and maintain authorized users of federal cyber systems;
3. Secure federal wireless local area networks;
4. Improve security in government outsourcing and procurement; and
5. Encourage state and local governments to consider establishing information technology security programs and participate in information sharing and analysis centers with similar governments.

PRIORITY V: NATIONAL SECURITY AND INTERNATIONAL CYBERSPACE SECURITY COOPERATION   America's cyberspace links the United States to the rest of the world. A network of networks spans the planet, allowing malicious actors on one continent to act on systems thousands of miles away. Cyber attacks cross borders at light speed, and discerning the source of malicious activity is difficult. America must be capable of safeguarding and defending its critical systems and networks. Enabling our ability to do so requires a system of international cooperation to facilitate information sharing, reduce vulnerabilities, and deter malicious actors.

The National Strategy to Secure Cyberspace identifies six major actions and initiatives to strengthen U.S. national security and international cooperation:

1. Strengthen cyber-related counterintelligence efforts;
2. Improve capabilities for attack attribution and response;

3. Improve coordination for responding to cyber attacks within the U.S. national security community;
4. Work with industry and through international organizations to facilitate dialogue and partnerships among international public and private sectors focused on protecting information infrastructures and promoting a global "culture of security";
5. Foster the establishment of national and international watch-and-warning networks to detect and prevent cyber attacks as they emerge; and
6. Encourage other nations to accede to the Council of Europe Convention on Cybercrime, or to ensure that their laws and procedures are at least as comprehensive.

A National Effort

Protecting the widely distributed assets of cyberspace requires the efforts of many Americans. The federal government alone cannot sufficiently defend America's cyberspace. Our traditions of federalism and limited government require that organizations outside the federal government take the lead in many of these efforts. Every American who can contribute to securing part of cyberspace is encouraged to do so. The federal government invites the creation of, and participation in, public–private partnerships to raise cybersecurity awareness, train personnel, stimulate market forces, improve technology, identify and remediate vulnerabilities, exchange information, and plan recovery operations.

For the foreseeable future two things will be true: America will rely upon cyberspace and the federal government will seek a continuing broad partnership with the private sector to develop, implement, and refine a National Strategy to Secure Cyberspace.

INFORMATION COMPROMISE–GUIDANCE FOR BUSINESSES

These days, it is almost impossible to be in business and not collect or hold personal identifying information—names and addresses, Social Security numbers, credit card numbers, other account numbers—about customers, employees, business partners, students, or patients. If this information falls into the wrong hands, it can put these individuals at risk for identity theft.

Still, not all personal information compromises result in identity theft, and the type of personal information compromised can significantly affect the degree of potential damage. What steps should a manager take, and whom should he or she contact if personal information is compromised? Although the answers vary from case to case, the following guidance from the Federal Trade Commission (FTC), the nation's consumer protection agency, can help you make smart, sound decisions. Check federal and state laws or regulations for any specific requirements for your business.

Notifying Law Enforcement

When the compromise could result in harm to a person or business, call the local police department immediately. Report the situation and the potential risk for identity theft. The sooner law enforcement learns about the theft, the more effective they can be. If the local police are not familiar with investigating information compromises, contact the local office of the FBI or the U.S. Secret Service. For incidents involving mail theft, contact the U.S. Postal Inspection Service.

Notifying Affected Businesses

Information compromises can affect businesses other than yours, such as banks or credit issuers. If account access information—say, credit card or bank account numbers—has been stolen, but the business does not maintain the accounts, notify the institution that does, so that it can monitor the accounts for fraudulent activity. If the business collects or stores personal information on behalf of other businesses, also notify them of any information compromise.

If names and Social Security numbers have been stolen, contact the major credit bureaus for additional information or advice. If the compromise may involve a large group of people, advise the credit bureaus if the company is recommending that people request fraud alerts for their files. The notice to the credit bureaus can facilitate customer assistance (Federal Trade Commission 2007).

If the information compromise resulted from the improper posting of personal information on the company website, immediately remove the information from the site. Be aware that Internet search engines store, or "cache," information for a period of time. You can contact the search engines to ensure that personal information that was posted in error is not archived.

Notifying Individuals

Generally, early notification to individuals whose personal information has been compromised allows them to take steps to mitigate the misuse of their information. In deciding whether notification is warranted, consider the nature of the compromise, the type of information taken, the likelihood of misuse, and the potential damage arising from misuse. For example, thieves who have stolen names and Social Security numbers can use this information to cause significant damage to a victim's credit record. Individuals who are notified early can take some steps to prevent or limit any harm.

When notifying individuals, the FTC recommends that the company:

- Consult with law enforcement about the timing of the notification so that it does not impede the investigation.
- Designate a contact person within the organization to release information.
- Give the contact person the latest information about the breach, your response, and how individuals should respond.
- Consider using letters, websites, and toll-free numbers as methods of communication with those whose information may have been compromised.

It is important that the notice:

- Describes clearly what the company knows about the compromise.
- Includes how it happened; what information was taken, and, if known, how the thieves have used the information; and what actions have been taken already to remedy the situation.
- Explain how to reach the contact person in the organization.
- Consult with local law enforcement contact on exactly what information to include, so the notice does not hamper the investigation.

- Explain what responses may be appropriate for the type of information taken. For example, people whose Social Security numbers have been stolen should contact the credit bureaus to ask that fraud alerts be placed on their credit reports. See www.consumer.gov/idtheft for more complete information on appropriate follow-up after a compromise.
- Include current information about identity theft. The FTC's website, at www.consumer.gov/idtheft, has information to help individuals guard against and deal with identity theft.
- Provide contact information for the law enforcement officer working on the case (as well as the case report number, if applicable) for victims to use. Identity theft victims often can provide important information to law enforcement. Victims should request a copy of the police report and make copies for creditors who have accepted unauthorized charges. The police report is important evidence that can help absolve a victim of fraudulent debts.
- Encourage those who discover that their information has been misused to file a complaint with the FTC at www.consumer.gov/idtheft or at 1-877-ID-THEFT (877-438-4338).
- Information entered into the Identity Theft Data Clearinghouse, the FTC's database, is made available to law enforcement.

Summary

- The information infrastructure is not an engineered system, and it was not designed with security in mind.
- The infrastructure is a prime target for terrorist actions.
- Although the security concerns of wireless networks mirror those of wired networks, the security solutions are different.
- Computer viruses are the most common form of attack on computer systems.
- Although the computer has changed the capability of management to store, retrieve, and use date, it has also provided new opportunities to misuse that information.
- Most information networks have been attacked in one form or another.
- The typical computer criminal is well educated, has not previously been involved in criminal activity, and is relatively young.
- For a successful data and network security program, members of the management team must be convinced that they have a vested interest in preventing misconduct.

- A data and network security program should include protection against unauthorized use or disclosure of sensitive data, data changes or movement, destruction or theft of hardware, and misuse of physical assets.
- The first phase of a successful data security planning should be directed toward determining the overall structure of the system.
- Passwords should be used and changed frequently.
- The security program should include provisions for the disposal of printed or recorded data, used computers, hard drives, and other devices.
- Investigate customer complaints and incident reports for possible irregularities in the information system.
- Auditing should be expanded to all records, not just those that pertain to financial matters.
- One of the most frequent attacks to a system comes in the form of messages.
- Laptops and the data on them must be regulated, and physical protection is necessary for them.

Review Questions

1. Why are computers and data systems prime targets for terrorists?
2. What constitute a good data security system?
3. How should passwords be regulated?
4. What is cracking, and why is it a problem?
5. What measures should be taken to physically secure your hardware?

Class Exercises

1. Assign class members to hunt out newspaper articles involving computer misconduct and present them to the class.
2. Have class members explain how an unethical employee could disrupt the operation of an organization by destroying computer files.

References

Calgary Public Safety Committee. 2005. *Laptop theft in the commercial high-rise.* Calgary, Canada: BOMA Safety Committee.

Department of Homeland Security. 2007. www.ojp.usdoj.gov/newsroom/2006/BJS06024.htm, retrieved June 22, 2007.

Federal Trade Commission. 2007. Facts for business, www.ftc.gov/bcp/edu/pubs/business/idtheft/bus59.shtm, retrieved March 18, 2008.

Ilett, Dan. 2007. Instant messaging poses a big risk. *Financial Times Digital Business,* June 13, 5.

Institute for Information Infrastructure. 2003. Cyber security research and development agenda, www.security-management.com/library/I3P_cybersecurity0403.pdf, retrieved April 1, 2007.

CHAPTER 9

Criminal Issues in Private Security

CHAPTER OUTLINE

OBJECTIVES

After completing this chapter, you will be able to:

•. Discuss the rights of security personnel to arrest or detain individuals.

•. Describe the elements of an arrest by a private person.

•. Explain how to handle evidence.

•. Define what constitutes probable cause.

•. Describe what constitutes a search.

•. Explain the difference between a tort and a criminal act.

•. Explain under what circumstances a private security officer may use force.

•. Discuss the importance of handling evidence correctly.

•. Describe the most common criminal incidents that security officers are involved with.

In May 2007, a security officer was convicted of reckless discharging a firearm in the accidental shooting of a bank customer in Kansas City, Missouri. Clifford O'Rear was sentenced to three years' probation for shooting a bank customer after thinking the man's cane was a shotgun while O'Rear was working at a Bank Midwest branch. Mr. O'Rear was subject to both criminal and civil liability for the shooting. The criminal liability is discussed in this chapter and the civil liability in Chapter 10.

In this chapter we explore the criminal issues involved in private security. The issues discussed include the right of security personnel to arrest or detain, to conduct a search, use of force to protect property, and investigations. Generally, criminal law issues in private security center around trying to help convict a person of committing a crime, such as theft of merchandise, destruction of property, or disrupting the activities of a business, or around the issue of whether a security person is subject to criminal liability for acts committed in the course of his or her security duties.

Often, the security professional is assisting the police or the prosecutor in a criminal action. For example, in the Petrosian case, a drug possession case discussed later in this chapter, the security personnel turned over to the police drugs that they had taken from the defendant. A similar situation exists when security catches an individual stealing from a business. In both of these situations, the security professional is assisting the state in the conviction of an individual for a criminal offense. Although the security professional may be assisting the prosecution, the security officer's real goal is to protect the organization's property or other rights. Of course, there are exceptions to the general rule, as noted in the chapter opening, which discusses a bank guard's criminal liability for shooting a bank customer.

An illegal action by a security professional may be both a criminal act and a private tort. For example, the Kansas City bank security officer discussed in the chapter opening was convicted of a crime when he shot the bank customer after he mistook the customer's walking cane for a weapon. The security officer and the bank were also liable in a civil court for the tortuous conduct of negligently inflicting an injury on the customer.

Criminal offense:
A criminal offense is a wrong against the public that the state prosecutes. It is also the violation of a criminal law.

A *tort* is an act that injures someone in some way, and for which the injured person may sue the wrongdoer for damages. Legally, torts are called *civil wrongs,* as opposed to criminal ones. (Some acts, such as battery, may be both torts and crimes; the wrongdoer may face both civil and criminal penalties.) A *criminal act* constitutes a violation of a criminal law. A *tort action* refers to an action by a private individual or entity in civil court for a wrong committed against the individual or entity. Tort law is the name given to a body of law that creates, and provides remedies for, civil wrongs that do not arise out of contractual duties. For example, in the above scenario, the security officer committed a criminal act when he shot the customer. He was also liable in a civil action for the civil tort of assault.

SEARCHES

Assume you are the security manager for a major casino in Atlantic City. One of the security personnel informs you that a customer has a pocket full of counterfeit chips and that the individual is being detained on the casino floor. What actions should you take? Can you legally arrest the customer? Can you legally search the individual?

Search:
A government intrusion into an area where an individual has a reasonable expectation of privacy.

In the study of the right to search, it is important to remember that individuals who are not connected with a law enforcement agency are considered to be private citizens. In most situations like that above, if the individual does not agree to allow you to look in his or her pockets, because of civil liability concerns, it is probably wise to detain the individual and request law enforcement assistance.

The Fourth Amendment Diagramed

- The right of the people to be secure in their
  - Persons
  - Houses
  - Papers
  - And effects
against unreasonable searches and seizures, shall not be violated; and

- No warrant shall issue, but
  - Upon probable cause
  - Supported by oath or affirmation
  - Particularly describing the
    - Place to be searched
    - And the persons or things to be seized

Any examination of the restrictions on searches must begin with a review of the Fourth Amendment to the U.S. Constitution. The Fourth Amendment, with its convoluted word structure, is not a model of clarity. The Amendment has two key clauses; the first clause, known as the *search clause,* protects individuals from unreasonable searches and seizures of their persons, houses, papers, and effects. The second clause, known as the *warrant clause,* sets forth the requirements for and restrictions on issuing a warrant. (Note that although an arrest is a seizure within the meaning of the Fourth Amendment, arrests will be discussed in separate sections of the chapter.)

Note that the Amendment does not prohibit all searches and seizures, but only "unreasonable" ones. What constitutes an unreasonable search is discussed later in the chapter. Also note that the Amendment states that only persons, houses, papers, and effects are protected. The present trend in criminal cases is to protect the right to privacy rather than property rights. And while the warrant clause describes the requirements and limitations of a warrant, it does not require that a warrant be issued in all cases before conducting a search. The warrant requirement is also discussed later in this chapter.

What Constitutes a Search?

Unless the incident qualifies as a search or seizure, it is not restricted by the Fourth Amendment. The U.S. Supreme Court presently uses the "privacy approach" in deciding what constitutes a search.

The privacy approach was first formulated by the Court in the case of *Katz v. United States,* 389 U.S. 347 (1967). In *Katz,* federal agents suspected illegal activities and installed an electronic listening device outside a public telephone booth that Katz frequently used. At trial, when Katz moved to exclude intercepted conversations, the government argued that there was no search of a person, house, papers, or effects, and therefore the Fourth Amendment did not apply. The government also contended that the telephone booth was a public place and not subject to the Amendment's restrictions.

The Supreme Court held that listening to private conversations between people constituted a search. The Court stated that the Fourth Amendment protects people, not property. The Court stated: "What a person knowingly exposes to the public, even in his own home or office, is not a subject of the Fourth Amendment protection. . . . But what he seeks to preserve as private, even in an area accessible to the public, may be constitutionally protected."

What Constitutes a Search Under *Katz*?

A search is

- A government intrusion
- Into area or interest

- Where a person has
- A reasonable expectation of privacy.

Is It a Search?

Would the results in the *Katz* case been different had the government, rather than placing a listening device outside the telephone booth, positioned an undercover agent dressed as a homeless person near the booth in such a manner that the agent could hear the conversation? Under this scenario, the government's actions would probably not be considered a search, because talking on a telephone within the hearing distance of another person (the apparent homeless person) would not constitute a reasonable expectation of privacy.

Note that the *Katz* definition of what constitutes a search requires government action. Therefore, a search by a private security individual, unless the individual is acting as an agent of government, is not governed by the Fourth Amendment. If the individual conducting the search is an off-duty police officer, then the courts may consider the individual as an agent of government, based on the theory that every off-duty officer has a duty to prevent crime. Private security employees generally have problems with civil liability issues rather than with whether the evidence seized in a search is admissible in court. The civil liability issues may include assault and battery in the search of a person, invasion of privacy in the search of a person's property, and false arrest or false imprisonment if an individual is retained during the search. These issues are discussed in Chapter 10.

Exclusionary rule:
A rule of evidence that excludes evidence from being admitted in a criminal trial on the question of defendant's guilt or innocence that was obtained in violation of the defendant's constitutional rights.

Prohibited by the Fourth?

In the *Katz* case, federal agents attached the listening device to the telephone booth. What would have been the results if Katz's girlfriend had placed the listening device in an attempt to catch him cheating on her? And if, after the girlfriend intercepted the messages, she turned them over to the federal agents? Note: A prohibited search is based on a "government intrusion." Under this scenario, there was no government intrusion, so the intercepted conversations would not be prohibited by the Fourth Amendment. If, however, the federal agents had influenced the girlfriend to place the listening device on the booth, this would constitute a government intrusion based on the concept that the girlfriend was acting as an agent for the government.

Reasonable Expectation of Privacy

One of the definitional requirements of the Second Amendment, as noted earlier, is the requirement of a "reasonable expectation of privacy." Included within the reasonable expectation of privacy is the requirement that society accept the expectation as reasonable. The expectation of privacy is an objective expectation. Consider this scenario: John lives in a suburban area. He has purchased a large amount of illegal drugs and is in the process of dividing them into smaller bags for retail sale. Does John have a reasonable

People v. Petrosian, 2005 Cal. App. Unpub. LEXIS 5983, (2005)

Hagop Jack Petrosian appealed his case after a jury convicted him of two counts of possession of a controlled substance. He argued that the trial court erred in denying his motion to suppress the evidence, because the search conducted by private security officers amounted to state action for purposes of the Fourth Amendment to the U.S. Constitution. The court found no merit in this argument and affirmed his conviction.

Facts of the case: Upon entering the Galaxy Concert Theater, Petrosian was searched by security personnel consistent with their practice of searching all guests for contraband. About two hours later, the security personnel approached Petrosian while he was sitting at a table. According to Petrosian, the security personnel "physically manhandled" him, dragged him outside, cursed at him, and handcuffed him. The security officers interrogated and searched him. Upon discovering illegal drugs, the security personnel notified the Santa Ana, California, Police Department and detained Petrosian until officers arrived. The security personnel gave the officers the contraband they had found.

Petrosian was charged with two counts of possession of a controlled substance, methamphetamine and ecstasy [Calif. Health & Saf. Code, §11377, subd. (a)]. Petrosian filed a motion to suppress. At the hearing on the motion, defense counsel mentioned several internal reports from the security company. The reports indicated there were a number of citizen arrests arising from non-theater-related offenses, including narcotics and burglary, on or about the time of Petrosian's arrest.

In denying Petrosian's motion, the trial court judge stated: "Based upon my analysis of the stipulated facts, I don't see any government involvement in this, the seizure of the property. This basically happened at a nightclub. A security officer comes up and searches Petrosian. The police are called only after the fact to come in and basically get the property from the security officer." The trial court failed to find any government activity in this that would call into question the restrictions in the Fourth Amendment. The jury convicted Petrosian of both counts. Petrosian was sentenced to seven days in the county jail and placed on probation for three years.

The appellate court affirmed Petrosian's conviction and stated that the exclusionary rule did not apply because there was no government action involved in the security officers' search of the defendant. Note, however, that Petrosian may have had a civil cause of action against the security personnel and the theater for the alleged assault and battery, if he was, as he claimed, subjected to excessive force.

expectation of privacy if he is dividing and repackaging the drugs in his front room with the windows open and he can be observed from the sidewalk? It is unlikely that a court would hold that this expectation of privacy was objectively reasonable.

Suppose that instead of dividing the drugs in his living room, John does the work in his bathroom. There is only one small window in the bathroom, and a person would have to stand on a drainage pipe in order to look into the bathroom window. In this situation, a court would probably hold that John had a reasonable expectation of privacy.

Standing

The legal concept of "standing" is based on the rule that a defendant generally must assert his or her own legal rights and interests, and cannot rest his or her claim to relief on the legal rights or interests of another person. This rule assumes that the party with the right has the appropriate incentive to challenge (or not challenge) governmental action and to do so with the necessary zeal and appropriate presentation. It represents a concern that if the claim is brought by someone other than one at whom the constitutional protection is aimed, the courts might be called on to decide abstract questions of wide public significance even though other governmental institutions might be more competent to address the questions and even though judicial intervention might be unnecessary to protect individual rights [*Warth v. Seldin,* 422 U.S. 490, 498 (1975)].

Standing:
The legal concept of "standing" is based on the rule that a defendant generally must assert his or her own legal rights and interests, and cannot rest his or her claim to relief on the legal rights or interests of another person.

To have standing to object to a search, your constitutional rights must be violated. For example, Covington's home was illegally searched and the evidence was used to convict Brown of receiving stolen merchandise. Brown could not object to the illegal search of Covington's home because Covington's constitutional rights, not Brown's, were violated.

Probable Cause

As noted earlier, the Fourth Amendment provides that "no warrant shall issue but upon probable cause." In addition, the Supreme Court has required probable cause before many authorized warrantless searches may be made. Generally, when we discuss probable cause, it is in reference to a search or arrest warrant. There are four basic situations when probable cause is an issue: arrests with warrants, arrests without warrants, searches and seizures with a warrant, and searches and seizures without warrants.

Probable cause:

It exists where the facts and circumstances within an officers' knowledge and of which he or she had reasonably trustworthy information are sufficient to warrant a person of reasonable caution in the belief that an offense has been or is being committed.

What constitutes probable cause is difficult to explain. As the Pennsylvania Supreme Court noted in *Commonwealth v. One 1958 Plymouth Sedan,* 211 A.2d 536 (Pa. Sup. Ct. 1965), "Probable cause is exceedingly difficult to explain and to apply to the facts and circumstances of a particular case." Justice Rutledge, in *Brinegar v. U.S.,* 338 U.S. 160 (1949), stated that in "dealing with probable cause . . . as the very name implies, we deal with probabilities. These are not technical; they are the factual and practical considerations of everyday life on which reasonable and prudent men, not legal technicians, act."

As noted by the Pennsylvania Supreme Court, in *McCarthy v. De Armit,* 99 Pa. 63 (1920), "The substance of all the definitions of probable cause is a reasonable ground for belief of guilt." The U.S. Supreme Court stated in *Carroll v. United States,* 267 U.S. 132 (1925), "Probable cause exists where the facts and circumstances within the officers' knowledge and of which they had reasonably trustworthy information are sufficient in themselves to warrant a man (person) of reasonable caution in the belief that an offense has been or is being committed."

The Pennsylvania Court also noted in *De Armit* that "Many years ago this Court stated that probable cause depends upon an honest and reasonable belief and must be judged by the totality of the circumstances existing at the time of the search and seizure." The Pennsylvania Court noted that probable cause has been said to exist where the facts and circumstances within the arresting officers knowledge and of which they had reasonably trustworthy information are sufficient in themselves to warrant a person of reasonable caution in the belief that an offense has been or is being committed and that the person to be arrested has committed or is committing the offense.

Judge Learned Hand, speaking for the U.S. Court of Appeals, Second Circuit, in *U.S. v. Heitner,* 149 F.2d 105, 106 (2nd Cir. 1945), noted that it was well settled that an arrest or search may be based on hearsay evidence; and indeed, the probable cause necessary to support an arrest or search does not demand the same strictness of proof as the accused's guilt upon a trial.

An interesting case was *Colorado v. Pilkington,* 156 P.3d 477; 2007 Colo. LEXIS 353. Pilkington was the owner of City View Liquors in Thornton, Colorado. City View Liquors occupied a commercial building under a lease from the building's owner, Ed Ciancio. In the early morning hours of May 24, 2005, the Thornton Fire Department (TFD) responded to a fire alarm from City View Liquors and arrived to find smoke coming from the building. Firefighters promptly extinguished the fire inside. Shortly thereafter, Pilkington arrived at the scene and consented to TFD's search of the premises. TFD searched the building and initially concluded that a faulty light fixture caused the fire.

Later that morning, David Harvey, a private investigator, arrived at the scene. With Pilkington's verbal consent, Harvey began his investigation of the fire. Two hours later, Leon Beesley, a fire investigator for EMC Insurance, arrived and also began investigating the fire. There is no evidence in the record that Pilkington ever consented to Beesley's investigation. Harvey and Beesley both concluded that the fire had multiple points of origin, signifying arson as the cause. Beesley contacted TFD and suggested that it reconsider whether the fire was accidental.

TFD's investigation revealed additional evidence that the fire was deliberately set, and Pilkington subsequently was charged with two felony counts of arson. At a pretrial hearing, Pilkington moved to suppress the evidence gathered by TFD, Harvey, and Beesley on grounds that their respective searches of City View Liquors violated Pilkington's rights under the Fourth Amendment. Pilkington argued that Harvey and Beesley acted as agents of the government for purposes of the search and therefore were subject to the requirements of the Fourth Amendment.

The state did not dispute that the private investigators entered the premises without the defendant's consent. The state asserted that the Fourth Amendment did not apply to the investigators' search because they were not acting as agents of the government when collecting evidence at the scene. One was acting on behalf of the building owner and the other was acting on behalf of the insurance company. The reviewing court held that the Fourth Amendment did not apply to the search conducted by the investigators. The investigators had an independent motive to search the crime scene apart from assisting law enforcement. The record did not reveal that law enforcement

General Rules Involving Probable Cause That Apply to Both Searches and Arrests

- The magistrate, not the police or the individual conducting the search, makes the determination as to whether probable cause exists in warrant applications.
- Probable cause may be based on hearsay information or other evidence that may not be admissible in court.
- The phrase "person of reasonable caution" does not refer to a person with special legal training; it refers to the average person who under the circumstances would believe that the individual being arrested or searched had committed the offense or that the items to be seized would be found in a particular place.
- Probable cause requires an "honest and reasonable belief."
- Proof beyond a reasonable doubt is not required to establish probable cause.

- Probable cause may be established by an individual's own knowledge of certain facts and circumstances; by information given by informants; or by information plus corroboration.
- Probable cause cannot be based on the results of the search or arrest. For example, if the search of a person reveals the presence of drugs, that cannot be used to justify the search in the first place. Probable cause must exist before the search or the arrest.
- The experience of the individual requesting the warrant may be considered as one factor in establishing probable cause but cannot be the sole factor justifying the arrest or search.
- If the facts used to establish probable cause are provided by an informant, additional corroboration is required because of the inherent unreliability of informants.

officers encouraged or instigated the investigators to conduct the search to the degree necessary to establish that the investigators were acting as agents of the government. Absent such agency, the Fourth Amendment did not apply to the investigators' search.

Security Professional Participation in the Execution of a Warrant

Many cases have considered the issue of whether a civilian may participate in the execution of a search warrant. In some of those cases the civilian was a private security professional involved in the protection of the company's property. The restrictions on civilians being present during a search is based on the requirement that in executing a search warrant, government officials must ensure that the search is conducted in a way that minimizes unwarranted intrusions into an individual's privacy.

If the civilian participating in the execution of a search warrant was the victim of a theft who has been requested by police to point out property that has been stolen from the victim, the courts have unanimously held that the civilian's presence did not affect the propriety of the search [*United States v. Robertson,* 21 F.3d 1030 (10th Cir. 1994)]. A carjacking victim's presence in the defendant's residence was permitted to help identify items covered by warrant in *People v. Superior Court,* 598 P.2d 877, 878 (Cal. 1979). The People's case supported the proposition that a security professional may accompany the police to identify property stolen from a company.

Most courts have required that the civilian's role must be to aid the efforts of the police. In other words, civilians cannot be present simply to further their own goals. Note: The recovery of stolen property belonging to a company is considered as efforts to aid the police rather than the furtherance of a person's interest in recovering the stolen property. In *Wilson v. Layne,* 526 U.S. 603 (1999), the U.S. Supreme Court held that inviting media to "ride along" on execution of warrant violated the defendant's privacy rights. The Court noted that the officer must be in need of assistance. Police cannot invite civilians to perform searches on a whim; there must be some reason why a law enforcement officer cannot himself conduct the search or the need for the assistance of the civilian or some reason to believe that postponing the search until an officer is available might raise a safety risk. Third, the civilians must be limited to doing what the police have authority to do.

The use of civilians in the execution of federal search warrants is governed by federal statute, 18 U.S.C. §3105 (a search warrant may in all cases be served by any of the officers mentioned in its direction or by an officer authorized by law to serve such warrant, but by no other person, except in aid of the officer on his or her requiring it, he or she being present and acting in its execution).

ARREST AUTHORITY OF SECURITY PROFESSIONALS

Arrests by private persons are arrests by individuals who are not law enforcement officers. Every state recognizes the authority of private individuals to make arrests. This authority is commonly referred to as "citizen's arrest authority." The label is a misnomer because there is no requirement that the individual making the arrest be a citizen of any state or the United States. Second, when police officers make arrests, they are "citizens" even though they are acting in an official capacity. Any arrest by a private security professional will normally be considered an arrest by a private person.

There are some exceptions that are permitted by state law, such as those discussed later in this section involving a Michigan statute.

An arrest by a private person requires that the crime for which the arrest is made has been committed or attempted in the presence of the arresting person. The statutes in most states also provide for the private arrest of a felon even though the crime occurred in the absence of the private party. When an arrest is made, the person effecting the arrest must inform the arrested person of the reason for the arrest.

The idea that citizens are responsible for policing their communities dates back to before the Norman Conquest of England in 1066, when the shire reeve (similar to a present-day sheriff) could call on any free male subject to serve on a posse. The free males were expected to constrain felons and in some cases to administer justice. As noted in Chapter 1, the concept of private security is older that the concept of an organized police force, which is a relatively recent development.

Private arrests frequently turn into a "he said, she said" confrontation. For example, in November 2005, an angry motorist in Sacramento, California, tried to make a private arrest of one Jason Meggs, who was demonstrating to promote the rights of cyclists as a member of an organization called Critical Mass. Meggs and his cohorts retaliated by trying to arrest the original arresting party (Marsh 2004).

The number of private arrests differs wildly from state to state and even from city to city. In 2006, the Washington, D.C., police department reported no private arrests, while the Los Angeles Police Department reported 6441 arrests—all for misdemeanor offenses. For the most part, private arrests are made by security professionals employed by private industries in response to shoplifting and employee thefts. The records of one national drug store chain reflect that the security professionals of that chain of stores average more than 12,000 private person arrests annually.

In *Hamburg v. Wal-Mart Stores, Inc.,* 116 Cal. App. 4th 497 (Cal. App. 1st Dist. 2004), protestors, arrested for trespass after they refused to leave the business premises of a store, filed suit against the store and its manager for false arrest and violation of their constitutional rights, alleged as an intentional tort. The protestors had been collecting signatures on petitions to qualify a voter initiative and carrying signs bearing messages such as "Free Speech" on a median approximately 25 feet from the store's entrance and on the sidewalk along the front of the store. They did not use the four-by-six area designated by the store for expressive activities. The manager asked the protestors to leave, and when they refused, placed them under citizen's arrest, which resulted in their being taken into custody by the city police.

The Court of Appeal held that the reasonableness of the store's time, place, and manner restrictions and the protestors' refusal to be bound by them did not establish that the protestors committed a crime for which they were placed under citizen's arrest. Because the arrests, which were central to both claims made by the protestors,

General Rules for Security Professionals

Security professionals may

- Temporarily detain an individual suspected of shoplifting

- Arrest an individual who commits a felony or misdemeanor in their presence
- Arrest an individual who has committed a felony

were made by the store security manager, a private citizen, it was necessary for the offenses to have been committed in the manager's presence.

In some states, such as Michigan, the state has given additional powers to licensed security officers. For example, Michigan Compiled Laws §338.1080 (2008) provides as follows:

> **§338.1080. Private security police officers; arrest powers; limitations.**
>
> Sec. 30. A private security police officer who is properly licensed under this act has the authority to arrest a person without a warrant as set forth for public peace officers in section 15 of chapter IV of the code of criminal procedure, 1927 PA 175, MCL 764.15, when that private security police officer is on the employer's premises. Such authority is limited to his or her hours of employment as a private security police officer and does not extend beyond the boundaries of the property of the employer and while the private security police officer is in the full uniform of the employer.

Based on that statute, a licensed security officer in Michigan has statutory authority to arrest without warrant in the same manner as a public police officer when the security officer is on the employer's property and in full uniform [*People v. Eastway* (1976) 67 Mich App 464, 241 NW2d 249.] In one case, a Michigan court held that security officers who worked for the defendant, a private casino, were state actors for purposes of 42 USCS §1983 because they were properly licensed security officers who had police powers pursuant to MCLS §338.1080 (*Romanski v. Detroit Entm't,* L.L.C. (2003, ED Mich) 265 F Supp 2d 835).

Pennsylvania has a similar statute, and the Pennsylvania state attorney general opined that for a licensed private security police officer to possess limited police powers under the 1968 PA 330, §30 statute, the officer must be a citizen of the United States (Op Atty Gen, May 9, 1980, No. 5705). The state attorney general also opined that qualified private security officers have the same authority to make arrest without warrant as peace officers (Op Atty Gen, April 27, 1977, No. 5126).

USE OF FORCE

Security professionals have only limited authority to use force. Any force utilized must be reasonable under the circumstances. Security professionals may use deadly force only when it is reasonably necessary to protect a life. The *Landry* case, discussed later in this section, provides a good summary of the authority of a security professional making a private person's arrest. If the force used by the professional is not authorized or is excessive, the action will be an assault or battery or both. The threat or attempt to use unlawful force by an individual may be an *assault*. A *battery* is the unconsented, offensive touching of another person, either directly or indirectly.

In *Landry v. Naghizadeh,* 2004 Cal. App. LEXIS 1556 (2004), the court held that a private person may lawfully arrest someone committing or attempting a public offense or felony in his or her presence. The term *public offense* includes misdemeanors. An *arrest* is made by an actual restraint of the person, or by submission to the custody of an individual. The person arrested may be subjected to such restraint as is reasonable for his or her arrest and detention. Force utilized must be reasonable. As with a citizen's arrest, the separate right of a merchant to detain a customer is limited to "a reasonable amount of non-deadly force for self-protection or to prevent escape of the person detained or loss of property." Use of unreasonable force constitutes an assault or battery.

CRIMINAL OFFENSES

As noted in the previous section, the unreasonable use of force by a security officer may constitute an assault or battery. Assault and battery, false imprisonment, and firearm violations are the most common criminal liability situations that security officers face. Consider the following scenario: A bank security officer sees a customer entering the bank. The officer recognizes the customer as his neighbor, whom he dislikes. To "teach the neighbor a lesson," he draws his pistol and points it at the neighbor in a threatening manner. Because the security officer had no authority to use force, his use of his pistol in a threatening manner constitutes the crime of assault and also the civil tort of assault. The security officer could be prosecuted for the assault. In addition, the neighbor could sue the officer in civil court for the assault.

Assault and Battery

Assault and battery are frequently considered the same offense, although they are separate and distinct. A battery consists of the unjustified offensive touching of another. An assault is either an attempted or a threatened battery. The critical difference between assault and battery is that battery requires an actual or constructive touching of the person. In some aggravated assault crimes, the "assault" actually refers to battery. For example, the crime of assault causing serious bodily injury is actually a battery rather than an assault (see the discussion of aggravated assault).

Battery

The unjustified offensive touching is the *actus reus* (the Latin term for the act that constitutes a crime) of the crime of battery. In most states, no actual bodily injury is necessary to constitute battery. The Model Penal Code (American Law Institute 1982), however, requires at least a slight bodily injury to constitute the crime of battery. It is not necessary that the victim actually fear physical harm as the result of the touching. For example, offensively touching the breasts of a woman or kissing her may be a battery. Note: The Model Penal Code (MPC) is a statutory text that was developed by the American Law Institute (ALI) in 1962 and updated in 1981. The purpose of the MPC was to stimulate and assist legislatures in updating and standardizing the penal laws of the United States.

In many cases, it is unclear whether the touching should be considered offensive. For example, a hug or kiss from an elderly aunt may be offensive to a child, but it is certainly not criminal. The test generally used is whether a reasonable person would consider the touching offensive.

It is immaterial how the offender causes the offensive touching. For example, it can be firing a weapon or hitting with a fist. There is no requirement to actually touch the person; a constructive touching is sufficient. In one famous case, the accused was convicted of battery when he hit the horse that the victim was riding. In another case, a defendant was convicted of battery when he convinced a six-year-old girl to touch his sexual organs.

Assault

There are two standard types of assault: (1) the attempted battery and (2) placing a person in fear of a battery by menacing behavior. In several states, such as California, the second type of behavior is not an assault. In those states, assault is only an attempted battery. Because an assault is in many cases an attempted battery, a defendant may in most cases be convicted of an assault even though a battery was actually committed.

Aggravated Assault and Battery

Aggravated assaults or batteries are assaults and batteries with aggravating factors— for example, assault with the intent to commit rape, assault with a motor vehicle, assault on a peace officer, and assault with a dangerous weapon. In cases of aggravated assault or battery, there must be either the intent to commit a specific crime, such as rape; the use of a deadly weapon; or the infliction of serious bodily harm.

In most cases, an assault unaccompanied by a battery is only a misdemeanor. We often describe those as "simple assaults." Aggravated assaults, which are felonies, are often referred to as "felonious assaults." For purposes of aggravated assaults, a dangerous weapon is generally defined as an instrument likely to cause serious bodily injury.

Intent

In most states, the courts have extended battery to include not only intentional conduct but also those situations where the defendant has acted in a criminally negligent fashion. Normally, criminal negligence is conduct that the accused knew or should have known would result in harm to others. Several states have limited battery to situations where the accused acted in a willful, wanton, or reckless manner.

Transferred Intent

The doctrine of transferred intent is applied to those cases where the offender intends to injure one person and by mistake or accident injures another. The intent to injure is *transferred* to the actual victim. The doctrine is based on an old English case regarding an individual who threw a firecracker at another person. The other person, in a reflex action, threw the firecracker in a different direction, consequently injuring a passerby. The person who first tossed the firecracker was convicted of battery of the passerby. The intent may still be used to establish an assault on the intended victim. For example, suppose a security officer wrongly shoots at X, intending to kill her. He misses and hits V. The officer is guilty of assault on X and battery on V. The battery of V is based on the doctrine of transferred attempt.

False Imprisonment

The Model Penal Code requires that to constitute false imprisonment, the restraint must substantially interfere with the victim's liberty. For example, preventing an individual

Model Penal Code

Section 212.2 Felonious Restraint

A person commits a felony of the third degree if he knowingly:

   a. restrains another unlawfully in circumstances exposing him to risk of serious bodily injury; or
   b. holds another in a condition of involuntary servitude.

Section 212.3 False Imprisonment

A person commits a misdemeanor if he knowingly restrains another unlawfully so as to interfere substantially with his liberty.

---

from crossing the street at one location would be insufficient to constitute false imprisonment. But restraining the individual in a small area might constitute a crime. The force used may be physical force or threat of physical force to the victim or another. False imprisonment may be established if a security officer, without authority, orders a person to get into a car (and the person obeys), when the officer knows that he or she does not have the right to so order the person to get into the car. The MPC also establishes the crime of "felonious restraint" for aggravated false imprisonment.

Recklessly Discharging a Firearm

In Mr. O'Rear's case, discussed in the opening of the chapter, the defendant willfully shot the bank customer, thinking that the customer had a shotgun. What about when a security officer accidentally discharges his or her weapon? In *Minnesota v. Engle,* 743 N.W.2d 592; 2008 Minn. LEXIS 4, the Minnesota Supreme Court reviewed defendant Engle's conviction for recklessly discharging a firearm in a municipality while on duty as a private security officer. The court noted that the statute did not require proof of an intentional discharge, but rather required proof of a conscious or intentional act, in connection with the discharge of a firearm, that creates a substantial and unjustifiable risk that the defendant is aware of and disregards. In the Engle case the intentional act was the carrying of a loaded firearm in a vehicle and the accidental discharging of it.

The court noted that "recklessness" often describes conduct that exceeds ordinary negligence in two respects: a higher degree of risk, and a higher degree of fault, in that the actor must be subjectively aware that his or her conduct creates the risk. A person acts recklessly with respect to a result or to a circumstance described by a statute defining an offense when he or she is aware of and consciously disregards a substantial and unjustifiable risk that such result will occur or that such circumstance exists. The court noted that a defendant has the requisite mental state for Minn. Stat. §609.66, subd. 1a(a)(3), if he commits a conscious or intentional act in connection with the discharge of a firearm that creates a substantial and unjustifiable risk that he is aware of and disregards.

The court had granted review of the case to determine whether a conviction under Minn. Stat. §609.66, subd. 1a(a)(3) (2006), which proscribes recklessly discharging a firearm in a municipality, requires proof that the firearm was intentionally discharged.

Facts of the case: On November 2, 2003, Engle, a private security officer, arrived at a St. Paul housing complex to assist a fellow security officer in apprehending a suspected thief. The suspect attempted to flee, but eventually the officers held him at gunpoint, sitting in the driver's seat of a stolen car. Somehow, in the course of removing the suspect from the car, Engle discharged his gun, shooting and paralyzing the suspect. Both parties concede that the discharge was unintentional.

After a bench trial [trial by judge alone], the district court found Engle guilty of recklessly discharging a firearm within a municipality. The court stayed imposition of Engle's sentence and placed him on probation for two years.

The appellate court noted that "reckless" was an ambiguous term. It was not defined in the Minnesota criminal code. The term has not always been used consistently, although it is generally used to define a level of culpability more serious than ordinary negligence and less serious than specific intent to harm. "Recklessness" often describes conduct that exceeds ordinary negligence in two respects: a higher degree of risk, and a higher degree of fault—the actor must be subjectively aware that his or her conduct creates the risk.

The court held that a person is said to act recklessly when he or she consciously disregards a substantial and unjustifiable risk that an injury will occur, or when his or her action is grossly heedless of consequences. The policy of the statute—protecting the community from death or injury by firearms—"is best served by holding actors responsible for consciously disregarding risks of harm, whether they do so by intentionally pulling the trigger or by another act that increases the likelihood that the gun will discharge accidentally, involuntarily, or reflexively."

Possession of an Illegal Weapon

In *Bohn v. State,* 651 S.W.2d 274 (1983 Tex. App. Dallas), defendant Bohn sought review of a judgment from a County Court of Dallas County (Texas) that convicted him of unlawfully carrying a weapon in violation of Tex. Penal Code Ann. §46.02. The defendant urged a "mistake of fact" defense, in that he believed he was acting as an appointed peace officer, and further claimed that his possession of the prohibited weapon was only momentary, and therefore not criminal.

A private security officer enlisted Bohn's aid to quell a disturbance in a bar. For this purpose the security officer handed Bohn a blackjack. Bohn did not surrender the blackjack until challenged by a police officer some minutes later. The court affirmed the conviction. The court held that the trial court was entitled to disregard Bohn's defensive evidence completely. Even if the trial court had believed his evidence, the court concluded that the private security officer was not a peace officer as defined in Tex. Code Crim. Proc. Ann. art. 2.12 (1977). The trial court noted that Tex. Penal Code Ann. §46.03 (Supp. 1982–1983) made the offense of unlawful carrying of weapons, Tex. Penal Code Ann. §46.02, inapplicable to peace officers at all times, but inapplicable to private security officers only if they were on duty, in uniform, and the weapon was in plain view. This, according to the trial court, negated the notion that a private security officer was *ipso facto* a peace officer. As a result, the private security officer could not have appointed Bohn as a peace officer to assist him. Bohn's possession of the weapon lasted too long to be temporary, and was not for an innocent purpose.

Bohn was convicted, after a nonjury trial, of unlawfully carrying a weapon, for which he was sentenced to confinement of thirty days (probated) and a fine of $400. Although he admitted all elements of the offense during his trial testimony, he argued that his guilt was not established for two reasons: first, because he believed that he was

acting as an appointed peace officer, and second, because his possession of the prohibited weapon was only momentary. The appellate court affirmed (approved) the
judgment of the trial court.

The appellate court noted that the facts were not in dispute. During the early
morning hours of June 8, 1981, a Dallas police officer saw Bohn on the parking lot of
a local club holding in his hand what appeared to be a gun. As the officer approached
him, Bohn put the object in his rear pants pocket and pulled his shirt tail down over it.
The officer asked what he had placed in his pocket and recovered a club described as
a blackjack or black leather slapper.

Before the arrival of the officer, Bohn was assisting a private security officer on
duty at the club with a disturbance involving an intoxicated customer. The security
officer had asked the customer to leave; the customer not only refused, but armed himself with a two-by-four piece of wood, which he brandished "like a baseball bat."
When the customer was reinforced by the arrival of a friend from inside the club, the
security officer requested Bohn's assistance and handed him the blackjack for protection. The confrontation lasted until the customers left, a period of several minutes.

Although Bohn had a commission as a private security officer, he was not on
duty or in uniform on this occasion. He had worked at this club, but on this particular
night he was there as a customer to visit the security officer on duty. Bohn had the prohibited weapon in his possession for a total of ten to twelve minutes from the time the
security officer gave it to him until the police officer recovered it.

Bohn first argued that he believed that the security officer he was aiding had
appointed him a peace officer, and that this good-faith belief relieved him of culpability. The appellate court stated that the private security officer whom Bohn was aiding
before his arrest was not a peace officer. Therefore, his argument that he was legally
obligated to assist a peace officer must necessarily fail. The court held that the private
security officer, who was licensed under Tex. Rev. Civ. Stat. Ann. art. 4413(29bb)
(Vernon 1976 & Supp. 1982–1983) was not a peace officer under Tex. Code Crim.
Pro. Ann. art. 2.12(13) (Vernon 1977) and that, as a result, he could not have appointed
appellant as a peace officer to assist him.

Bohn next argued that §46.02 of the Penal Code does not prohibit temporary
possession of, as distinguished from carrying, a weapon. He cited numerous cases for
the proposition that temporary possession of a weapon, for an innocent purpose, does
not constitute an offense.

As to this argument, the appellate court found that the possession of the weapon
was more than momentary, that he had the club for twelve minutes and never voluntar-
ily relinquished it, even after arrival of the police officer. The conviction was affirmed
(approved).

Impersonating a Law Enforcement Officer

Often, security officers' uniforms look like police officers' uniforms. This looka-
like situation can be the basis of criminal liability. In *Ohio v. Taylor,* 2005 Ohio
App. LEXIS 6240 (2005, Ohio), defendant Taylor appealed a judgment from
the Youngstown Municipal Court of Mahoning County (Ohio), which convicted
him of impersonating a peace officer, in violation of Ohio Rev. Code Ann.
§2921.51(B).

The defendant was charged with impersonating a peace officer while he was providing security at a drinking establishment. He was wearing black military tactical pants, boots, had an Ohio State Police Constable badge hanging from his neck, and was wearing a hat with a patch printed "Constable Ohio State Police." Based on a complaint, police officers went to the bar and observed the defendant, who was dressed like a peace officer. After a jury trial, the defendant was convicted, and he appealed. The defendant contended that he was in fact a private policeman and thus could not be convicted of impersonating a peace officer or private policeman.

The appellate court found that there was sufficient evidence to support the defendant's conviction, as his attire closely resembled that of a peace officer, and he was not licensed as a peace officer under Ohio Rev. Code Ann. §4749.03. The fact that he was lawfully employed did not insulate him from compliance with the laws. The court noted that Ohio Rev. Code Ann. §2921.51(B) prohibited one from wearing the uniform or any part of the uniform, or displaying the identification of a peace officer, with the purpose of making another person believe that the actor is that particular person or is a member of that class of persons. The essence of an impersonation offense pursuant to §2921.51(B) is to prohibit individuals from acting in a manner consistent with those of a peace officer, which includes wearing the uniform, assuming the identity, or displaying the identification of a peace officer. The court held that, pursuant to Ohio Rev. Code Ann. §2921.51, it was possible for a lawfully employed security guard to be convicted of impersonation of a peace officer. The court noted that acting as a security officer to protect drinking establishments and their patrons is a lawful endeavor if an individual is actually a licensed private security officer. Ohio Rev. Code Ann. §4749.03 required private security guard providers to be licensed. The appellate court noted, however, that Ohio Rev. Code Ann §2921.51(A) defined a peace officer as follows:

> "Peace officer" means a sheriff, deputy sheriff, marshal, deputy marshal, member of the organized police department of a municipal corporation, or township constable, who is employed by a political subdivision of this state, a member of a police force employed by a metropolitan housing authority . . . a member of a police force employed by a regional transit authority . . . a state university law enforcement officer . . . a veterans' home police officer . . . a special police officer employed by a port authority . . . , or a state highway patrol trooper and whose primary duties are to preserve the peace, to protect life and property, and to enforce the laws, ordinances, or rules of the state or any of its political subdivisions.
>
> "Impersonate" means to act the part of, assume the identity of, wear the uniform or any part of the uniform of, or display the identification of a particular person or of a member of a class of persons with purpose to make another person believe that the actor is that particular person or is a member of that class of persons.

The appellate court noted that the essence of an impersonation offense pursuant to Ohio Rev. Code Ann §2921.51(B) is to prohibit individuals from acting in a manner consistent with those of a peace officer, which includes wearing the uniform, assuming the identity, or displaying the identification of a peace officer. His act of wearing an official-looking uniform and badge depicting the state seal was an attempt to signify that he was a peace officer representing a state authority.

Question: Would he have been convicted had he only worn the uniform, without the badge? Probably not.

HANDLING EVIDENCE

Many defendants have escaped punishment because the evidence was mishandled. The security professional who discovers or takes evidence needs to ensure that when it is transferred to a law enforcement agent, the proper steps are taken. Two major principles apply in the control of evidence: continuity and security. *Continuity* of evidence means that there is a clearly documented record of where a piece of evidence has been, a record of who handled it, and why, from the time that the evidence is taken from the crime scene until it appears in court. This is generally accomplished by collecting the evidence in sealed containers to prevent contamination and marked for identification. In addition, a chain of custody of the evidence is maintained. Any break in continuity may provide the defense with grounds to have the evidence excluded (Thibault 2004, 281).

The *security* of the evidence is also paramount. Special background checks are normally made on individuals who are assigned responsibility for the security of evidence. Even small qualities of drugs offer a temptation for quick money for any individual with access to the evidence.

Requirement for Miranda Warnings by a Security Officer

Is a security officer required to give Miranda warning before questioning an individual being detained by the security officer? In *New York v. Huff,* 604 N.Y.S. 2d 1024 (1993), defendant Huff was charged with violating Penal Law Section 165.40 when he allegedly took a "red machine" from a Water Pollution Control Plant. At about 6:00 AM on that day, one of the plant employers got on a "walkie talkie" and announced that an unknown person was walking out with private property belonging to the plant. Jesus Serrano, a security officer employed by a private security company, responded to the area immediately and saw the man walking out of the gate. The officer also noticed that the gate chain and the padlock were on the floor. Serrano asked the defendant where he had acquired the machine, and he told Serrano that he found it in the water treatment plant. Serrano then detained the defendant but never gave the defendant a Miranda warning. Serrano did recover other physical property from the defendant and asked him a few questions relating to the incident. A police officer arrived at the scene shortly thereafter and placed the defendant under arrest on the city-owned land.

On appeal, the defendant contended that his statement to the security officer should not be admitted into evidence because the security officer had never advised him of his Miranda rights before the questioning.

The court held that the rights that Miranda warnings are designed to protect did not apply when a private security guard employed at a public water treatment plant questioned the defendant about the machine he was removing from the plant. Private conduct may become so pervaded by governmental action as to pierce the shield of

Chain of custody:
A document or testimony that establishes the control and possession of evidence from the time of possession until it is entered into evidence in court.

private investigation into public constitutional scrutiny where there is a clear nexus between the policy and a private investigation. In this case, there was no evidence of public involvement in the private investigation and detainment of the defendant. The mere fact that the land where the alleged offense took place was publicly owned did not alone constitute government action necessitating that Miranda warnings be given to the defendant. Additionally, the private surveillance, apprehension, and questioning of the defendant was in no way instigated by a police officer or undertaken at the official behest of a law enforcement agency.

The exclusionary rule that protects persons against unlawful search and seizure is inapplicable when a private security officer stops an individual, detains him, and recovers certain properties from the person. According to the court, the origin and history of the Fourth Amendment showed that it was intended as a restraint on the activities of sovereign authority, and was not intended to be a limitation on other than governmental agencies.

The court concluded that a private security officer, securing an area that is publicly owned, is not working closely with the police department or any other governmental law enforcement agency. This private security officer is no more subject to the restrictions of the Fourth Amendment than the department store security manager, the safety official at a state psychiatric center, or the faculty member of a high school in charge of discipline. Such individuals, operating in a private capacity, are completely distinguishable for Fourth Amendment purposes from those who have an obvious nexus to governmental police enforcement or are otherwise obviously working with the police.

Therefore, the defendant's application to suppress any physical evidence seized by the security officer was denied. Even if the exclusionary rule were to be applicable here, the circumstances of the defendant being seen by the officer exiting a gate where the lock had been broken, the officer observing the defendant pushing a wagon with a red machine inside it, and the announcement of a person walking out of the plant with private property, gave the officer more than enough reasonable suspicion to stop, detain, and frisk the defendant.

Show-ups Conducted by Security Officers

A *show-up* is a one-on-one confrontation between a suspect and a witness or victim that is held shortly after the crime and normally at the crime scene. If a security officer conducts a show-up without the involvement of law enforcement, is the evidence of the identification admissible in court? That issue was litigated in *New York v. Brown,* 174 A.D.2d 370; 571 N.Y.S. 2d 450 (1991 N.Y. App.). Defendant Brown was convicted after a jury trial of grand larceny in the fourth degree and was sentenced to two to four years' imprisonment. The New York appellate court affirmed his conviction.

Evidence adduced at trial was that on the afternoon of May 2, 1988, the defendant approached one William Ahdout at the Madison Square Garden mall, snatched concert tickets out of his hand, and fled. The incident was observed by a private security officer, who recognized and identified defendant at trial, as did the complaining witness, Ahdout. The appellate court held that the evidence was properly admitted and noted that the issue of possible suggestiveness of a show-up procedure arranged by private security personnel was fully explored by defense counsel on cross-examination, and any inconsistencies in the testimony were for the jury to resolve. The appellate court affirmed the conviction.

Summary

- Private security professionals are involved in both criminal and civil court trials, generally as a witness for the prosecution in criminal cases or as defendants in civil liability cases.
- A search is a governmental intrusion into an area where a person has a reasonable expectation of privacy. The U.S. Supreme Court currently uses the privacy approach in deciding what constitutes a search.
- The reasonable expectation of privacy is an objective expectation.
- Standing is a legal concept and is based on the rule that before a person may complain of the violation of a right, the person's right must be involved.

- The concept of probable cause is complex. Probable cause exists where the facts and circumstances within an individual's knowledge and of which he or she has reasonably trustworthy information are sufficient for a reasonable person to conclude that an offense has been committed or is being committed.
- Under limited circumstances, a security professional may participate in the execution of a search warrant.
- A security professional has only limited authority to arrest and detain a person. A similar restriction exists on the use of force.
- Two major principles apply in the control of evidence: continuity and security.

Review Questions

1. What are the differences between crimes and torts? When can the same conduct be considered as both a crime and a tort?
2. What authority does a private security person have the right to arrest an individual?

3. Under what circumstances may a private security person use force?
4. When may a private security person participate in the execution of a search warrant?

Class Exercises

1. Role playing: Assign members of the class to act as a shoplifter, a store clerk, and a private security officer and have them enact the detention of a suspected shoplifter.

2. Have class members demonstrated how they would handle evidence taken from an individual found on the premises of the company.

References

American Law Institute. 1982. Model Penal Code (revised). Chicago: American Law Institute.

Marsh, Kathryn. 2004. Playing police. *Legal Affairs*, July, 16–20.

Thibault, Edward T. 2004. *Proactive police management*, 6th ed. Upper Saddle River, NJ: Prentice-Hall.

CHAPTER 10

Civil Liability Issues in Private Security

CHAPTER OUTLINE

Objectives

Civil Liability

Liability Based on Negligent Acts

Strict Liability

Intentional Torts

Protection of Others

Summary

Review Questions

Class Exercises

OBJECTIVES

After completing this chapter, you will be able to:

- List the elements of a negligence tort.
- List the elements of an intentional tort.
- List the common types of civil liability suits that involve private security individuals.
- Describe the situations in which there is a duty to protect others.
- Explain whether actual damages are required.

Tort:
A civil wrong for which a private party may sue the tort feasor for restitution.

In this chapter we will explore the issues involving civil liability and private security. It is important to understand the legal restrictions under which private security professionals operate and how they can protect themselves from civil lawsuits. Unfortunately, in civil cases, the security professionals and/or their employers are normally defendants. They may be personally liable for false arrest, false imprisonment, assault and battery, defamation, failure to act, and excessive use of force. The basis of most civil actions is the tort action. A *tort* is a private wrong, for which an individual may sue another individual, organization, or both for money damages or restitution.

CIVIL LIABILITY

There are three categories of civil liability: intentional tort, negligence, and strict liability. An *intentional tort* involves an intentional act or wrong. Intentional torts include a security officer wrongly arrested someone, willfully inflicting injury on a person, or wrongly detaining a person.

The "intentional" aspect of the tort refers to intentionally committing the act or the wrong. It does not matter that the security officer honestly believed he or she had the authority to detain a person or to use the force. The elements of recovery or the items that a plaintiff must establish in court to recover under an intentional tort are that:

- The defendant or tort feasor committed an intentional act.
- The act was wrong.
- The plaintiff suffered injuries or damages.

Tort feasor:
An individual who commits a tort.

The elements of negligent liability include:

- Existence of a duty
- Foreseeability of the likelihood of the injury occurring
- Failure to meet a reasonable standard of care
- Proximate results of the injury
- Injury or damages

Duty refers to the obligation not to injure another person or damage another person's property. It also refers to the duty of an employer to protect his or her employees. Other duties include the duty of an automobile driver to drive safely, the duty of a bank security officer not to negligently injure a bank customer, and the duty of a business not to cause injury or damage to customers and others visiting the business.

The U.S. Supreme Court, although it decides few cases involving civil liability, is the supreme law of the land, and its decisions constitute a significant part of the law of civil liability.

Duties are established based on the relationship between the actor and the injured party, for example, the duty of a parent to protect his or her children; by statute, for example, the duty of a driver not to drive in excess of the speed limit; or by custom, for example, the duty of a landowner to keep his or her property in a safe condition.

Consider this hypothetical situation: A ten-year-old child is drowning in the lake. Joe, an adult, is standing on the shore. Near him is life-saving equipment that he could toss to the child and save the child's life. Joe does nothing. Has he committed a tort? The answer to this question depends on whether Joe has a duty to the child. If Joe is the parent of the child or the caretaker, or if there is a statute that requires adults to render life-saving efforts, then Joe has a duty to save the child. In addition, if Joe is responsible for the child's situation—for example, he accidentally pushes the child into the lake—he has a duty to rescue. If Joe is a security officer and is assigned to ensure the safety of the users of the lake, he has a duty because of his employment situation to rescue the child. If Joe is a stranger and has no duty to the child, Joe does not commit a tort by failing to rescue the child, even though his actions are morally wrong.

A security professional may be subject to civil litigation in any of three situations:

1. A civil action based on an intentional tort—for example, battery, false arrest, infliction of mental distress, or conversion of property.
2. A civil action based on negligence—for example, negligent driving, negligent discharge of a firearm, or negligence in the use of lawful force to effect an arrest.
3. A civil action based on an infringement of a constitutional right—for example, illegal search, denial of right to counsel, or illegally preventing a person from exercising a constitutional right.

LIABILITY BASED ON NEGLIGENT ACTS

Wrongful death:
A civil court action in which it is alleged that the tort feasor, by his or her actions, caused the death of a person.

The first element of a negligent tort recovery is duty, as we have discussed. The second element is a *foreseeable likelihood* that the incident would occur. An actual case that highlights this element is *Birge v. Dollar Gen. Corp.,* 2006 U.S. Dist. LEXIS 29 (2006). This case was about a child's claim for the wrongful death of his father, Dexter Birge. The robbery and murder of Dexter Birge occurred in 2004 at a Dollar General store located in Memphis, Tennessee. After purchasing some items from the Dollar General store, Mr. Birge exited the store to go to his vehicle in the store parking lot. Mr. Birge was robbed and shot in parking lot. Mr. Birge made his way back into the Dollar General store, where he collapsed and later died. The Plaintiff (the child) contended that criminal acts against customers were reasonably foreseeable by Dollar General and that Dollar General failed to take reasonable steps to protect its customers from criminal acts of others.

The child's attorney contended that Dollar General knew, or had reason to know, from past experience that criminal acts against its customers were reasonably foreseeable, either generally or at some particular time, and that Dollar General was guilty of negligence in failing to follow its own internal criteria for posting security officers. And had Dollar General followed its own criteria, Dollar General would have posted a security officer. The child's attorney also claimed that Dollar General had failed to properly train its employees regarding security measures, failed to share internal information about crimes that had occurred at its store with its employees, and failed to make known to its employees Dollar General's internal criteria for posting security officers. Finally, the attorney claimed that Dollar General failed at each and every level of its management hierarchy to determine and know what crimes were occurring at its store.

The court stated that the foreseeability of harm and the gravity of harm must be balanced against the commensurate burden imposed on the business to protect against that harm. In cases in which there is a high degree of foreseeability of harm and the probable harm is great, the burden imposed on the business may be substantial. Alternatively, in cases in which a lesser degree of foreseeability is present or the potential harm is slight, less onerous burdens may be imposed. By way of illustration, using surveillance cameras, posting signs, installing improved lighting or fencing, and removing or trimming shrubbery might, in some instances, be cost-effective and greatly reduce the risk to customers.

The court noted that a business ordinarily has no duty to protect customers from the criminal acts of third parties that occur on its premises. The business is not to be regarded as the insurer of the safety of its customers, and it has no absolute duty to implement security measures for the protection of its customers. However, a duty to take reasonable steps to protect customers arises if the business knows, or has reason to know, either from what has been or should have been observed or from past experience, that criminal acts against its customers on its premises are reasonably foreseeable, either generally or at some particular time. The factual issue before the court was whether Dollar General, because of previous crimes at the location, could reasonably foresee the death of the child's father. The court decided that this factual issue should be determined by a jury. Apparently, the case was then settled between the parties, because there is no reported final decision in the case.

Failure to meet a reasonable standard of care is the third element of a negligent tort. In the Dollar General case, one of the primary issues was whether Dollar General's actions to protect its customers were reasonable. As noted earlier, the court stated that it was a question for the jury as to whether the store had take reasonable steps to protect customers based on what management knew or should have known about the crime activity at that location. On the issue of meeting a reasonable standard of care, examine the conduct of Mr. O'Rear, the Kansas City bank guard who shot a customer, described at the beginning of Chapter 9. The case discussed was a criminal one, but the conduct of Mr. O'Rear also created a possible tort liability action. If a judge in a civil case faced the same fact situation, the judge would probably instruct the jury that they must decide whether Mr. O'Rear exhibited a reasonable standard of care when he mistook the customer's walking cane for a weapon and shot the customer. The trial judge would probably also instruct the jury that when you use a dangerous weapon such as a firearm, the standard of care before using the dangerous weapon is very high. Conversely, if the weapon was not a dangerous weapon, the standard of care required to be exhibited before using the weapon would be less.

The fourth element of a negligent tort action is that the negligence was *the proximate result of the injury*. The concept of proximate cause is confusing and very difficult for first-year law students. Referring again to the Dollar General case, what if the murder was the result not of a robbery but of a contract killing, and the killer had been

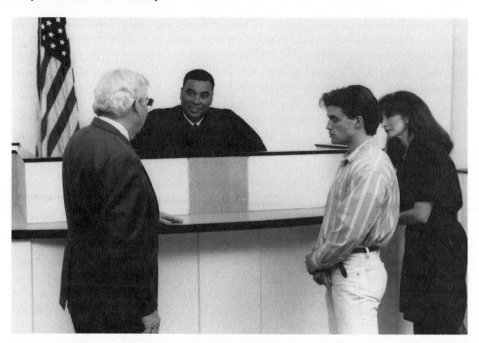

An attorney discusses the rules of court with the judge.

tracking the decedent looking for an opportunity to kill him. Under this fact situation, any negligence of Dollar General would not have been the proximate cause of the decedant's death. According, if the deceased would have been killed regardless of the actions of the store's employees, then his death was not the proximate cause of any failure on the part of Dollar General.

What if the decedent in the Dollar General case had only been wounded and was taken to a hospital, where he died as a result of negligent medical treatment. Courts would probably hold that both the original negligence and the negligent medical treatment were proximate causes of the death. The reason the original negligence is considered one of the proximate causes is that it is reasonably foreseeable that if you injure a person, that person might receive negligent medical treatment.

The final element needed for tort recovery is that there must be some *injury or damage*. If, in the Dollar General example, there had been no injuries to anyone nor damages to any property, then the store would not be liable regardless of the degree, if any, of its negligence. The courts are divided on whether physical injury or damage is necessary. A few courts have held that psychological damages are sufficient. The general rule is that psychological damages are recoverable only if there were also physical injuries or damages.

STRICT LIABILITY

The third type of civil liability is based on strict liability. *Strict liability* is based on instances in which an individual or business may be held liable without the need to prove an intentional act or negligence. For example, selling adulterated food opens a grocery store to civil liability for a strict liability tort in most states, based on the concept that such stores have a high standard of care to individuals who purchase their food products. Another area where strict liability may be imposed is when the activity involved is a very dangerous activity. For example, work that involves the use of explosives falls into this class. For the most part, security professionals will seldom be involved in strict liability situations.

INTENTIONAL TORTS

In this section, we will look at some of the typical situations in which a security professional may be subject to civil liability.

Assault or Battery

Consider the following actual situation: One day in 1963, a customer entered a restaurant and ordered a $3.25 dinner special, specifying Roquefort dressing for his salad. After finishing his dinner, he was presented the bill, including an extra 35-cent charge for the Roquefort dressing. When he objected to this charge, a private security officer was summoned. At this point, testimony conflicts, each party's witnesses insisting that the other was abusive. In any case, the customer left the restaurant, refusing to sign for or pay the check and apparently intent on consulting the manager of the adjacent motel (a distinct operation, which, by arrangement, would include guests' restaurant bills on their motel account). The security officer followed the customer to the motel office and gave the desk clerk the bill, instructing the clerk to put it on the customer's account. According to the testimony, the motel manager was in the restaurant at the time of the incident. Both the customer and the officer apparently became increasingly angry. The customer and the desk clerk testified that the security officer asked the customer to "step outside." All witnesses agreed that the customer made a sweeping motion toward the security officer and cursed at him. The security officer then struck the customer on the back of the head with an ashtray. The trial court's judgment, awarding the customer damages against the security officer and the restaurant, was approved on appeal based on the fact that the officer had no authority to hit the customer in the head. [Facts from *Columbia v. Petty,* 1963 Fla. App. LEXIS 3244 (Fla. Dist. Ct. App. 2d Dist. 1963).]

False Imprisonment

Randall's Food Mkts. v. Johnson, 891 S.W.2d 640 (Tex. 1995) contains an excellent discussion on the intentional torts of false imprisonment and the intentional infliction of emotional distress.

Johnson, a manager of a Randall's store, purchased several items from the store but did not pay for a large Christmas wreath that she was holding. Davis, the checkout clerk, did not charge Johnson for the wreath because, after ringing up her other items, the clerk asked her if there was anything else, and she replied that there was nothing else. Davis reported Johnson's failure to pay him for the wreath to management. The store's security officer investigated the incident.

One question before the court was whether the employer's request that the employee stay away from a particular area of the business premises during work hours constituted false imprisonment. The second question was whether the employer's questioning of Johnson about the possible theft constituted "extreme and outrageous conduct," necessary to state a claim for intentional infliction of emotional distress. The court answered both questions in the negative.

The court stated that the essential elements of false imprisonment were (1) willful detention, (2) without consent, and (3) without authority of law. A detention may be accomplished by violence, by threats, or by any other means that restrains a person from moving from one place to another. Where a detention is effected by a threat, the plaintiff must demonstrate that the threat was such as would inspire in the threatened person a just fear of injury to her person, reputation, or property. The court held that Randall's did not willfully detain Johnson and only prevented Johnson from returning to the store.

False Arrest

In *Cervantez v. J. C. Penney,* 24 Cal. 3d 579 (1979, Cal.), Cervantez sued the J.C. Penney department store for false arrest, malicious prosecution, assault and battery, intentional infliction of emotional distress, and negligence. The record indicated that at the time of the arrest, the security officer was an off-duty, full-time peace officer with a local police department. The security officer, being suspicious of the plaintiff and his companion because of their behavior, had followed them throughout the store. He observed them place several items in a bag and leave the store, and he placed them under arrest after they left. The theft charges against the plaintiff were eventually dismissed.

The legal issue in the case concerned the jury instructions. The appellate court held that it was prejudicial error to instruct the jury that Cervantez had the burden to prove the unlawfulness of the arrest because the burden was on business to prove justification for the arrest. In an arrest by a peace officer, the burden to establish that the arrest was unjustified is on the individual being arrested. However, in the case of an arrest by an off-duty police officer who was employed as a private security officer, the burden on proving the justification for the arrest is with the business.

The appellate court noted that a peace officer may arrest a person without a warrant whenever he has probable cause to believe that the person has committed a misdemeanor in his presence [Cal. Penal Code §836(1)]. A private citizen, however, may arrest another for a misdemeanor only when the offense has actually been committed or attempted in his presence [Cal. Penal Code §837(1)].

An off-duty police officer who is acting within the scope of his employment as a private security officer is not engaged in the performance of his duties as a peace officer for purposes of application of the enhanced punishment provisions of Cal. Penal Code §243 for battery on a peace officer.

The Private Investigator and Adjuster Act, Cal. Bus. & Prof. Code §7500 et seq., provides that no person subject to its regulatory provisions may use a title, or wear a uniform, or use an insignia, or use an identification card, or make any statement with the intent to give an impression that he is connected in any way with any political subdivision of a state government [Cal. Bus. & Prof. Code § 7538(e)].

Peace officers are subject to the regulatory provisions of the Private Investigator and Adjuster Act, Cal. Bus. & Prof. Code, §7500 et seq., when they are employed during their off-duty hours as private security officers. A police officer is thus prohibited from wearing his uniform or indicating in any way that he is a police officer when he is acting within the scope of his private employment as a security officer. The fact of private employment operates to prevent a peace officer from acting in what would otherwise be his official capacity.

Cal. Penal Code §490.5(e) provides in part that a merchant may detain a person for a reasonable time when he has probable cause to believe the person is shoplifting, that he may use reasonable nondeadly force in effecting such a detention, that he may examine any items in plain view that he has reasonable cause to believe have been unlawfully taken from his premises, and that it shall be a defense to an action for false arrest or imprisonment based on such a detention that the merchant had probable cause to believe the person detained had stolen or attempted to steal merchandise and that the merchant acted reasonably under the circumstances.

A cause of action for false imprisonment is stated where it is alleged that there was an arrest without process, followed by imprisonment and damages. Upon proof of those facts, the burden is on the defendant (J.C. Penney) to prove justification for the arrest.

Many states have eliminated the difference between false arrest and false imprisonment. As one Kentucky appellate court noted, there was no distinction between false arrest and false imprisonment in cases involving arrests, and "that reference books have even abandoned a separate title for False Arrest and all of these cases are indexed under False Imprisonment" (*Lexington-Fayette Urban County Gov't v. Middleton,* 555 S.W.2d 613, 619 (Ky. Ct. App. 1977).

Most states have statutes similar to Georgia's Code Ann. §105–1005, which provides that a plaintiff may not recover damages against the operator of a mercantile establishment for false arrest where it is established by competent evidence that the plaintiff had so conducted himself, or behaved in such manner, as to cause a person of reasonable prudence to believe that the plaintiff was committing the offense of shoplifting or provided that the manner of such detention or arrest and the length of time during which the plaintiff was detained was under all of the circumstances reasonable. The determination of whether the defendant acted with reasonable prudence or whether the manner and length of the detention were reasonable are matters for the jury, not the court, to determine.

In some states the rule is that damages may be recovered for false arrest even though the plaintiff has failed to show actual injuries, but many states require some actual damages before allowing a recovery. As one Georgia court noted: "Recovery of damages where the only injury is to the plaintiff's peace, feelings or happiness is allowed only under the same circumstances in which punitive damages would be allowed, i.e., where there is evidence of willful misconduct, maliciousness, or wanton disregard for consequences" [*Westview Cemetery v. Blanchard,* 234 Ga. 540, 545 (1975)].

Malicious Prosecution

To establish a cause of action for malicious prosecution, the plaintiff must prove the following elements to succeed in a claim for malicious prosecution: (1) the institution of original judicial proceedings, either civil or criminal; (2) by or at the encouragement of the defendant; (3) the termination of such proceedings in the plaintiff's favor; (4) malice in the institution of the proceeding; (5) want or lack of probable cause for the proceeding; and (6) the suffering of damage as a result of the proceeding.

In *Murillo v. Moore,* 2005 U.S. Dist. LEXIS 11759 (2005, WD. KY), the defendant, a private security officer at a Sam's Club store in Louisville, Kentucky, arrested the plaintiff on July 15, 2001. As the plaintiff was leaving the store, the defendant detained him and placed him under arrest, charging him with disorderly conduct, resisting arrest, and terroristic threatening. The charges were later dismissed by the Jefferson District Court when the security officer did not appear in court. As the result, the store and the officer were sued in court for malicious prosecution, false imprisonment, and battery.

The court stated that under Kentucky law, to prove a claim for battery, a plaintiff must show that the defendant intended to commit an offensive touching and that the touching occurred. When a police officer has no legal justification for an arrest or uses more force than is necessary to effect the arrest, the battery is an excessive use of force.

To sustain his claim for false imprisonment, the plaintiff must show that he was detained and that his detention was unlawful. In other words, the plaintiff must have been deprived, through an exercise of force, of his liberty to leave the store when he wished to do so.

The court noted that there was no factual dispute that the plaintiff was detained. He was arrested and taken to the Jefferson County Metropolitan Correctional Jail. The plaintiff established that he was subjected to criminal prosecution instituted by the defendant and that the proceeding ended in his favor when the charges were dismissed. The plaintiff, however, failed to establish that the defendant acted with malice. The court noted that the question as to whether a defendant acted with malice involves a subjective intent.

A paramedic testifies regarding an injury to a customer.

Intentional Infliction of Emotional Distress

Refer to the *Randall's Food Mkts. v. Johnson* facts as given in the previous section. The court noted that to recover for intentional infliction of emotional distress, a plaintiff must prove that (1) the defendant acted intentionally or recklessly, (2) the defendant's conduct was extreme and outrageous, (3) the defendant's actions caused the plaintiff emotional distress, and (4) the emotional distress suffered by the plaintiff was severe. The tort of intentional infliction of emotional distress includes the definition of extreme and outrageous conduct as conduct that is "so outrageous in character, and so extreme in degree, as to go beyond all possible bounds of decency, and to be regarded as atrocious, and utterly intolerable in a civilized community." The court held that evidence established that Randall's conduct was not "extreme and outrageous," an essential element of the tort of intentional infliction of emotional distress.

Defamation

Evans v. Keystone, 884 F. Supp. 1209 (C.D. Ill. 1995), is an interesting case involving the intentional tort of defamation. Evans was a former employee of Keystone who was fired as a result of an incident. Evans, although not scheduled to work, was on Keystone's premises in the early morning hours of October 24, 1992. At approximately 1:30 AM on this day, an on-duty private security officer received an anonymous call in which the caller stated that the officer would find "interesting" what was occurring in the locker room.

The officer reported this call to his dispatcher, requested that a second security officer assist him in investigating the call, and proceeded to the wire mill foreman's locker room via a patrol vehicle. En route to the locker room, the officer was joined by a female security officer at Keystone. As the two entered the locker room, they discovered Evans, a female, and a male Keystone employee together. Just how together was disputed. The security officer filed a report that stated that Evans and the male were involved in a sexual act in the locker room.

Evans was fired. She denied having sex in the locker room and filed the present case in response to her being discharged. The court noted that to state a claim for defamation under Illinois state law, a plaintiff must present facts sufficient to show that the defendants made a false statement concerning her, that there was an unprivileged publication to a third party with fault by the defendants, which caused damage to the plaintiff. Should the defamation claim arise within the context of an employer–employee relationship, the publication of the statement may be subject to a qualified privilege under Illinois law. An employer has a qualified privilege to communicate or publish allegedly defamatory statements to those in the company who have a legitimate employment interest in the statements. To overcome such a qualified privilege, a plaintiff would be required to prove that the statements were made with actual malice, because the defendants were acting within the course and scope of their employment by uttering the statements in an attempt to benefit their employer.

The court noted that because there was a legitimate employment interest in the statement, actual malice was required to establish liability. The court held that under Illinois state law, "actual malice" requires a person to prove that the statement was made with knowledge of its falsity or in reckless disregard of whether it was true or false.

Invasion of Privacy

A case involving the intentional tort of invasion of privacy is *Brooks v. Lady Foot Locker,* 2005 Ohio App. LEXIS 2281 (Ohio Ct. App., Summit County May 18, 2005). The Lady Foot Locker store did not have surveillance cameras or theft-deterrent sensors on the merchandise. A private security officer became suspicious when he noticed stacks of shirts and a rack of clothes in disarray. He did not see the two shoppers dishevel the clothes or put any unpurchased merchandise in their bags. The officer believed that some shirts were missing.

After the shoppers headed out of the store, the officer followed them. He them approached them and said, "Excuse me. I need to look in your bags." It is undisputed that the officer did not see the shoppers steal anything.

The shoppers argued that the officer invaded their privacy by following them closely through the mall and accusing them of stealing. The court noted that invasion of privacy claims involve the wrongful intrusion into one's private activities in such a manner as to outrage or cause mental suffering, shame, or humiliation to a person of ordinary sensibilities. One who intentionally intrudes, physically or otherwise, on the solitude or seclusion of another or his private affairs or concerns is subject to liability to the other for invasion of his privacy, if the intrusion would be highly offensive to a reasonable person. The court held that the employee did not invade the two girls' privacy by walking close to them in the mall and then requesting to look through their bags.

How to Invite a Civil Law Suit

Cases like *Jones v. Wet Seal Retail, Inc.,* 519 F. Supp. 2d 1164 (D. Kan. 2007), provide an excellent example of how not to handle a confrontation with a suspected shoplifter. Plaintiff Jones, a woman, was stopped for shoplifting. Defendant Arden B operated a retail business at the Oak Park Mall Shopping Center ("Oak Park Mall") in Johnson County, Kansas. Defendant ERMC provided security services at Oak Park Mall.

Jones alleged that on July 22, 2006, the defendants verbally accused her of stealing and/or shoplifting one or more bracelets from Arden B's retail store. Jones stated that she advised the defendants they were mistaken, the jewelry/bracelets they were accusing her of stealing were not Arden B's property, but that she had purchased them on a previous occasion from another store. Jones stated that she told the defendants her jewelry did not look like Arden B jewelry and that if the defendants checked a display jar located at or near the Arden B cash register, the allegedly stolen property would be found.

Jones alleged that various Oak Park Mall security officers physically restrained her (binding her hands behind her back with handcuffs), physically removed her against her will from the public area of the mall, and confined her in an isolated office in the mall that was restricted from public access. Jones claimed that one of the security officers who detained her was an off-duty reserve police officer for the City of Overland Park, Kansas ("City"), who was wearing a City police uniform with a City-issued police badge. Jones asserted that during her detention, the defendants advised her that she was going to be arrested by the police and prosecuted for shoplifting. Jones asserted that while she was restrained, the defendants made racial slurs to her, an African American, including numerous references to "white power," and that she was in fear for her physical safety.

After an indeterminate period of time, Jones was advised by the defendants that they had made a mistake and that she would not be arrested or prosecuted for shoplifting. An employee or agent of the defendants apologized for the mistake. Jones asserted that the defendants, however, continued to restrain her against her will in the secluded office and refused to remove her handcuffs. After another indeterminate period of time, a female Overland Park police officer, Deborah Swanson, appeared. The defendants requested that Officer Swanson arrest Jones and charge her with "causing a verbal disturbance." Officer Swanson refused the defendants' request, removed the handcuffs, and released Jones.

PROTECTION OF OTHERS

What if a security officer at a building notices that one driver exiting the building is under the influence of some type of drug or alcohol? Does the security officer have a legal duty to prevent the driver from leaving and driving on a public street? That was one of the questions considered in *Sports, Inc. v. Gilbert,* 431 N.E.2d 534 (1982, CA, IN). The defendant business appealed the decision of the Clark Circuit Court (Indiana), which entered a judgment upon a jury verdict against it in a personal injury and wrongful death action.

Sports, Inc. security officers questioned but did not arrest a third party who was found intoxicated on its premises. Subsequently, the third party left the premises in an automobile and caused injury to the plaintiffs, the injured parties, and the deaths of their children. The injured parties contended that the business owed a duty to protect them from the acts of the third party. The appellate court disagreed and found that the business's actions did not increase the risk of harm to the injured parties, that the injured parties did not rely on the business's undertaking, or that it undertook a duty owed by the third party. Further, the business had no duty to control the third party because there was no special relationship between them. The third party did not have a right to protection from the business and the business citizen had no right to intervene and control his actions. Thus, the business's conduct could not constitute negligence. Further, the business had no duty to make a citizen's arrest because it would have been liable for false imprisonment under these facts. The judgment of the trial court was reversed and the cause remanded for entry of judgment in Sports, Inc.'s favor.

Sports, Inc. owns and operates an automobile racetrack known as the Sportsdome Speedway (speedway). It employs a security force consisting of off-duty police officers and special deputies who control traffic and crowds on the premises. There is a parking lot outside the speedway, and the racetrack area itself is surrounded by a fence. This was not a case in which Sports, Inc. had sold intoxicating beverages or drugs to the third party. Most states have "dram act" statutes that may subject taverns and bars to civil and criminal liability if they sell drinks to intoxicated individuals. The majority of jurisdictions follow a general rule regarding the duty to control the conduct of a third person. This rule is

> There is no duty so to control the conduct of a third person as to prevent him from causing physical harm to another unless
>
> **a.** a special relation exists between the actor and the third person which imposes a duty upon the actor to control the third person's conduct, or
>
> **b.** a special relation exists between the actor and the other which gives to the other a right to protection. (*Birge v. Dollar Gen. Corp,* 2006)

The court noted that Indiana imposes civil liability against anyone who supplies alcoholic beverages to a minor or an intoxicated adult who causes personal injuries while driving under the influence. In these cases, liability stems from a duty imposed by statute. However, Riggs (the third party) did not consume alcohol at the speedway. In Indiana and elsewhere, the courts have shown great reluctance to require an individual to take any action to control a third party when there is no special relationship between them. When a special relationship does exist, the responsibilities it engenders are limited.

In *Shockley v. Zayre of Atlanta, Inc.* (1968) 118 Ga. App. 672, 165 S.E.2d 179, Zayre's duty to protect its business invitees did not extend to a situation in which a third party attacked a customer out of personal animosity toward the customer. In *Ambrose v. Kent Island Yacht Club, Inc.,* (1974) 22 Md. App., the plaintiff's daughter was injured during a game of catch at a yacht club picnic. The court held that the yacht club security officers were not negligent in failing to anticipate the negligence of the ball players.

The court noted that in all of the cases imposing liability for the failure to control the conduct of a third party, there were similar factors supporting the imposition of a duty. There was a person in need of special supervision or protection (i.e., a child, a drunkard, a business invitee) from someone who was in a superior position to provide it (parent, supplier of alcohol, business owner, hospital). This dependency is part of the special relationship. The other part of this special relationship is the right to intervene or control the actions of a third person. The court stated that it knew of no case from any jurisdiction that imposed a duty to control a third person when no right to control exists. The right to control another person's actions is essential to the imposition of this duty. If Sports had no right to control Riggs, its conduct cannot constitute negligence.

Summary

- The three types of civil liability are intentional torts, negligence, and strict liability.
- Intentional torts refer to willful acts, even those acts that a person honestly believed that he or she could lawfully commit.
- Negligence torts require a violation of a standard of care, the breech of a duty, proximate cause, foreseeability, and damages or injuries.

- Strict liability refers to liability without fault and normally does not involve security professionals.
- Negligence torts require a violation of a standard of care, the breech of a duty, proximate cause, foreseeability, and damages or injuries.
- Strict liability refers to liability without fault and normally does not involve security professionals.

Review Questions

1. What constitutes a false arrest?
2. Under what circumstances may a business detain a suspected shoplifter?
3. When can a security officer arrest an individual?
4. Under what circumstances does a business have a duty to protect a customer from actions of a third party?
5. If a security officer uses excessive force in arresting an individual, what torts has she committed?

Class Exercises

1. Have the class develop guidelines as to when a security officer may arrest a customer.
2. Have several members of the class act out a situation in which a customer is apparently shoplifting merchandise and explain the proper procedures that should be taken.

CHAPTER 11

Testifying in Court

CHAPTER OUTLINE

OBJECTIVES

After completing this chapter, you will be able to:

- Explain the necessity of making good reports.
- Understand the purpose of rules of evidence.
- Explain what constitutes hearsay evidence.
- Define what constitutes expert testimony.
- Explain how evidence is admitted.
- Know what to do to prepare to testify in court.
- Know what is expected of witnesses during direct examination.
- Know what occurs during cross-examination.

> *Students who want to make good grades hit the books prior to taking a test. Witnesses who expect to be called to present evidence in court should take their cues from college kids and study the material that's likely to be part of the court case.*
>
> —*Carole Moore (2005)*

This chapter provides an overview of the complicated rules of evidence and information related to testifying in court. Security personnel are often required to collect evidence or to testify in court. For example, an elaborate scheme to steal merchandise from a warehouse may result in the security director having to testify at trial to explain how he or she discovered the scheme, and evidence that a scheme existed will be needed in court. Generally, in these situations, the witness testifies as a witness for the prosecution in a criminal case. Another frequent situation in which security personnel are involved as witnesses in court cases occurs in civil actions, when an individual is either injured on the business premises or was detained or searched based on the security manager's determination that criminal misconduct was occurring, and the individual brings a civil action against the business for violation of his or her rights.

Numerous television shows attempt to portray what courtrooms are like. Police and security personnel are sometimes shown as cool professionals who do not recant their positions under fierce cross-examination. Unfortunately, real life bears little resemblance to television. Many times, witnesses become frustrated and flustered on the witness stand, especially if they have not prepared properly for the hearing. In court, witnesses have identified the wrong person as the perpetrator or individual involved, forgotten to mention important details, and made other embarrassing and avoidable mistakes. Many of the mistakes made during court hearings are the direct result of a witness's either failing to prepare for court or failing to discuss the case with the prosecutor or the business's counsel before taking the stand.

The following dialogue is an example of what can happen in court if key words are spelled incorrectly in the report submitted by a director of security. In this case, an incident occurred in which a woman customer was assaulted by another customer.

> ATTORNEY (DEFENSE ATTORNEY): Now sir, will you explain to the court why you attacked the victim after she had already been injured?
>
> WITNESS (DIRECTOR OF SECURITY): I did not attack the victim.
>
> ATTORNEY: But isn't this your signature on the report as the reporting individual?
>
> WITNESS: Yes.
>
> ATTORNEY: Now, sir, your report reads, "I raped her in a blanket and called for an ambulance."
>
> WITNESS: But sir, I meant wrapped.
>
> ATTORNEY: How many other errors are in your report?

The legal system is notorious for moving slowly. Days, weeks, or months may pass before a witness is called on to appear in court. For a security manager or other witness for the prosecution, the court appearance is the final step in the criminal justice process. It will tax the witnesses's communication skills to the limit.

REPORT WRITING

The following excerpts are from reports, many of which were approved by supervisors.

> Prieto threatened that Bach was going to hers and the police were going to charged also.
>
> They put the victim on a heart monitor and received a negative heatbeat.
>
> Capt. Crane showed me the locatioon of the victim's location.

Rp said the victim was pronunced dead by himself at 0200 hrs today.

The rear driver's side tire was flat but I could not find an entry or exit wound through the tire.

Not only do some security officers have difficulty writing a simple sentence, their spelling can cause laughter or professional embarrassment. Writing is an art, but with patience and attention to detail, effective reports can be developed. Reports are read by fellow officers, supervisors, and other professionals in the field. If you have not yet mastered the English language and spelling, now is the time to start. As a professional, you will be using written communications for the rest of your career.

Field notes are the notes an officer takes at the scene or immediately after leaving the scene. Field notes provide the basis for most incident reports. Field notes should be taken as soon as practicable after an incident. The notes should be made in some type of notebook. Some organizations specify notebook types that officers must use for recording field notes. Most officers prefer to use a loose-leaf notebook because it is easy to organize and pages can be removed for use in writing other reports and to refer to when testifying in court. Field notes should list the facts in the order in which they occurred or presented themselves. Because they are taken at the time the officer learns or observes the facts, they tend to be taken as the most accurate report of the incident. It is important that the field notes contain an unbiased report of the facts.

Different reports are used for different purposes. However, all initial reports should contain certain building blocks of information. This information can be organized under six separate headings: *who, what, when, where, how,* and *why.* Officers should use these heading as a guide to ensure that all the important information is included in their reports. In the following paragraphs, we use writing a report on a crime as an example. A similar approach can be used to write a report about an incident other than a crime.

Who

Who is much broader than who committed the crime or the incident in question. It is an all-inclusive category that requires special attention by the responding officer. The question of who is not answered by simply listing the name of the person involved.

Who requires the officer to identify all persons involved in the offense. Who is the victim? Many times, officers respond to a call and talk to a witness to a potential crime but discover that finding the victim may be time-consuming and, in some situations, futile.

Who is the offender? Is the person known to the victim, the witness, or other persons? Can the officer obtain a name, a description, or other information that may identify the offender?

Who are potential witnesses? Will they volunteer information, or are they afraid of retaliation by the offender? Witnesses should be identified by name, address, employment, and other information that will assist other officers if a follow-up investigation or a second interview of the witnesses is required.

Answering the question of who involves identifying the complaining party, the victim, the suspect, the witnesses, and any law enforcement personnel involved. This identification should include home and work addresses and telephone numbers, physical descriptions, and occupations when appropriate.

What

What is a broad question that covers a number of areas. The officer must ensure that all these areas are answered in any report. Injuries, damage, or other physical aspects of the crime or the crime scene that are observed by the officer must be included in any report.

The officer must determine what evidence is available and what evidence was not obtained. The evidence may be oral, visual, or physical. What was done with any evidence? Is there a chain of custody? Has it been properly marked, tagged, stored, and disposed of according to relevant policy and regulations?

The officer must also review what, if any, further actions are required. What agencies responded to the call? What agency assumed jurisdiction for the crime? What section or officers will conduct any necessary follow-up investigation?

What type of offense was committed? Was it a crime against a person or property? Was it an accident, a natural disaster, or an intentional act?

When

When means more than the date, day, and time of the incident. The officer must examine this question from the perspectives of the offense, the citizens involved in the incident, and the law enforcement agency that responds to the call for assistance. Each of these areas should be reviewed and basic information documented.

When was the offense committed or discovered? When was it reported? Was there a significant delay between discovery and reporting? If so, the officer needs to inquire into the reasons for the delay.

What persons were observed at the scene of a crime is a critical piece of information. What time did they arrive? How long did they stay? When did they leave? These are questions to which the officer should seek answers. Was the victim already at the scene, or did he or she arrive at that location at a certain time? Did any witnesses have an opportunity to view the scene of the crime before the officers arrived? If so, what was the time and how long did they view the scene? Did they observe the incident? If so, for how long and from what location?

When did police officers arrive at the scene of the crime? How much time had passed since the commission of the crime, the report of the crime, and the arrival of the police? When did the officer contact the police, the witnesses, or other parties and take their statements? Recording this information may be critical if a victim or witness later changes the story. The fact that the officer obtained a statement within minutes, hours, or days immediately after the incident, when the crime was fresh in these individuals' minds, may become important in court if the witnesses or the victim testify differently during the trial.

Where

Where must cover the offense, the persons involved in the incident, and police agencies. In the police report, the officer must answer questions about the location of all these variables.

The most obvious question to be asked is where the offense was committed. The officer should not automatically assume that the location of the property or the body is where the offense occurred. Where the crime occurred, where it was discovered, and where it was reported may be three distinct locations. For each of these factors, the officer should ensure that any report clearly indicates the location and type of activity involved.

The location should be described by street address, intersection, or exact location in any building. The officer should ensure that the location is clear and understandable by any person who reads the report. For example, what is the difference between a living room and a family room?

The officer should ensure that all available information is obtained about persons involved in the incident. The locations of the victim, the witnesses, and the suspect are critical to any investigation. Where they reside, their work addresses, all telephone numbers, and other information necessary to get in contact with them should be gathered and recorded by the officer. In addition, the locations of all the parties at the time of the crime are important. Exactly where they were located may have a significant impact on the admissibility of their testimony. For example, a witness who was located across the street would probably not have been able to observe the suspect's eye color.

The locations and activities of the police should also be carefully recorded. Where they interviewed victims, witnesses, and suspects is important.

How

How the offense was committed is important for *modus operandi* files. What tools were used and how they were used are often critical pieces of evidence that may link the offense to other, similar crimes. How was the offense discovered? How was it reported?

How various persons were involved in the crime is often overlooked by inexperienced officers. How was the victim transported to the hospital? How did the suspect arrive and depart the crime scene? How did witnesses happen to be at the location of the incident?

How police agencies responded at the scene of the crime is also important. How did the officer identify the victim, the suspect, and the witnesses? How did the officer locate these individuals?

Why

Motive, or *why* a person commits a crime, is not traditionally one of the elements of an offense. However, prosecutors and jurors want to know why the crime was committed; therefore, officers should attempt to answer this question if possible. Why was the offense reported? Was it for insurance purposes, to seek revenge, or for other reasons? Why did the suspect commit the crime in that manner? Was an easier method available to accomplish the crime, and why did the suspect not use it? Why did witnesses come forward? Is there any bias, prejudice, or motive to their cooperation?

As the preceding discussion indicates, there are several ways of asking the same question. If the officer approaches report writing using this method, there will be no gaps or missing pieces of information in the report. Gathering information is only the first step in writing a complete report. Once the information is obtained, the officer must organize it.

RULES OF EVIDENCE

The study of evidence is a study of regulation of the process of proving facts. Evidence law was originally almost entirely decisional law. Now, it is codified in statutes and court rules. For purposes of this chapter, we will examine evidence based on the federal rules. The federal rules do not depart significantly from common law decisions. Most state rules of evidence are based on the federal rules, with only slight differences among the states. Evidence is a very complex and difficult subject. In this chapter, we will cover only the highlights to acquaint readers with the subject.

"Evidentiary rules should be construed in a manner to attempt to secure fairness in administration, elimination of unjustifiable expense and delay, and promotion of growth and development of the law of evidence to the end that the truth may be ascertained and proceedings justly determined" [*United States v. Haddad,* 10 F.3d 1252, 1257 (7th Cir. 1993)]. The two basic themes found in the federal rules are that:

- The rules favor admissibility of evidence.
- The trial judge has considerable discretion as to the admissibility of evidence.

A trial judge has the authority (discretion) to fashion evidentiary procedures to deal with situations not specifically covered by the rules. In interpreting the rules, it is important for judges to differentiate when Congress or the legislatures have spoken and finally determined an issue and when they have left room for judicial interpretation. As the Third Circuit stated in *United States v. Pelullo* [964 F.2d 193, 3rd. Cir. (1993)], while the rules "are to be liberally construed in favor of admissibility, this does not mean that we may ignore requirements of specific provisions merely because we view the proffered evidence as trustworthy."

Federal Rule 102 establishes a principle of flexibility in the application of the Federal Rules of Evidence. Most states have a similar rule. The U.S. Supreme Court has stated that judicial flexibility has no place when the "plain meaning" of a Federal Rule of Evidence mandates a certain result. However, cases such as *Daubert v. Merrell Dow Pharmaceuticals Inc.* [509 U.S. 579 (1993)] and *United States v. Mezzanatto* [513 U.S. 196 (1995)] indicate that the Supreme Court is sometimes willing to employ a more flexible approach than a rigid adherence to plain meaning would seem to allow.

The Hearsay Rule

Hearsay is a statement other than one made by the declarant while testifying at a trial or hearing, which is offered in evidence to prove the truth of the matter asserted. A statement is not hearsay if:

Statement:

An an oral or written assertion, or nonverbal conduct of a person, if it is intended by the person as an assertion.

Declarant:

A person who makes a statement.

- The declarant testifies at the trial or hearing and is subject to cross-examination concerning the statement, and the statement is (A) inconsistent with the declarant's testimony, and was given under oath subject to the penalty of perjury at a trial, hearing, or other proceeding, or in a deposition, or (B) consistent with the declarant's testimony and is offered to rebut an express or implied charge against the declarant of recent fabrication or improper influence or motive, or (C) one of identification of a person made after perceiving the person; or
- *Admission by party-opponent.* The statement is offered against a party and is (A) the party's own statement in either an individual or a representative capacity or (B) a statement of which the party has manifested an adoption or belief in its truth, or (C) a statement by a person authorized by the party to make a statement concerning the subject, or (D) a statement by the party's agent or servant concerning a matter within the scope of the agency or employment, made during the existence of the relationship, or (E) a statement by a coconspirator of a party during the course and in furtherance of the conspiracy. The contents of the statement shall be considered but are not alone sufficient to establish the declarant's authority under subdivision (C), the agency or employment relationship and scope thereof under subdivision (D), or the existence of the conspiracy and the participation therein of the declarant and the party against whom the statement is offered under subdivision (E). [*United States v. Haddad,* 10 F.3d 1252, 1257–58 (7th Cir. 1993)]

General Rule on Hearsay

Hearsay is inadmissible unless an exception is applicable. Exceptions to the hearsay rule include:

- Affidavits to show grounds for issuing warrants.
- Affidavits to determine issues of fact in connection with motions.
- A statement describing or explaining an event or condition made while the declarant was perceiving the event or condition, or immediately thereafter.
- A statement relating to a startling event or condition made while the declarant was under the stress of excitement caused by the event or condition.
- A statement of the declarant's then existing state of mind, emotion, sensation, or physical condition (such as intent, plan, motive, design, mental feeling, pain, and bodily health), but not including a statement of memory or belief to prove the fact remembered or believed unless it relates to the execution, revocation, identification, or terms of declarant's will.
- Statements made for purposes of medical diagnosis or treatment and describing medical history, or past or present symptoms, pain, or sensations, or the inception or general character of the cause or external source thereof insofar as reasonably pertinent to diagnosis or treatment.

- A memorandum or record concerning a matter about which a witness once had knowledge but now has insufficient recollection to enable the witness to testify fully and accurately, shown to have been made or adopted by the witness when the matter was fresh in the witness' memory and to reflect that knowledge correctly. If admitted, the memorandum or record may be read into evidence but may not itself be received as an exhibit unless offered by an adverse party.
- A memorandum, report, record, or data compilation, in any form, of acts, events, conditions, opinions, or diagnoses, made at or near the time by, or from information transmitted by, a person with knowledge, if kept in the course of a regularly conducted business activity, and if it was the regular practice of that business activity to make the memorandum, report, record or data compilation. The term "business" includes business, institution, association, profession, occupation, and calling of every kind, whether or not conducted for profit.
- Evidence that a matter is not included in the memoranda reports, records, or data compilations, in any form, to prove the nonoccurrence or nonexistence of the matter, if the matter was of a kind of which a memorandum, report, record, or data compilation was regularly made and preserved, unless the sources of information or other circumstances indicate lack of trustworthiness.
- *Records, reports, statements, or data compilations,* in any form, of public offices or agencies, setting forth (A) the activities of the office or agency, or (B) matters observed pursuant to duty imposed by law as to which matters there was a duty to report, excluding, however, in criminal cases matters observed by police officers and other law enforcement personnel, or (C) in civil actions and proceedings and against the Government in criminal cases, factual findings resulting from an investigation made pursuant to authority granted by law, unless the sources of information or other circumstances indicate lack of trustworthiness.
- *Records of vital statistics.* Records or data compilations, in any form, of births, fetal deaths, deaths, or marriages, if the report thereof was made to a public office pursuant to requirements of law.
- *Absence of public record or entry.* To prove the absence of a record, report, statement, or data compilation, in any form, or the nonoccurrence or nonexistence of a matter of which a record, report, statement, or data compilation, in any form, was regularly made and preserved by a public office or agency, evidence in the form of a certification in accordance with rule 902, or testimony, that diligent search failed to disclose the record, report, statement, or data compilation, or entry.
- *Records of religious organizations.* Statements of births, marriages, divorces, deaths, legitimacy, ancestry, relationship by blood or marriage, or other similar facts of personal or family history, contained in a regularly kept record of a religious organization. Marriage, baptismal, and similar certificates. Statements of fact contained in a certificate that the maker performed a marriage or other ceremony or administered a sacrament, made by a clergyman, public official, or other person authorized by the rules or practices of a religious organization or by law to perform the act certified, and purporting to have been issued at the time of the act or within a reasonable time thereafter.

- *Family records.* Statements of fact concerning personal or family history contained in family Bibles, genealogies, charts, engravings on rings, inscriptions on family portraits, engravings on urns, crypts, or tombstones, or the like.
- *Statements in ancient documents.* Statements in a document in existence twenty years or more the authenticity of which is established.
- *Judgment of previous conviction.* Evidence of a final judgment, entered after a trial or upon a plea of guilty (but not upon a plea of nolo contendere or no contest), adjudging a person guilty of a crime punishable by death or imprisonment in excess of one year, to prove any fact essential to sustain the judgment, but not including, when offered by the Government in a criminal prosecution for purposes other than impeachment, judgments against persons other than the accused. The pendency of an appeal may be shown but does not affect admissibility. [*United States v. Haddad,* 10 F.3d 1252, 1259 (7th Cir. 1993)]

The following are not excluded by the hearsay rule if the declarant is unavailable as a witness:

1. ***Former testimony.*** Testimony given as a witness at another hearing of the same or a different proceeding, or in a deposition taken in compliance with law in the course of the same or another proceeding, if the party against whom the testimony is now offered, or, in a civil action or proceeding, a predecessor in interest, had an opportunity and similar motive to develop the testimony by direct, cross, or redirect examination.

2. ***Statement under belief of impending death.*** In a prosecution for homicide or in a civil action or proceeding, a statement made by a declarant while believing that the declarant's death was imminent, concerning the cause or circumstances of what the declarant believed to be impending death.

3. ***Statement against interest.*** A statement which was at the time of its making so far contrary to the declarant's pecuniary or proprietary interest, or so far tended to subject the declarant to civil or criminal liability, or to render invalid a claim by the declarant against another, that a reasonable person in the declarant's position would not have made the statement unless believing it to be true. A statement tending to expose the declarant to criminal liability and offered to exculpate the accused is not admissible unless corroborating circumstances clearly indicate the trustworthiness of the statement. [*United States v. Haddad,* 10 F.3d 1252, 1259 (7th Cir. 1993)]

Redirect examination:
The prosecutor's opportunity to clarify any issues raised during cross-examination.

Rulings on Evidence

Rulings on evidence cannot be assigned as error on appeal unless (1) a substantial right is affected, and (2) the nature of the error was called to the attention of the judge, so as to alert him or her to the proper course of action and enable opposing counsel to take proper corrective measures. The objection and the offer of proof are the techniques for accomplishing these objectives. An exception to this requirement is the "plain error" rule. Under the plain error rule, an appellate court may consider a judicial ruling on the evidence if the ruling was clearly wrong and prejudiced the defendant.

In jury cases, proceedings regarding evidentiary questions are generally conducted, to the extent practicable outside the presence of the jury, so as to prevent inadmissible evidence from being suggested to the jury by any means, such as making statements or offers of proof or asking questions in the hearing of the jury.

In some states, each time that the evidence is offered or referred to, the opposing party must renew any objections to the evidence. Most courts take a more flexible approach, holding that the renewal of objections is not required if the issue decided is one that (1) was fairly presented to the trial court for an initial ruling, (2) may be decided as a final matter before the evidence is actually offered, and (3) was ruled on definitively by the trial judge [*Rosenfeld v. Basquiat,* 78 F.3d 84 (2d Cir. 1996)]. Other courts distinguished between objections to evidence, which must be renewed when evidence is offered, and offers of proof, which need not be renewed after a definitive determination is made that the evidence is inadmissible.

Preliminary Questions

Preliminary questions concerning the qualification of a person to be a witness, the existence of a privilege, or the admissibility of evidence is determined by the court (trial judge). For example, the first question asked a witness, usually "What is your name?" is considered as preliminary question.

Hearings on the admissibility of confessions should be conducted out of the hearing of the jury. Hearings on other preliminary matters should also be conducted outside the hearing of the jury when the interests of justice require, or when an accused is a witness and so requests. The accused does not, by testifying on a preliminary matter, become subject to cross-examination as to other issues in the case.

Limited Admissibility

When evidence that is admissible as to one defendant or for one purpose but not admissible as to another defendant or for another purpose is admitted, the court, on request, will restrict the evidence to its proper scope and instruct the jury accordingly. For example, when evidence that a witness has made a prior inconsistent statement is admitted, the judge will generally instruct the jury that the prior statement was admitted only for the purpose of attacking the creatability of the witness and not for the purpose of showing that the prior statement was true. Federal Rule 195 allows for admission of the evidence for a limited purpose but provides protection by way of limiting instruction to the non-offering party who will be prejudiced by the evidence.

Burden on Parties to Object

When evidence is admitted for a limited purpose, or against only one party, the judge should instruct the jury as to the proper scope of the evidence. The burden is on the party who wants the instruction to ask for it.

Nothing prohibits a trial judge from providing a limiting instruction *sua sponte* (on the judge's own action) [*United States v. Mark,* 943 F.2d 444 (4th Cir. 1991)]. There is often good reason for a trial court judge to avoid giving an instruction that is not requested. The party who is otherwise entitled to an instruction may have made a strategic decision that he or she is better off without one—that is, that an instruction would only serve to emphasize the evidence that the jury has heard, and may suggest a use to which the evidence could be put that the jury might not even have thought about.

The fact that evidence is admissible for a limited purpose does not require that the evidence be admitted. If the prejudicial effect of evidence substantially outweighs its probative value, despite a limiting instruction, then the non-offering party can argue that the evidence should be completely excluded because any limiting instruction would be inadequate.

A trial judge, in determining the prejudice to be suffered from the offered evidence, must necessarily take into account whether this prejudice can be sufficiently ameliorated by a limiting instruction. A trial judge is required to restrict the evidence to its proper scope and to instruct the jury accordingly if a request is made, but it does not articulate the requirements of a proper request.

Admission of Part of a Document

When a writing or recorded statement or part thereof is introduced by a party, an adverse party may require the introduction at that time of any other part or any other writing or recorded statement that ought in fairness to be considered contemporaneously with it. The rule is an expression of the rule of completeness. The rule is based on two considerations. The first is the misleading impression created by taking matters out of context. The second is the inadequacy of repair work when delayed to a point later in the trial.

The rule of completeness does not prevent the other party from developing the matter on cross-examination or as part of his or her own case. The rule is limited to writings and recorded statements and does not apply to conversations. The rule applies to separate writings and recordings as well as to excised portions of a single writing or recording.

Oral Statements

When a party introduces a portion of an oral statement, the adversary is entitled to have omitted portions introduced at the same time, insofar as that is necessary to correct any misimpression that the initially proffered portion would create [*United States v. Haddad,* 10 F.3d 1252, 1259 (7th Cir. 1993)].

"Fairness"

The "fairness" rule requires admission of completing evidence only when it ought "in fairness" to be considered with the admitted statement [*United States v. Wright,* 826 F.2d 938 (10th Cir. 1987)]. For example, the rule does not require that "portions of writing which are neither explanatory of the previously introduced portions nor relevant to the introduced portions be admitted" [*United States v. Wright,* 826 F.2d 938, 941 (10th Cir. 1987)]; the rule does not mean that if any part of a statement is to be admitted, then the entire statement is to be admitted. Sometimes it is difficult to determine whether "fairness" mandates the admission of allegedly completing evidence.

A good example of the rule's fairness principle arose in *United States v. Haddad.* Haddad was being prosecuted for a firearms offense. In a postarrest confession, he stated that he knew that marijuana was under his bed, but that he did not know that a gun was under the bed. At trial, the inculpatory statement was admitted as an admission, but the exculpatory statement was excluded as hearsay. The Court of Appeals found that the confession had been improperly (though harmlessly) redacted (edited) to exclude the exculpatory statement about the gun. The court noted that ordinarily, a defendant's self-serving, exculpatory, out-of-court statements would not be admissible. But here the exculpatory remarks were part and parcel of the very statement a portion of which the Government was properly bringing before the jury, that is, the defendant's admission about the marijuana.

Judicial Notice

The concept of judicial notice is used when a relevant fact is so well known that to require that it be proved would be a waste of time. For example, a trial judge may take judicial notice that July 4th is a court holiday. A judicially noticed fact must be one that is not subject to reasonable dispute in that it is either (1) generally known within the territorial jurisdiction of the trial court or (2) capable of accurate and ready determination by resort to sources whose accuracy cannot reasonably be questioned. A party is entitled upon timely request to an opportunity to be heard as to the propriety of taking judicial notice and the tenor of the matter noticed. In the absence of prior notification, the request may be made after judicial notice has been taken. Judicial notice may be taken at any stage of the proceeding.

RELEVANT EVIDENCE

Evidence is relevant when it has some tendency as a matter of logic and human experience to make the proposition for which it is advanced more likely than that proposition would appear to be in the absence of that evidence. To identify logically irrelevant evidence, ask, "Does the evidence assist in proving the fact that one party is trying to prove?" (Paciocco and Stuesser 1996, xvii). Problems of relevancy call for an answer to the question whether an item of evidence possesses sufficient probative value to justify receiving it in evidence. For example, evidence that a person purchased a revolver shortly before a fatal shooting with which he is charged is considered relevant because it may prove the person was guilty of the fatal shooting if the gun used in the shooting is the same gun that was purchased.

Under the concept of "conditional" relevancy, probative value depends not only on satisfying the basic requirement of relevancy as described above but also on the existence of some matter of fact. For example, if evidence of a spoken statement is relied on to prove notice, probative value is lacking unless the person sought to be charged heard the statement. Does the item of evidence tend to prove the matter sought to be proved?

Exclusion of Relevant Evidence

Although it is relevant, evidence may be excluded if its probative value is substantially outweighed by the danger of unfair prejudice, confusion of the issues, or misleading the jury, or by considerations of undue delay, waste of time, or needless presentation of cumulative evidence. Case law recognizes that certain circumstances call for the exclusion of evidence that is of unquestioned relevance. These circumstances entail risks that range all the way from inducing decision on a purely emotional basis at one extreme, to nothing more harmful than merely wasting time, at the other extreme. Situations in this area call for balancing the probative value of and need for the evidence against the harm likely to result from its admission.

Exclusion for risk of unfair prejudice, confusion of issues, misleading the jury, or waste of time all find ample support in the authorities. "Unfair prejudice" within its context means an undue tendency to suggest decision on an improper basis, commonly, though not necessarily, an emotional one. Surprise is generally not a ground for exclusion under this concept, but unfair surprise may be a ground for exclusion if it is coupled with the danger of prejudice and confusion of issues.

Character Evidence Not Admissible to Prove Conduct

Evidence of a person's character or a trait of character is not admissible for the purpose of proving action in conformity therewith on a particular occasion, except:

- Character of accused. Evidence of a pertinent trait of character offered by an accused, or by the prosecution to rebut the same, or if evidence of a trait of character of the alleged victim of the crime is offered by an accused and admitted, evidence of the same trait of character of the accused offered by the prosecution.
- Evidence of a pertinent trait of character of the alleged victim of the crime offered by an accused, or by the prosecution to rebut the same, or evidence of a character trait of peacefulness of the alleged victim offered by the prosecution in a homicide case to rebut evidence that the alleged victim was the first aggressor.
- Evidence of the character of a witness may be admissible to impeach the witnesses' testimony.
- Evidence of other crimes, wrongs, or acts is not admissible to prove the character of a person in order to show action in conformity therewith. It may, however, be admissible for other purposes, such as proof of motive, opportunity, intent, preparation, plan, knowledge, identity, or absence of mistake or accident, provided that, upon request by the accused, the prosecution in a criminal case shall provide reasonable notice in advance of trial, or during trial if the court excuses pretrial notice on good cause shown, of the general nature of any such evidence it intends to introduce at trial. (Roberson 2008, 131–3).

Character questions arise in two fundamentally different ways: (1) Character may itself be an element of a crime, claim, or defense. A situation of this kind is commonly referred to as *character in issue*. Illustrations include the competency of the driver in an action for negligently entrusting a motor vehicle to an incompetent driver. No problem of the general relevancy of character evidence is involved, and the rule therefore has no provision on the subject. (2) Character evidence is susceptible of being used for the purpose of suggesting an inference that the person acted on the occasion in question consistently with his character. This use of character is often described as *circumstantial*. Illustrations are evidence of a violent disposition to prove that the person was the aggressor in an affray, or evidence of honesty to disprove a charge of theft. This circumstantial use of character evidence raises questions of relevancy as well as questions of allowable methods of proof (Roberson 2008).

In most jurisdictions today, the circumstantial use of character is rejected, but with important exceptions: (1) An accused may introduce pertinent evidence of good character (often misleadingly described as "putting his character in issue"), in which event the prosecution may rebut with evidence of bad character; (2) an accused may introduce pertinent evidence of the character of the victim, as in support of a claim of self-defense to a charge of homicide or consent in a case of rape, and the prosecution may introduce similar evidence in rebuttal of the character evidence, or, in a homicide case, to rebut a claim that deceased was the first aggressor, however proved; and (3) the character of a witness may be gone into as bearing on his credibility.

Character evidence is of slight probative value and may be very prejudicial. It tends to distract the jury from the main question of what actually happened on the particular occasion. It subtly permits the jury to reward the good person or to punish the bad person because of their respective characters despite what the evidence in the case shows actually happened.

WITNESSES

Every person is competent to be a witness except as otherwise provided in these rules.

—Federal Rule 601

General Rule of Competency

In common law, only certain individuals were qualified to testify as witnesses. The present rule is that every person is competent to be a witness except as otherwise provided in the rules. This general ground-clearing eliminates all grounds of incompetency not specifically recognized. Disqualifications under common law included religious belief, conviction of crime, and connection with the litigation as a party or interested person or spouse of a party or interested person. U.S. jurisdictions generally have ceased to recognize these grounds. In *United States v. Ramirez* [871 F.2d 582, 584 (6th Cir. 1989)], the Court of Appeals held that the trial court did not abuse its discretion in admitting the testimony of a cocaine addict.

No mental or moral qualifications for testifying as a witness are specified. Standards of mental capacity have proved elusive in actual application. Discretion is regularly exercised in favor of allowing the testimony. The question is one particularly suited to the jury as one of weight and credibility, subject to judicial authority to review the sufficiency of the evidence. Standards of moral qualification in practice consist essentially of evaluating a person's truthfulness in terms of his or her own answers about it.

Competency of Hearsay Declarants

Because a trial judge has the authority in extreme cases to exclude a witness on grounds of incompetency, a question arises whether the witness's hearsay statements should be excluded as well, even if they would otherwise fit a hearsay exception. This problem occurs fairly frequently in cases that raise issues of child abuse, when the child victim has made hearsay statements that would be admissible under a hearsay exception—most commonly Federal Rule 803(2), 803(4), or 807—and yet the child is too young to appreciate the consequences of the oath and the responsibilities of being a witness. Most courts have held that a person's incompetence to testify as a witness has no bearing on the admissibility of the hearsay statement. The reasoning is that the grounds for admitting the hearsay statement have nothing to do with the witness's ability to appreciate the oath and the consequences of testifying. For example, if the hearsay statement is an excited utterance of a young child, its truthfulness is supported by the fact that the child made the statement while under the influence of a startling event. If this is so, it does not matter that the child has no appreciation of the consequences of the oath; the hearsay statement is reliable anyway [*United States v. Dorian,* 803 F.2d 1439 (8th Cir. 1986)].

Non-Expert Witness's Lack of Personal Knowledge

A witness may not testify to a matter unless evidence is introduced sufficient to support a finding that the witness has personal knowledge of the matter. Evidence to prove personal knowledge may, but need not, consist of the witness's own testimony. This rule is subject to the provisions of Federal Rule 703, relating to opinion testimony by expert witnesses.

The rule requiring that a witness who testifies to a fact that can be perceived by the senses must have had an opportunity to observe, and must have actually observed the fact is a "most pervasive manifestation" of the common law insistence on "the most reliable sources of information." These foundation requirements may, of course, be furnished by the testimony of the witness himself or herself; hence personal knowledge is not an absolute but may consist of what the witness thinks he or she knows from personal perception (Roberson 2008). A witness need not be absolutely certain of the event related in order to satisfy the personal knowledge requirement. It is enough that a reasonable juror could find that the witness perceived the event. Moreover, perfect knowledge is not required—the witness can be vague about certain details and still have enough knowledge to testify. A problem in the witness's perception generally goes to weight and not admissibility. For example, the fact that a witness cannot recall specific dates does not require exclusion of that testimony, because inability to recall specific dates does not demonstrate an absence of personal knowledge [*United States v. Powers,* 75 F.3d 335 (7th Cir. 1996)].

Oath or Affirmation

Before testifying, a witness is required to declare that the witness will testify truthfully, by oath or affirmation administered in a form calculated to awaken the witness's conscience and impress the witness's mind with the duty to do so. Along with cross-examination, the requirement of an oath is designed to ensure that every witness gives accurate and honest testimony. The idea behind the oath requirement is to preserve the integrity of the judicial process by awakening the witness's conscience and making the witness amenable to perjury prosecution if he fibs [*United States v. Zizzo,* 120 F.3d 1338 (7th Cir. 1997)]. Federal Rule 603 states that a witness need not swear an oath but may merely affirm that he or she will testify truthfully. The affirmation can be given in any form calculated to awaken the conscience of the witness and impress on the witness the duty to tell the truth. By permitting affirmation as well as oath, many of the difficulties faced by certain members of some religious groups should be alleviated.

In *United States v. Ward* [989 F.2d 1015 (9th Cir. 1993)], the defendant refused to testify because the trial judge did not permit him to take an altered version of the standard oath. The defendant would have taken an oath that substituted the term "fully integrated honesty" for the word "truth." The Court of Appeals held that the trial court was in error for refusing to accede to the defendant's demand. It found the defendant's objection to the standard oath to be based on "beliefs that are protected by the First Amendment." The Court noted that there is no rigid formula for an acceptable oath. For example, a proffered oath that "I would not tell a lie to stay out of jail" has been properly rejected, because the witness could later say that he lied for some purpose other than to stay out of jail, such as to protect a relative [*United States v. Fowler,* 605 F.2d 181 (5th Cir. 1979)].

Impeachment of a Witness

Impeachment is a legal term referring to the process of attacking the credibility of a witness. The rules provide that the credibility of any witness may be attacked by any party, including the party calling the witness. Under common law, a party who called a witness could not impeach that witness unless the court declared the witness a "hostile witness." This is no longer the rule in most jurisdictions. The rationale for the common law rule rested on assumptions concerning a party's presumptive support of a witness called by that party, and the need to protect the witness from harassment. The Federal Rules recognize that a party does not necessarily vouch for a witness; in fact, a party may have no choice but to call an adverse witness in order to prove a case.

Evidence of Character and Conduct of Witness

The credibility of a witness may be attacked or supported by evidence in the form of opinion or reputation, but subject to these limitations: (1) the evidence may refer only to character for truthfulness or untruthfulness, and (2) evidence of truthful character is admissible only after the character of the witness for truthfulness has been attacked by opinion or reputation evidence or otherwise.

Specific instances of the conduct of a witness, for the purpose of attacking or supporting the witness's character for truthfulness, may, at the discretion of the court, if probative of truthfulness or untruthfulness, be inquired into on cross-examination of the witness (1) concerning the witness's character for truthfulness or untruthfulness, or (2) concerning the character for truthfulness or untruthfulness of another witness as to which character the witness being cross-examined has testified.

Impeachment by Evidence of Conviction of Crime

Evidence that a witness other than an accused has been convicted of a crime is admissible, if the crime was punishable by death or imprisonment in excess of one year under the law under which the witness was convicted, and evidence that an accused has been convicted of such a crime shall be admitted if the court determines that the probative value of admitting this evidence outweighs its prejudicial effect to the accused; and evidence that any witness has been convicted of a crime shall be admitted if it involved dishonestly or false statement, regardless of the punishment (Roberson 2008).

Evidence of a conviction is not admissible if a period of more than ten years has elapsed since the date of the conviction or of the release of the witness from the confinement imposed for that conviction, whichever is the later date, unless the court determines, in the interests of justice, that the probative value of the conviction supported by specific facts and circumstances substantially outweighs its prejudicial effect. However, evidence of a conviction more than ten years old is not admissible unless the proponent gives to the adverse party sufficient advance written notice of intent to use such evidence to provide the adverse party with a fair opportunity to contest the use of such evidence (Roberson 2008).

Evidence of a conviction is not admissible under this rule if the conviction has been the subject of a pardon, annulment, certificate of rehabilitation, or other equivalent procedure based on a finding of the rehabilitation of the person convicted, and that person has not been convicted of a subsequent crime that was punishable by death or imprisonment in excess of one year, or the conviction has been the subject of a pardon, annulment, or other equivalent procedure based on a finding of innocence.

Evidence of juvenile adjudications is generally not admissible. The court may, however, in a criminal case allow evidence of a juvenile adjudication of a witness other than the accused if conviction of the offense would be admissible to attack the credibility of an adult and the court is satisfied that admission in evidence is necessary for a fair determination of the issue of guilt or innocence.

Mode and Order of Interrogation and Presentation

The court exercises reasonable control over the mode and order of interrogating witnesses and presenting evidence so as to (1) make the interrogation and presentation effective for the ascertainment of the truth, (2) avoid needless consumption of time, and (3) protect witnesses from harassment or undue embarrassment.

Cross-examination should be limited to the subject matter of the direct examination and matters affecting the credibility of the witness. A court may, in the exercise of discretion, permit inquiry into additional matters as if on direct examination.

Leading questions should not be used on the direct examination of a witness except as may be necessary to develop the witness's testimony. Ordinarily, leading questions should be permitted on cross-examination. When a party calls a hostile witness, an adverse party, or a witness identified with an adverse party, interrogation may be by leading questions.

A witness may be cross-examined on any matter relevant to any issue in the case, including credibility. In the interests of justice, the judge may limit cross-examination with respect to matters not testified to on direct examination.

Prior Statements of Witnesses

In examining a witness concerning a prior statement made by the witness, whether written or not, the statement need not be shown nor its contents disclosed to the witness at that time, but on request the same shall be shown or disclosed to opposing counsel. Evidence of a prior inconsistent statement by a witness is not admissible unless the witness is afforded an opportunity to explain or deny the same and the opposite party is afforded an opportunity to interrogate the witness thereon, or the interests of justice otherwise require.

One of the traditional ways of impeaching a witness is by introducing evidence of a prior inconsistent statement. Under common law, the examining party was required to lay an adequate foundation for the statement at the time the witness testified. This was referred to as "the rule in Queen Caroline's case." That rule required the cross-examining party to confront the witness directly on cross-examination with the inconsistent statement. At that point, the witness would have an opportunity to explain, repudiate, or deny the statement. If the witness denied making the statement, then the trial court could, at its discretion, permit the cross-examining party to prove that the statement was made.

Federal Rule 613 provides that when a witness is examined concerning a prior statement, this statement need not be shown to the witness at the time of the examination. However, before evidence of the statement can be introduced, the witness must be given some opportunity, at some point in the trial, to explain, repudiate, or deny the statement.

Upon request of opposing counsel, the contents of the statement must be disclosed, so that opposing counsel may protect his case against unwarranted insinuations that a statement has been made. The time for the showing or disclosure is when the witness is examined about the prior statement, assuming that a proper request is made.

Opportunity for Witness to Explain or Deny the Statement

The basic common law foundation consists of affording the witness an opportunity of either admitting or denying that a prior inconsistent statement was made and, if he admits it, of explaining the circumstances of the statement. The traditional method of confronting a witness with his inconsistent statement prior to its introduction is the preferred method of proceeding. In fact, where the proponent of the testimony fails to do so, and the witness subsequently becomes unavailable, the proponent runs the risk that the court will properly exercise its discretion to not allow the admission of the prior statement.

Exclusion of Witnesses (Invoking the Rule)

At the request of a party, the court shall order witnesses excluded so that they cannot hear the testimony of other witnesses, and it may make the order of its own motion. This rule does not authorize exclusion of (1) a party who is a natural person, or (2) an officer or employee of a party that is not a natural person designated as its representative by its attorney, or (3) a person whose presence is shown by a party to be essential to the presentation of the party's cause, or (4) a person authorized by statute to be present.

The sequestration of prospective witnesses is a common method of discouraging or preventing collusion and exposing inaccuracies in testimony. Federal Rule 615 provides that, at the request of a party, or on its own motion, the court can order witnesses excluded so that they cannot hear the testimony of other witnesses. Where a victim of a crime is a witness in a criminal case, the sequestration power set forth in Rule 615 has been substantially changed by legislation.

In a criminal case, the Sixth and Fourteenth Amendments entitle a defendant to be present, although the defendant may "waive" that right in several ways. It is generally held that the police officer in charge of the investigation is within the "officer or employee" exception provided in Rule 615. As noted by the Appellate Court in *United States v. Payan* [992 F.2d 1387 (5th Cir. 1993)], a defendant has no right to sequestration of the officer in charge of the investigation.

Opinion Testimony by Lay (Non-Expert) Witnesses

If a witness is not testifying as an expert, the witness's testimony in the form of opinions or inferences is limited to those opinions or inferences that are (1) rationally based on the perception of the witness, and (2) helpful to a clear understanding of the witness's testimony or the determination of a fact in issue, and (3) not based on scientific, technical, or other specialized knowledge. Witnesses often find difficulty in expressing themselves in language that is not that of an opinion or conclusion. Although the courts have made concessions in certain recurring situations, necessity as a standard for permitting opinions and conclusions has proved too elusive and too unadaptable to particular situations for purposes of satisfactory judicial administration. For example, law enforcement agents can testify that the defendant was acting suspiciously, without being qualified as experts; however, the rules on experts are applicable where the agents testify on the basis of extensive experience that the defendant was using code words to refer to drug quantities and prices. Courts have permitted lay witnesses to testify that a substance appeared to be a narcotic, so long as a foundation of familiarity with the substance is established. For example, two lay witnesses who were heavy amphetamine users were permitted to testify that a substance was amphetamine; but it was error to permit another witness to make such identification where she had no experience with amphetamines [*United States v. Westbrook,* 896 F.2d 330 (8th Cir. 1990)]. Such testimony is not based on specialized knowledge, but rather is based on a layperson's personal knowledge. If, however, that witness were to describe how a narcotic was manufactured, or to describe the intricate workings of a narcotic distribution network, then the witness would have to qualify as an expert [*United States v. Figueroa-Lopez,* 125 F.2d. 1241 (9th Cir. 1997)]. In *State v. Brown* [836 S.W.2d 530, 549 (1992)], the trial court declared that the distinction between lay and expert witness testimony is that lay testimony "results from a process of reasoning familiar in everyday life," whereas expert testimony "results from a process of reasoning which can be mastered only by specialists in the field." The court in *Brown* noted that a lay witness with experience could testify that a substance appeared to be blood, but that a witness would have to qualify as an expert before he or she could testify that bruising around the eyes is indicative of skull trauma.

Testimony by Experts

If scientific, technical, or other specialized knowledge will assist the jury to understand the evidence or to determine a fact, a witness qualified as an expert by knowledge, skill, experience, training, or education may testify thereto in the form of an opinion or otherwise, if (1) the testimony is based on sufficient facts or data, (2) the testimony is the product of reliable principles and methods, and (3) the witness has applied the principles and methods reliably to the facts of the case.

The fields of knowledge that may be drawn on are not limited merely to the "scientific" and "technical" but extend to all "specialized" knowledge. Similarly, the expert is viewed, not in a narrow sense, but as a person qualified by "knowledge, skill, experience, training,or education." Thus, within the scope of the rule are not only experts in the strictest sense of the word—for example, physicians, physicists, and architects—but also the large group sometimes called "skilled" witnesses, such as bankers or landowners testifying to land values.

The *Daubert* test set forth a nonexclusive checklist for trial courts to use in assessing the reliability of scientific expert testimony [*Daubert v. Merrell Dow Pharmaceuticals, Inc.,* 509 U.S. 579 (125 L. Ed. 2d 469) (1993)]. The specific factors explicated by the *Daubert* court are (1) whether the expert's technique or theory can be or has been tested—-that is, whether the expert's theory can be challenged in some objective sense, or whether it is instead simply a subjective, conclusory approach that cannot reasonably be assessed for reliability; (2) whether the technique or theory has been subject to peer review and publication; (3) the known or potential rate of error of the technique or theory when applied; (4) the existence and maintenance of standards and controls; and (5) whether the technique or theory has been generally accepted in the scientific community.

The courts both before and after *Daubert* have found other factors relevant in determining whether expert testimony is sufficiently reliable to be considered by the trier of fact. These factors include:

- Whether experts are proposing to testify about matters growing naturally and directly out of research they have conducted independent of the litigation, or whether they have developed their opinions expressly for purposes of testifying.
- Whether the expert has unjustifiably extrapolated from an accepted premise to an unfounded conclusion.
- Whether the expert has adequately accounted for obvious alternative explanations.
- Whether the expert is being as careful as he would be in his regular professional work outside his paid litigation consulting.
- Whether the field of expertise claimed by the expert is known to reach reliable results for the type of opinion the expert would give. (Roberson 2008).

A review of the case law after *Daubert* shows that the rejection of expert testimony is the exception rather than the rule. The court in *Daubert* stated: "Vigorous cross-examination, presentation of contrary evidence, and careful instruction on the burden of proof are the traditional and appropriate means of attacking shaky but admissible evidence" (509 U.S. at 595).

When a trial court rules that an expert's testimony is reliable, this does not necessarily mean that contradictory expert testimony is unreliable.

The facts or data in the particular case on which an expert bases an opinion or inference may be those perceived by or made known to the expert at or before the hearing. If of a type reasonably relied on by experts in the particular field in forming opinions or inferences on the subject, the facts or data need not be admissible in evidence in order for the opinion or inference to be admitted. Facts or data that are otherwise inadmissible shall not be disclosed to the jury by the proponent of the opinion or inference unless the court determines that their probative value in assisting the jury to evaluate the expert's opinion substantially outweighs their prejudicial effect.

Facts or data on which expert opinions are based may, under the rule, be derived from three possible sources. The first is the first-hand observation of the witness, with opinions based thereon traditionally allowed. A treating physician affords an example. The second source, presentation at the trial, also reflects existing practice. The technique may be the familiar hypothetical question or having the expert attend the trial and hear the testimony establishing the facts. The third source consists of presentation of data to the expert outside of court and other than by his or her own perception.

An expert may testify in terms of opinion or inference and give reasons therefore without first testifying to the underlying facts or data, unless the court requires otherwise. The expert may in any event be required to disclose the underlying facts or data on cross-examination.

DOCUMENTS

Requirement of Original

To prove the content of a writing, recording, or photograph, the original writing, recording, or photograph is required, except as otherwise provided. Federal Rule 1002 is the "Best Evidence Rule," which requires the production of an original in order to prove the contents of writing, recording, or photograph, unless an exception is provided in another rule. The traditional rationale of the best evidence rule is that accuracy is promoted by production of the original, because the process of copying creates a risk of error.

An exception to the best evidence rule is police testimony as to the contents of a confession. Officers who heard a defendant confess may testify to what they heard even if there is a recording of the confession and a transcript of that recording. A duplicate is admissible to the same extent as an original unless (1) a genuine question is raised as to the authenticity of the original or (2) in the circumstances it would be unfair to admit the duplicate in lieu of the original.

The original document is not required, and other evidence of the contents of a writing, recording, or photograph is admissible if:

1. Originals lost or destroyed—All originals are lost or have been destroyed, unless the proponent lost or destroyed them in bad faith.
2. Original not obtainable—No original can be obtained by any available judicial process or procedure.
3. Original in possession of opponent—At a time when an original was under the control of the party against whom offered, that party was put on notice, by the pleadings or otherwise, that the contents would be a subject of proof at the hearing, and that party does not produce the original at the hearing.
4. Collateral matters—The writing, recording, or photograph is not closely related to a controlling issue.

The contents of an official record, or of a document authorized to be recorded or filed and actually recorded or filed, including data compilations in any form, if otherwise admissible, may be proved by copy, certified as correct or testified to be correct by a witness who has compared it with the original. If a copy that complies with the foregoing cannot be obtained by the exercise of reasonable diligence, then other evidence of the contents may be given.

The contents of voluminous writings, recordings, or photographs that cannot conveniently be examined in court may be presented in the form of a chart, summary, or calculation. The originals, or duplicates, shall be made available for examination or copying, or both, by other parties at reasonable time and place. The court may order that they be produced in court.

Requirement of Authentication or Identification

One of the general requirements of introducing real evidence, including writings, at trial is that the evidence must be authenticated. This means that someone must lay a sufficient foundation so that the jury is able to determine that the evidence is what it is supposed to be. Similarly, when a witness testifies to statements made by someone else, the witness must be able to identify the person from whom the statements emanated so that the trier of fact is able to properly attribute the statements.

The requirements for authenticating evidence are not burdensome, but they often require that foundational evidence be presented. Courts will not assume that evidence is what the proponent claims simply because on the face of the evidence it is apparent that it might be. In *United States v. Skipper* [74 F.3d 608 (5th Cir. 1996)]), Skipper was charged with and convicted of possession of crack cocaine with intent to distribute. Police stopped the car that Skipper owned because he was changing lanes erratically. A plastic bag containing crack cocaine was thrown from the driver's side of the car shortly after the lights of the patrol car were activated. Skipper was arrested. At trial, the prosecution introduced criminal evidence of two other convictions for crimes allegedly committed by Skipper. Government Exhibit No. 3 was a certified copy of a judgment against "John Derrick Skipper," indicating that the defendant in that case had pleaded guilty to possession of a controlled substance. An expert testified that the fingerprints on this conviction matched Skipper's fingerprints. Government Exhibit No. 2 was a certified copy of a deferred adjudication order indicating that "John D. Skipper" was placed on ten-year probation for possession of a controlled substance. However, Exhibit No. 2 bore no fingerprints and the government did not otherwise identify Skipper as the person named in the order.

The Court of Appeals held that the trial judge erred, but the error was harmless, in admitting Exhibit No. 2, because the prosecution failed to produce evidence proving that the defendant was the actual "John D. Skipper" named in the deferred adjudication order. The Court held "that the mere similarity in name between a criminal defendant and a person named in a prior conviction alone does not satisfy the identification requirement."

Chain of Custody

In criminal cases, a question of authenticity arises when something is seized from a defendant and then introduced at trial, and the defendant disputes that it is his or argues that the thing has been altered in some way. One way for the prosecution to authenticate the evidence in these circumstances is to establish a chain of custody. Courts have been permissive in determining whether the government has established a sufficient chain of custody. The standard rule is that gaps in the chain of custody go to weight and not admissibility [*United States v. Miller,* 994 F.2d 441 (8th Cir. 1993)]. For example, a one-year gap in the chain of custody for contraband goes to the weight and not the admissibility of the evidence; there was no showing of bad faith on the part of government officials, who are entitled to a presumption that they did not alter the proffered evidence.

The most important chain of custody is the one from the original seizure of the evidence to the analysis of the substance. Given the fungibility of drugs, it is essential to make a connection between the substance seized from the defendant and the substance actually tested. Any substantial gap in this chain of custody or any indication of alteration should be treated as fatal, because otherwise there is an unacceptable risk that the test does not reflect the contents of the substance seized [*United States v. Casamento,* 887 F.2d 1141 (2d Cir. 1989)]. A gap in the chain occurring after testing can be treated more permissively, given the admissibility of the testing procedure itself and the fact that the only purpose for introducing the substance in court is to illustrate the testimony of government witnesses.

Testimony of a witness who has personal knowledge as to a piece of evidence is a classic way of authenticating the evidence. Someone who is an eyewitness to the signing of a document may authenticate the document. A layperson can identify handwriting based on familiarity with the handwriting. A signature may be identified by testimony of a person familiar with the signature. It is not essential that the witness have been present when the signature was executed.

Handwriting, fingerprints, blood, hair, clothing fibers, and numerous other things can be authenticated by comparison with specimens that have been authenticated. Sometimes the comparison can be done by the jury; at other times, an expert witness will be required, especially when scientific knowledge is needed to make a valid examination of the samples. The trial judge has discretion to exclude specimens when questions as to their authenticity will be confusing and excessively time-consuming.

Sometimes the characteristics of an item will themselves serve to authenticate the item. A letter may be authenticated, for example, by content and the circumstances indicating it was a reply to a duly authenticated letter.

One who is familiar with the voice of another may authenticate a conversation or identify the speaker on a tape or other recording. However, if the tape or recording is offered for its truth, hearsay problems still will exist and must be solved following the satisfaction of the authentication requirement.

COURT APPEARANCE

Effective witnesses do not simply arrive in court the day of the trial, do battle with the defense attorney or attorney for the opposing party, and convince the jury they are telling the truth and the defendant or witness for the other party is not being entirely truthful. Effective witnesses prepare for court. During their careers, security managers and other security personnel can be expected to testify in court. Although the magnitude of the cases may differ, the principles for effective witness preparation are the same.

Preparing for Court

Before going to court, the witness should review in detail any reports or statements that he or she may have previously made. A witness cannot expect to sit in front of a judge in a court trial, or a jury in a jury trial, and read the previous statement or report.

Depending on the seriousness of the case and how well the witness remembers the scene, he or she may wish to drive by the scene before going to court. The witness should also be able to pronounce the names of key individuals involved in the case and be familiar with any other unique pronunciations of words. Doing so adds to the witness's credibility.

Dress regulations for court appearances vary according to the jurisdiction. An effective witness strives for a professional, conservative look. Remember, the jurors should pay attention to the testimony and not what the witness is wearing. Flashy clothes, rings, gold chains, or other out-of-the-ordinary dress may cause a juror to concentrate on the witness's clothing at a critical part of the testimony instead of listening. The witness does not have to wear a three-piece suit with a white shirt, but he or she should dress in a manner acceptable for court. Cowboy boots, jeans, or a leather miniskirt is unsuitable.

On receiving the summons to appear in court, the witness should attempt to contact the prosecutor or attorney for the party that is calling him or her as a witness. In most large cities and counties, prosecutors—like the police—are overworked and understaffed and may not return telephone calls before meeting the witness in the court hallway. The witness should not depend on the prosecutor or counsel to make the job of testifying easy. The attorney may not have examined the file before appearing in court and may be depending on the witness to carry the day. If a critical aspect of the case is not evident from reading previous reports or statements, the witness should ensure that the attorney is informed of this fact *before* the start of the trial—not just before the witness takes the stand. The reason is this: The attorney may be engaged in last-minute plea bargaining, settlement discussions, or may make an opening statement to the judge or jury that will later prove to be false if he or she is not made aware of all the important facts surrounding the case.

After discussing the case with the attorney, the witness will await his or her turn to testify. Depending on the nature of the case, and the attorney's preference, the witness may testify first or last. Although jurors are told not to consider anything that is not admitted into evidence, they will sometimes form unofficial opinions of persons on the basis of their observations. If the witness is required to remain outside the courtroom, he or she should also remain attentive and professional. In addition, the witness should avoid joking with other witnesses—and especially avoid laughing with the defense attorney or attorney for the opposing side. Jurors who observe these antics may believe that the witness is not serious about what is occurring in the courtroom and therefore may discount his or her testimony.

Having reviewed any previous reports or statements, refreshed the memory, and talked with the attorney, the witness is ready to take the stand and testify.

TESTIMONY IN COURT

Some individuals are uncomfortable standing or sitting in front of a group and talking. However, this skill is exactly what is needed to be an effective witness. Occasionally, a witness may be required to testify in a deserted courtroom with only the court personnel present, such as in a closed hearing. However, the majority of a person's testimony will occur in public. Moreover, the witness will be subjected to cross-examination by the opposing attorney, who will attempt to destroy the witness's credibility.

Even if you were not a member of the debating team in high school or college, you may, with proper training, learn to communicate in a professional manner while testifying. This oral skill can be mastered with practice, but only if you are familiar with the purposes of both direct examination and cross-examination. In the following subsections, we briefly discuss this aspect of the judicial process.

Direct Examination

Direct examination:
The prosecutor's opportunity to present favorable evidence to the jury; questions are open-ended and do not suggest the answer to the person being questioned.

UNDERSTANDING THE GOALS OF DIRECT EXAMINATION   To testify in court effectively, witnesses should understand the aims or goals of direct examination. Most attorneys who call witnesses attempt to satisfy two generally accepted objectives during direct examinations:

1. To present all legally sufficient evidence to support the charges or claims filed against the opposing party or defendant
2. To convince the fact finder of the integrity of the evidence and, ultimately, the truth of the charge or claim

Direct examination is an attorney's opportunity to present favorable evidence to the jury. The witness is responsible for telling the truth and leaving the jury with a good impression of professionalism and honesty. Many attorneys hand out to lay witnesses lists outlining what is expected of them during direct and cross-examination.

KNOWING THE "TEN COMMANDMENTS" FOR WITNESSES   Following is a list of what have been called the "Ten Commandments" for witnesses:

1. *Tell the truth.* In a trial, as in all other matters, honesty comes first.
2. *Do not guess.* If you do not know, say so.
3. *Be sure you understand the question.* You cannot possibly give a truthful and accurate answer unless you understand the question.
4. *Take your time and answer the question asked.* Give the question as much thought as is required to understand it, formulate your answer, and then give the answer.
5. *Give a loud, audible answer.* Everything you say is being recorded. Do not nod your head yes or no.
6. *Do not look for assistance when you are on the stand.* If you think you need help, request it from the judge.
7. *Beware of questions involving distance and time.* If you make an estimate, make sure everyone understands that you are making an estimate.
8. *Be courteous.* Answer yes or no, and address the judge as *Your Honor.*
9. *If asked if you have talked to the prosecutor, admit it freely if you have done so.*
10. *Avoid joking and making wisecracks.* A lawsuit is a serious matter. (County of San Diego, CA, District Attorney's Office, 1995)

These commandments are as valid for a seasoned witness as they are for a first-time witness. Each rule is based on both common sense and years of court experience by attorneys. The first and most basic rule of testimony requires that the witness tell the truth. Although the idea that witnesses should always tell the truth seems obvious, reality and emotions can sometimes cause individuals to slant their testimony to assist an attorney or to ensure that the defendant is portrayed in a bad light. Failure to testify truthfully has several consequences. The most obvious issue is that the witness is sworn to tell the truth. Violation of this oath can lead to criminal charges or the destruction of the person's reputation. In addition, the witness's credibility may be destroyed in front of the court or jury, with the result that they disbelieve all of the witness's testimony and find for the other party. This result is the exact opposite of what was intended by slanting or stretching the truth to help out the attorney or place the defendant in an unfavorable light. Who can forget the problems caused in the O. J. Simpson case when everyone learned that Detective Mark Fuhrman of the Los Angeles Police Department had "forgotten" using racial slurs in the past?

Close to the first rule is the second, which requires that the witness not try to help the case by guessing. If the witness is unsure, a simple statement to this effect is sufficient. Such a statement shows the jury that the witness is human and may not have all the answers to every question.

The third rule simply requires that the witness understand the exact question that is asked. At first glance, this rule appears simple to follow; however, many times attorneys will ask several questions in one sentence. If the witness is unsure of the exact question, a request should be made to repeat or clarify the question.

The fourth rule requires the witness to think through both the question and the answer instead of blurting out a response. Taking a few seconds to form your answer in your mind before responding to the question is a good practice.

The fifth requirement mandates that the witness answer in a loud and clear voice. Remember, appellate courts have only the written transcript of what occurred when they review a case on appeal. The court reporter will not transcribe a nod of the head or estimate the distance between the witness's hands when he or she is demonstrating a gesture or an action of the witness. If the witness uses motions during the testimony, they should be accompanied by an accurate oral description.

The sixth commandment may seem harsh, but it exists for the witness's benefit. The witness must understand that no one but the judge can intervene during direct examination or cross-examination. The attorneys may raise objections, but the court must decide whether the objections are valid.

The seventh rule is one that most witnesses will violate at least once. Typically, the witness states a distance during direct examination. For example, in response to the prosecutor's question about the distance between the witness and the defendant, the witness may state, "The defendant was twenty feet from me when I observed the weapon." On cross-examination, the defense attorney may ask the witness to point out an object in court that is twenty feet from the witness stand. If the witness is mistaken about this distance, the defense attorney will clearly point out this mistake and will then ask how the witness could be certain about the distance between the witness and the defendant on the night in question when he or she cannot even make an accurate estimate in the calm and secure setting of a courtroom.

The eighth commandment is also basically common sense, but it can also build an witness's credibility. The witness should be seen as a professional and not as someone who does not respect authority.

The ninth rule ties in with the first rule because it requires the witness to answer a question truthfully. Discussing the case with the attorney who called before you testify is not improper.

The last commandment also pertains to the witness's credibility. The defendant's liberty is at stake during the trial. The witness should be professional and calm when answering every question.

BEING ON THE WITNESS STAND   Once called to testify, the witness should approach the witness chair or, as it is sometimes called, the *witness box,* and turn to the clerk or judge to be sworn in. The witness will be asked to swear or affirm to tell the truth, the whole truth, and nothing but the truth. Once the witness is sworn in, the attorney, clerk, or judge will tell him or her to be seated.

The witness should wait for this invitation because doing so shows respect for the court and allows the attorney to appear to be in control of the courtroom. Once the witness is seated, the prosecutor will ask a series of questions about the witness's knowledge of the crime, one of the individuals involved in the case, or the incident. This questioning is known as *direct examination.* Following is a series of preliminary questions most attorneys use to start the questioning:

- Would you state your full name for the record?
- What is your occupation?
- How long have you been employed by ____?
- On the (date and time in question), what was your assignment?
- On that date and time, did you observe anything unusual?
- At what location did you observe this occurrence?
- Is that location in the (city, county, state) of X?

Foundational questions:
Preliminary questions that most attorneys use to start the direct examination.

The purpose of these questions is to allow the witness to become comfortable on the stand and to give the jury some background information about the witness. Such questions also set the stage for the more critical testimony about the witness's observations and reactions. In some jurisdictions these questions are known as *foundational questions* because they establish the witness's jurisdiction and authority to act.

When a party calls a witness, the party is allowed to ask only direct questions (with some minor exceptions that are not relevant to this text). Such questioning is accomplished through direct examination. A direct question is open-ended and does not suggest the answer to the person being questioned. Once the attorney finishes with direct examination, the attorney for the other side has a right to cross-examine. *Cross-examination* allows asking either direct or leading questions. A *leading question* is phrased in a way that suggests an answer to the person being questioned.

Cross-examination:
The defense attorney's opportunity to attack a witness's credibility or establish a motive or bias on the witness's part; questions are either direct or leading questions.

After establishing the jurisdiction for the witness to act, the attorney will question the witness about his or her knowledge of the case. The witness should listen to each question and ensure that he or she understands what is being asked. If not clear what the exact question is, the witness should state this fact and ask the prosecutor to restate the question. "I'm not certain I understand your question; would you please restate it?" is one way to ask for clarification.

Leading question:
A question phrased in a way that suggests an answer to the person being questioned.

If the question is understood, the witness should pause for a second and then answer. This pause should follow every question; as is discussed subsequently, it becomes extremely important during cross-examination.

When answering a question, the witness should answer only what was asked. Following is an example of a witness answering more than was asked:

Question: Did you observe anyone at that location?

Answer: Yes, as I pulled up to the service station, he saw me and fled from the scene. I then lost sight of him for several minutes, but observed him one block from the scene of the crime.

Not only is the witness's response defective on several grounds, it creates more questions than it answers. Furthermore, without clarifying some of the issues in the witness's answer, the attorney may have opened the door for the other attorney to question whether a certain individual was the same person who fled from the service station. Following is a specific series of questions dealing with the issues the witness raised.

Question: Did you observe anyone at that location?

Answer: Yes, I did.

Question: Whom did you observe?

Answer: I saw the defendant.

Question: Would you point to that person if he or she is in court and, for the record, describe what the person is wearing?

Answer: Yes, it is the person sitting next to the defense attorney, wearing a blue suit.

Question: How far away were you when you saw the defendant?

Answer: I was about fifteen feet from him.

Question: What was he doing when you first saw him?

Answer: He was backing out of the service station office.

Question: What, if anything, did he do next?

Answer: He looked toward me and fled.

Question: Where did he go?

Answer: He ran south on Broadway Street.

Question: What did you do at that time?

Answer: I entered the service station to check on the welfare of the people inside and was informed by Mr. Smith that the defendant had just robbed them at gunpoint.

Question: Once you heard this, what did you do?

Answer: I called the police.

The difference between the two sets of questions and answers is apparent. The second set provides the jury with more complete facts about the incident and establishes why the witness could recognize the defendant even though he lost sight of the defendant for several minutes.

Cross-Examination

Once the witness has answered the questions posed by the attorney, the attorney for the other party has the right to ask questions on cross-examination. Unlike trials in the movies, cross-examination seldom results in witnesses' breaking down and recanting their previous testimony. Rather, it is a series of questions designed to attack the credibility of witnesses by showing weaknesses in their original testimony or by establishing a motive or bias on their part.

Cross-examination has several purposes. All witnesses should be aware of these objectives so that they can better understand the questions being asked of them by defense attorneys. Depending on the jurisdiction, some questions or issues may not be raised on cross-examination. However, the general objectives of cross-examination include, but are not limited to, the following nine points:

1. To develop favorable matters that were left unsaid on direct examination
2. To introduce all of a conversation or document, if the witness has testified to only a part of the content
3. To demonstrate that the witness is lying
4. To establish that the witness could not have seen or heard what he or she has claimed
5. To test the witness's ability to hear, see, remember, and relate facts with accuracy
6. To establish the witness's bias or prejudice
7. To establish any interest the witness may have in the outcome of the case
8. To impair the witness's credibility
9. To impeach the witness by any means permitted by law

Just as with direct examination, the witness should pause before answering any question. This pause is critical because it allows the other attorney to object to the question and prevent its answer from coming before the jury. Attorneys, during cross-examination, can and will use numerous tactics or techniques to discredit the witness's testimony.

The witness should know the facts surrounding the case. An unprofessional and embarrassing response by the witness is to say, "I don't recall, but I put it in my report." Rest assured, the attorney for the other party will know the facts—and will have the opportunity to read the report again while the witness is testifying. In addition, the opposing attorney has the other party's version to draw on. Even though parties do not always tell their attorneys the complete truth, the defense is provided with another perspective on the facts that can be used to attack the witness.

Furthermore, the witness should always maintain a professional, courteous attitude. Some attorneys will argue with witnesses, others will be condescending, and some may even sneer. No matter what tactic is used, the witness should never lose his or her temper. The witness must be prepared for these types of ploys and respond in a positive manner. Positive responses in such situations reinforce in the jury's mind that the witness is a professional simply doing a job.

If the witness makes a mistake during testimony and is caught by the opposing attorney, the witness should readily admit to the mistake. Nothing damages your credibility more than letting an opposing attorney lead you down a path of rationalizations in an attempt to justify an obvious mistake.

The witness's voice and body language should convey the attitude of a calm professional. The voice should be loud enough for all the jurors to hear, but not so loud as to distract from what is being said. The witness should also avoid squirming on the witness stand. If the testimony has proceeded for more than two hours and the witness must use the rest room, the witness should politely ask for a brief recess.

The witness should not despair if the defense attorney appears to be "winning." After cross-examination, the prosecutor is allowed to conduct a *redirect examination,* which is the prosecutor's opportunity to clarify any issues raised during cross-examination.

Preparing for and testifying in court are everyday experiences for some witnesses. Even when it becomes a common occurrence, the witness must understand that unless the information can be conveyed to the jury in the proper manner, all the work done during the arresting, questioning, and charging of the defendant may be wasted.

Summary

- The study of evidence is a study of regulation of the process of proving facts. Evidence law is codified in statutes and court rules.
- Hearsay is inadmissible unless an exception is applicable.
- The two basic themes found in the federal rules are:
  - The rules favor admissibility of evidence.
  - The trial judge has considerable discretion as to the admissibility of evidence.
- Rulings on evidence cannot be assigned as error on appeal unless a substantial right is affected, and the nature of the error was called to the attention of the judge, so as to alert him or her to the proper course of action and enable opposing counsel to take proper corrective measures.
- The fact that evidence is admissible for a limited purpose does not require that the evidence be admitted. If the prejudicial effect of evidence substantially outweighs its probative value, despite a limiting instruction, then the non-offering party can argue that the evidence should be completely excluded because any limiting instruction would be inadequate.

- Before a witness's testimony, the witness should carefully prepare for this event and always remember to present a professional image to the court and the jury.
- The witness's professional reputation goes on the line every time the witness testifies.
- Preparing to testify is as important as the actual testimony.
- The witness must never assume that the case will be easy or that the opposing attorney will not attack the witness's credibility.
- Whenever possible, the witness should discuss the case with the attorney who is calling the witness before entering the courtroom.
- Direct examination and cross-examination have distinct purposes. The witness should be prepared for both types of questioning and follow the "Ten Commandments" as closely as possible.
- All witnesses should remember certain techniques when testifying. These will become second-nature to most witnesses after they have testified in court several times.

Review Questions

1. How do you define *hearsay*?
2. Under what circumstances is relevant evidence not admissible in court?
3. When may a lay witness state an opinion while testifying in court?
4. Explain the "Best Evidence Rule."
5. What is the most appropriate attire for a witness testifying in court? Why?
6. Which of the "Ten Commandments" is the most important? Why?
7. If you had to delete one of the "Ten Commandments," which would you delete? Why?
8. Which is more important—direct examination or cross-examination? Why?
9. What effect can a simple reporting error have on a witness's testimony?

Class Exercises

1. Have students practice testifying in court by using a mock court trial.

2. Have students watch a civil court trial and report back to the class.

References

County of San Diego, CA, District Attorney's Office. 1995. Direct Examination Workshop Handout.

Moore, Carole. 2005. Taking the stand. *Law Enforcement News,* www.officer.com/publication/article.jsp? pubId=1&id=25198, retrieved July 30, 2007.

Paciocco, D., and L. Stuesser. 1996. *The law of evidence.* Concord, CA: Irwin Law.

Roberson, Cliff. 2008. *Extraneous offenses & uncharged misconduct,* 5th ed. Ft. Worth, TX: Knowles.

CHAPTER 12

Recruiting, Selecting, and Training Security Personnel

CHAPTER OUTLINE

OBJECTIVES

After completing this chapter, you will be able to:

- Explain the difference between recruitment and selection.

- Identify and discuss the activities in the security officer recruiting process.

- Identify and discuss the general steps in the security officer selection process.

- Understand the role that the Equal Employment Opportunity Commission guidelines play in the selection of security professionals.

- Identify the best method by which a background investigator can glean the most useful information when conducting a reference check.

- Identify and discuss the pros and cons of using the polygraph as a preemployment selection tool.

- Identify and discuss private security training curricula.

- Explain liability issues that center on improper training of private security officers.

- Identify and discuss training delivery methods.

A man can seldom—very, very, seldom—fight a winning fight against his training; the odds are too heavy.

—*Mark Twain*

One of the best ways to avoid potential misconduct on the part of security officers is to hire only honest employees, and the most qualified. This may seem to be a difficult task, but careful screening and selection of private security job applicants will result in hiring fewer dishonest or troublesome employees as well as improving the quality of the security service.

Proper recruitment, selection, and training of security personnel are critical to the effectiveness and efficiency of the organization. It takes only one misfit who is allowed to gain employment in the security service, and who subsequently engages in misconduct, to cost the security organization dearly in terms of money paid out as the result of a lawsuit, credibility, and the ability to attract and retain new clients.

Private security organizations are profit-driven, so it is important that they have sound reputations in the industry. It is also crucial that security personnel receive the proper training before starting security duties. All too often, security officers are hired and assigned to another security officer for a few days of on-the-job training. This is a backward and unwise practice and should be discontinued. Private security officer selection and training criteria vary from state to state. In some states the training requirements are minimal; in others they entail comprehensive training for every private security officer. This chapter provides an overview of the recruitment, selection, and training of security personnel. First, before we examine recruitment, selection, and training, we briefly discuss perhaps the most important question that many students have—Will there be jobs available in private security when I graduate?

CAREERS IN PRIVATE SECURITY

Osama bin Laden has probably been the biggest boost for private security employment ever.

—*Kirk Barner, private security agent, 2007*

According to the U.S. Department of Labor (2008), employment of private security personnel is expected to grow 18 percent over the next ten years, faster than the average for all occupations. Increased demand for private security officers will result from heightened security concerns, increased litigation, and the need to protect confidential information and property of all kinds. The proliferation of criminal activity through the Internet, such as identity theft, spamming, and email harassment, will also increase the demand for private security personnel.

According to the Department of Labor, median annual earnings of salaried private security officers and investigators were $33,750 in 2006. The middle 50 percent earned between $24,180 and $47,740. The lowest 10 percent earned less than $19,720, and the highest 10 percent earned more than $64,380. Earnings of private detectives and investigators vary greatly by employer, specialty, and geographic area (U.S. Department of Labor, 2008).

The range of jobs under the private security umbrella is quite diverse; people with all kinds of interests can find something that appeal to them. Corporations in the manufacturing and retail sectors are continually concerned with loss prevention and risk management, while the increased emphasis on homeland security has Fortune 500 companies concerned with the safety and security of their business and employees. These trends have led to an increasing need for qualified security professionals in a variety of industries. The types and requirements for security professionals are too varied and job-specific to list, but the following are some of the most common career positions available:

- Administrator/manager
  - Leadership position that entails the ability to make policy decisions
  - Consults and advises superiors in upper management
  - Responsible for personnel administration
- Investigator
  - Must be able to deal with people and collect evidence
  - Must be able to work well under pressure
- Security technician
  - Must have a working knowledge of how technological equipment operates
- Protective specialist
  - Specialized knowledge in protective tactics needed
- Gaming surveillance officers, also known as surveillance agents, and gaming investigators act as security agents for casino managers and patrons. Using primarily audio and video equipment in an observation room, they observe casino operations for irregular activities, such as cheating or theft, by either employees or patrons. They keep recordings that are sometimes used as evidence against alleged criminals in police investigations. Some casinos use a catwalk over one-way mirrors located above the casino floor to augment electronic surveillance equipment. Surveillance agents occasionally leave the surveillance room and walk the casino floor.

RECRUITMENT OF SECURITY PERSONNEL

It is through recruitment and selection that the future of the security agency is determined. Of those recruited and selected for employment into the security service, some will gravitate to specialized investigative positions, some will lead others as supervisors, still others will make it to management and administrative positions, while a few may go on to become owners of a security business.

The stakes are high when recruiting security officers. According to one report, as a rule of thumb, the wrong person costs an organization three times his or her annual salary; for example, a $50,000 employee with poor job performance actually costs the company $150,000 (*Executive Focus* 2004). Additionally, there is lost opportunity as well as negative public perception if the public becomes aware of a security officer's poor performance. Even worse, a lawsuit might result if the officer willfully breaks the law and injures a citizen or engages in some other form of gross misconduct. Sacrifices in quality today may be felt for many years into the future.

In order for security agencies to hire the best qualified personnel, a comprehensive recruitment program is essential. Recruitment and selection, while sometimes used interchangeably, are actually different in scope and purpose. *Recruitment* is the

Recruitment:
The process of locating, identifying, and attracting capable applicants who have the minimum qualifications to be eligible for the selection process.

process of locating, identifying, and attracting capable applicants who have the minimum qualifications to be eligible for the selection process. *Selection*, which is discussed latter in this chapter, involves subjecting security applicants to what amounts to a specific testing protocol. Selection is an exercise that seeks to predict which applicants will be successful if hired and to weed out the unqualified candidates. A good recruitment program usually results in better-quality applicants from which to select. Security executives should avoid the tendency to relax standards to hire security officers who will be earning minimal wages. Regardless of the salary, only the most qualified should be selected for the security service.

The scope of the recruitment program and the amount of effort devoted to it will be largely influenced by the size of the security organization. In general, the larger the security organization, the easier it is to recruit applicants. Larger security organizations are more visible to potential applicants and may be perceived as offering more opportunities as well as higher starting wages. Recruitment should be an ongoing, year-round process; if continuous recruiting is not conducted, the organization risks losing qualified candidates.

Recall that the purpose of recruitment is to attract qualified individuals to apply for security positions. The term *qualified* denotes those individuals who possess, or who can acquire through entry-level training, the required skills, knowledge, abilities, and job behaviors to perform the tasks and duties of a security officer successfully. Effective recruiting may involve advertising employment opportunities both within the immediate geographic area as well outside the area. To attract the most qualified candidates, security officials must not be afraid to travel to other states for recruiting purposes. The organization must be willing to go anywhere to seek out applicants with high potential.

Birzer and Roberson (2007, 183) in their book, *Policing Today and Tomorrow,* provide an overview of recruitment activities that public police agencies use in a comprehensive recruitment program. These same recruitment activities are also appropriate for recruiting applicants for private security positions:

- Advertisements in professional publications, with college and university placement services, and in local, state, and regional newspapers
- Interviews with students enrolled in criminal justice internship programs
- Internal and external searches
- Inquiries and referrals
- Professional contacts with community organizations promoting interests of minority groups
- Publications and pamphlets
- Special activities and events for prospective applicants
- Audiovisual packages
- Internet advertising

The Vacancy Announcement

The goal of vacancy announcements is to reach as many men and women as possible in order to attract the best candidates for the job. There are some legal precautions to consider when announcing security officer vacancies. Any recruitment activity that intentionally restricts or affects a protected classification under Title VII of the Civil

What Qualifications do I Need for a Career in Private Security?

Generally, there are no formal education requirements for most private detective and investigator jobs, although many applicants have college degrees, and it is highly recommended. Courses in criminal justice, police studies, and security administration are helpful to aspiring private security officers. Although related experience is usually required, some people enter the occupation directly after graduating from college, generally with an associate's or bachelor's degree in criminal justice or in police or security studies. Most corporate investigators are required to have a bachelor's degree, in criminal justice, security administration, or a business-related field. It is not uncommon for some corporate investigators to have a master's degree or a law degree; others are certified public accountants.

Rights Act of 1964 is unlawful. In other words, the recruitment activities of an organization must not discriminate on the basis of race, sex, national origin, religion, or ethnicity.

Advertisements

Effective advertising is about reaching and influencing security officer applicants. Advertising is about delivering the right message to the right audience in the right media—newspapers, trade publications, radio, or the Internet. The job advertisement should include job qualifications, required job experience, job skills needed, and salary and benefits package.

The benefit of widespread advertising is that a large population or specific groups can be targeted; however, this can be a double-edged sword, inasmuch as wide advertising distribution can also generate many unqualified applicants. Nevertheless, proper advertising can be an invaluable tool for attracting large numbers of potential security officer applicants.

In the age of technology, the Internet has become increasingly popular as a recruiting device; and the broadest geographic reach for recruitment is, of course, the Internet. Many security organizations have their own Internet Web page with links to employment information that potential applicants can log onto and learn about what is required for the job. Security organizations should increasingly explore the Internet as a mechanism to allow applicants to submit their employment applications online.

Although the latest and farthest-reaching job search medium is the Internet, the long-standing tradition of placing employment advertising in metropolitan Sunday newspapers continues be an effective recruitment source. Recruiting ads should be placed in the local newspaper whenever possible. Publishing job openings in a good-sized newspaper ensures reaching a large and diverse audience. In a world of high-tech information, newspapers are trying out innovative approaches to remain competitive. There is no getting around the fact that when people hunt for jobs, a great many of them look in the local newspaper.

Brochures are another medium for recruiting. An attractive brochure should be colorful and include photographs and information about salary, benefits, working conditions, promotional and career opportunities, contact information for questions, basic minimum qualifications, and where to apply. If the recruiting brochure includes photographs, it should reflect diversity. A brochure that depicts both male and female

Security Officer Job Advertisement

Company Overview

As an industry leader with 30 years of experience, eFunds provides leading technology and proven solutions in financial risk management and electronic payments to financial services, retailers, governments and other businesses worldwide. Backed by a broad range of business process outsourcing, as well as comprehensive business and IT consulting services, our solutions strengthen customers' overall profitability by increasing revenue, reducing costs, streamlining operations and maximizing technology performance.

Description

Patrol a facility or man a post as instructed by security management. Acts as a general security presence to deter, detect and identify suspicious activities and criminal acts or rule infractions that may be a threat to the property, visitors, contractors, or employees.

Position Qualifications Required

Must be at least 18 years of age or

Must have a high school diploma or GED.

At least one verifiable employer.

No criminal convictions and successful completion of an eFunds designated background check.

Ability to communicate effectively both orally and in writing for the purpose of public interaction and report writing.

Must have a working knowledge of Microsoft Windows operating system and Microsoft Office software.

Authorized to work in the United States.

Ability to perform essential functions of the position with or without reasonable accommodation.

Negative result on pre-employment drug screen.

Successful completion of a basic skills test including a writing sample and computer skills test.

Ability to maintain satisfactory attendance and punctuality standard.

Neat and professional appearance.

Friendly and professional demeanor.

Ability to providing quality customer service.

Ability to handle typical and crisis situations efficiently and effectively.

Willing to submit to background procedures including drug screen and background check, and periodic unannounced drug screening.

Position Qualifications Preferred

A current state guard card is preferred but not required.

Military experience preferred but not required.

Source: www.careerbuilder.com/JobSeeker/Jobs/JobDetails.

security officers may attract underrepresented groups to the security occupation and gives the impression that the organization is open to these groups. Where ethnic minorities normally speak languages other than English, a brochure translated into the languages that are commonly spoken locally may be useful. In areas where there is a large population of Spanish speakers, for instance, a brochure printed in Spanish can help get the word out.

Employee Referrals

Employee referrals result when security officers recruit by word of mouth. The security organization may offer recruitment incentive plans for employees. For example, if an employee successfully refers a qualified security applicant who is then hired, the employee receives time off with pay or some other monetary reward. This is usually a highly effective way to recruit.

College students in line
at career fair.

College and University Recruiting

College and university campuses are ideal recruiting locations. Many colleges and universities hold job or career fairs, which attract large numbers of potential employers to the campus. Not only are college and university job fairs excellent sources for recruiting, many universities offer internship programs for students. Security executives are encouraged to work with local universities to sponsor internship opportunities for students. A student completing an internship with a security company may become a viable candidate for employment. Likewise, many college and university criminal justice programs now offer specializations and degrees in security operations and management. These programs offer an excellent venue to security officials for recruiting.

Military Installations

Security officials should make an effort to recruit military personnel, especially those who have military police or security experience. For example, the United States Air Force Security Force members provide resource protection for vital national security assets, including aircraft, nuclear bombs, and nuclear missiles. Their main function is protection for all Air Force personnel, property, and operations. In order to perform these important functions, Air Force Security Force members complete extensive training that includes, basic military police functions, missile security, convoy actions, capture and recovery of nuclear weapons, law enforcement, and directing traffic. Air Force Security Force members also undergo training in nonlethal tactics, such as using pepper spray and pressure-point control tactics. This experience would assuredly look good on a private security job application. Upon completion of their military service, many of these military personnel seek jobs in law enforcement or the security industry.

The security training that they received while in the military gives them a clear advantage in the civilian private security industry.

Law Enforcement Agencies

You would probably be amazed at the number of former and retired law enforcement officials who work in the private security industry. Many law enforcement officials find it more profitable to leave law enforcement for the private security industry. It is possible to earn significantly higher wages in corporate security than can be made in public law enforcement. One of the authors of this textbook interviewed several former Midwestern police officers who left police service to work in the private security industry at local aircraft manufacturing plants. They related that after only a few years, their salary had nearly doubled from what it had been in law enforcement. Many law enforcement officers also seek private security employment after they retire from policing, as a second career. Security officials should target recruiting efforts at law enforcement agencies. Former and retired police officers usually do very well in security careers as a result of their law enforcement training and experience.

THE SELECTION PROCESS

Selection:
The process that begins after recruitment, by which a security job applicant is subjected to testing and screening processes that may include job-related written tests, background investigation, and psychological assessment.

After security officer applicants have been recruited, the selection process begins. Selection is the screening of job applicants to ensure that the most qualified candidates are hired. Selection is an exercise in prediction; in other words, the selection process seeks to predict who will be successful if hired for security work. It is an absolute necessity that the most qualified men and women are selected for the security service. Sometimes selection is viewed as a multiple-hurdle process because applicants have to successfully pass one test (or hurdle) in order to go to the next phase (or next hurdle). A number of selection testing devices are used to screen out unqualified candidates while at the same time identifying qualified candidates.

The Employment Application

A comprehensive application form can be a valuable tool that reveals not only the abilities of the applicant but also his or her personality. When the application is received from the applicant, he or she should be advised that, before being hired, a thorough background investigation and reference checks will be made and any offer of employment will be contingent on a satisfactory verification of the information given in the application. Review of the application is the very first step in the selection process.

The employment application form offers an often-overlooked device to determine an applicant's qualifications. The application form can be reviewed relatively quickly to determine whether the applicant meets the minimum qualifications for the job. Job requirements usually include such criteria as minimum age, minimum education (such as high school diploma or its equivalent), no felony convictions, a valid driver's license, and U.S. citizenship or permanent residence status. Applicants who do not meet the minimum requirements are disqualified early in the process, thus saving the applicant and the security organization valuable time. For example, if an applicant

Suggested Minimum Standards for Private Security Officers

The Private Sector Liaison Committee of the International Association of Chiefs of Police has worked to build lines of communication and cooperation with the private sector. As a result, a document was prepared as a set of guidelines for meaningful security officer standards in the areas of private security and public safety. According to the report, all private security officers must meet the applicable statutory requirements and the established criteria of the employer, which may exceed minimum mandated requirements. Federal law mandates that candidates for employment must be citizens or possess legal-alien status prior to employment. All applicants who are hired or certified as a private security officer should meet the following minimum criteria:

1. Be at least 18 years of age, "unarmed" private security officer.
2. Be at least 21 years of age, "armed" private security officer, and comply with U.S. Public Law 104-208 Section 658 (The Omnibus Consolidated Appropriations Act of 1997).
3. Possess a valid state driver's license (if applicable).
4. Not have been:
   a. Convicted or pled guilty or *nolo contendere* to a felony in any jurisdiction;
   b. Convicted or pled guilty or *nolo contendere* to a misdemeanor involving moral turpitude acts of dishonesty or acts against governmental authority, including the use and/or possession of a controlled substance within a seven-year period;
   c. Convicted or pled guilty or *nolo contendere* to any crime in any jurisdiction involving the sale, delivery, or manufacture of a controlled substance; or

   d. Declared by any court to be incompetent by reason of mental disease or defect that has not been removed or expunged.
5. Submit two sets of classifiable fingerprints and two passport-sized photographs, along with applicant's name, address, date of birth, social security number, citizenship status, and a statement of conviction of crimes in order to conduct a state criminal record check, and a FBI criminal history check, prior to permanent employment as a private security officer. In all instances, these actions must be taken prior to the private security officer's being armed;
6. Furnish information about all prior employment through the employer making a reasonable effort to verify the last seven years of employment history, and checking three personal references; and
7. Successfully pass a recognized preemployment drug screen.

Suggested nonregulated preemployment applicant criteria include the following:

1. High school education or equivalent
2. Military discharge records (DD 214);
3. Mental and physical capacity to perform duties for which being employed;
4. Armed applicants shall successfully complete a relevant psychological evaluation to verify that the applicant is suited for duties for which being employed.

Source: International Association of Chiefs of Police, www.theiacp.org/documents/pdfs/Publications/privatesecurityofficer.pdf.

is only 17 years of age and the minimum age requirement is 18, the applicant is directed out of the selection process and encouraged to apply once he or she reaches the age of 18.

The applicant should be required to sign a statement at the end of the application form giving the security employer permission to check all items of information provided in the application and any other information provided by the applicant. The employment application should contain a warning that falsification of information either on the application or presented during the subsequent selection process will be sufficient grounds to withdraw an offer of employment or, if discovered after employment, to terminate the employment.

General Requirements

It is wise practice to establish a requirement that candidates be at least 18 years of age for unarmed security, and 21 years of age for armed security, with provisions that the candidate must be able to perform the duties required of the position. It is also important to establish a requirement that candidates be citizens of the United States, lawful permanent residents, or aliens authorized to work.

Candidates should possess a high school diploma or equivalent. The applicant should demonstrate an ability to read, write, and speak English and the language(s) most appropriate to his or her assigned duties. It is now common to see college education required for certain security fields, especially security officials working in corporations. Criminal justice programs in many colleges and universities now offer specializations or entire degree programs in security management. For example, the Eastern Kentucky University College of Criminal Justice offers a bachelor's degree in Safety, Security, and Emergency Management. Within the program there are several specialty areas on which students can focus their studies, including assets protection and security, emergency medical care, fire and safety engineering technology, homeland security, and traffic safety.

Fingerprinting

Requiring that candidates submit a fingerprint card or electronic fingerprint to be processed for a criminal history check is sound practice. Whenever possible, consideration should be given to using a national fingerprint database.

Past Employment

Hiring personnel should be able to verify a candidate's current and previous employers' addresses and phone numbers for at least the last seven years. Candidates with prior military service should be required to provide form DD-214.

Illustration, index finger being pressed down on chart of fingerprints. Security applicants have their fingerprints taken and checked during selection process.

Written Examination

Some security companies require applicants to take a written examination. The written examination is usually administered early in the selection process, after the initial application form has been completed and checked for minimum qualifications. The written examination is a cost-effective means of screening large numbers of applicants. If the security organization utilizes a written examination, federal law requires that it be job-related.

Some types of written tests, such as intelligence tests, may create legal challenges for the organization. Security executives should be cautious about using intelligence tests with a minimum quotient cutoff score. The 1971 *Griggs v. Duke Power Company* (401 U.S. 424) decision prohibits such tests when adverse impact occurs. In the *Griggs* decision, the court makes clear that the employer has the burden of showing that any job requirement has a manifest relationship to the job in question when the requirement tends to reduce job opportunities because of race. A key element of the court's holding in *Griggs* was that good intent or the absence of discriminatory intent does not redeem testing procedures that have adverse impact on protected classes but that are unrelated to measuring job capability.

There are two approaches to using a written examination as a selection device. In one approach, applicants take the examination and their score is factored into a constellation of all tests administered during the selection process; in other words, the test itself is not used as a disqualifying device. The benefit to this approach is that it allows the applicant to continue in the selection process regardless of test score.

In the second approach, there may be a minimum passing score for the examination; if an applicant fails to reach the minimum score, he or she is disqualified from further consideration. For example, suppose a security organization sets 70 percent as the minimum passing test score and the applicant scores 60 percent; the applicant is disqualified from the remaining selection process. The advantage to this approach is that it narrows a large pool of candidates down quickly and early in the selection process. The disadvantage is that it may disqualify an otherwise qualified applicant based solely on written test performance.

Polygraph Screening

I don't know anything about lie detectors other than they scare the hell out of people.

—President Richard M. Nixon

The polygraph test, also known as a lie detector test, is the most famous of the trust verification devices on the market. The number of businesses using polygraph examinations has increased tenfold in the past decade. Although they were prohibited from use in the private sector by the Employee Polygraph Protection Act of 1988, government organizations can use polygraph testing. However, the law also specified that certain occupations outside of government organizations can use the polygraph. One of the specified occupations is security organizations who employee personnel whose duties include protecting facilities significant to the safety of any state, water supply facilities, nuclear and conventional power plants, and public transportation facilities.

Polygraph:
A device that measures and records several physiological variables such as blood pressure, heart rate, respiration and skin conductivity while a series of questions is being asked, in an attempt to detect lies.

Most people have strong feelings regarding use of polygraph tests. Supporters claim a very high accuracy rate and recommend its use in business. Critics state that polygraph examinations wrongfully deny large numbers of persons employment each year, either because they refuse to take the exam or because of inaccuracies in reading the results of the exam. Some critics claim that with poorly trained operators the error rate can exceed 50 percent.

A polygraph test records the body's involuntary responses to an examiner's questions in order to ascertain deceptive behavior. The test measures physiological data from three or more systems of the human body, generally the respiratory, cardiovascular, and sweat gland systems. The underlying theory of the polygraph is that when people lie, they also get measurably nervous about lying; as a result, their heartbeat increases, blood pressure goes up, breathing rhythms change, perspiration increases, and so on. A baseline for these physiological characteristics is established by asking the subject questions whose answers the investigator knows.

Preemployment polygraph screening is generally used to verify information in a job application and to learn if some relevant information has been omitted. Of particular concern is the applicant's past criminal activity, drug usage, and job history. The preemployment polygraph examination should be considered a separate phase from the background investigation; however, these two stages are mutually reinforcing when used correctly. The polygraph test is designed to query areas that normally cannot be examined during the background investigation (a background investigation cannot yield information that only the applicant would know), and it enables the examiner to solicit and gain relevant information regarding an applicant's behavior and character.

Security officer applicant undergoing polygraph testing.

TO USE OR NOT TO USE THE POLYGRAPH   According to proponents of the polygraph, the advantages of using the polygraph in employment are that it (1) results in honest or more honest employees, (2) is a constant deterrent to employee misconduct, (3) prevents hiring of dishonest persons and drug addicts, (4) prevents honest employees from unjust accusations, and (5) is cheaper to use than supporting criminal activities of dishonest employees would be.

The disadvantages of using a polygraph are that (1) it is dehumanizing, (2) its accuracy is questionable, (3) improper use may subject the company to criminal or civil liability, and (4) there is a stigma attached to the use of the polygraph.

Oral Interview

The oral interview gives security executives an opportunity to meet and observe the communication skills of the applicant. During the interview, the applicant is usually asked about background information he or she provided on the application form. The applicant may also be asked to respond to several hypothetical scenarios, which are used to assess how the candidate would respond to stressful situations as well as to assess problem-solving skills.

There are generally two types of oral interviews, nonstressful and stressful. In a nonstressful interview, the candidate is asked general questions about his or her background and is asked several hypothetical questions. There is no attempt to place pressure or stress on the candidate.

On the other hand, the interviewer may place a great amount of stress on the candidate and may try to force the candidate into making a disqualifying mistake. In a stressful interview, the interviewer may actually take a hostile or adversarial position against the candidate. The focus in this kind of interview is emotional. The interviewer attempts to push the candidate verbally into an emotional outburst of some kind. These types of interviews were once common in law enforcement selection. Many law enforcement organizations have discontinued use of the stressful interview, believing that it is a poor way to measure problem-solving skills on the part of the candidate and that it is difficult to find any justification for its use. Security executives should rethink the stressful interview if it is being used in the selection process. It is questionable whether the stressful interview actually indicates candidates' ability to respond under stress.

Psychological Assessment

Psychological testing is usually conducted after a conditional offer of employment is made to the applicant, because it tends to be expensive to give and have interpreted by a qualified psychologist or psychiatrist. A conditional offer of employment occurs when the applicant is offered security employment contingent on passing the remaining selection tests.

Conditional job offer: An offer of employment made to an applicant contingent on him or her successfully completing the rest of the testing process, which usually includes psychological examination and medical and drug screening.

Psychological tests are written, visual, or verbal evaluations administered to assess the cognitive and emotional functioning of private security officer applicants. More specifically, psychological tests are used to assess a variety of mental abilities and attributes, including achievement and ability, personality, and neurological functioning. Psychological tests used in security officer selection may include the Minnesota Multiphasic Personality Inventory (MMPI), the California

Personality Inventory (CPI), Rorschach "inkblots," figure drawings, and sentence-completion tests.

One of the more popular psychological tests used in the employment screening process is the Minnesota Multiphasic Personality Inventory (MMPI). The MMPI is used by many behavioral scientists to study the psychological makeup of persons. There are 550 questions or statements on the test to which a person responds "true," "false," or "cannot say." Dispersed throughout the test are questions or statements designed to measure particular personality characteristics of the applicant. There are also statements and questions designed to reveal false responses or lies by the test taker. Many of the questions and statements appear to be nonsense, but, according to its supporters, the test is effective in classifying a person's personality as well as honesty character traits.

All psychological tests should be administered, scored, and interpreted by a trained professional, preferably a psychologist or psychiatrist with expertise in the appropriate area. Psychological tests are only one element of a psychological assessment. They should never be used alone but should be one of several devices in the selection process.

Preemployment psychological testing is an effective way of screening out security officer applicants who present high risks of personality traits related to psychological distress. Psychological factors have been found to have an effect on many factors including workplace stress, judgment, illnesses, and injuries.

There is always concern about employing an individual who has the potential to break down in a stressful situation or who has a psychological disorder that may prevent him or her from functioning effectively as a security officer. Preemployment psychological testing, in part, can assist in identifying applicants with serious psychological disorders. One significant problem with preemployment psychological screening, however, is that it only depicts what the applicant is like at the time of hire. Research is inconclusive regarding the usefulness of psychological tests in predicting future employee performance. Nevertheless, psychological screening can be an important selection device in identifying persons with dangerous personality disorders.

Background Investigation

The background investigation is literally an investigation into an applicant's background. It provides a wealth of insight into the candidate's personal and professional

---

Major Providers of Psychological Tests

- California Psychological Inventory: Consulting Psychologists, 577 College Avenue, Palo Alto, CA 94306.
- Minnesota Multiphasic Personality Inventory: MMPI Psychological Corporation, 757 Third Avenue, New York, NY 10017.
- Personnel Selection and Inventory: London House Consultants, 1550 Northwest Highway, Park Ridge, IL 60068.
- Reid Report: John E. Reid and Associates, 233 North Michigan Avenue, Chicago, IL 60601.
- Stanton Analysis Test: The Stanton Corporation, 407 South Dearborn Avenue, Chicago, IL 60605.
- Trustworthiness Attitude: Personnel Security Corporation, 1301 West 22nd Street, Oakbrook, IL 60521.

life and may provide some of the most important indicators of job success. Established past bad behavior has a tendency to repeat itself, and the background investigation assists in identifying patterns of bad behavior. Performing background checks on applicants is one of the most effective tools available to assist in making good hiring decisions. A properly conducted background investigation may take several weeks or even months to complete, and should naturally be carried out toward the end of the selection process. In some organizations, the background investigation is conducted after a conditional offer of employment is made.

The background investigation usually concentrates on the following areas: information from employers, neighbors, acquaintances, and former teachers, references provided by the applicant, credit checks, military records, and civil court records, information about drug use or abuse and habitual use of intoxicants, and investigation into past criminal behavior. The background investigation concentrates on obvious and not-so-obvious character qualities.

As part of the background investigation, reference checks are generally conducted; however, the information they provide is sometimes questionable. Generally, references furnished by the applicant provide little useful information for the selection decision. Most references furnished by the applicant will provide biased information about the applicant. Imagine yourself applying for a security position; you will most likely list only references who will provide glowing information about your character, work habits, and attitude.

More useful information will be gleaned from references that are not provided directly by the applicant but are developed from listed references. For example, the investigator asks the listed references for the names of other persons who know the applicant. When the investigator develops references from references, there is a much more likelihood of finding out revealing information about the character of the applicant. The farther you move out from listed references, the more revealing and useful information you are likely to obtain.

Former employers are also contacted during the background investigation. Like personal references, the accuracy or usefulness of information from past and present employers is questionable. Past and present employers are often reluctant to give candid evaluations of the applicant's job performance for fear of legal repercussions (Robbins and Coulter 1999). A recent survey found that only 55 percent of human resources executives would "always" provide accurate references to potential employers. What is more surprising is that 7 percent reported that they would never give an accurate reference (Robbins and Coulter 1999). Laws in some states permit employers to sue other employers if, during employment background checks, they omit or lie about serious employee acts, especially if the employee again commits the same or similar acts on the job.

A major company in Dallas, Texas, instructed all its managers not to talk to anyone regarding former employees of the company. The company established the policy of providing only dates of employment and job titles. Nothing else is permitted to be stated about former employees. The company justifies its actions as necessary to lessen the chances of being sued based on any information provided. This appears to be the trend in the United States.

Any discrepancies noted between the information furnished by the applicant and that discovered in the background investigation should be carefully noted and investigated. Because employee screening can be both costly and time-consuming, it is recommended that verification be conducted after a tentative employee is selected but before the final job offer is made.

Examine closely the employment history of an applicant. Gaps in employment, periods of self-employment, and employment with relatives should be verified. These terms quite often are used to hide periods of unemployment, jail sentences, or unpleasant job experiences. If there are lingering questions about an applicant's character after the background investigation is completed, it should always be decided in favor of the security organization.

Credit Check

The credit check is normally part of the background investigation. In public law enforcement it has become a standard part of the selection process. Similarly, credit checks of private security applicants are becoming more common. The rule of thumb on credit checks is simply that the organization should be cautious about hiring a candidate who has established a questionable credit record. Not only may this be an indicator of a larger problem such as a lack of personal responsibility, dependability, or maturity on the part of the applicant, it may also tempt the individual after he or she is hired to steal or embezzle money from the security organization, or the company that he or she is assigned to provide security for. As previously pointed out, the gold standard is to make the employment decision that is in the best interest of the organization. The credit check may also be useful because the credit report may list employers who are not otherwise reported by the applicant.

The federal Fair Credit Reporting Act of 1970 requires that if an employer obtains the credit record of a job applicant and decides not to hire the person because of adverse information noted in the credit report, the employer must notify the applicant of the nature, substance, and source of the information. At least fourteen states have enacted similar legislation.

Medical and Drug Screening

Medical and drug screening is one of the last tests in the selection process and is usually administered after a conditional offer of employment has been made to the applicant. During the medical screening, a designated physician performs a physical examination of the applicant to ensure that the applicant has no underlying medical condition that would prevent or limit him or her from performing the essential functions of the job.

Drug testing is usually conducted as part of the medical screening. Preemployment drug testing has become a very common selection device for security employment. It is best to obtain consent from the applicant and to clearly indicate that drug testing is a requirement for employment. Most drug testing is done by sending an applicant to a collection site where a urine sample is obtained, which is sent to a certified laboratory for analysis. Negative results are normally available within twenty-four hours.

Legal Considerations

Security organizations, like many other organizations, operate in a legal vacuum. In other words, the law dictates what they can and cannot do when making employment hiring decisions. In 1964 the U.S. Congress established the Equal Employment

Opportunity Commission (EEOC). The EEOC is charged with the responsibility for administering the provisions of the Civil Rights Act. The Civil Rights Act makes it illegal for employers to discriminate against persons on the basis of race, sex, color, religion, or national origin. All criteria for hiring must be based on a bona-fide occupational qualification (BFOQ). A BFOQ is any physical attribute and/or skill that an employer has proven is necessary for satisfactory performance of a particular job. According to the EEOC guidelines, the use of any selection procedure that has an adverse impact on the hiring, promotion, or other employment opportunities of members of any race, sex, or ethnic group is considered to be discriminatory.

Bona-fide occupational qualification:
Any physical attribute and/or skill that an employer has proven is necessary for satisfactory performance of a particular job, as distinguished from characteristics that have sometimes been required, such as race, height, gender, property-owning status, or passing grades on tests, but that cannot be shown to be related to job performance (Rush 2003).

TRAINING SECURITY PERSONNEL

After the recruitment and selection of security personnel, training is one of the most important functions of a security organization. It is through training that neophyte security officers learn the skills of the security job, and it is through training that veteran security officers learn new techniques while at the same time hone existing skills. The need for security officers to continually stay abreast with the latest technology and advancements in the field, and the need to stay proficient in job-related skills, are among the reasons that security officers find themselves in the classroom.

Training Versus Education

Often, the terms *training* and *education* are incorrectly used interchangeably. Training and education differ in terms of scope and objectives; also, the purpose of education is broader and more general than that of training. Education is concerned with the development of the mind (of the intellect), whereas training deals with learning specific skills.

New security officers walking to a training session.

Education is a more personal activity in that its main purpose is enhancement of an individual's ability to use his or her mind for personal pleasure or gain; training means developing skills that will be used more for social and economic reasons than for personal purposes. Education should come first, and then training should follow. Our primary focus in the section of the chapter is on security officer training—that is, the acquisition of the requisite skills and competencies required to carry out the security job.

The State of Private Security Training

Training:
Teaching security officials the job skills and competencies necessary to perform the job.

For some time, the private security industry has been criticized for lacking sound training programs for employees. The industry has relied primarily on on-the-job training. In other words, a security officer is hired and assigned to work alongside a more experienced officer for a few days or weeks with little other training. In 1976, a National Advisory Committee report recommended a minimum of eight hours of training before security officers enter the field, with a further requirement that security officers receive thirty-two hours of additional formal training within three months. The report also stated that a maximum of sixteen of these hours can be supervised on-the-job basic training hours (U.S. Department of Justice 1976).

In today's complex society, the need for highly trained security professionals is critical. The skills necessary to be a successful security officer are similar to those needed by a police officer. Superior judgment, a willingness to adjust to the personality of the client, good vision, and first-rate communication skills are all very important. For certain types of security jobs, an ability to work alone, and to understand and operate surveillance systems, computers, and photography equipment, is also required.

THE RAND STUDY   Private security training has been a topic of interest and much debate for many years. Various studies and research efforts have been undertaken to better define the role of the private security officer and also to provide agencies with information needed to select and train such officers. One of the earlier studies of interest on this subject was Kakalik and Wildhorn's (1971) report for the Rand Corporation, *Private Police in the United States: Findings and Recommendations*. This report provided one of the first descriptions of private security in this country and continues to be referred to as the baseline research on this subject. Of interest in the Rand report is the criticism that was brought to light regarding the lack of training for security personnel, especially firearms training. The reports asserted that "at the heart of the concern over the arming of security guards is the belief that security guards are often not adequately training to use firearms (Kakalik and Wildhorn 1971, 143). The report stated:

> Many persons now entering security work have no prior experience with firearms, and of those who do claim experience, it is usually of a casual nature rather than any development of expertise. Some security guards do come from the armed forces and from police departments, but this is not generally typical, despite what many people may believe; thus, those who lack experience with firearms would require intensive training prior to their induction into an armed security department. (p. 143)

The security profession can be a hazardous profession, in many cases just as hazardous as the law enforcement profession. The inherent dangers of the job make it imperative that security officers receive comprehensive training that may save their lives if they should encounter a dangerous situation. Security officers should know exactly how to respond instantaneously in a given situation. Whether it is a door found open on a business after hours, a suspicious person sitting in a parking lot of a convenience store, or a suspected shoplifter wandering down the aisles of the department store, the security officer must be properly trained on how to respond to such situations. Much like a police officer, the security officer never knows what he or she will encounter in from one situation to the next.

Basic Certification Training

Many states and local jurisdictions require that security officers receive a specific number of training hours to be certified. In some jurisdictions the local police department offers a private security training course that security officers are required to attend in order to receive their security permit. The number of training hours and the content of training curriculum varies among states and local jurisdictions.

ASIS International (formerly the American Society for Industrial Security), which is the largest professional organization in the security field, established guidelines that called for a formal mechanism to establish minimum training requirements certified by a regulatory body in each of the fifty states (ASIS 2004). The guidelines were established in early 2001 in response to a concerted need for a protocol regarding security issues in the United States. According to the ASIS, regulatory bodies should mandate the minimum training requirements, and there should be cooperative efforts by these bodies to mandate consistent requirements state to state. The ASIS recommended that all entities or persons providing security officer training should be certified by a regulatory body.

The guidelines prescribe specific recommended hours of training and acknowledge different ways in which a security officer may receive this training or demonstrate proficiency to perform the duties of a private security officer. Training may consist of computer-based training, classroom training, self-study, or other methods of delivery. The ASIS recommends that each private security officer receive forty-eight hours of training within the first one hundred days of employment. Training should include the following core topics:

- Nature and role of private security officers
  - Security awareness
    - Private security officers and the criminal justice system
    - Information sharing
    - Crime and loss prevention
  - Legal aspects of private security
    - Evidence and evidence handling
    - Use of force and force continuum
    - Court testimony
    - Incident scene preservation
    - Equal opportunity (EEO) and diversity
    - State and local laws

- Security officer conduct
  - Ethics
  - Honesty
  - Professional image
- Observation and incident reporting
  - Observation techniques
  - Note taking
  - Report writing
  - Patrol techniques
- Principles of communication
  - Interpersonal skills
  - Verbal communication skills
  - Customer service and public relations
- Principles of access control
  - Ingress and egress control procedures
  - Electronic security systems
- Principles of safeguarding information
  - Proprietary and confidential
- Emergency response procedures
  - Critical incident response (e.g., natural disasters, accidents, human-caused events)
  - Evacuation processes
- Life safety awareness
  - Safety hazards in the workplace/surroundings
  - Emergency equipment placement
  - Fire prevention skills
  - Hazardous materials
  - Occupational safety and health requirements (e.g., OSHA-related training, blood-borne pathogens, etc.)
- Job assignments and post orders
- Employer orientation and policies
  - Substance abuse
  - Communications modes (e.g., telephones, pagers, radios, computers)
- Workplace violence
- Conflict resolution awareness
- Traffic control and parking lot security
- Crowd control
- Procedures for first aid, cardiopulmonary resuscitation (CPR), and automatic external defibrillators (AEDs)
- Crisis management
- Labor relations (strikes, lockouts, etc.)

Another report, by the International Association of Chiefs of Police (IACP), also recommends minimum basic and in-service training requirements for private security officers (IACP 2004). According to the IACP, private security officer basic or in-service training should be based on needs analysis related to job function, which may include unarmed security officers, armed security officers, unarmed nonsworn alarm responders, armed nonsworn alarm responders, and armored car guards. The IACP report states that security officers' training should be addressed under topic areas as appropriate, for example, legal, operational, firearms, administrative, electronic, armored transport, and use of force.

Field Training

If a jurisdiction or security agency requires that security officers complete preservice classroom training, then it is important upon graduation that they also complete a field training program. The field training of new security officers is a vital supplement to the classroom training. The initial exposure to security operations provided through the field training program plays a significant role in shaping the future careers of new security officers and provides them with their first opportunity to practice what has been learned in the formal classroom. In the field training program, a new security officer who has recently completed classroom training is assigned to work with a field training officer, who directs and evaluates the performance of the new security officer for a specified period of time.

FAILURE-TO-TRAIN LIABILITY

Another important reason for private security management to ensure that their security personnel are properly trained is the legal environment. Simply put, security management can be sued for failing to provide adequate training for their personnel. The courts are seeing more and more cases involving injuries to citizens caused by private security personnel. A significant number of these cases arise from actions such as assault, battery, false arrest, and false imprisonment. However, the facts of these cases usually reveal a lack of proper training of the private security officer involved. In cases in which negligent training is alleged, the courts have made clear that a lack of training is a basis of support for a cause of action for injury by private security personnel (Moore 1988).

Imagine, for example, that Security Officer John Smith has been issued a new PR-24 baton by his security company. Security Officer Smith begins to wear his shiny new baton on security patrol but has not received any formal training in how to use the baton. One week after being issued the baton, he is checking a business late one evening and comes across a homeless man sleeping under the business's loading dock. Security Officer Smith orders the man to get up. The man continues to lie on the ground and ignore the order. After several commands to get up, the homeless man suddenly leaps up and begins to kick Smith. Security Officer Smith retrieves his PR-24 baton and strikes the man several times. The homeless man falls to the ground and begs Smith to stop. Officer Smith continues to strike the homeless man in the face and head, which results in a deep laceration to the man's head. The man falls into unconsciousness and begins to bleed profusely, and he has to be transported to a hospital for medical attention that ends up being a five-day hospital stay. In this scenario, did Security Officer Smith do anything wrong? Can he or the security company be held liable?

The short answer is yes! Both federal and state laws can hold security officers and security management accountable for negligence on the part of security officers. Not only may there be civil liability, in this scenario there may be criminal liability too. This accountability underscores the importance of effective training. The failure of security management to provide their officers with proper training can result in lawsuits that may ultimately cost the security agency thousands or even millions of dollars.

Direct Liability

Direct liability:
Liability incurred by the
actions of supervisors and
managers themselves.

Security management may face two distinct forms of liability, direct liability and indirect liability. *Direct liability* is liability incurred by the actions of supervisors or managers themselves. For direct liability to exist, security managers usually must have engaged directly in the activity.

Indirect Liability

Indirect liability:
Also referred to as vicarious
liability. Liability that
supervisors and managers
may face for the actions of
their employees.

Indirect liability, or *vicarious liability,* as it is sometimes called, is the liability that supervisors and managers face because of the actions of their employees. For example, let's apply indirect liability to the previous hypothetical case of Security Officer Smith, who was issued a PR-24 baton but not provided any formal training in how to use it, and who seriously injured a homeless man with the baton. In this case, security management might be held vicariously liable under indirect liability.

TRAINING DELIVERY METHODS

Those authorities responsible for training security officers must ensure that training delivery methods are effective. Strict lecture formats should be used with caution, and trainers should, whenever possible, use approaches that actively engage security officers in the learning process.

Adult Learning Model

Andragogy:
A theory of teaching and
learning related to adults,
developed by adult education
scholar Malcolm Knowles.

Adult education scholar Malcolm Knowles argues that adults must be taught differently than children and that the learning process of adults is drastically distinct when compared to that of children or the traditional pedagogical or lecture approach (Knowles 1980). Knowles, a strong proponent of self-directed learning and the teacher's role as a facilitator in the process of adult education, is well known for his theory of andragogy. According to Knowles, andragogy is a theory that is vastly different from the traditional lecture model; instead, it advocates both self-directed learning and the teacher as a facilitator of learning (Knowles 1990).

Knowles (1990, 60) contended that adults are motivated to devote energy to learn something to the extent that they perceive it will help them perform tasks or deal with problems they confront in their life situations. Furthermore, they learn new knowledge, understandings, skills, values, and attitudes most effectively when these are presented in the context of application to real life situations.

The training of private security officers should be made experiential, interactive, and participatory. Every aspect of security training should include simulation exercises and problem-solving activities that help develop communication and language skills. Security trainers can be used as actors to construct, for example, a shoplifting scenario involving a non-English-speaking suspect. Learners might then be required to bring to bear their experience, powers of observation, and communication skills to solve the problem. Situations should be designed so that learners can use previous knowledge and can connect theory and practice.

Role playing and improvisations are not new adult learning techniques, but they are often relegated to one or two hastily conceived practical skills sessions that are poorly performed, monitored, and evaluated. Properly prepared activities lead to increased retention. Thus, security officers are more likely to understand legal concepts and may be able to better empathize with citizens they encounter on the street because of their classroom experience.

Problem-Based Learning

Problem-based learning is an instructional method that challenges students to "learn to learn," working cooperatively in groups to seek solutions to real-world problems (Stepien and Gallagher 1993). Problems are presented in training to engage students' curiosity and to initiate their learning of the subject matter. Problem-based learning prepares security officers both to think critically and analytically, and to find and use appropriate learning resources. Problem-based learning is ideal for field training of new security officers.

Problem-based learning is a curriculum development and delivery system that recognizes the need to help security officers develop problem-solving skills as well as acquire necessary knowledge and skills. The first application of problem-based learning was in medical schools, which rigorously tested the knowledge base of graduates. Problem-based learning utilizes real-world problems, not hypothetical case studies with neat, convergent outcomes. It is in the process of struggling with actual problems that students learn both content and critical thinking skills.

Case Study Method

The case study method is an instructional technique based on real-life examples. Case studies stimulate the real world, and they can be used to orient trainees to ethical dilemmas in the security profession. The case study method was developed by Christopher Langdell of Harvard University School of Law in the 1880s and later introduced into Harvard Business School.

Case studies have been used in a wide variety of professional training programs; for example, in law schools, cases are frequently the backbone of a course, with various cases used throughout the course. Case studies help future lawyers organize complex bodies of facts and information on their own, arrive inductively at principles, and apply them to new situations. The central aims of the case study are to stimulate self-development in a blend of understanding that combines intellectual ability (the power to think clearly, incisively, and reasonably about specific facts and about abstractions) and to develop practical judgment and social awareness (Marsick 1998). Cases typically include three interrelated components: a case study or report, case analysis, and case discussion.

In private security training, security officers might be required to read a factual case situation and then identify the key issues of the case; present a rationale of whether, for example, a suspect should be detained, and support the rationale with the appropriate security policy and procedure or statutory laws or local ordinances. The case study method makes training both realistic and active. Designing case studies will also serve to break the monotony of the lecture. The technique should include essential lectures and then use of the case study method.

The case study method requires the facilitator to allow enough time for trainees to fully understand the nature of the problem or case scenario. Using a video or other relevant audiovisual will cut down on the time needed for understanding but will increase the design time. The case study method usually works best when trainees work together in groups.

Summary

- Recruitment and selection is an important activity. It is through recruitment and selection that the future of the security agency is determined.
- Recruitment is the process of locating, identifying, and attracting capable applicants who have the minimum qualifications to be eligible for the selection process.
- Recruitment involves many activities and may include advertisements in professional publications, with college and university placement services, and advertisements in local, state, and regional newspapers. Recruiting may also include professional contacts with community organizations, publications and pamphlets, special activities and events for prospective applicants, audiovisual packages, and Internet advertising.
- The selection process is the process by which security officer applicants are subjected to specific testing protocols. Selection is an exercise that seeks to predict which applicants will be successful if hired and to weed out the unqualified candidates.
- The employment application form offers an often-overlooked device to determine an applicant's qualifications. The application form can be reviewed quickly to determine whether the applicant meets the minimum qualifications for the job.
- If a security company requires applicants to take a written test, the test should be administered early in the selection process but after the initial application form has been completed and checked to ensure minimum qualifications. A written examination is an effective and cost-effective method of screening large numbers of applicants. If the security organization utilizes a written examination, federal law requires that it be job-related.
- Preemployment polygraph screening may be used to verify information contained on a job application and to learn whether some relevant information has been omitted. The private sector is usually prohibited from using the polygraph according to the Employee Polygraph Protection Act of 1988. However, the law specified that certain occupations outside government organizations can use the polygraph. One of the specified occupations is security organizations that employee personnel whose duties include protecting facilities significant to the safety of any state, water supply facilities, nuclear and conventional power plants, and public transportation facilities.
- Psychological tests are written, visual, or verbal evaluations administered to assess the cognitive and emotional functioning of security officer applicants.
- Psychological tests used in security officer selection may include the Minnesota Multiphasic Personality Inventory (MMPI), the California Personality Inventory (CPI), Rorschach "inkblots," figure drawings, and sentence-completion tests.
- A background investigation is an investigation into an applicant's background. It provides a wealth of insight into the candidate's personal and professional life and provides some of the most important indicators of job success. A credit check of the applicant may be part of the background investigation.
- Medical and drug screening is one of the last tests in the selection process and is usually administered after a conditional offer of employment has been made to the applicant.
- Training is the life blood of the security organization. Proper training is the root of efficiency. In the past, the private security industry has been criticized by the lack of sound training criteria.
- Training and education differ in terms of scope and objectives. The purpose of education is

broader and more general than that of training. Education is concerned with development of the mind (of the intellect), whereas training deals with learning specific skills.

- Classroom training should be supplemented with a field training program whenever possible. In a field training program, a new security officer who has completed classroom training is assigned to ride with a field training officer, who directs, evaluates, and correct the performance of the new security officer.
- ASIS International has established guidelines that call for a formal mechanism to establish minimum training requirements certified by a regulatory body in each state. The guidelines prescribe specific recommended hours of training, and acknowledge different ways in which a security officer may receive this training.

- To protect themselves from potential costly legal settlements, security companies should ensure that their security officers are properly trained.
- Direct liability is incurred when a security supervisor or manager participants directly in inappropriate conduct. Indirect liability or vicarious liability occurs when security supervisors or managers are held liable for the actions of their employees.
- Authorities responsible for training security officers should use a number of different approaches that have been shown to be effective when training adults. Andragogic (adult education) methods work best when training adults. Training methods such as problem-based learning and case studies are effective techniques that can be used in training security officers.

Review Questions

1. Discuss effective recruiting strategies.
2. Identify the steps in the selection process.
3. Identify some types of psychological tests that may be used in the selection process.
4. Discuss the differences between education and training.
5. Define bona-fide occupational requirements.
6. Define direct liability and indirect liability.

7. Describe the andragogy learning model.
8. What do proponents of polygraph testing argue regarding the use of the polygraph as a selection tool?
9. Describe failure-to-train liability.
10. Describe the case study method.
11. Explain problem-based learning.

Class Exercises

1. In small groups, discuss the qualifications you think are necessary to become a private security officer.
2. In small groups, discuss the advantages and disadvantages of the polygraph for preempolyment screening of security officers.

3. Discuss the types of courses that you think should be included in a security officer training curriculum.
4. Pick up recruiting brochures from various security companies and compare them in class. How are they different; similar?

References

ASIS International 2004. *Private security officer selection and training.* www.asisonline.org/guidelines/guidelinesprivatefinal.pdf, retrieved October 6, 2007

Birzer, M. L., and C. Roberson. 2007. *Policing today and tomorrow.* Upper Saddle River, NJ: Prentice-Hall.

Executive Focus. 2004. Hiring the wrong person costs you three times their annual salary. *Executive Focus,* June, 33–4.

International Association of Chiefs of Police. 2004. *Private security officer selection, training and licensing guidelines.* Alexandria, VA: International Association of Chiefs of Police.

Kakalik, J. S., and S. Wildhorn. 1971. *Private police in the United States: Findings and recommendations.* Santa Monica, CA: Rand Corporation.

Knowles, M. S. 1980. *The modern practice of adult education: From pedagogy to andragogy.* Chicago: Follett.

Knowles, M. S. 1990. *The adult learner: A neglected species.* Houston, TX: Gulf.

Marsick, V. J. 1998. Case study. In *Adult learning methods,* 2nd ed., ed. M. W. Galbraith, 241–3. Malabar: FL: Krieger.

Moore, R. H. 1988. Civil liability and negligent and inadequate training: A private security problem. *Journal of Contemporary Criminal Justice* 4(2): 106–18.

Pigors, P. 1976. Case method. In *Training and development handbook: A guide to human resource development,* ed. R. L. Craig, 173–5. New York: McGraw-Hill.

Robbins, S. P., and A. Coulter, A. 1999. *Management.* Upper Saddle River, NJ: Prentice-Hall.

Rush, G. E. 2003. *The dictionary of criminal justice,* 6th ed. New York: Dushkin/McGraw-Hill.

Stepien, W. J., and S. A. Gallagher. 1993. Problem-based learning: As authentic as it gets. *Educational Leadership* 50(7), 25–8.

U.S. Department of Justice. 1976. U.S. Department of Justice Law Enforcement Assistance Administration, National Advisory Committee on Criminal Justice Standards and Goals. *Report of the task force for private security: Private security.* Washington, DC: U.S. Government Printing Office.

U.S. Department of Labor. 2008. *Occupational outlook handbook: 2008–2009 edition.* www.bls.gov/oco/home.htm, retrieved March 21, 2008.

CHAPTER 13

Drug and Alcohol Issues for Private Security

CHAPTER OUTLINE

OBJECTIVES

After completing this chapter, you will be able to:

- Identify commonly abused drugs.
- Discuss the purpose of the Drug Free Workplace Act of 1988.
- Describe private security's role in creating a drug-free workplace.
- Discuss what is involved in creating a drug-free workplace.
- Identify the various types of drug abuse detection methods in the workplace.
- Discuss the signs of drug-related activities that private security officers should recognize in the field.
- Discuss the pros and cons of drug testing in the workplace.
- Describe the purpose of employee assistance programs.
- Discuss drug field testing.

*The loss to companies in the United States due to alcohol and drug-related
abuse by employees totals $100 billion a year.*

—*National Clearinghouse for Alcohol and Drug Information (2008)*

Illicit drug:

*A drug or chemical substance
whose possession and use are
regulated under the federal
Controlled Substances Act.*

D rug and alcohol abuse is a serious problem for employers, and it occurs at all
levels of the workforce. For example, in one case, the manager of a company
that grossed in excess of $140 million annually was arrested at a local hotel
and charged with the possession of cocaine and drug paraphernalia (Roberson 2005).
Although alcohol abuse has long been a problem at the managerial level, it now
appears that drug abuse, especially the use of cocaine, is increasing among managers.
In addition, security officers may encounter illicit drugs or a person intoxicated on
alcohol in the performance of their duties. These encounters may take place when
security officers are in the field performing security checks of buildings and apartment
complexes, or perhaps in a corporate security position when they are summoned by
management because an employee has shown up for work under the influence or in
possession of an illicit drug and/or alcohol. Research has shown that the majority of
heavy drinkers and users of illicit drugs are employed adults, yet there is a lack of
sophisticated substance abuse prevention efforts in the workplace (Cook, Back, and
Trudeau 1996). Security officials, especially those working in corporate and business
security environments, play an invaluable role in convincing management of the
importance of ensuring an effective substance abuse prevention plan is in place.

Narcotic offenses run the gamut from simple possession of marijuana to the sale
of heroin. Offenders vary from a person supplying marijuana for an afternoon party to
a drug lord planning distribution of heroin throughout the United States. Security officers must have some basic knowledge of illicit drugs and substance abuse to perform
their jobs effectively. This chapter provides a brief overview of private security's role
in dealing with illicit drugs or alcohol abuse. In addition, the chapter discusses some
of the more common types of drugs that security officials may encounter.

PREVALENCE OF DRUG AND ALCOHOL ABUSE

Marijuana:

*The most used drug. A drug
from the leaves of the
flowering top of the hemp
plant, Cannabis sativa, also
known as Indian hemp,
thought to have originated in
the mountainous districts of
India, north of the Himalayan
Mountains.*

According to a recent national survey conducted by the U.S. Department of Health
and Human Services (2007), over 19.5 million Americans, representing 8.2 percent of
the population aged 12 and older, use illicit drugs such as marijuana, cocaine, and
heroin on a regular basis. Almost half of all Americans have used an illicit substance,
most likely marijuana, at least once. It is clear that marijuana is the most popular illicit
drug. Approximately 14.6 million Americans or 6.2 percent of the population report
that they have used marijuana on a regular basis. Furthermore, alcohol and drug abuse
are said to cost U.S. industry more than $100 billion annually (Schuler 1995, 281).

Most drug users are employed, but those who are unemployed use illicit drugs at
substantially higher rates. An estimated 18.2 percent of unemployed adults aged 18
and older used illicit drugs on a current basis, compared with 7.9 percent of those
employed full time and 10.7 percent of those employed part-time. According to the
2006 National Survey on Drug Use and Health (U.S. Department of Health and
Human Services 2007), 7.0 million persons (2.8 percent of the populatiion) aged 12 or
older used prescription-type psychotherapeutic drugs nonmedically in the past month.

Variety of illicit drugs discovered by a security officer.

Of these, 5.2 million used pain relievers, an increase from 4.7 million in 2005. In terms of new substance abuse users, the survey indicates that the nation faces major challenges, perhaps epidemics, of misuse of prescription drugs, ecstasy, marijuana, and cocaine.

Alcohol Abuse

Security officers need to be thoroughly versed regarding the magnitude and scope of alcohol abuse and the use of illegal drugs in the workplace. Nearly three-quarters of those who use illegal drugs also work, and alcohol remains the leading drug of abuse: One in every ten people in the United States has an alcohol problem (U.S. Department of Labor 2008). People don't check their substance abuse problems at the door when they enter the workplace. Workers who abuse alcohol and other drugs affect everyone around them. Substance abuse can affect all segments of the workforce, from employees performing tedious repetitive tasks to managers under stress.

Alcohol abuse: Frequent intake of large amounts of alcohol, typically distinguished by decreased health and physical and social/job functioning impairment.

In the U.S. Department of Health and Human Services survey (2007), slightly more than half of Americans aged 12 or older reported being current drinkers of alcohol. This translates to an estimated 125 million people. More than one-fifth (23.0 percent) of persons aged 12 or older reported that they had participated in binge drinking (having five or more drinks on the same occasion on at least one day in the thirty days prior to the survey). This translates to about 57 million people.

In 2006, heavy drinking was reported by over 6 percent of the population aged 12 or older, or 17 million people. Heavy drinking is defined as binge drinking on at least five days in the past thirty days. In 2006, among young adults aged 18 to 25, the rate of binge drinking was about 42 percent and the rate of heavy drinking was over 15 percent.

TYPES OF ILLICIT DRUGS

This section provides a brief overview some of the more common drugs used in our society. It is not intended to be an exhaustive review all of the various types of drugs that may be encountered by security officials, but rather it should be used as an introduction to the vast array of drugs that are available on the streets of our nation.

A drug originally was classified as a narcotic if it was habit-forming and tended to cause a state of drowsiness (Abadinsky 1993). The habit-forming requirement has been modified in recent years to include not only those drugs that are physiologically habit-forming but also those that are psychologically habit-forming. In addition, the term *narcotic* now includes drugs that produce feelings of excitement. Narcotics are generally either depressants or stimulants. *Depressants* lessen physical activity and tend to produce drowsiness. The most common depressants are morphine, heroin, codeine, and opium. *Stimulants,* which produce feelings of excitement, include methamphetamine and cocaine.

Narcotic:
An addictive drug, such as opium, that reduces pain, alters mood and behavior, and usually induces sleep or stupor. Natural and synthetic narcotics are used in medicine to control pain.

Depressant:
An agent, especially a drug, that decreases the rate of vital physiological activities. In street lingo often referred to as a "downer."

Stimulant:
A drug that excites the central nervous system. Over-the-counter decongestant medications commonly contain stimulate properties.

Cocaine

Cocaine is a powerful stimulant. It is a by-product of the cocoa plant and is freely cultivated in South America. It comes in white powder or crystal form. It has a bitter taste and produces a peculiar tingling sensation on the tongue. It is normally inhaled (snorted) through the nostrils, where it is absorbed by the mucous membranes. To obtain faster results, some users take it by injection or rub it on their gums. It provides a feeling of increased physical strength and mental resources.

Coca Cola once contained cocaine, but its use in the beverage was discontinued in the early 1900s. Cole Porter's great song, "I Get a Kick Out of You," at one time contained the line, "I get no kick from cocaine, but I get a kick out of you." Cocaine was used in the 1920s mainly by musicians to enhance their performance. Now it has become the drug of the young professional businessperson.

"Speedballing" is the practice of mixing cocaine and heroin for the purpose of obtaining a distinct high. "Freebasing" refers to the conversion of street cocaine to freebase, or pure cocaine. This substance is then sprinkled on a cigarette or smoked in a pipe. Freebase enters the bloodstream through the lungs, and the high is felt before the smoke is exhaled.

Crack is refined cocaine that comes in rock form. Crack is an off-white color and sometimes resembles pieces of soap. The word "crack" comes from the crackling sound made when it is smoked or from its occasional resemblance to cracked plaster. Crack is popular because it can be smoked, which produces an immediate high.

Ecstasy

MDMA (3,4-methylenedioxymethylamphetamine), most commonly known today by the street name ecstasy (often abbreviated to E, X, or XTC) is a synthetic, psychoactive (mind-altering) drug with amphetamine- and hallucinogen-like properties. It almost always comes in a pill or capsule, and the normal dose is 100 to 125 milligrams. The drug produces a euphoric effect—it makes the user very happy. It is not uncommon for an ecstasy user to experience heightened feelings of empathy, emotional warmth, peacefulness, and self-acceptance. It is considered a recreational drug and a mood elevator, and has had a strong association with the rave and club culture. Security officials who work in night club environments are likely to come into contact with a person under the influence of ecstasy.

Methamphetamines

Methamphetamines are a form of amphetamine that has been sometimes called the poor man's cocaine. It has various street names, including meth, speed, or crystal. It has been produced illegally for decades and may be manufactured in home laboratories. It may be injected, inhaled, or taken orally.

Ice is a smokable form methamphetamine. Ice was initially reported in Hawaii in 1985 and supposedly has become that state's greatest problem drug. The street name "ice" comes from the drug's appearance, generally a clear, crystal-shaped form that looks like glass. In some areas this narcotic is also known as crank. Ice has the same properties as methamphetamine, but through a recrystallization process, the rocklike crystals can be smoked. The ice form of methamphetamine is highly addictive.

LSD

LSD (lysergic acid diethylamide-25) is a synthetic drug that stimulates cerebral sensory centers and promotes a full range of visual hallucinations. The drug may induce feelings of anxiety and panic, and some users have experienced flashbacks long after discontinuing use of the substance.

Peyote

The peyote is a small cactus that grows naturally in Mexico and the southwestern portion of the United States. It contains mescaline, a hallucinogenic substance named after the Mescalero Apaches, who first used it. Peyote produces a wide range of hallucinations, including colors, geometric patterns, and out-of-body sensations.

Morphine

Morphine is the principal psychoactive alkaloid in opium. It was first produced in 1805. It was named after the Greek god of dreams, Morpheus. Morphine is ten times stronger than opium and is used by physicians to relieve pain. It produces an elevation of spirits and then drowsiness. Morphine is a highly addictive drug.

Codeine

Codeine is a derivative of opium that may be used legally under a doctor's orders. It is present in many pain-relieving prescription drugs. It can produce drug dependence of the morphine type and therefore is considered highly addictive.

Heroin

Heroin was first produced in 1874 by an Englishman, D. P. Wright, and is twenty-five times stronger than morphine. It is one of the more commonly used illegal drugs in the United States. Users quickly build up a tolerance and must use more of the drug to obtain the same effect. It is sold as a powder and mixed before being injected into the bloodstream. There are numerous forms of heroin: "Mexican Brown" is sold in the western United States and is pink-brown in color. It is usually a fine powder with dark brown flecks. The color may vary from light brown to chocolate. "Persian Heroin" is tan or reddish in color. It is not water-soluble; lemon juice or vinegar is added before cooking in the traditional spoon. "Black Tar Heroin" began appearing in the United States about 1979. This drug is especially desired on the streets because of its purity, about 93 percent. There are numerous street names for Black Tar, including gum, goma, and Mexican mud.

Methadone

Methadone is a synthetic drug that is used to assist heroin users in breaking their habit. Some states have established methadone clinics where heroin users may go to obtain the drug legally in lieu of purchasing heroin on the streets. Methadone is considered highly addictive. The withdrawal following extended use of methadone is more prolonged but less intense than that of heroin.

Demerol

Demerol is in a class of drugs called narcotic analgesics. Demerol is a synthetic drug that is used by the medical profession. It is usually administered before and after operations as a method of controlling pain.

Phencyclidine (PCP)

PCP (phencyclohexyl piperidine monohydrochloride) is a synthetic drug. It was first discovered in 1956 by researchers at the Parke-Davis pharmaceutical company (now a division of Pfizer). The PCP sold in the United States is made in illegal laboratories. PCP in its pure state is a clear liquid. In solid form, it is a powder that may be white or have a yellowish or brownish tint. It may act as a depressant, a stimulant, a psyche-delic, and a tranquilizer. It also removes the feeling of physical pain. The user's pain threshold is dramatically increased, and therefore traditional police restraints may be ineffective against a person under the influence of PCP.

Marijuana

Marijuana is the most commonly used illicit drug in the United States. More than 94 million Americans (40 percent) age 12 and older have tried marijuana at least once, according to the 2006 National Survey on Drug Use and Health (U.S. Department of Health and Human Services 2007). According to the National Institute of Justice Arrestee Drug Abuse Monitoring Program, which collects data on the number of adult arrestees who test positive for various drugs, on average, 41 percent of adult male arrestees and 27 percent of adult female arrestees tested positive for marijuana. On average, 57 percent of juvenile male and 32 percent of juvenile female arrestees tested positive for marijuana (National Institute of Justice 2003).

Marijuana, a dry, shredded green/brown mix of flowers, stems, seeds, and leaves of the plant *Cannabis sativa,* is usually smoked as a cigarette (joint, nail), or in a pipe (bong). Marijuana is a strong hallucinogenic drug and can have affect short-term

Cannabis sativa—the marijuana leaf.

memory, verbal skills and judgment, and can distort perception. The marijuana plant is grown in many regions of the United States, Mexico, and Southeast Asia, among other places. It may be chewed, smoked, mixed in a beverage, or baked in cookies.

The major active chemical in marijuana is delta-9-tetrahydrocannabinol (THC), which causes the mind-altering effects of marijuana intoxication. The amount of THC (which is also the psychoactive ingredient in hashish) determines the potency and, therefore, the effects of marijuana. Marijuana, like alcohol, can be either a depressant or a stimulant, depending on the personality of the user.

EFFECTS OF DRUG ABUSE

Drug abuse can cause poor job performance and lead to drug intoxication on the job, possession or selling of drugs during company time, and stealing from the company to support a drug habit. For example, some studies on marijuana use indicate that its effects can last up to twenty-four hours. Thus, if employees smoke marijuana during nonworking hours, in most cases they will still be under its effects when they report for work the next day. In one study, airplane pilots who were experimental marijuana smokers were tested at intervals of one hour, four hours, and twenty-four hours after

Drug intoxication:
Stupefaction or excitement caused by the action of a chemical substance upon ingestion of a drug. Drug intoxication may cause exhilaration, excitement, or euphoria. Street lingo refers to drug intoxication as "getting high."

Street Names of Various Drugs

Methamphetamine: speed, meth, ice, crystal, chalk, crank, tweak, uppers, black beauties, glass, bikers coffee, methlies quick, poor man's cocaine, chicken feed, shabu, crystal meth, stove top, trash, go-fast, yaba, yellow bam

    Cocaine: blow, nose candy, snowball, tornado, wicky stick

    Heroin: smack, thunder, hell dust, big H, nose drops

LSD: acid, blotter acid, window pane, dots, mellow yellow

Marijuana: grass, pot, weed, bud, Mary Jane, dope, indo, hydro

MDMA (ecstasy): MDMA, ecstasy, XTC, E, X, beans, adams, hug drug, disco biscuit, go

smoking marijuana (Yesavage, Leirer, Denari, and Hollister 1985). The researchers found "significant impairments in a variety of landing tasks when compared to pre-smoking performance." The pilots' impaired ability to control the airplane persisted up to twenty-four hours after they used the drug. This study concluded that the results suggest concern for the performance of employees entrusted with complex behavioral and cognitive tasks. Marijuana use also may affect the use of complicated or dangerous equipment.

SCHOOLS OF THOUGHT ON DRUG ABUSE

Courts and labor arbitrators have tended to adopt one of three schools of thought when considering an employer's right to fire or otherwise discipline an employee who uses illegal drugs. The rule in most states is that an employer has the right to fire an employee who abuses drugs or alcohol. Security officials should caution management, however, to seek legal advice before taking action in such cases. Preventive legal advice will save money in the long run.

The first school of thought is the traditional one that, if an employee cannot perform his or her job assignment, then the employer can take the necessary corrective action.

The second school of thought is that drug use is a form of illness and therefore should be handled as a medical problem. Numerous attempts have been made to classify drug abuse as a medical handicap. In most cases, the courts have failed to consider it a medical handicap. In one case, two unsuccessful applicants for employment as fire fighters were denied employment when they were tested twice for drug abuse and both tests indicated the presence of marijuana. The court, in upholding the right of the city to deny them employment, indicated that, even if it were considered a medical handicap, the impaired ability of an abuser rendered him or her unsuitable for employment.

The third school of thought is that the drug-abusing employee should be given an opportunity to receive professional help to overcome the problem without jeopardizing his or her job. Thus, the employee is given a second chance. The problem with this approach is that most drug abusers will deny a drug problem and therefore will not seek assistance to handle the problem.

Drug abuse includes the abuse of legally prescribed drugs and over-the-counter drugs as well as illegal drugs. Legal drugs can have the same effects on employees as illegal ones, but the employer's right to discharge an employee who abuses legal drugs is not as clear. For example, most courts have upheld the right of an employer to terminate an employee who is convicted of illegal drug-related conduct. The court decisions are unclear as to the right to fire employees for abuse of prescribed or over-the-counter drugs.

ALCOHOLISM VERSUS DRUG ABUSE

A question now plaguing employers is whether it is unfair or illegal to treat drug abuse differently from alcohol abuse. From a practical point of view, an employee with either a drug abuse problem or an alcohol abuse problem creates similar work-related problems. Alcohol abuse represents serious consequences for workplace behavior just as other forms of drug abuse do (Greenberg and Grunberg 1995). We are, however, more familiar with alcoholism and tend to accept it much more than drug abuse, which is often mistakenly thought of as a product of a subculture. Several recent court cases have indicated that it is illegal for a company to punish a drug abuser more heavily than it does someone who abuses alcohol. Although this requirement of equal treatment for drug and alcohol abuse is not accepted by most courts, management needs to exercise caution before establishing different policies for treating drug abusers and alcoholics.

CUES TO DRUG ABUSE

A person under the influence of drugs exhibits definite clues. Because some drugs act as stimulants and others as depressants, not all of the following clues will be present in each case and, in many cases, a person may be under the influence of a drug without exhibiting any of the clues. The following performance and behavior problems, however, are common to many employed individuals who abuse alcohol and/or other drugs. It is important to note that if an employee displays these symptoms, it does not necessarily mean that he or she has a substance abuse problem.

1. The person appears to be intoxicated, but the smell of alcohol is absent.
2. The person is in a state of restlessness, drowsiness, or exultation.
3. The pupils of the person's eyes are dilated or are not affected by changes in lighting.
4. The person walks rapidly.
5. The person exhibits an inability to concentrate.
6. Strong body odors emanate from the person.
7. The person exhibits mental or physical disorientation.

Other cues include:

1. Inconsistent work quality
2. Lowered work productivity
3. Increased absenteeism from the job
4. Errors in judgment
5. Needless risk taking
6. Frequent financial problems
7. Blaming others for own problems and shortcomings
8. Deterioration in personal appearance
9. Complaints about problems at home
10. Complaints and excuses of vaguely defined illnesses

Cues for Security Officers Working in the Field

Security officers should be aware of specific signs that may indicate the prevalence of drug activity in housing communities, apartment complexes, or other residential areas. Some of these signs include:

1. An unusually large amount of traffic coming to the house or apartment building, in cars, taxis, or walking, often at strange hours. The traffic is usually quick, and people stay only a short time. They often don't go inside the residence; someone comes out to meet them.
2. Renters who reportedly always pay in cash.
3. Finding drugs or drug paraphernalia (syringes, pipes, baggies, etc.) in the area.

4. Repeated, observable items being exchanged between individuals, especially where money is visible.
5. Reports from citizens that someone offered to sell them drugs, or conversations about drugs that they overheard.
6. Houses or buildings where extreme security measures seem to have been taken, such as bars over the windows or doors, and vicious dogs positioned near the doors. Curtains and blinds are blacked out.
7. Houses or buildings where no owner or primary renter is apparent, and no home activity such as painting or yard work has taken place. In other words, the property looks run down and is an eyesore.
8. Noxious strong odors such as cat urine, ether, ammonia, acetone, rotten eggs, or dirty diapers (may indicate a methamphetamine lab).
9. Dumped items in the garbage container such as red, chemically stained coffee filters, drain cleaner, duct tape, antifreeze and lantern fuel cans (may indicate a methamphetamine lab).

CREATING A DRUG-FREE WORKPLACE

Drug-free workplace:
Workplaces at which
employees are prohibited
from engaging in the
unlawful manufacture,
distribution, dispensing,
possession, or use of any
controlled substance.

Security officials have an important responsibility to business management to foster a culture of a drug-free workplace. Often, this task falls exclusively on the security team. As pointed out previously, drug abuse on the part of employees is linked to numerous problems in business and industry, includng employee theft, absenteeism and tardiness, poor job performance, and poor morale. A drug-free workplace policy forms the foundation for a drug-free workplace program; however, it is not the same as a drug-free workplace program. Rather, it is one of five components. The U.S. Department of Labor (2008) recommends that, in addition to a policy, a comprehensive drug-free workplace program should include supervisor training, employee education, employee assistance, and drug testing.

Although programs can be effective without all five of these components, all five should at least be explored when developing a program. Effective program planning is critical to success. Security officials, employers, and employees should work together to examine each component and design a balanced, fair program suited to the unique needs and challenges of their workplace. Once again, often security officials are tasked with developing a comprehensive drug-free workplace policy that includes training the company's supervisors, educating employees, employee assistance, and drug testing.

Training Supervisors

After developing a drug-free workplace policy statement, security officials may be tasked with training those individuals closest to the workforce—supervisors. Training supervisors is an integral part of every drug-free workplace program. Supervisors should be provided with basic information about your drug-free workplace program and their role in its implementation. The U.S. Department of Labor (2008) recommends that, at a minimum, supervisor training should include a review of:

1. The drug-free workplace policy
2. The supervisor's specific responsibilities in implementing the policy

3. Ways to recognize and deal with employees who have job performance problems that might be related to alcohol and other drugs.

Security officials should reinforce to supervisors that they have a responsibility to monitor employees' performance while staying alert to and documenting performance problems and enforcing the drug-free workplace policy. Security officials and/or supervisors should not be expected to diagnose alcohol- and drug-related problems or to provide counseling to employees who may have them.

Documentation of, and intervention into, an employee's substance abuse problem is critical. If substance abuse is contributing to an employee's poor performance, ignoring or avoiding the issue will not help the situation. An employee's use of alcohol or drugs may be the root of the performance problem; however, substance abuse on the part of someone close to the employee also could be the source. Regardless, as pointed out throughout this chapter, abuse of alcohol or other drugs inevitably leads to costly and potentially dangerous consequences in the workplace unless action is taken to confront the issue.

Educating Employees

The purpose of employee training is to familiarize them with the company's drug-free workplace program and to provide general awareness education about the dangers of alcohol and drug abuse. Research has shown that educating both employees and management may be the best way to help employees who suffer from substance abuse problems (Bennett and Lehman 2001). As part of the education process, every employee should receive a copy of the drug-free workplace policy. Security officials should ensure that each employee signs a form acknowledging that he or she has received a copy of the policy. The objectives of the training are to inform employees about:

1. The requirements of the organization's drug-free workplace policy
2. The prevalence of alcohol and drug abuse and their impacts on the workplace
3. How to recognize the connection between poor performance and alcohol and/or drug abuse
4. The progression of the disease of alcohol and drug addiction
5. What types of assistance may be available

The security officials who conduct the employee education should be thoroughly familiar with each component of the organization's drug-free workplace policy and prepared to lead a discussion about the questions the following questions:

1. What is the purpose and intent of the program?
2. Who will be covered by the policy?
3. When will the policy apply?
4. What behavior will be prohibited?
5. Will employees be required to notify you of drug-related convictions?
6. Will the policy include searches?
7. Will the program include drug testing?
8. What will the consequences be if the policy is violated? Will there be return-to-work agreements?
9. What type of assistance will be available?

10. How will employee confidentiality be protected?
11. Who will be responsible for enforcing the policy?
12. How will the policy be communicated to employees?

Employee Assistance Programs

A critical component of a drug-free workplace program is providing assistance or support to employees who have problems with alcohol and other drugs. Employee assistance programs (EAPs) are generally the most effective vehicle for addressing poor workplace performance that may stem from an employee's personal problems, including the abuse of alcohol or other drugs. EAPs are an excellent benefit to employees and their families and clearly demonstrate employers' respect for their staff (Yandrick 1995). They also offer an alternative to dismissal and minimize an employer's legal vulnerability by demonstrating efforts to support employees. In addition to counseling and referrals, many EAPs offer other related services, such as supervisor training and employee education. Employee assistance programs ideally target employees whose performance shows a pattern of decline that is not readily explained by job circumstances, and employees who are aware of personal problems that may or may not be affecting their performance. Current research has substantiated employee assistance programs have the potential to save significant dollars through early intervention and prevention efforts, as well as creating a sense of caring for the employees. This will enable the employer to develop interventions that aid in preventing or reducing workplace problems, as well as employee risk. Security officials should be well versed in the benefits of EAPs and encourage the organization's management to establish an EAP if the copmany does not have one.

Employee assistant program: A program designed specifically to assist employees with chronic personal problems such as drug or alcohol abuse that may hinder their work performance.

As a minimum, businesses should maintain a resource file through which employees can access information about community-based resources and treatment programs. According to the U.S. Department of Labor (2008), security officials and employers implement EAPs to accomplish a variety of goals:

- Identify employee personal problems at an early stage, before there is a serious impact on the job.
- Motivate employees to seek help through easy access to assessment and referral.
- Direct employees to the best source of help and high-quality providers.
- Limit health insurance costs through early intervention.
- Reduce workers' compensation claims by encouraging easy access to help.
- Decrease employee turnover.
- Offer an alternative to firing valuable employees.
- Provide employees with support and demonstrate that a company is a caring employer.

An employee assistance program should include these essential components:

- A policy statement that defines how employees access the EAP, the services provided, and how confidentiality is protected
- Consultation and training services for supervisors and managers on how to manage and refer troubled employees to the EAP
- Promotional activities that ensure the EAP is highly visible and easily accessible to employees
- Educational programs for employees on relevant issues such as alcohol and drug addiction

- Problem identification and referral services provided directly to individual employees (and often to family members)
- Identification and maintenance of a current, annotated directory of qualified providers of treatment or assistance to enable prompt referral of employees to appropriate resources

The following is a sample employee assistance program suggested by the U.S. Department of Labor. It may not suit your business environment; do not adopt this policy unless you are sure that your EAP operates according to the statements it contains.

Employee Drug Testing

The majority of employers across the United States are not required to test employees for the presence of drugs, and many state and local governments have statutes that limit or prohibit workplace testing, except as required by state or federal regulations for certain jobs. Furthermore, drug testing is not required under the federal Drug Free Workplace Act of 1988. The Drug Free Workplace Act requires some federal government contractors and all fund recipients to implement workplace drug prevention programs (Falcone 2002). Under this act, employers or contractors are required to:

- Certify that you will provide a drug-free workplace.
- Publish a statement notifying your employees that the unlawful manufacture, distribution, dispensing, possession, or use of a controlled substance is prohibited in the workplace and stating what action will be taken against your employees for violations.

Model Employee Assistance Program

Our organization supports the drug-free workplace program by offering an Employee Assistance Program (EAP). The EAP is designed to assist employees with personal concerns that may impact their job performance. These concerns include but are not limited to health, marital, family, financial, emotional, alcohol abuse and drug use. We believe that all of us, at one time or another, have serious problems to deal with. It is important to seek help for such problems. Your EAP can help assess the problem, offer guidance and provide a referral to quality care.

We consider the abuse of alcohol and prescription drugs and the use of illegal drugs to be treatable conditions. We encourage employees to seek assistance for these problems on a confidential self-referral basis.

Participation in the EAP, on a voluntary basis, will not jeopardize an employee's opportunities for promotion or employment. Employees can contact the EAP directly. Their contact, participation in the EAP and any recommended treatment is confidential and will not be disclosed to the organization.

Employees may be referred to the EAP by their supervisor on the basis of job performance problems. When the employee follows through with the referral, the supervisor will be notified that the employee has made contact, but the exact nature of the problem will not be disclosed.

Employee Assistance Policy services are available to the employee without charge, however, the cost of referrals to treatment or rehabilitation is the responsibility of the employee if the cost is not completely covered by insurance. In support of our drug-free workplace, our insurance plans include some coverage for the treatment of addiction.

*Include if testing is performed by the organization: An employee who tests positive on an alcohol and/or drug test may be referred to the EAP for assessment and rehabilitation recommendations. The employee's decision to participate in the recommended treatment, successful completion of the program and additional treatment recommendations will be communicated to the organization.

Source: U.S. Department of Labor (2008).

- Establish an ongoing, drug-free awareness program.
- Require each employee directly involved in the work of the contract or grant to notify you of any criminal drug statute convictions for a violation occurring in the workplace.
- Notify the federal government of such a violation.
- Require the imposition of sanctions or remedial measures for an employee convicted of a drug abuse violation in the workplace.
- Continue in good faith to comply with the above requirements (U.S. Department of Labor 2008).

The current law in the private sector generally permits nonunion companies to require applicants and/or employees to take drug tests. All employers should consult with legal advisors to ensure that they comply with any applicable state or local laws and design their testing programs to withstand legal challenges. In unionized workforces, the implementation of testing programs must be negotiated. Even when testing is required by federal regulations, certain aspects of how the policy is implemented must be agreed on through collective bargaining. Drug testing such as urine specimens taken from employees to check for drugs may seem like an intrusion but may be effective at identifying chronic abusers. Research has concluded that workplace urine surveillance is successful in detecting employees with significant substance abuse-related problems, and that referral to standard treatment was associated with substantial improvements in those problems (Lawental et al. 1996). Likewise, when companies do perform random preventive drug testing, the prevalence of marijuana use is the highest (Osterloh and Becker 1990).

There has been a slight increase in drug testing of employees, and this can be attributed to the growing awareness by employers that approximately one of every ten employees is a substance abuser. Substance abuse refers to the abuse of drugs, alcohol, or both. The federal Bureau of Business Practices estimated that substance abuse costs businesses approximately $16 billion a year, and that on-the-job drug and alcohol abuse causes accidents, increased worker's compensation claims, employee thefts, lower productivity, poor quality control, and absenteeism (Roberson 2005).

One railroad company started testing its employees after a train accident in which seven people were killed; evidence was discovered that some of the employees involved were under the influence of marijuana and alcohol. The Federal Aviation Administration established a drug and alcohol testing program in 1985 after three air traffic controllers were fired as the result of an investigation of cocaine and marijuana use. In Houston, Texas, employees of the Metropolitan Transit Authority are subject to tests for drugs or alcohol (Roberson 2005).

An additional justification for the use of testing is to provide legal evidence of drug or alcohol abuse. For example, one city, after paying damages to six ex-employees who were fired for drug and alcohol abuse, instituted a drug testing program for certain classes of its employees. The city was required to pay the damages to the ex-employees when a jury determined that the city had failed to establish that the ex-employees were under the influence of drugs or alcohol at the time they were fired. Had the city used a substance abuse testing program before the firing, it probably would have been able to produce sufficient evidence of substance abuse (Roberson 2005). One study indicated that substance abuse costs an employer at least 25 percent of an employee's salary in poor attendance, inefficiency, and medical benefits (Roberson 2005).

Drug testing first began in the military in the late 1970s. Now substance abuse testing is mandatory for police officers and firefighters in many cities. As mentioned earlier, the Federal Aviation Administration has issued guidelines for testing air traffic controllers, and the Department of Defense has issued similar guidelines for testing civilian employees in the Pentagon.

Many federal employees and state employees are screened for substance abuse. A Drug Enforcement Administration report listed fifty major corporations and industry groups that test for drug use. This is a fivefold increase over the past three years. One-third of the thirty-five largest corporations now request a urine sample from their employers or use comparable tests to detect drugs and or alcohol. Federal agencies conducting drug testing must follow standardized procedures established by the Substance Abuse and Mental Health Services Administration, part of the U.S. Department of Health and Human Services (U.S. Department of Labor 2008).

Most defense contractors and drug manufacturers test their employees. Many the high-tech firms also use drug testing. Researchers foresee a rapid rise in the number of businesses that use drug testing over the next few years because of the increasing availability of inexpensive substance abuse testing methods.

It is not uncommon for employers to have private security officials design and implement a drug testing program for the organization. Drug testing of employees is implemented for a variety of reasons, such as deterring and detecting drug use as well as providing concrete evidence for intervention, referral to treatment, and/or disciplinary action. Before deciding to conduct testing, however, employers should consider a few factors, including:

- Who will be tested? Options may include all staff, job applicants, and/or employees in safety-sensitive positions.
- When will tests be conducted? Possibilities including preemployment, upon reasonable suspicion or for cause, after an accident, randomly, periodically, and postrehabilitation.
- Which drugs will be tested for? Options including testing applicants and employees for illegal drugs and testing employees for a broader range of substances, including alcohol and certain prescription drugs.
- How will tests be conducted? Different testing modes are available, and many states have laws that dictate which may and may not be used.

Security officials and employers also must be familiar with any local, state, or federal laws or any collective bargaining agreements that may affect when, where, and how testing is performed. It is strongly recommended that legal counsel be sought before starting any testing program.

Criticisms of Testing

Substance abuse testing is described by many as an unwarranted invasion of privacy. For example, an American Civil Liberties Union attorney has stated that businesses should not screen all employees; that the screening of employees without reason to believe they are intoxicated or using drugs is an invasion of privacy (Roberson 2005).

Some critics question the accuracy of the routine drug tests currently being used. For example, critics claim that the error rate for urine testing can be as high as 25 percent and that most employers who use these tests are not aware of their inaccuracy. Critics contend that an over-the-counter cold medicine can give a false reading indicating the presence of amphetamines.

Several of the tests being used are criticized for being too sensitive to be useful in that they will test positive even if an employee was merely in the same area as a person smoking marijuana. Another problem with drug testing is the lack of an acceptable scale for measuring the effects of drugs on an employee. A group of toxicologists concluded that it is impossible to establish as the result of urine testing that a person is adversely affected by the drug used. At most, the test indicates only that a drug has been used by a person, unlike the blood alcohol concentration test, for example, which tests the ability of a person under the influence of alcohol to perform certain functions. Some argue that there is no solid empirical evidence that drug testing is associated with enhanced organizational productivity and safety (Comer 1994).

Many critics contend that testing is not cost-effective. For example, some critics say that there is no evidence that the millions of dollars being spent on screening programs have reduced the abuse problem on the job. Some researchers disagree with the claimed inaccuracy of drug screening tests and contend that the actual error rate in a properly administered test is nil. One drug expert says that, before administration of the test, the employee should be asked to list any medicine or drugs that he or she has taken within the past week. Persons who test positive should be immediately retested. The retest procedure will weed out most of the false positives.

Establishing that a person under the influence of drugs has impaired ability is a problem. The fact that drugs are present and that they most likely will impair a person's ability to function on the job can be presumed only from past experience. Studies referred to later in this chapter discuss the effects of drugs on job performance.

Proponents of substance abuse testing claim that if an initial test indicates the presence of drugs or alcohol, a subsequent test using more sophisticated equipment or procedures will reduce the error rate to less than 1 percent. As to the contention that abuse testing is not cost-effective, supporters state that preliminary screening costs only a few dollars per test and that more sophisticated follow-up testing costs only about $50 to $100 per test. These costs, they say, will be recovered in the reduction of absenteeism, medical costs, and employee mistakes.

Testing Procedures

The most common drug test presently in use is urine testing. Other types being used test breath and blood. Although the current tests are highly accurate in determining the presence of a drug, none of them can evaluate the effects of that drug on the individual employee. However, we caution that many of these tests such as the urine testing are controversial, and security officials should advise their clients to seek legal advice before implementing a drug testing program. Organizations such as mining copanies, communications businesses, transportation establishments, and public utilities are more likely to have drug testing programs because of governmental regulatory requirements (Gatewood and Field 1994).

Most drug tests will detect the presence of marijuana for up to three weeks after the drug has been used, but cocaine can only be detected for twenty-four to forty-eight hours after use. Many companies that use drug testing consult with the employee the first time that a test indicates a positive (drug traces) result and offer counseling or rehabilitation. Employees who do not follow up on the counseling service or rehabilitation program or who later test positive a second time are terminated.

Before instituting a drug testing program, check with your attorney regarding local restrictions on drug testing. Establish clear company policies and publicize them to all company employees. Indicate the procedures to be taken when an employee is determined to have a drug in his or her system.

Ask new employees to sign a consent agreement before being employed, granting permission to submit to reasonable drug testing, with the proviso that if they do not submit to such tests they will lose their jobs. No employee should be forced to take these tests, but refusing to submit to a test may be an adequate basis to terminate an employee. Check with your attorney before actually terminating an employee for failure to submit to the requested tests.

Avoid lawsuits by double-checking positive test samples (traces of drugs present). This is necessary because there are reported cases of false positives, which are test samples that indicate falsely the presence of drug traces.

Keep in mind that, although the "high" produced by some drugs lasts only a few hours, traces of the drug may remain in the bloodstream for many days and you

Bozarth v. Atlantic Richfield Oil Company

Supreme Court of Alaska 833 P.2d 2 May 18, 1992, Decided

The employer discharged the employee [Bozarth] because the employee refused to participate in the employer's random drug-testing program. The employee's administrative proceeding for state unemployment insurance was denied. The employee brought a wrongful discharge action against the employer for retaliatory discharge on the grounds that he was discharged for having complained about the employer's unsafe practices. The trial court granted summary judgment to the employer and the employee appealed. The court held that: (1) the employer's testimony that the discharge was due to employee misconduct. . . .

John Bozarth, a pilot for Atlantic Richfield Company (ARCO), was fired after he refused to participate in ARCO's random drug-testing program. Bozarth sued, claiming that the dismissal was really in retaliation for whistle-blowing. Bozarth had repeatedly complained about unsafe practices in ARCO's aviation department.

We affirm the decision of the trial court on the grounds that there were no genuine issues of material fact. The record demonstrates that the decision to fire Bozarth was made by Camron Cooper, a senior vice-president of ARCO, and that she made that decision solely on the basis of his refusal to participate in ARCO's drug-testing program. Cooper asserted that she knew nothing about Bozarth's safety complaints or about other conflicts with his immediate supervisors. This assertion stands unrebutted in the record.

A private employer may, with notice, require its employees to take a test for drugs. Luedtke v. Nabors Alaska Drilling, Inc., 768 P.2d 1123 (Alaska 1989). Failure of an employee to comply with a reasonable order of his employer is cause for discharge. Central Alaska Broadcasting v. Bracale, 637 P.2d 711 (Alaska 1981). Bozarth was ordered to submit to a drug test after being notified of ARCO's drug-testing program, and he refused to submit. Under the above authorities, this failure was a legitimate basis for Bozarth's discharge.

AFFIRMED.

do not control the off-duty hours of an employee. Care should be taken to avoid the possibility of a lawsuit. When in doubt, consult with the proper legal authorities.

Confidentiality

To prevent potential legal problems, keep the results of a drug test private. Only persons who have a definite need to know about the test results should be informed of them. The employee, however, has a right to know the results of his or her own test.

Many state statutes protect the confidentiality of employee and job applicant health records. Most courts that have taken up this issue have concluded that the confidentiality requirements of health records include the results of drug abuse testing. In addition, all companies receiving federal funds or federal assistance, either directly or indirectly, are required by Title 21, U.S. Code, Section 1175, to keep confidential all records regarding the identity, diagnosis, or treatment of drug testing or abuse. The results may be released to third parties only on written consent of the employee or in cases of medical emergency.

Other Detection Methods

In addition to urinalysis drug screening, other methods of monitoring substance abuse among employees include the use of searches, interrogation, and surveillance. Surveillance should not include wiretapping or eavesdropping on an employee's private conversations. This practice could subject security officials and the business that they are contracted to provide security services for to legal litigation.

Several court cases have upheld the firing of an employee because it appeared to management that the employee was under the influence of some unknown substance. In these cases, the employer was able to establish that the reflexes or other physical actions of the employee appeared to support the fact that he or she was under the influence of some type of drug or alcohol.

Some large firms are now using narcotics-sniffing dogs to detect the presence of drugs in employee lockers and personal effects. The dogs become alert when they smell the presence of drugs.

Many police officers have testified in court that they have smelled marijuana or marijuana smoke. However, experts contend that there is no acceptable evidence to conclude that an untrained human is capable of reliably distinguishing the smell of marijuana. For example, pharmacologists, as the result of their investigations, have concluded that the courts should not accept as evidence the smell of marijuana or marijuana smoke by a human being (Roberson 2005).

FINAL THOUGHTS ON PREVENTION PROGRAMS

The following are some collaborative steps that security authorities and the company's management team can work toward in an effort to reduce the affects of substance abuse at a place of business.

1. Issue clear and concise policy statements on substance abuse. Indicate that substance abuse will not be tolerated, and put employees on notice as to the

consequences of job-related drug abuse. (The recommended policy is to offer drug counseling or treatment programs in lieu of termination in most cases.) Be specific in your policies regarding which instances will result in an employee's termination and which will result in a request to the employee to participate in a treatment program, including the results of the employee's failure to satisfactorily complete the drug treatment program.

2. Educate all employees through the use of special classes on the problems associated with substance abuse.
3. Train key personnel to detect substance abuse and how to handle an abusing employee.
4. Consider the possibility of instituting urinalysis testing at regular intervals. Before testing, consult with proper legal authorities for specific guidelines.
5. Send high-level management personnel to drug abuse seminars. If 10 percent of the employees are involved in substance abuse, managers need professional training to deal with them.

NARCOTICS FIELD TESTING

Many security officers have access to narcotics field testing kits. Narcotics field testing kits allow security officers to do a quick test or a presumptive test of suspected illicit drugs. For example, suppose that a security officer is summoned by the organization's management and advised that they have found a small bag of green botanical substance in an employee's workspace. The security officer can perform a test on the substance to make a probable determination that the substance is, in this case, marijuana. Narcotics field kits use reagents and can give clues about the identity of drugs. Field testing kits are easy to use and have evolved over the past few years.

It is very important that security officers avoid direct skin contact with suspected narcotics. Always wear disposable gloves when handling suspected drug evidence. It is possible that some drugs will penetrate the skin and could result in a potentially dangerous situation for the security officer. Furthermore, field tests should not be conducted at the security officer's desk or work area. Usually these same areas contain some form of drink (coffee, soda, etc.) as well as potentially some food items. The imminent danger of this practice is too risky. Any small slip or transfer of the controlled substances to your food or drink could lead to ingestion of the substance. After performing the field test, the gloves and the field test kit should be disposed of. All field testing procedures should be documented and a copy turned over to the public police authorities if they are called.

The chemical reagents used to test suspected illicit drugs are housed inside glass ampoules located in clear hard plastic packets. There are usually one or two glass ampoules inside each of the tubes. To perform the test, a small sample of the drug is placed inside the tube while ensuring that the drug falls to the bottom of the packet. The first ampoule is broken and then the tube is shaken to mix it with the drug. The ampoule is observed for color changes. If there is a second ampoule, follow the directions for the individual test as to the timing of the breakage of the second ampoule. Once the second ampoule is broken, shake the tube again and observe for any color changes. The specific color change will depend on the drug being tested for. A positive

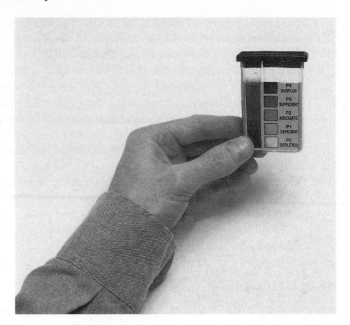

Narcotics field test kit
with color squares.

color indicator is located on the packet to assist in interpreting the reaction. Field tests are available for a wide variety of drugs that security officers may come into contact with. A field test, however, is not a substitute for a test performed in the laboratory by a qualified chemist.

Summary

- Drug and alcohol abuse continues to be a serious problem in our society, and security authorities are not immune from dealing with these problems. Security officials may encounter drugs while working in the corporate or business security industry. Security officers who work in the field may also encounter illegal drugs and persons under the influence of these drugs, much as a police officer may while patrolling in the field.
- The most popular illicit drug is marijuana. Approximately 14.6 million Americans report that they have used marijuana on a regular basis. Furthermore, alcohol and drug abuse are said to cost U.S. industry more than $100 billion annually.
- A drug originally was classified as a narcotic if it was habit-forming and tended to cause a state of drowsiness. The habit-forming requirement has been modified in recent years to include not only those drugs that are physiologically habit-forming but also those that are psychologically habit-forming.
- The term *narcotic* now includes drugs that produce feelings of excitement. Narcotics are generally either depressants or stimulants.
- Depressants lessen physical activity and tend to produce drowsiness. The most common depressants are morphine, heroin, codeine, and opium. Stimulants, which produce feelings of exultation, include methamphetamine and cocaine.
- A person under the influence of drugs may exhibit certain cues. Because some drugs act as stimulants and others as depressants, cues may vary and may not be present in every case. A person

may be under the influence of a drug without exhibiting any of the cues.

- Security officials have an important responsibility to work with management to foster a culture of a drug-free workplace. A drug-free workplace may prevent or reduce problems such as employee theft, absenteeism and tardiness, poor performance on the job, and poor morale.
- Educating employees and management about the hazardous effects of drugs and substance abuse is an important mandate of private security officials.
- Security officials should encourage business and industry management to implement employee assistant programs.
- Employee assistance programs are generally the most effective vehicle for addressing poor workplace performance that may stem from an employee's personal problems, including the abuse of alcohol or other drugs.

- Employee drug testing is one mechanism to identify and address substance abuse in the workplace. Security officials should be well versed in the legal requirements and prohibitions in conducting drug tests.
- Other methods of identifying employees who have substance abuse problems are by interrogation and surveillance techniques. Security officials should only conduct those interrogation and surveillance techniques that are lawful. Security officials are never justified in forcibly coercing an employee into confessing a substance abuse problem.
- Wiretaps and other listening devices are illegal and should not be used.

Review Questions

1. What do narcotics offences include?
2. What is the most used drug? Discuss why you think this drug is used so much?
3. Identify and list the various kinds of abused drugs.
4. Describe the Drug Free Workplace Act of 1988.
5. Describe security officials' role in illicit drug enforcement in corporate and private business security.
6. Describe the symptoms of someone under the influence of an intoxicating substance.
7. Discuss the problems that drugs and substance abuse create in the workplace.
8. Discuss the purpose of employee assistant programs.
9. What are narcotics field testing kits, and what do they do?
10. Identify and discuss the various type of employee drug testing.

Class Exercises

1. Interview a private security officer about his or her experiences with encountering a person under the influence of alcohol or drugs.
2. Log onto the Bureau of Justice website and peruse the drug and crime link, www.ojp.usdoj.gov/bjs/drugs.htm. Discuss the patterns or trends you identify.
3. If you hold a job outside of school, ask your supervisor whether the company has a drug-free workplace policy. Obtain a copy and read it, then discuss the policy in class.
4. In small groups of three or four students, write a model drug testing policy for a fictitious company. Share your policy with other groups. Discuss whether you think the policy would survive legal scrutiny.

References

Abadinsky, H. 1993. *Drug abuse*. Chicago: Nelson-Hall.

Bennet, J. B., and W. E. Lehman. 2001. Workplace substance abuse prevention and help seeking: Comparing team-oriented and informational training. *Occupational Health Psychology* 6: 243–54.

Comer, D. R. 1994. A case against workplace drug testing. *Organizational Science* 5: 259–67.

Cook, R. F., A. Back, and J. Trudeau. 1996. Substance abuse prevention in the workplace: Recent findings and an expanded conceptual model. *The Journal of Primary Prevention* 16: 319–39.

Falcone, P. 2002. *The hiring and firing question and answer book*. New York: American Management Association.

Gatewood, R. D., and H. S. Field. 1994. *Human resource selection*. Fort Worth, TX: Harcourt Brace.

Greenberg, E. S., and L. Grunberg. 1995. Work alienation and problem alcohol behavior. *Journal of Health and Social Behavior* 361: 83–102.

Lawental, E., T. A. McLellan, G. R. Grissom, P. Brill and C. O'Brien. 1996. Coerced treatment for substance abuse problems detected through workplace urine surveillance: Is it effective? *Journal of Substance Abuse* 81: 115–28.

National Clearinghouse for Alcohol and Drug Information. 2008. *Alcohol and drug information*. National Clearinghouse for Alcohol and Drug Information, U.S. Department of Health and Human Services, http://ncadi.samhsa.gov/about, retrieved August 14, 2008.

National Institute of Justice. 2003. *Arrestee Drug Abuse Monitoring Program: Preliminary data on drug use and related matters among adult arrestees and juvenile detainees*. Washington, DC: U.S. Department of Justice.

Osterloh, J. D., and C. E. Becker. 1990. Chemical dependency and drug testing in the workplace. *Western Journal of Medicine* 152: 506–13.

Roberson, Cliff. 2005. *Preventing employees from ruining your business*. Boston: Booklocker.

Shuler, R. S. 1995. *Managing human resources,* 5th ed. Minneapolis/St. Paul: West.

U.S. Department of Health and Human Services, Substance Abuse and Mental Health Services Administration. 2007. *Results from the 2006 National Survey on Drug Use and Health: National findings,* NSDUH Series H-32, DHHS Publication No. SMA 07-4293. Rockville, MD: Office of Applied Studies.

U.S. Department of Labor. 2008. *Drug free workplace advisor,* www.dol.gov/workingpartners/welcome.html, retrieved March 17, 2008.

Yandrick, R M. 1995. Behavior risk management: The preventive approach to reducing workplace problems. *Behavioral Healthcare Tomorrow* 45: 30–5.

Yesavage, J. A., V. O. Leirer, M. Denari, and L. E. Hollister. 1985. Carry-over effects of marijuana on aircraft pilot performance: A preliminary report. *Journal of the American Psychiatric Association* 142: 1325–9.

CHAPTER 14

Ethical Issues in Private Security

CHAPTER OUTLINE

OBJECTIVES

After completing this chapter, you will be able to:

- Explain what constitutes the study of ethics.
- Define key terms in ethics.
- Explain what constitutes ethical behavior.
- Define what constitutes lying.
- Discuss ethical issues involved in lying and deception.
- Define and discuss values and the role they play in shaping our conduct.
- Explain how ethics acts as a restriction on human behavior.
- Define and explain Kantian ethics.
- List the sources of ethical problems.
- Discuss the concepts involved in moral development theory.

In this chapter, the ethical concerns usually encountered in security and risk management are discussed. Students often use the term "dead Greeks" when studying ethics. They are referring to the fact that the theoretical concepts of ethics are based largely on the writings of Plato and Socrates (dead Greeks). For example, many theoretical ethical discussions are based on Socrates' famous credo that "A life unexamined is not worth living" (Souryal 2003, 4).

The goal of this chapter is to introduce issues involving ethics and provide a basic framework for understanding ethical issues and the choice of actions based on those principles. Except for a brief discussion of what constitutes ethics, Socrates' credo is not the focus of this chapter; rather, we will examine practical issues involving private security.

Ethics has a jargon of its own. Following are a few of the key terms used in discussing ethical issues.

Ethics:

A philosophy that examines the principles of right and wrong, good and bad. Ethics has also been defined as standards of fair and honest conduct.

Ethics: A philosophy that examines the principles of right and wrong, good and bad.

Morality: The practice of moral principles on a regular basis.

Ethical egoism: The view that human conduct should be based exclusively on self-interest.

Utilitarianism: A theory that attempts to determine what makes an action good by evaluating the sum total of the pleasures and pain that a course of action would bring.

Departmental values: The values that are expressed though the actions of the department.

Moral development: The theory that we develop morally just as we develop physically. The theory contends that we are not born with the ability to understand and apply moral standards to our actions; we develop it in the same way we learn to do physical things such as riding a bicycle.

Values: Those concepts we value. Values are beliefs that guide a person's or an organization's behavior.

WHAT IS ETHICS?

Ethics deals with values, with good and bad, with right and wrong. We cannot avoid involvement in ethics, for what we do—and what we don't do—is always a possible subject of ethical evaluation. Anyone who thinks about what he or she ought to do is, consciously or unconsciously, involved in ethics.

—*Peter Singer (1991, v)*

It is necessary only for the good man to do nothing for evil to triumph.

—*Edmund Burke, 1729–1797 [quoted in Somerset 1957, 4]*

Ethics examines issues involving right and wrong, good and bad, virtue and vice. Ethics has also been defined as standards of fair and honest conduct. To many, the word *ethics* suggests a set of standards by which a particular group or community decides to regulate its behavior to distinguish what is legitimate or acceptable in pursuit of its aims from what is not (Flew 1999, 23). For example, the American Bar Association has ethical standards for attorneys.

The terms *morality* and *ethics* are frequently used interchangeably. According to Muraskin and Muraskin (2001), ethics is a philosophy that examines the principles of right and wrong, good and bad. Morality, on the other hand, is the practice of these principles on a regular basis, culminating in a moral life. Accordingly, morality is conduct that is related to integrity. Under this definition, a person may be viewed as ethical by virtue of knowing the principles of right and wrong, but only those who internalize the principles and faith and fully apply them in their relationships with others should be considered moral (Muraskin and Muraskin 2001). Based on the foregoing, consider the following questions: Can a person be ethical and immoral? Can a person be moral without understanding the ethical issues involved? In the latter situation, would the person be considered unethical and moral?

Although many writers, like the Muraskins, make a distinction between ethics and morality, the two terms are used interchangeably in common practice and are treated as equivalent in this chapter. There are two basic questions involving ethics: What should I do? How should I be? Under this approach, ethics involves the evaluation of actions and lives, choices and characters. This orientation is a rational argument toward the production of reasons to support one's choices of action (Ryan 2001, 7–8). The use of the rational argument approach indicates that individuals should develop their own moral reasons to guide their conduct rather than merely parroting the views of others. For example, why is stealing unethical or immoral? The rational argument approach would use rational arguments to support answers to this question. To state that stealing is unethical because it is a violation of the law would be to parrot the views of the lawmakers (Muraskin and Muraskin 2001).

The problems of ethics are problems about human conduct at the individual level. Like all members of our society, some individuals, because of their positions in society, have obligations that need to be considered in formulating choices of action. Some of these obligations are placed on the person by being a member of society. Some are placed on the individual based on ethical decisions that the person has made. In addition, many obligations are placed on a person by accepting a position of trust, such as a law enforcement officer. When a person enters into a marriage, the person promises to perform certain obligations. The law enforcement officer promises to support and enforce the laws of the government when the officer accepts his or her position. These obligations place additional restrictions on our choices of ethical courses of action.

What are the consequences of our actions that should be considered in determining the ethical course of action? A central feature of ethics is that it should make us consider the results of our chosen course of action and the effects of that action on others. Accordingly, the welfare of others is critical in our ethical evaluations. For example, the decision of an officer as to whether to fire his or her weapon at an escaping criminal should include consideration of whether an innocent bystander might be harmed by the discharge of my weapon. If it is possible that firing will hurt some innocent person, is it ethical to ignore that risk and fire at the suspect?

WHAT CONSTITUTES ETHICAL BEHAVIOR?

John Stuart Mill contended that it is the business of ethics to tell us what our duties are, or by what test we may know them; but no system of ethics requires that the sole motive of all we do should be a feeling of duty; on the contrary, ninety-nine one-hundredths of all our actions are done from other motives, and rightly so, if the rule of duty does not condemn them (Mill 1863, 419–20). Everyone has an opinion as to what constitutes ethical conduct. As Aristotle stated centuries ago: "It is hard to be accounted an expert in ethics because every person seems to think he knows something about it. In fact, everyone does" (Souryall 2003, 7).

Ethics is often erroneously considered the practice of telling or counseling people how to act. Ethics, however, is not intended to instruct people on how to act. Ethics is also not concerned with values clarification. The real concern of ethics is not what one values, but what one should value. The immediate goal of ethics is knowledge—not forcing, causing, or encouraging people to act in certain ways (Facione, Scherer, and Attig 1978, 10). Once a person has the knowledge, then the knowledge can serve as a guide to help program behavior.

The traditional approach to ethics is an individualistic one. Our notions of good and bad, moral and amoral, are based primarily on our considerations of a person as an individual. Accordingly, the morality of any profession, including security, cannot be separated from the morality of the individuals who constitute that entity, and the entity and the individuals who make up that entity need to be studied together.

ETHICS AS A RESTRICTION ON BEHAVIOR

It is often stated that ethical restrictions on behavior are unconscious—that is, when we alter our behavior for ethical reasons, often we do not realize that it is our values and morals that guide our action. Does it matter that our values and moral guidelines are not consciously held? According to one philosopher:

> Ethics, like metaphysics, is no more certain and no less dangerous because it is unconsciously held. There are few judges, psychoanalysts, or economists today who do not begin a consideration of their typical problems with some formula designed to cause all moral ideals to disappear and to produce an issue purified for the procedure of positive empirical science. But the ideals have generally retired to hats from which later wonders will magically arise. (Cohen 1959, 3)

One of the important questions that should be examined in any study of ethics is this: Is ethics a fundamental component of the decision making, or only a narrowly defined constraint on individual conduct? *Ethical egoism* describes the view that human conduct should be based exclusively on self-interest. This concept is a normative statement regarding the best way to lead a life and what makes human conduct good or bad. Ethical egoism implies that the right thing to do is always to pursue self-interest. Can people ever act on motives other than those of self-interest? Can a security officer ever act on motives other than those of self-interest? The Greek philosopher Epicurus (341–270 BC) taught that human beings come to exist simply as parts of nature and, like other natural things, seek their own self interest (Facione et al. 1978, 39). According to Epicurus, self-interest is self-pleasure and is naturally desirable. Epicurus also taught that true pleasure is achieved with peace of mind and that other things such as wealth, political power, or fame do not guarantee pleasure.

Utilitarianism is another ethical theory that, among other things, attempts to answer the question: What makes an action good or bad? The classical utilitarian, Jeremy Bentham, attempted to provide an objective means for making value judgments. According to Bentham, two important questions face utilitarians: (1) good or bad

Utilitarianism:
A theory that attempts to answer what makes an action good by evaluating the sum total of the pleasures and pain that a course of action would bring.

consequences for whom and (2) how we calculate the value of the consequences. Two general theories of utilitarianism have developed. The first, Bentham's, holds that pleasure is the only thing of intrinsic value to people and thus worthy of pursuit. The second, developed by John Stuart Mill, states that happiness is the only thing of intrinsic value and that happiness is not merely the sum total of our pleasures of whatever variety.

Under Bentham's concept, also referred to as *hedonistic utilitarianism,* actions and practices are right if they lead to pleasure or prevent pain. They are wrong if they lead to pain or prevent pleasure. The measure to use in calculating pleasure and pain depends on their intensity and duration. The present-day approach using Bentham's theory would be to use a cost–benefit analysis of proposed conduct.

According to Mill, the good that is happiness is not merely the sum total of pleasures, because there are important qualitative as well as quantitative differences among pleasures. Accordingly, two lives of equal quantitative pleasures may have different values because one may include pleasures of a higher quality. Mill contended that higher pleasures, such as those of intellect or spirituality, are preferable to more sensual pleasures such as eating and sex.

KANTIAN ETHICS

One popular approach to solving ethical problems was developed by the eighteenth-century German philosopher Immanuel Kant. Kant's approach relies on fundamental principles to define what is permissible and what is prohibited. To Kant, the essence of morality is strict respect for certain duties, and such respect supersedes any other goal. Kant contended that one's duty in a given situation could be deduced from fundamental *a priori* principles that were open to the careful inquirer, and that such principles were independent of experience. According to him, duty is distinct from pleasure, moral virtue is the supreme good, and moral worth is measured neither by the consequences of a person's actions nor by his or her benevolence but, rather, by the person's intention to obey the moral laws. Accordingly, certain self-evident truths provide the "categorical imperative" for moral behavior (Walton 1988). Examination of Laura Nash's approach to solving ethical behavior, presented later in this chapter, indicates that her approach is Kantian. A similar influence can be noted in the approaches recommended by Benson and Gilbert, also discussed later in this chapter.

Laura Nash (1981), in a widely read *Harvard Business Review* article, listed twelve questions that individuals should pose in examining the ethics of a decision. She contends that the guidelines are a practical approach to considering the ethical dimensions of a decision:

1. Have you defined the problem accurately? [Obtain a clear understanding of the problem. The more facts that are collected and the more precise the use of the facts, the less emotional that your approach to the problem will be.]

Sources of Ethical Problems

- Personal gain involving activity of a dubious nature
- Individual values in conflict with departmental goals
- Competitive pressures
- Cross-cultural considerations

2. How would you define the problem if you stood on the other side of the fence? [Look at the issue from the perspective of those who may question your conduct or those who are most likely adversely affected by your decision.]

3. How did the situation occur? [Look into the history of the situation and make certain that you are dealing with a problem not a symptom.]

4. To whom and what do you give your loyalties as a person and a member of the organization? [Individuals and supervisors must ask to whom or what they owe the greater loyalty.]

5. What is your intention in making this decision? [Ask yourself, "Why am I really doing this?" If you are uncomfortable with the answer, don't make the decision.]

6. How does this intention compare with likely results? [Often, regardless of the intent, the results are likely to be harmful. Accordingly, it is important to think through the likely outcome.]

7. Whom could your decision injure? [Even though an action may have a legitimate use, what is the likelihood that it could cause harm to some.]

8. Can you discuss the problem with the affected persons before making a decision? [If your decision will harm others, can you discuss it with them first and obtain their views on it.]

9. Are you confident that your position will hold up in the long run? [Will today's decision be tomorrow's bad decision?]

10. Could you disclose without qualm your decision or action to your supervisor? [Would you be comfortable in seeing your action reported on television?]

11. What is the symbolic potential of your action if misunderstood? [How will others perceive your actions?]

12. Under what conditions would you allow exceptions to your stand? [What conflicting principles, circumstances, etc., provide a morally acceptable basis for making an exception to one's normal institutional codes?]

MORAL DEVELOPMENT

Moral development:
The theory that we develop morally in the same way we develop physically. The theory contends that we are not born with the ability to understand and apply moral standards to our actions, we develop it in the same way we learn to do physical things such as riding a bicycle.

An awareness of the patterns of moral development may help one understand what is involved in developing a moral position and how to formulate one's own moral positions.

According to Lawrence Kohlberg, we develop morally just as we develop physically. We are not born with the ability to understand and apply moral standards to our actions; we develop it in the same way we learn to ride a bicycle or play baseball. Kohlberg, after years of research, devised a sequence of six stages in the development of a person's ability to reason regarding moral matters (Kohlberg 1986, 36–51). He grouped the maturation of moral development into three levels, each with two stages. A summary of the six stages follows (Velasquez 1982, 132):

- *Level One: Preconventional Stages.* These are the first stages, and they are characterized by unquestioning obedience and the gratification of one's own needs.
  - *Stage One: Punishment and Obedience Orientation.* At this stage, the physical consequences of an act wholly determines the goodness or badness. The operative rule may be stated as "Do the right thing and defer to the superior physical power of authorities in order to avoid punishment."

- *Stage Two: Instrument and Relativity Orientation.* This is the stage where the child identifies right and wrong according to whatever satisfies the desires or needs that the child cares about. The operative rule may be stated as "Respect the needs and desires of others in order to get the best for you."
- *Level Two: Conventional Stages.* At the conventional stages, the individual recognizes that meeting expectations of others, such as family, peer groups, friends, or employees, is valuable in its own right.
  - *Stage Three: Interpersonal Concordance Orientation.* The right conduct at this stage is that conduct is viewed as what pleases and helps others and/or elicits social approval, for example, being the "good son" or "good daughter"—The Charlie Brown of *Peanuts* approach (Barry 1985, 15). The operative rule for this stage is "Do the right thing to please others in order to be good in your own eyes."
- *Level Three: Postconventional Stages.* This stage represents the higher level of values. These stages are the autonomous or principle stages. At this level there is a questioning of the existing social and legal system in the light of social utility and abstract principles such as justice and human dignity. At this stage, we no longer accept the values and norms of our group but attempt to view situations in ways that impartially take into consideration everyone's interest.
  - *Stage Four: Law and Order Orientation.* The perceived conduct explained in Stage Three is broadened to include one's own nation. At this stage the individual is still authority-oriented but also recognizes a personal stake in the maintenance of law and order. The operative rule for stage four should be "Be duty bound to society's norms and respect the law in order to maintain social harmony."
  - *Stage Five: Social Contract Orientation.* This stage is characterized by the recognition of social contract, an implicit agreement between individual and society. Accordingly to Kohlberg, Stage Five is expressed in the U.S. Constitution and represents the "official morality" of the U.S. government. He believes that less than a majority of people reach this level.
  - *Stage Six: Universal Ethical Principles Orientation.* The final stage of Kohlberg's moral development includes the formulation of abstract moral principles. Right action is viewed in terms of universal ethical principles because of their logical comprehensiveness. At this stage, the individual acts in a certain way because the action is perceived as conforming to moral principles that he or she believes as the legitimate criteria for evaluating all other moral rules and arrangements. According to Kohlberg, few individuals reach this stage.

The six stages according to Kohlberg are sequential in that people must pass though each of the earlier ones before advancing to the next higher level. According to Kohlberg, the majority of American people never advance beyond Stages Three and Four.

VALUES

The term *value* is used in many different ways. Some of its meanings are subjective and some are objective. For example, in economics, *valus* refers to the utility or usefulness of something or some person. *Value* also has subjective meanings in philosophy.

Philosophical values are judgments about classes of objects or phenomena. Philosophers debate whether the value of truthfulness is absolute or situational—that is, it is good to be truthful, but there are situations where truth might do more harm than good. There is one common core to the various uses of the term *value*. Value refers to the "worth" to a system, object, and so on (Tracy 1989). In this chapter, when we speak of values, we are referring to moral values.

Values:
Those concepts we value. Values are beliefs that guide a person or organization's behavior.

Arnold Mitchell states that values are, more than anything else, what we believe, what we dream, and what we value (Mitchell 1986, 33). Values are those concepts that we value. They act as filters, standards of behavior, and conflict resolvers. Values are also the forces that cause or motivate us to act. Values underpin our attitudes.

Our values are primarily acquired during our early formative years. They do, however, change over time. Most people believe that our moral values are learned and that we generally acquire them from our parents, teachers, clergy, and peers. The learning process may be formal, as in school, or informal.

Conflict among values is inevitable. Our innate values often conflict with one another. To resolve value conflicts, we prioritized our competing values. For example, we may value life, but our values regarding our duties as a security officer may require us to place our life in danger in order to perform our duties. Accordingly, we must prioritize our conflicting values of continuing our own life and providing protection to others.

Paul Whisenand (1982, 411) lists the following general propositions regarding human values:

- The actual number of values that we possess is relatively small when compared to our interests, attitudes, and motives.
- Human beings tend to have similar values.
- Values are organized into hierarchical "value systems."
- The origin of our values can be traced back to our formative years, our culture, institutions, and society.

Misfeasance:
The performance of a duty or act that one is obligated or permitted to do in a manner that is improper, sloppy, or negligent (e.g., report writing, unsafe operation of motor vehicle, aggressively "reprimanding" a citizen, improper searching of arrestees).

Management Tools

Organizational values can be important management tools in three circumstances:

- When management's values are incorporated into the administrative systems and culture of the organization and thereby become work ethics for the organization

The Validity of Values of Others

The focus should not be so much on how to change other people to conform to our standards and our values. Rather, we must learn how to accept and understand others in their own right, acknowledging the validity of their values, their behavior. American Indians believed that "to know another . . . you must walk a trail in his moccasins." This is a classic challenge for understanding others. If we can understand and respect other people and their values, then we can interact with them in a more effective manner.

—Morris Massey (1979, 79–80)

- When management values are suited to the challenges and tasks facing the organization and thereby lead to organizational success
- When the management, through values, is superior to any other kind of management control (Wasserman and More 1988, 213)

Organizational Culture

Organizational culture represents a complex pattern of beliefs and expectations shared by its members. It is often defined as the shared philosophies, ideologies, values, beliefs, assumptions, expectations, attitudes, and norms (Hellriegel, Slocum, and Woodman 1991, 302). The dimensions of an organizational culture include:

- Behavioral regularities that are observable: commonly used language, rituals, and ceremonies
- Shared norms
- Dominant values
- Accepted rules of the game that newcomers must learn
- The feeling or climate conveyed by the physical manner in which the organization interacts with outsiders (p. 302)

Individual Guidance

There are some basic ethics tests that individuals may use for guidance in questionable situations. The tests recommended by Benson and Skinner (1988) include:

- *Common sense test:* Does the questioned act make sense?
- *Publicity test:* Would you be embarrassed if the conduct was reported on the front page of your paper?
- *One's best self test:* Does the conduct fit your concept of your best self?
- *Most admired personality test:* What would your father or mother do in this situation?
- *Hurting someone else test:* Does your conduct cause "internal pain" to someone else?
- *Foresight test:* What are the long-term effects of your conduct?

If your proposed conduct fails any of these tests, then don't take the action.

Leadership Roles

Most researchers contend that supervisors set the moral tone of the department and that top management serves as a key reference point for all subordinates (King 1991, 24). If that is so, then supervisors are obligated to set an ethical example for others to follow. In addition, top administrators should be willing and able to discipline violators of ethical standards. Often, inaction by those in key positions is considered as approval of the conduct in question. A key duty of executives is to evaluate what is expected and then communicate clearly and inculcate values—that is, fairness, honesty, reliability, and accountability—to the others in the department.

Leaders have the responsibility to develop an ethical environment that eliminates public suspicion and lessens the temptations toward unethical conduct.

Nonfeasance:
The failure to perform an act that one is obligated to do either by law or directive due to omission or failure to recognize the obligation (e.g., failure to file a report).

Organizational culture:
Often defined as the shared philosophies, ideologies, values, beliefs, assumptions, expectations, attitudes, and norms of an organization.

LYING AND DECEPTION

False words are not only evil in themselves, but they infect the soul.

—*Socrates*

A good man does not lie. It is this intuition that brings lying so naturally within the domain of things that are categorically wrong. Yet many lies do little if any harm, and some lies do real good. How are we to account for this stringent judgment on lying, particularly in face of the possibly trivial, if not positively beneficial, consequences of lying (Fried 1978, 54)?

Sissela Bok (1999) distinguishes between two conceptual domains; the abstract question of truth and falsity, and the moral question of intended truthfulness or deception. She contends that veracity cannot be established by the truth or falsity of what one says, but on the basis of whether one intends to mislead. In Bok's first edition of *Lying: Moral Choice in Public and Private Life* (1978), she stated that there had been a relatively small number of studies on the concept of the issues of truthfulness and deceit. In her second edition (1999), she noted that since her first edition these issues had received considerable debate (Bok 1999, xiii).

Bok (1999, 14) describes a deceptive person as not one who is merely wrong or mistaken, but one who is intentionally deceitful or treacherous. She defines a liar as one who intentionally undertakes to deceive others by communicating messages that are intended to mislead them. She notes that a lie may be verbal, written, or conveyed via sign language. For example, the shaking of one's head may constitute a lie. Bok's definition of a lie is this: "A lie is a statement, believed by the liar to be false, made to another person with the intention that the person be deceived by the statement" (Bok 1999, 17). Note that her definition of what constitutes a "statement" is very broad. For example, the nodding of your head may be a statement under her definition. Under Bok's definition of a lie, intention is a key element. Accordingly, it appears that if my statement is in fact true, but I believe it to be false when I make it, then I am telling a lie.

Bok's "principle of veracity" is the principle that establishes a very strong moral presumption against lying. Under her principle there is a strong presumption that any lie is wrong. She asks the rhetorical question of what it would be like to live in a world in which truth telling was not the common practice. She makes it clear that we benefit enormously by living in a world in which the practice of truth telling is widespread. She also notes that the social practice of truth telling has great value both generally and personally. Her principle of veracity is a moral principle because it tells you not to lie even when you could get away with it. There are two steps to defending the principle: (1) the fact that each of us personally benefits from a system that we want others to do their part in maintaining; and (2) a principle of reciprocity that requires each of us to do our part in maintaining the system of truth telling.

Are Some Lies Justified?

Samuel Johnson, a nineteenth-century English scholar, is reported to have made the following statement: "The general rule is that truth should never be violated; there must, however, be some exceptions. What if a murderer should ask you which way a man has gone?" (Bok 1999, 40). Immanuel Kant would have disagreed. Kant saw the formal duty of an individual to everyone as to be truthful. He contended that truthfulness in a statement cannot be avoided, however great the disadvantage may be. According to Kant, the duty to be truthful is absolute. Kant stated: "By a lie a man throws away and, as it were, annihilates his dignity as a man" (Kant 1797, 123.)

As noted earlier, Bok's principle of veracity has a strong presumption against lying. Lying is usually wrong, but not always. The presumption can be overcome. The problem under Bok's principle is deciding when lying is morally justified. She offers a mechanical procedure for deciding this question under her scheme of applied publicity. Her scheme has an introspective and an active part.

Under the introspective part, you must ask the following questions:

- Are there truthful alternatives?
- What is the context of the lie, that is, the relationship between the liar and the person being lied to?
- What are the effects of the lie? The good? The bad?
- Considering the context of the lie and the relationship of the parties, and so on, what are the arguments for and against the lying?
- What are the effects on the practice of veracity itself?
- When you weigh the considerations and decide on a conclusion, how would your conclusion and the reasons you made it impress other reasonable persons?

Under the active part, you need to see how an actual audience responds to your reflections. Would they agree with your conclusions? Your aim is to arrive at a decision that would be acceptable to a reasonable public. Bok sees the active part as a check on the introspective part. She notes that the active part cannot actually be carried out most of the times. When it is impracticable, you need to fall back on your judgment as to how an actual audience would respond to your conclusions.

Discussion Questions and Class Exercises

1. Your personal hall of fame: Make a list of the ten persons you admire most. Then make a list of qualities that you admire most regarding the persons listed. Examine the list. The items listed probably reflect character traits, abilities, and so on, that you admire and therefore place a high value on.

2. Make a list of the ten things that you enjoy (value) most. Rank the list from 1 to 10, with 1 being your most valued activity. Next, place an "a" by those activities that you have done in the last two weeks; a "b" by those you have done within the last three months; a "c" by those things that you have not done within the last year; and a "d" by those things that you have not done within the past two years. Examine the list. How does the assigned letter compare with the assigned number; for example, do your 1s and 2s have an "a" designation? Are there any patterns in your list? Do you need to reassign your rankings? What does the list demonstrate regarding where your values lie?

3. Explain the differences between ethics and values.

References

Barry, Vincent. 1985. *Applying ethics: A text with readings,* 2nd ed. Belmont, CA: Wadsworth.

Benson, Bruce L., and Gilbert H. Skinner. 1988. Doughnut shop ethics: There are answers. *The Police Chief* 55(12): 32–3.

Bok, Sissela. 1999. *Lying: Moral choice in public and private life,* 2nd ed. New York: Vintage Books.

Cohen, Felix S. 1959. *Ethical systems and legal ideals.* Ithaca, NY: Cornell University Press.

Facione, Peter A., Donald Scherer, and Thomas Attig. 1978. *Values and society*. Englewood Cliffs, NJ: Prentice-Hall.

Flew, Anthony. 1999. *A dictionary of philosophy*, 2nd ed. New York: Gramercy.

Frankenhause v. Rizzo, 59 R.F.D. 339 E.D. Pa., 1973.

Fried, Charles. 1978. *Right and wrong*. Cambridge, MA: Harvard University Press.

Hellriegel, Don, John W. Slocum, Jr., and Richard W. Woodman. 1991. *Organizational behavior*, 5th ed. St. Paul, MN: West.

King, Vane R. 1991. Rededicating ourselves to leadership and ethics in law enforcement, *FBI Law Enforcement Bulletin*, January, 24–6.

Kohlberg, Lawrence. 1976. Moral stages and moralization: The cognitive-development approach. In *Moral development and behavior: Theory, research, and social issues*, ed. Thomas Lickona, 31–52. New York: Rinehart & Winston.

Massey, Morris. 1979. *The people puzzle: Understanding yourself and others*. Reston, VA: Reston.

Mill, John Stuart. 1863. *Utilitarianism*. Republished in *The utilitarians*. New York: Dolphin Books, 1961, 419–20.

Mitchell, Arnold. 1986. *The nine American lifestyles*. New York: Macmillan.

Muraskin, Roslyn, and Matthew Muraskin. 2001. *Morality and the law*. Upper Saddle River, NJ; Prentice-Hall.

Nash, Laura L. 1981. Ethics without the sermon. *Harvard Business Review*, November–December, 78–90.

Ryan, Kevin. 2001. Doing right, being good: The socratic question and the criminal justice practitioner. In *Morality and the law,* ed. Roslyn Muraskin and Matthew Muraskin, 7–31. Upper Saddle River, NJ: Prentice Hall.

Singer, Peter. 1991. *A companion to ethics*. Oxford, England: Basil Blackwell.

Somerset, H. V. F, ed. 1957. *A notebook of Edmund Burke*. Cambridge, England: Cambridge University Press.

Souryall, Sam S. 2003. *Ethics in criminal justice: In search of the truth*, 3rd ed. Cincinnati: Anderson.

Tracy, Lane. 1989. *The living organization*. New York: Prager.

Velasquez, Manuel G. 1982. *Business ethics: Concepts and cases*. Englewood Cliffs, NJ: Prentice-Hall.

Walton, Clarence C. 1988. *The moral manager*. New York: Harper & Row.

Wasserman, Robert, and Mark H. More. 1988. Values in policing. *Perspectives on Policing No. 8,* U.S. Department of Justice.

Whisenand, Paul. 1982. *The effective police manager*. Englewood Cliffs, NJ: Prentice-Hall.

GLOSSARY

Alcohol abuse: Frequent intake of large amounts of alcohol, typically distinguished by decreased health and physical and social/job functioning impairment.

Andragogy: A theory of teaching and learning related to adults, developed by adult education scholar Malcolm Knowles.

Antiterrorism: Defensive measures used to reduce the vulnerability of individuals and property to terrorist acts, to include limited response and containment by local military forces.

Associative evidence: Any evidence that can link a suspect to a crime.

Battle of Homestead: An infamous incident between mill laborers and Pinkerton security officers.

Biochemicals: The chemicals that make up or are produced by living things.

Biological weapons agents: Living organisms or the chemical compounds derived from them that cause disease or disrupt physiological activity in humans, animals, or plants, or that cause deterioration of material. Biological agents may be dispersed as liquid droplets, aerosols, or dry powders.

Biological weapons: The intentional use of biological agents as weapons to kill or injure humans, animals, or plants, or to damage equipment.

Bioterrorism: The illicit use of biological agents (e.g., bacteria, viruses, and parasites or their by-products) to cause illness and spread fear.

Bona-fide occupational qualification: Any physical attribute and/or skill that an employer has proven is necessary for satisfactory performance of a particular job, as distinguished from characteristics that have sometimes been required, such as race, height, gender, property-owning status, or passing grades on tests, but that cannot be shown to be related to job performance (Rush 2003).

Broken windows theory: This theory uses the analogy that if a few broken windows on a vacant residence is left unrepaired, the tendency is for vandals to break more windows. Eventually, they may even break into the building and possibly take up residence in the building or light fires inside. The idea is that small disorder problems should be addressed promptly, or they may lead to more serious crime problems.

Burglary: The unlawful entry of a structure with the intent to commit a felony or theft.

Chain of command: The line of authority and responsibility in an organization along which orders are passed.

Chain of custody: A document or testimony that establishes the control and possession of evidence from the time of possession until it is entered into evidence in court.

Check kiting: The practice of issuing a check from an account for which the endorser knows sufficient funds are not available to cover the encumbrance, but with the faith that funds will become available to pay the amount by the time the check clears. It is essentially a fraudulent method of obtaining credit by kiting (Falcone 2005).

Class characteristics: Evidence that has characteristics that are common to a group of similar objects. Examples of evidence with class characteristics include soil, glass, and paint.

Coactive security: When security organizations, police, the community, and other public and private resources work together to solve crime and community problems.

Community partnerships: The premise that the police and the community work together to solve community crime- and disorder-related problems.

Community policing: A strategy, and how all department members from top to bottom, sworn and nonsworn, view their job. The strategy must permeate the entire organization, local government, and the community, not just the community policing officers or the patrol division. Community policing entails problem solving, community partnerships, and organizational change.

Conditional job offer: An offer of employment made to an applicant contingent on him or her successfully completing the rest of the testing process, which usually includes psychological examination and medical and drug screening.

Corporate security: Security departments in businesses or corporations.

Counterterrorism: Operations that include the offensive measures taken to prevent, deter, preempt, and respond to terrorism.

Crime prevention: Any action taken to reduce crime risks and build individual and community safety.

Crime prevention through environmental design (CPTED): A multidisciplinary approach to deterring criminal behavior. CPTED strategies rely on the ability to influence offender decisions that precede criminal acts.

Most implementations of CPTED occur solely within the built environment.

Crimes against persons: A category of crimes that includes robbery, simple assault, aggravated assault, sexual assault, and murder.

Criminal offense: A criminal offense is a wrong against the public that the state prosecutes. It is also the violation of a criminal law.

Crisis management: Measures to identify, acquire, and plan the use of resources needed to anticipate, prevent, and/or resolve a threat or an act of terrorism. Crisis management is predominantly a law enforcement response, most often executed under federal law.

Cross-examination: The defense attorney's opportunity to attack a witness's credibility or establish a motive or bias on the witness's part; questions are either direct or leading questions.

Cryptography: The art and science of "secret writing," through which the meanings of messages are concealed from unintended recipients. The actual method of concealing a message, or plaintext, as it is commonly referred to, is called *enciphering* or *encryption*.

Cybercrime: Criminal offenses carried out using computers. Financial crimes, cyber pornography, sale of illegal articles, online gambling, intellectual property crimes, email spoofing, cyber defamation, and cyber stalking are all examples of cyber crimes.

Cyberterrorism: Computer-based attack or threat of attack intended to intimidate or coerce government or societies in pursuit of goals that are political, religious, or ideological.

Cyberwars: Disruption to the flow of information, principally through computer viruses that eat data or freeze up systems and logic bombs that force machines to try to do something they can't.

Declarant: A person who makes a statement.

Depressant: An agent, especially a drug, that decreases the rate of vital physiological activities. In street lingo often referred to as a "downer."

Deterrence: A theory of justice whereby the aim of punishment is to prevent or deter persons from engaging in future criminal behavior because of the consequences associated with their being detected.

Differential association theory: A theory developed by Edwin Sutherland during the 1930s and 1940s that proposes that criminal behavior is learned through interaction with others.

Direct examination: The prosecutor's opportunity to present favorable evidence to the jury; questions are open-ended and do not suggest the answer to the person being questioned.

Direct liability: Liability incurred by the actions of supervisors and managers themselves.

Drug intoxication: Stupefaction or excitement caused by the action of a chemical substance upon ingestion of a drug. Drug intoxication may cause exhilaration, excitement, or euphoria. Street lingo refers to drug intoxication as "getting high."

Drug-free workplace: Workplaces at which employees are prohibited from engaging in the unlawful manufacture, distribution, dispensing, possession, or use of any controlled substance.

Embezzlement: The fraudulent appropriation by a person to his or her own use of property or money entrusted to that person's care but owned by someone else, including an employee who steals assets or funds of a company.

Employee assistance program: A program designed specifically to assist employees with chronic personal problems such as drug or alcohol abuse that may hinder their work performance.

Ethics: A philosophy that examines the principles of right and wrong, good and bad. Ethics has also been defined as standards of fair and honest conduct.

Evangelical Police: A private police force in the Colonies whose function was to act as a watchdog over the lower class and to enforce Puritan propriety.

Evidence: Anything that assists in proving or disproving a fact. Any object that can establish that a crime has been committed, or any object that can link a suspect to a crime, or can provide a link between the victim and a crime. The weapon used in a homicide is considered evidence that can assist in proving the crime of murder.

Exclusionary rule: A rule of evidence that excludes evidence from being admitted in a criminal trial on the question of defendant's guilt or innocence that was obtained in violation of the defendant's constitutional rights.

Fear management: Comprises the programs that reduce the incidence of adverse psychological effects following a disaster.

Fingerprint evidence: Fingerprints collected at a crime scene or on items of evidence from a crime scene. Fingerprint evidence can assist in identifying the perpetrator of a crime.

Forgery: The process of making or counterfeiting objects, documents, or personal signatures with the intent to defraud.

Foundational questions: Preliminary questions that most attorneys use to start the direct examination.

Fraud: The unlawful deception of another, intended to wrongfully obtain money or property from the reliance of another on the deceptive statements or acts, believing them to be true.

General deterrence: A punishment with the objective of deterring other persons from following the example of the offender, for fear of the same consequences that have been inflicted on the offender. The theory of general deterrence is not concerned with the future behavior of the offender but rather with deterring others from committing criminal offences.

Graffiti: Illegal or unauthorized defacing of a building, wall, or other structure or object by painting, drawing, or otherwise marking it with words, pictures, or symbols. Graffiti is often painted on property by gang members, who use it as a means to mark their territory and communicate with rival gang members.

Hazardous material (HAZMAT): Any substance or material in a quantity or form that may be harmful or injurious to humans, domestic animals, wildlife, economic crops, or property when released into the environment. The four traditional classes are chemical, biological, radiological, and explosive.

Homeowners' associations: Organizations formed to maintain, enhance, and protect the common areas and interests of an association (also called a subdivision or neighborhood). The transfer of deeds to houses in new developments almost always include limitations on how the property can be used. Usually these limitations, called covenants, conditions, or restrictions, put decision-making rights into the hands of the homeowners' association. Some associations enforce every rule, while others are run in a more relaxed way. Most associations try to make decisions that will enhance the value of the homes.

Hue and cry: A call to citizens to assist in an emergency situation.

Illicit drug: A drug or chemical substance whose possession and use are regulated under the federal Controlled Substances Act.

Incapacitation: A component of deterrence proposing that if the offender is locked up in jail or prison, he or she cannot commit crimes.

Incident management: A national comprehensive approach to preventing, preparing for, responding to, and recovering from terrorist attacks, major disasters, and other emergencies. Incident management includes measures and activities performed at the local, state, and national levels and includes both crisis and consequence management activities.

Index crimes: The eight major crimes included in Part I of the FBI's Uniform Crime Report: criminal homicide, forcible rape, robbery, aggravated assault, burglary, larceny theft, motor vehicle theft, and arson.

Indirect liability: Also referred to as vicarious liability. Liability that supervisors and managers may face for the actions of their employees.

Individual characteristics: Evidence that has characteristics that are unique to a given object and set it apart from similar objects. Examples of evidence with individual characteristics include fingerprints, palm prints, and footprints.

Keystroke logging (also known as key logging): A diagnostic tool used in software development that captures the user's keystrokes. Keystroke logging can be useful. For instance, it is sometimes used to measure employee productivity on certain clerical tasks or for law enforcement. However, keystroke logging is also used by individuals to spy on computers by providing a means to obtain passwords or encryption keys. Unfortunately, keystroke loggers are widely available on the Internet.

Leadership: The ability to lead others to accomplish the mission, goals, and objectives of an organization.

Leading question: A question phrased in a way that suggests an answer to the person being questioned.

Learning organization: An organization where people continually expand their capacity to create the results they truly desire, where new and expansive patterns of thinking are nurtured, where collective aspiration is set free, and where people are continually learning to see the whole together (Senge 1990).

Malware: Short for malicious software, an umbrella term for any software that may be harmful to a computer user. Malware includes computer viruses, worms, Trojan horses, and also spyware, programming that gathers information about a computer user without permission.

Management by Objectives (MBO): A systematic and organized approach that allows management to focus on achievable goals and to attain the best possible results from available resources.

Manager: A member of an organization who coordinates the work of others through planning, organizing, directing, budgeting, and controlling.

Marijuana: The most used drug. A drug from the leaves of the flowering top of the hemp plant, *Cannabis sativa,* also known as Indian hemp, thought to have originated in the mountainous districts of India, north of the Himalayan Mountains.

Misfeasance: The performance of a duty or act that one is obligated or permitted to do in a manner that is improper, sloppy, or negligent (e.g., report writing, unsafe operation of motor vehicle, aggressively "reprimanding" a citizen, improper searching of arrestees).

Moral development: The theory that we develop morally in the same way we develop physically. The theory contends that we are not born with the ability to understand and apply moral standards to our actions, we develop it in the same way we learn to do physical things such as riding a bicycle.

Narcotic: An addictive drug, such as opium, that reduces pain, alters mood and behavior, and usually induces sleep or stupor. Natural and synthetic narcotics are used in medicine to control pain.

National Crime Victimization Survey (NCVS): Conducted by the Bureau of Justice Statistics and the U.S. Census Bureau. The survey consists of questions asked of a carefully selected sample of victims regarding their experiences with criminal activity.

National critical infrastructure and key assets: The infrastructure and assets vital to a nation's security, governance, public health and safety, economy, and public confidence. They include telecommunications, electrical power systems, gas and oil distribution and storage, water supply systems, banking and finance, transportation, emergency services, industrial assets, information systems, and continuity of government operations.

National Security Emergency: Events include nuclear, conventional, chemical, biological warfare, civil disorder, terrorism, and/or energy shortages.

Neighborhood associations: Groups of citizens that form and meet periodically for the purpose of disseminating relevant information regarding a specific neighborhood. Neighborhood associations promote programs, services, and activities aimed at encouraging connections between neighbors and fostering civic involvement in the community.

Neighborhood watch: A citizens' organization devoted to preventing crime and vandalism in their neighborhood.

Nonfeasance: The failure to perform an act that one is obligated to do either by law or directive due to omission or failure to recognize the obligation (e.g., failure to file a report).

Organization: An entity that has a deliberate structure and includes organized groups of people working toward a common purpose and objective.

Organizational change: Sometimes referred to as organizational reengineering. Organizational change may include changes in policy and procedures, organizational values, organizational structure, management, and leadership.

Organizational culture: Often defined as the shared philosophies, ideologies, values, beliefs, assumptions, expectations, attitudes, and norms of an organization.

Paramilitary: An organization organized in a military fashion, or a group of civilians organized to function like a military unit. Paramilitary organizations often use military titles and terminology.

Pharming: A scheme whereby criminal crackers redirect Internet traffic from one website to a different, identical-looking site in order to trick the user into entering a username and password into the database on the fake site. Unbeknownst to the user, these crackers have hijacked the computer into going to the fake site or hijacked the DNS server on the intended site.

Phishing: Scam artists send emails that contain links to malicious websites to obtain personal information. Computer users follow the link, which directs them to a website designed to capture personal information. According to the FBI, phishing has become the leading type of Internet-based fraud, with financial institutions accounting for approximately 90 percent of all phishing attacks.

Polygraph: A device that measures and records several physiological variables such as blood pressure, heart rate, respiration and skin conductivity while a series of questions is being asked, in an attempt to detect lies.

Positional asphyxia: Most simply defined as death that occurs because the position of a person's body interferes with respiration (breathing), and the person cannot get out of that position. Death occurs because of the person's inability to breath. A body position that obstructs the airway or that interferes with the muscular or mechanical means of getting air into and out of the body will result in a positional asphyxia death, if the person cannot get out of it.

Private security: The wide range of activities used by non-government organizations and persons to protect themselves from criminal endeavors.

Proactive security: When security organizations work to prevent crime.

Probable cause: It exists where the facts and circumstances within an officers' knowledge and of which he or she had reasonably trustworthy information are sufficient to warrant a person of reasonable caution in the belief that an offense has been or is being committed.

Problem solving: The systematic identification and analysis of the actual and potential causes of crime and conflict within the community, with the results guiding development of measures to address the problems in the short, medium, and long term. Problem solving also involves conflict resolution and other creative methods to address service delivery and police–community relations problems.

Property crime: A category of crime that includes burglary, larceny, theft, auto theft, arson, shoplifting, and vandalism.

Property crime involves only the taking of money or property and does not involve force or threat of force against a victim.

Reactive security: When security officers respond for security purposes after a crime has been attempted or committed.

Recruitment: The process of locating, identifying, and attracting capable applicants who have the minimum qualifications to be eligible for the selection process.

Redirect examination: The prosecutor's opportunity to clarify any issues raised during cross-examination.

Restraint asphyxia: Restraining an offender in a manner that physically restricts the body's movement. The factor that distinguishes a restraint asphyxia death from a positional asphyxia death is that some form of restraint is the reason the victim could not escape the asphyxiating position.

Robbery: The unlawful taking of another's property by force or threat of force.

Search: A government intrusion into an area where an individual has a reasonable expectation of privacy.

Selection: The process that begins after recruitment, by which a security job applicant is subjected to testing and screening processes that may include job-related written tests, background investigation, and psychological assessment.

Shoplifting: The theft of merchandise from a commercial business establishment. In street slang referred to as "five-finger discount." Most shoplifting is committed by amateurs, who use unorganized and sometimes haphazard methods. Professional shoplifters are methodical and sophisticated in their methods. Professional shoplifters are sometimes referred to as "boosters."

Single-use plan: A plan developed for a specific one-time event, such as a large sporting event.

Situational crime prevention: Seeks to reduce opportunities for specific categories of crime by increasing the associated risks and difficulties and reducing the rewards. Situational prevention focuses on reducing opportunities to commit crimes rather than on the characteristics of offenders or potential offenders.

Special deterrence: Focuses on the individual offender. The aim of punishment is to discourage the offender from performing future criminal acts by instilling an understanding of the consequences.

Spyware: An umbrella term for any technology that gathers information about people or organizations without their knowledge. Advertisers or other interested parties often use spyware programming to gather and relay information.

Standard operating procedures: A written and codified manual of a security organization—a roadmap that guides officers in the field.

Standing: The legal concept of "standing" is based on the rule that a defendant generally must assert his or her own legal rights and interests, and cannot rest his or her claim to relief on the legal rights or interests of another person.

Statement: An oral or written assertion, or nonverbal conduct of a person, if it is intended by the person as an assertion.

Stimulant: A drug that excites the central nervous system. Over-the-counter decongestant medications commonly contain stimulate properties.

Strategic planning: Organization-wide plans to establish overall objectives and position the organization in terms of the internal and external environment.

Target hardening: A crime prevention technique that involves strengthening the security of a residence, business, or other structure with a view toward reducing or minimizing the risk of attack.

Terrorism: A violent act or an act that is dangerous to human life, in violation of the criminal laws of the United States or any segment thereof, to intimidate or coerce a government, the civilian population, or any segment thereof, in furtherance of political or social objectives (U.S. Department of Justice, FBI National Security Division 1996).

Testimonial evidence: Evidence that may be presented by witnesses at a trial or other type of hearing. Generally, testimonial evidence is given by a witness to the crime or by an expert.

Thames River Police: The first regular police force in London. It began as a private police force for Thames River merchants.

Theft: The wrongful taking of someone else's property without that person's willful consent.

Theory X: A management approach predicated on a negative view of people. Theory X managers assume that employees inherently dislike work, are lazy, and will avoid responsibility. Managers who subscribe to this view most likely supervise and direct employees closely to ensure that they get the job done. They have little trust in employees.

Theory Y: A management approach predicated on a positive view of people. Managers who subscribe to this assumption may empower employees to be creative. In turn, employees seek additional responsibility and exercise much self-direction.

Tort: A civil wrong for which a private party may sue the tort feasor for restitution.

Tort feasor: An individual who commits a tort.

Total Quality Management (TQM): A set of management practices geared to ensure that the entire organization consistently meets or exceeds customer requirements. TQM places strong focus on process measurement and controls as means of continuous improvement of services.

Tracing evidence: Evidence that results from the transfer of small quantities of materials. Tracing evidence is usually in the form of small particles and includes such items as hair, paint, glass, and fibers.

Training: Teaching security officials the job skills and competencies necessary to perform the job.

Trojan horse: A program that, unlike a virus, contains or installs a malicious program, sometimes called the payload or "trojan." A trojan horse can run autonomously, masquerading as a useful program, or it can hack into the code of an existing program and execute itself while that program runs.

Uniform Crime Report (UCR): Official data on crime that are reported to law enforcement agencies across the United States, which then provide the data to the FBI. The UCR is a summary-based reporting system, with data aggregated to the city, county, state, and other geographic levels.

Unity of command: A principle that states that all organizational personnel operate under a single commander with the requisite authority to direct personnel employed in pursuit of a common purpose.

Utilitarianism: A theory that attempts to answer what makes an action good by evaluating the sum total of the pleasures and pain that a course of action would bring.

Values: Those concepts we value. Values are beliefs that guide a person or organization's behavior.

Vandalism: Malicious and intentional destruction or defacing of property.

Viruses: Programs with the ability to replicate and install themselves, or infect a computer without the computer user's knowledge or authorization.

Wrongful death: A civil court action in which it is alleged that the tort feasor, by his or her actions, caused the death of a person.

INDEX